Freud and Religion

We live in an era that is often described as "therapeutic." Our culture is suffused with unconscious fantasies and psychoanalytic ways of thinking about self, other, and society. Aspects of the Freudian cultural universe have also had an impact on how we think about religion. In this volume, William B. Parsons explores the relationship between religion and psychoanalysis through multiple, linked investigations. Why did Freud write about religion and what did he say? What were the multiple critiques leveled at his work? What were the post-Freudian psychoanalytic advances? How can we still apply psychoanalytic ideas going forward? In answering these and related questions, Parsons distinguishes between classic-reductive, adaptive, and transformational psychoanalytic models. He also argues that the psychoanalytic theory of religion needs to integrate reflexive, dialogical, and inclusive elements as part of its toolkit. Offering illustrations and applications of such revisions, Parsons creates new capacities for thinking psychologically and critically about religion.

William B. Parsons is Professor of Religion at Rice University. He has authored nine books, including *The Enigma of the Oceanic Feeling* and *Religion and Psychology: Mapping the Terrain*.

Cambridge Studies in Religion, Philosophy, and Society

Series Editors

Paul K. Moser, Loyola University, Chicago
Chad Meister, Bethel College, Indiana

This is a series of interdisciplinary texts devoted to major-level courses in religion, philosophy, and related fields. It includes original, current, and wide-spanning contributions by leading scholars from various disciplines that (a) focus on the central academic topics in religion and philosophy, (b) are seminal and up-to-date regarding recent developments in scholarship on the various key topics, and (c) incorporate, with needed precision and depth, the major differing perspectives and backgrounds – the central voices on the major religions and the religious, philosophical, and sociological viewpoints that cover the intellectual landscape today. Cambridge Studies in Religion, Philosophy, and Society is a direct response to this recent and widespread interest and need.

Recent Books in the Series

Roger Trigg *Religious Diversity: Philosophical and Political Dimensions*
John Cottingham *Philosophy of Religion: Towards a More Humane Approach*
William J. Wainwright *Reason, Revelation, and Devotion: Inference and Argument in Religion*
Harry J. Gensler *Ethics and Religion*
Fraser Watts *Psychology, Religion, and Spirituality: Concepts and Applications*
Gordon Graham *Philosophy, Art, and Religion: Understanding Faith and Creativity*
Keith Ward *The Christian Idea of God: A Philosophical Foundation for Faith*
Timothy Samuel Shah and Jack Friedman *Homo Religiosus? Exploring the Roots of Religion and Religious Freedom in Human Experience*
Sylvia Walsh *Kierkegaard and Religion: Personality, Character, and Virtue*
Roger S. Gottlieb *Morality and the Environmental Crisis*
J. L. Schellenberg *Religion after Science: The Cultural Consequences of Religious Immaturity*
Clifford Williams *Religion and the Meaning of Life: An Existential Approach*
Allen W. Wood *Kant and Religion*
Charles Taliaferro and Jil Evans *Is God Invisible?*
Michael McGhee *Spirituality for the Godless: Buddhism, Humanism, and Religion*

Freud and Religion

Advancing the Dialogue

WILLIAM B. PARSONS
Rice University

CAMBRIDGE
UNIVERSITY PRESS

University Printing House, Cambridge CB2 8BS, United Kingdom

One Liberty Plaza, 20th Floor, New York, NY 10006, USA

477 Williamstown Road, Port Melbourne, VIC 3207, Australia

314–321, 3rd Floor, Plot 3, Splendor Forum, Jasola District Centre, New Delhi – 110025, India

79 Anson Road, #06-04/06, Singapore 079906

Cambridge University Press is part of the University of Cambridge.

It furthers the University's mission by disseminating knowledge in the pursuit of education, learning, and research at the highest international levels of excellence.

www.cambridge.org
Information on this title: www.cambridge.org/9781108429269
DOI: 10.1017/9781108554398

© William B. Parsons 2021

This publication is in copyright. Subject to statutory exception and to the provisions of relevant collective licensing agreements, no reproduction of any part may take place without the written permission of Cambridge University Press.

First published 2021

A catalogue record for this publication is available from the British Library.

Library of Congress Cataloging-in-Publication Data
NAMES: Parsons, William B., 1976- author.
TITLE: Freud and religion : advancing the dialogue / William B. Parsons, Rice University, Houston.
DESCRIPTION: Cambridge, United Kingdom ; New York, NY, USA : Cambridge University Press, 2021. | SERIES: Cambridge studies in religion, philosophy, and society | Includes bibliographical references and index. |
IDENTIFIERS: LCCN 2020048127 (print) | LCCN 2020048128 (ebook) |
ISBN 9781108429269 (hardback) | ISBN 9781108453707 (paperback) |
ISBN 9781108554398 (epub)
SUBJECTS: LCSH: Freud, Sigmund, 1856-1939–Religion. | Psychoanalysis and religion.
CLASSIFICATION: LCC BF109.F74 P37 2021 (print) | LCC BF109.F74 (ebook) | DDC 150.19/52–dc23
LC record available at https://lccn.loc.gov/2020048127
LC ebook record available at https://lccn.loc.gov/2020048128sss

ISBN 978-1-108-42926-9 Hardback
ISBN 978-1-108-45370-7 Paperback

Cambridge University Press has no responsibility for the persistence or accuracy of URLs for external or third-party internet websites referred to in this publication and does not guarantee that any content on such websites is, or will remain, accurate or appropriate.

Contents

	Introduction: Psychoanalysis and Religion in Context	1
1	Why Freud Wrote on Religion	29
2	Totem and Taboo: The Origin of Religion	51
3	Freud's *Moses*: The Advent of Monotheism	80
4	Future of an Illusion: The Secular Cure of Souls	95
5	Civilization and Its Discontents: The *Unbehagen* of Religion	133
6	Freud and Eastern Religions	151
7	Psychoanalysis and Religion beyond Freud	188
8	Revisions and Applications	221
	Conclusion: Psychoanalytic Spirituality	256

Bibliography 265
Index 273

Introduction

Psychoanalysis and Religion in Context

[T]o us he is no more a person
now, but a whole climate of opinion
under whom we conduct our different lives
      —W. H. Auden, "In Memory of Sigmund Freud"

We live in an era in modern Western countries that many culture theorists describe as "therapeutic." Among the most important of the figures who have contributed to this change is Sigmund Freud. It is beyond dispute that his theories and nomenclature have become a part of everyday life. Terms such as the unconscious, ego, and superego have been disseminated not only through psychoanalytic clinical sessions but also through movie screens, television, literature, and social media. Our shared public culture is suffused with unconscious fantasies and psychoanalytic ways of thinking about self, other, and society.

The psychoanalytic cultural universe has also impacted the way in which we think about religion. Ernst Jones, Freud's first biographer, pointed out that aside from sexuality no single topic in Freud's vast corpus has engendered more interest than his analysis of religion.[1] And, with regard to religion, the signature of Freud's influence can be summed up quite simply: religion is not from the hand of the divine but the very human projection of complex developmental issues and unconscious wishes. The philosopher Paul Ricoeur summed this up when he dubbed

---

[1] Ernest Jones, *The Life and Work of Sigmund Freud* (New York: Basic Books, 1957), 3: 349.

Freud's understanding of religion a "hermeneutics of suspicion" – one that has for many led to a mistrust of religious belief and its multiple social manifestations. It would not be an overstatement to say that this perspective looms large behind many contemporary critiques of religion within both academia and the general lay population.[2]

The chapters of this volume aim to illumine such vital aspects of contemporary life by tracing them back to what Freud and his heirs thought and wrote about religion. Why did Freud write about religion? What were his seminal texts and what has been their effect on our social world? What were the critiques of his various models of the mind and analysis of religion? What new psychoanalytic formulations did such critiques give rise to? What might a revised psychoanalytic theory of religion look like and how might it further the continued relevance of psychoanalysis for analyzing religious phenomena? In answering these and related questions, our aim is to enable a self-reflective awareness of the therapeutic atmosphere in which we live while heightening the capacity to think psychoanalytically about the dynamics of religion.

To facilitate this involves a delicate balance between presenting "experience-distant" (i.e., abstract theory) and "experience-near" (i.e., existentially meaningful) dimensions of psychoanalytic thought and application. In this regard it is important to remember that Freud's theories were born of his reflections on the suffering of patients in the clinical setting. It was his effort to understand the knots of suffering that led to theory-building. As the data (the sample size of the patients in the clinical setting) shifted and new observations came to the fore, so too did the theory change to accommodate such information. This falsification of theory was apparent not only during the course of Freud's own work but also in psychoanalytic reformulations after his death. Throughout this book we will strive to track Freud's own thoughts as well as subsequent developments in the psychoanalytic understanding of religion while balancing the two poles (experience-near and experience-distant) of psychoanalytic thought and practice.

FRAMING THE RELATION BETWEEN PSYCHOLOGY AND RELIGION: THE THREE ERAS

Psychoanalysis is hardly the sole player in the dialogue between psychology and religion during the past century. Before we delve into the details

---

[2] Paul Ricoeur, *Freud and Philosophy* (New Haven: Yale University Press, 1970).

of Freud and subsequent psychoanalytic formulations about religion, then, it would be helpful to offer a historical map, a bird's-eye view as it were, for situating psychoanalysis within an academic field that has been called the *psychology and religion movement* (a term that is further explained below).[3] How are we to understand the dynamics and evolution of the historical interplay between psychology and religion? Who were the major figures and theories? Where does Freud and psychoanalysis fit in this wider field? Answering such questions will afford us the opportunity to introduce the theoretical nomenclature that will be utilized throughout this volume. Additionally, it offers those maps and comparisons that will prove valuable for using and critiquing Freud's theories and subsequent developments in the psychoanalytic theory of religion in the chapters ahead.

A helpful way of thinking about the historical evolution of this intellectual field is to divide it into three eras: 1880–1944, 1945–1969, and 1970 to the present. Each of these eras can be further characterized with respect to its seminal figures and their creation of originative psychologies. For example, Freud (1856–1939) is considered to be one of most (if not *the* most) influential theorists of the initial, originative period, with Carl Jung (1875–1961) and William James (1842–1910) being universally cited as the other two crucial figures. Even a cursory glance at this originative period reveals it was international in scope, incorporating scholars and clinicians from North America, Europe, and even Asia. The best-known examples from North America would include William James, G. Stanley Hall (and his "Clark School"), E. D. Starbuck, James Leuba, James Bisset Pratt, George Coe, W. E. Hocking, and (from Canada) Richard Maurice Bucke. The best-known German contributions were that of Wilhelm Wundt (known as the founder of experimental psychology), his student Oswald Külpe (famous for his "Wurzburg School"), and Külpe's student Karl Girgensohn (who founded the "Dorpat School"). From France one could include Jean Martin Charcot

---

[3] The term was initially introduced by Peter Homans in his "The Psychology and Religion Movement," in *The Encyclopedia of Religion*, ed. Mircea Eliade (New York: Macmillan, 1987), 22: 64–77. Additional sophistication, particularly with respect to the "projects," stems from the map offered in Diane Jonte-Pace and William B. Parsons, eds., *Religion and Psychology: Mapping the Terrain* (New York: Routledge, 2001). See also William B. Parsons, "The Psychology of Religion: An Overview," in *Social Religion*, ed. William B. Parsons (New York: Macmillan, 2016), 3–22; William B. Parsons, "Psychology of Religion," in *The Encyclopedia of Religion*, 2nd ed., ed. Lindsay Jones (New York: Macmillan, 2005), 7473–7481.

FIGURE I.I Freud, Jung, and James at the 1909 Psychology Conference at Clark University.

and Pierre Janet, both of whom influenced Freud, as well as the Catholic researchers Henri Delacroix and Joseph Maréchal. While Carl Jung is cited as the most influential Swiss psychologist, one should also include his colleagues Theodore Flournoy and Ferdinand Morel. The British scholar Frederic Myers, who founded the Society for Psychical Research, and, from Asia, Girindrasekhar Bose (India) and Heisaku Kosawa (Japan) round out our survey of the more important figures of this first period. A survey of their written works reveals that they often cited each other, even borrowing and expanding on ideas rolling through their colleagues. The internationally based interaction between these men can be visually captured in the famous photograph, taken in 1909 at Clark University in Worcester, Massachusetts, of a group of significant figures of that time, including not only Freud, Jung, and James but also G. Stanley Hall (of Clark University) and multiple others (see Figure I.1).[4]

---

[4] For the details of the conference, see R. B. Evans and W. A. Koelch, "Psychoanalysis arrives in America: The 1909 Psychology Conference at Clark University," *American*

While this wide swath of figures is of interest to the specialized focus of scholars, for most in contemporary culture it is fair to say that the vast majority of them have been forgotten, buried by the tides of history. However, they remain relevant to us insofar as they had some influence on Freud's understanding of the psyche and analysis of religion. In this introductory chapter, our concern is with but two of them, Jung and James, not only because the latter two, along with Freud, are by far and away the best known and influential of the psychologists of this period, and not only because they heavily influenced each other, but also because all three figures are tied by the term "depth psychology" – a term coined by the Swiss psychiatrist Paul Eugen Bleuler (1857–1939) that, as the name suggests, has come to denote psychological models that articulate an area of the mind "below" that of normal waking consciousness. Importantly, the varying analyses and evaluation of religion found in the three men's works differ in part because they had very different theories of that "region below consciousness." As preparation for the chapters to come, it is to our benefit to show not only how Freud framed that region but also how it contrasted with that of James and Jung.[5] This is especially true insofar as post-Freudian developments in the psychoanalytic theory of religion tend to gravitate closer to the positions advocated by James and Jung, albeit in psychoanalytically specific ways.

Below Consciousness: Subconscious, Unconscious, and Collective Unconscious

William James's preferred way of conceptualizing that area was with the term *sub*conscious (or the *subliminal*, a term James appropriated from one of the figures mentioned above, the British researcher Frederic Myers). To utilize a helpful metaphor, imagine a beach at high tide. Let's call the line or "threshold" signifying how high the waves rush up on the beach the "liminal" (*limen*) threshold. Psychologically speaking, that line distinguishes what lies above that threshold (normal everyday consciousness) with that which lies below it (the *sub*liminal or

---

Psychologist 40, no. 8 (1985): 942–948. For more detail on the interaction between these early psychologists of religion, see Parsons, "Psychology of Religion," in *The Encyclopedia of Religion*, and David M. Wulff, "Psychology of Religion: An Overview," in *Religion and Psychology: Mapping the Terrain*, 15–29.

[5] The classic work on how the notion of the unconscious/subconscious/collective unconscious came to life in the nineteenth and twentieth centuries is Henri Ellenberger, *The Discovery of the Unconscious* (New York: Basic Books, 1970).

*sub*conscious). Utilizing a beach analogy, at low tide we can see for ourselves what lies "below": seaweed, shells, rocks, and so on. Similarly, James thought that there was a psychological form of the low tide (namely, the subconscious), in which psychological processes, unseen and unknown to the conscious mind, could incubate. When ripe enough, the latter could surge their way into the conscious mind to the extent that a new identity is born (as in the case of conversion), or, as in the case of mystical experiences or certain introspective exercises (like prayer or meditation), the normal threshold of consciousness could suddenly give way to the low tide of the subconscious, revealing a vast new territory that James colloquially referred to as the "More." James was willing to say that on *this side* of the More (the subconscious proper or, in our metaphor, the beach side), psychology had a lot to say about the various mechanisms and processes that determined how the subconscious works. At the same time, he was open to what other disciplines, such as theology, might say about the *farther* side of the More (i.e., the Ocean). Since this area below consciousness was deemed by James to be very rich and complex and, as a result, the origins of the religious life were obscured in the complexity of that mist, his criteria for evaluating the effects of religion were less *orginological* (i.e., determined solely by psycho-physical factors) than what he called *pragmatic*: immediate luminousness (which is to say, are we enlightened in any way by religious experience and insight?), philosophical reasonableness (i.e., do the religious ideas make sense?), and moral helpfulness (are they of value in living the good life?). In sum, he adopted a view that emphasized the famous "what are the fruits for life" or "adaptive" benefits of religion. As further evidence of James's open-mindedness, and with respect to religion's more fantastic (e.g., mystical, prophetic) claims, James advised being receptive to what he called "wild facts" (i.e., anomalous phenomena running counter or contradictory to the generally acknowledged nature and limits of reality). Such caution also authorized one to engage in a "radical empiricism" that values, as a part of theory-building and the interpretative task, personal experimentation (such as James's own encounter with nitrous oxide, where he came to see multiple dimensional realities, all separated by what he called the "filmiest of screens").[6] James use of nitrous oxide would be subsumed under the general heading of what scholars of religion call "entheogens," namely, those substances (such as peyote, ayahuasca, or

---

[6] See William James, *The Varieties of Religious Experience* (New York: Modern Library, 1929), 378.

psilocybin) that open up the subconscious to the workings of the divine, as is evident in multiple religious traditions.[7]

Although James was not always sure about Freud's characterization of the *un*conscious, he had occasion to cite psychoanalytic theories with great interest and optimism. For his part, Freud, initially aiming to become a medical doctor out of the University of Vienna in the 1880s, went to study with the aforementioned Pierre Charcot at the Salpêtrière (the premier French psychiatric hospital of Freud's time) and with Josef Breuer, an older established physician who took the young Freud under his wing. In particular, Freud and Breuer engaged patients afflicted with *hysteria*, a prevailing mental affliction of his time that can be generally described as the physical expression of unconscious psychological conflict (i.e., psychosomatic illness).[8] For example, Freud was once faced with a woman who had all the symptoms of hysteria, including psychosomatic, intermittent paralysis of her limbs. This woman, dubbed "Anna O" (later revealed to be the young Bertha Pappenheim, who went on to become a famous social pioneer, especially for women's rights), would enter into a period of absence during which some form of a daydream or fantasy was recounted, complete with amnesia as to what was said on return. This "chimney-sweeping," as it was initially called (later becoming the basis for Freud's term *catharsis*: the process of expressing repressed emotions and trauma), led to Anna O. being symptom free, if temporarily. Freud's observation of the patient's absence eventually became the basis for his postulation that there existed an unconscious dimension to the personality. At first Freud evoked the unconscious content of this absence in his patients through hypnosis (the agreed-on routine of his time). Because Freud ended up failing at hypnosis, he devised a new way to elicit unconscious material, which he called *free association*. Freud began

---

[7] For a survey of entheogens in American religious history, see Robert C. Fuller, *Stairways to Heaven* (Boulder, CO: Westview Press, 2000).

[8] Freud's initial attempt to analyze hysteria can be found (in brief) in his *Five Lectures on Psychoanalysis*, in *The Standard Edition of the Complete Psychological Works of Sigmund Freud*, 24 vols., trans. and ed. J. Strachey (hereafter referred to as S.E.) (London: Hogarth Press), 11: 3–56 (1910), and *Studies on Hysteria*, S.E. 2: 1–335 (1893). As with all things Freud, but especially with respect to hysteria (and Freud's case history of Dora), there has been a considerable amount of criticism. The initial salvo can be found in Jeffrey M. Masson, *The Assault on Truth: Freud's Suppression of the Seduction Theory*, 3rd ed. (New York: HarperCollins, 1992). More recently, a critical assessment of Freud and hysteria is offered by Mikkel Borch-Jacobsen, *Making Minds and Madness: From Hysteria to Depression* (Cambridge: Cambridge University Press, 2009), see esp. chapter 2.

by relaxing the patient and having them say whatever came into their mind. What he found was that all too often the patient would stop free associating, sometimes even becoming anxious. He used these observations to theorize that some mental censor (later to become the notions of the ego and super-ego) was *repressing* the conscious awareness and expression of the contents of the unconscious. The reason, as Freud came to observe, was that the daydreams/fantasies his patients recounted were often of a sexual, aggressive, or otherwise morally objectionable nature. In other words, it was for good reason that they needed to be repressed. Even so, Freud found that the patient in the clinical setting, perhaps without knowing the full extent of what they were expressing, would invariably project the various unconscious conflicts onto the analyst. This fact, which was instrumental to treatment, was what Freud would come to call *transference*.

Following the scientific motto of falsifiability, Freud knew that new clinical data necessitated the reformation of theory.[9] Jumping to the end of his career, he came to offer what is known as the "structural model" of the mind, which laid out the characteristics of and complex relationship between the unconscious (the German term was *das Es* or *id* ["the It"]), the ego (*das Ich* or the I), and the super-ego (*das Über-Ich*, literally the "over-I").[10] Freud held that the unconscious was based in somatic (bodily, biological) processes, being dynamic in nature and so seeking expression, pleasure, and satisfaction. To put it another way, the basis of unconscious processes was "instinctual" (Freud's original, more "experience-near" term was the German *triebe*, which is best translated as "drive"). We all know what it is to feel driven by desire, and for the "later" Freud those drives were basically two: *Eros* (sexuality and, more widely, the drive for ever greater and more complex forms of unity) and *Thanatos* (aggression and the eventual quiescence of death). Further, he

---

[9] A survey of the development of Freud's thought can be found in W. W. Meisner, *Freud and Psychoanalysis* (Notre Dame: University of Notre Dame Press, 2000). Once again, with respect to psychoanalytic models as a whole, there is no dearth of criticism. Throughout this volume we will note the more relevant debates, controversies, and scholarly rabbit-holes for those inclined to pursue them. For now, we can mention that on the far side of the negative ledger are studies that seek to dismiss him altogether (e.g., Frederick Crews, *Freud: The Making of an Illusion* [New York: Metropolitan Books, 2017], and Adolf Grünbaum, *The Foundations of Psychoanalysis* [Berkeley: University of California Press, 1984]).

[10] Freud's structural model is best articulated in his short essay "The Dissection of the Psychical Personality," in *New Introductory Lectures on Psycho-Analysis*, S.E. 22: 57–80 (1933).

characterized the unconscious as not so much immoral as amoral. It is ruled only by the "pleasure principle," which is to say that instincts seek one thing: satisfaction. At our biological core, then, we are highly animalistic and selfish. We literally "want," and the "mental" correlate of that somatically based desire is manifested in wishes and fantasies.

Freud supplemented this portrait of the unconscious by postulating a "developmental line" of the sexual instinct (i.e., *libido theory*). Somewhat scandalous for his time, Freud thought that mature forms of object-love had precursors (a developmental infrastructure) in the life of children. For example, in the first year of life the male child took pleasure in the mother's breast. This "oral stage" of sexual development had a pleasure zone (an "erotogenic zone"), namely, the mouth. Next was the anal stage, in which the child learns to defecate on their own (the first "gift" to the parents), the erotogenic zone being the anus. Then the phallic stage (the erotogenic zone being the genitals), and, after a latency period, puberty (the genital stage), where the emerging adolescent takes an object (a person) as their focus of desire. In addition to the possibility that one might, depending on various life events, become fixated at a particular developmental stage (which, in its extreme forms, leads to sexual perversions), during the course of development the male child is subject to the vicissitudes of the famous *Oedipus complex*. In its pure form this means that, on the one hand, the male child, through identification with the father, idealizes and identifies with him, seeking his protection, admiring his power, and wanting his love. On the other hand, the male child also sees the father as the major competitor for his first true love, the mother, and so the feelings of competition, fear (especially of castration), jealousy, and guilt (for wishing his death) are also part of, and in direct conflict with, his feelings of love and identification. The best outcome, thought Freud, would be if the male child identifies with and loves his father more than hates him, and renounces his love of the mother by "displacing" that affection onto a suitable substitute (hence the psychoanalytic view of the popular cultural phrase "I married someone just like dear old Mom").[11]

Females, thought Freud, have a different line of development. The latter was not, as some assume, simply the Oedipus complex reversed,

---

[11] Freud's major and early statement on the development of sexuality is his *Three Essays on Sexuality*, S.E. 7: 125–245 (1905). A brief and readable history of Freud's evolving theory of the instincts can be found in E. Bibring, "The Development and Problems of the Theory of the Instincts," *The International Journal of Psychoanalysis* 22 (1941): 102–131.

as if women had an "Electra complex" (a term coined by Jung and firmly rejected by Freud as psychoanalytically vague and inaccurate). Freud thought that girls, like boys, initially identified as "little men" in the initial oral phase of libidinal development. By the time they arrived at the third, phallic phase, however, girls realized they were castrated, a psychic scar that created "penis envy." The developmental challenge was thus far greater: the girl had to change her love object from the mother to the father and erotogenic zone from clitoris to vagina. Along the way, she would try to actualize her desire for a baby boy (and hence gain her "penis"), evincing the character traits of jealousy, envy, body narcissism, castration shame (Freud thought this was the psychological origin of the social institution of "weaving"), and perhaps even a professorship (a good cultural outcome for the sublimation of penis envy). Women were seen as less individuated, more narcissistic, and lacking in a sense of justice (which is to say, had a deficient super-ego), a logic that follows from the psychological reality of having been castrated (the latter obviates any strong need to follow the dictates of the super-ego). Such dictates are more effective for men precisely due to the fear of castration.[12]

If the unconscious is understood as rooted in biological processes, being "driven" to satisfaction, yet also amoral (with some of the instinctual wishes being socially unacceptable), then there must be a mental function that exists to square such transgressive wishes with a social reality that demands their renunciation. Here is where Freud's notions of the ego and super-ego come into play. Contrary to the id, Freud's ego is ruled by the "reality principle" and "secondary-process" thought (i.e., our reason). It helps the id get what it wants but, because it is informed with information about the social world, does so in a manner that mitigates and redirects the raw "want" of the id. The ego is characterized as operating primarily through a variety of "defense mechanisms," the most profitable of which are *repression* (the renunciation of the id's wants to the extent possible and in accordance with social mores), *projection* (where one denies one's own impulses and vulnerabilities by projecting them onto individuals and groups, exemplified in bullies and racists) and *sublimation* (a moral concept that redirects the desires of the id to socially

---

[12] Here again one finds no dearth of criticism as to Freud's views on female sexuality and development. His own views are best expressed in his later essay titled "Femininity," in his *New Introductory Lectures on Psychoanalysis*, S.E. 22: 112–135 (1933). A good introductory overview of the critiques that have been leveled at him can be found in Juliet Mitchell, *Psychoanalysis and Feminism*, 2nd ed. (New York: Basic Books, 2000).

productive pursuits). The extension of the ego to the super-ego, which is experienced as that moral voice "above" us (hence Freud's experience-near use of the term "Über-Ich" or "over-I"), happens in a developmental sense through identification with and internalization of the "dos" and "don'ts" of the parental units (who, it should be noted, are also informed by the mores of culture "behind" them). The super-ego internalizes (and is felt subjectively as) the moral rules by which one should abide (the abrogation of which is felt as guilt). These two component parts (ego and super-ego) of Freud's structural model, then, ensures (ideally at least) that the successful individual can exist in a group "with others" in a way that navigates their own preferences with those of others with an eye toward contributing to the common good. Of course, managing the desires of the unconscious is not always successful. Freud's structural model is clearly a *conflict model*: we are ambivalent beings whose wishes and wants do not always jibe with our internalized moral standards. Because unconscious desires are powerful and cannot be entirely repressed, contained, or sublimated, they are bound to leak through in some fashion: in dreams, in symptomatic acts, in slips of the tongue, in neurotic symptoms, and, as we shall see, in all forms of religion.

The following is a simple example of how this model might illumine an actual case history. A seventeen-year-old adolescent whose father (a Christian minister) had died five years earlier was brought to psychoanalytic therapy because of childish behavior, conflicts with authority, and various idiosyncratic, personal superstitious rituals. In the very first session the psychoanalyst asked him to free associate to his father. Immediately the patient recounted a kick-ball game two years before the death of his father in which he rebelled by stealing the ball. On persistent pleading from his father to release the ball, he threw it at him, hitting him in his solar plexus and knocking out his wind. On recounting this association the patient exhibited anxiety, which he dealt with by untying then retying his sneakers with greater force.

The psychoanalytic interpretation of this case is classically oedipal, as seen in the immediate association: the patient linked his father's death to his own guilt at "hurting him" (knocking out his wind). The emergence of this unconscious "forbidden wish" through free association led to anxiety (here understood in Freudian terms as the "signal" of the ego that unacceptable unconscious wishes were breaching the ego's defenses) and his subsequent "symptomatic act" (the retying of the shoes being a ritualized way of fortifying the inability of ego defenses to deal with the power of the unconscious). The ideal aim in therapy would be to help the patient build enough psychological structure so that they can explore the unconscious and its contents in an *ego-syntonic* way (which is to say, in a way that is accepted by the ego without undue anxiety), or what Freud dubbed in a pithy motto: "Where Id was, there Ego shall be." Over time and several sessions, this patient was deemed to suffer from an *obsessional neurosis*, defined as the presence of intrapsychic (id/ego/super-ego) conflict, the inability of the ego to manage sexual/aggressive instincts, and the corresponding need to perform personal rituals in a repeated, obsessional manner. Such rituals, as mentioned, needed to be constantly enacted to buttress a weak ego, as if they somehow aided in the defense against otherwise overwhelmingly powerful unconscious wishes. As the therapy proceeded, the patient gained more insight into the nature of the neurosis and was able to relinquish the superstitious rituals. Based on this clinical model, we can begin to see the outlines of what Freud's understanding of religious rituals will be (as we will see in the chapters ahead).

It should be apparent by now that Freud is miles away from James's understanding of the *sub*conscious. Most significantly, and contrary to James, for Freud there is no Ocean, no "farther side" of the subconscious More. Carl Jung, initially Freud's disciple and heir apparent to the psychoanalytic movement, broke with Freud in large measure because he, like James, tried to articulate the deeper, more spiritual side of the unconscious. Jung was the son of a Protestant pastor and from childhood on was deeply interested in religion. Throughout his long-written correspondence with Freud, Jung had occasion to say things like this: "I imagine a far finer and more comprehensive task for psychoanalysis than alliance with an ethical fraternity. I think we must give it time to infiltrate into people from many centres, to revivify among intellectuals a feeling for symbol and myth, ever to gently to transform Christ back into the soothsaying god of the vine, which he was."[13] Freud, for his part, did not waver in his response: "I am not thinking of a substitute for religion; this need must be sublimated. I did not expect the Fraternity to become a religious organization any more than I would expect a volunteer fire department to do so!"[14] Eventually, the two men parted, in part because Jung came to theorize a religious dimension to the unconscious. While he

---

[13] *The Freud-Jung Letters*, ed. William McGuire (Princeton: Princeton University Press, 1974), 294.

[14] Ibid., 295. A readable survey of Jung's basic theory and its relevance for religion can be found in Edward C. Whitmont, *The Symbolic Quest* (Princeton: Princeton University Press), 1991.

accepted the idea of a developmentally based personal unconscious and the power of sexuality and aggression (later integrated into what he called the "shadow archetype"), he also held that below the personal unconscious lay a universal *collective* unconscious. This deeper dimension to the unconscious had a religious, spiritual character, directing and guiding individuals through dreams, neuroses, physical symptoms, and even synchronistic events (i.e., "meaningful coincidences"). His view of the unconscious, then, was that it was wise, sending messages to us so that we might best actualize our unique potential. This developmental process, which Jung called *individuation*, involved an introspective path through which one would, on the one hand, free oneself from what could be a totalistic identification with that self created through the socialization process (i.e., *the persona*) and, on the other, gain insight into the archetypes (i.e., the psychological complexes that animate the collective unconscious). Archetypes were formed in the collective unconscious as the result of repeated experiences of humans over the course of generations. They were more philosophical in nature, on the order of Plato's Forms, being psycho-physical patterns that, while in themselves being empty as a result of being purely formal, were the source and ordering function (somewhat like a cookie-cutter) behind the images, symbols, and mythic expressions found in the world's religious traditions, fairy tales, literature, and folklore. For example, the repeated experiences of being mothered (both good and bad) have given rise to numerous images that represent that function, from the earth, sea, and the church to witches (think *Wizard of Oz*) and goddesses like the Hindu Kali. The archetypical expressions of wise men can be found in priests, wizards, and gurus; representations of the shadow in notions of original sin, the fall, and the devil; representations of the fully individuated self in Christ, Buddha, and mandalas. Jung thought that in order to individuate and fully flower as the unique person one was meant to be, one had to confront this deeper, collective layer of the unconscious. As a result, any religious tradition, understood as the public, social repository of archetypical material, is an invaluable aid to that psycho-religious process. Relative to his two major competitors (James and Jung), then, Freud was between the fabled rock and a hard place. He was the outlier, admitting that he had a "completely negative attitude to religion, in any form."[15]

---

[15] *Psychoanalysis and Faith: The Letters of Sigmund Freud and Oskar Pfister*, ed. H. Meng and E. L. Freud (New York: Basic Books, 1963), 110.

Psychology and Religion in the Second and Third Eras

By 1930 there was a general decline of interest in colleges and culture at large in the psychology of religion. Benjamin Beit-Hallahmi has adduced several factors for this, including the rise of National Socialism, the threat of war, the Great Depression, the rise of behaviorism (which eschewed introspection and subjectivity), theological neo-orthodoxy (a conservative theological movement that challenged the ability of psychology to apprehend religious truth), and the perception that the methods of psychology were less than competent, objective, and value-neutral. Nevertheless, even at the tail end of this era one can discern the beginnings of new theoretical models on which advances would be built.[16]

While our concern is not primarily with the assortment of non-psychoanalytic psychologies that proliferated during these two periods (i.e., 1945–1969 and 1970 to the present), a selective overview would have to include, in the second period, the continued influence of Jung's psychology, aided by Jung himself and followers such as Erich Neumann, James Hillman, and Joseph Campbell, as well as its empirical application through the creation of the Meyers–Briggs Type Indicator, an empirical test based on Jung's description of personality types. Also gaining ascendancy were other empirical formulas, the introduction of phenomenological-existential psychologies, and humanistic forms of the psychology of religion. The latter were paradigmatically evinced in Gordon Allport's (1897–1967) empirically based correlational scale (the Religious Orientation Scale), which measured extrinsic and intrinsic forms of religious behavior; Victor Frankl's (1905–1997) founding of an existential psychological system dubbed "logotherapy"; and Abraham Maslow's (1908–1970) inauguration of humanistic psychology. As with any science that valorizes the process of falsification, psychoanalysis was similarly fated to evolve in theory and technique. In the second era this initially fell to a group of theorists, headed by Freud's daughter Anna (1895–1982) and several pivotal theorists (Heinz Hartmann [1894–1970], Ernst Kris [1900–1957], and, above all, Erik Erikson [1902–1994]), who

---

[16] Benjamin Beit-Hallahmi, "Psychology of Religion 1880–1930: The Rise and Fall of a Psychological Movement," *Journal of the History of Behavioral Sciences* 10 (1974): 84–90.

developed *ego psychology*. Especially evident in the work of Erikson, modifications were made to Freud's theory on several levels: developmental (life-cycle theory), the unconscious (changes in the nature of the instincts), and the ego (its power and functions). Such formulations eventuated in an "executive ego" and a much more positive, adaptive view of religion, where religion was seen as potentially healing and socially constructive.

A cursory overview of the third, most recent period sees the continued development of empirical approaches: the Quest Scale (a more nuanced view of Allport's intrinsic forms of religious orientation), the Religious Viewpoints Scale (which distinguishes between committed, personal religious style and consensual, socially generated forms of religiousness), general attribution theory (which links religion with an attempt to find causes of behavior and life-events and thus intersecting with self-esteem, meaning, and control), and coping theory (which seeks to analyze religion as a means of coping with the existential and social exigencies of life). It has also seen the rapid development and application of neurocognitive brain mapping (formulated by theorists such as Robert Ornstein, Eugen D'Aquili, Andrew Newberg, Pascal Boyer, and Kelly Bulkeley) and the morphing of Maslow's humanistic psychology into transpersonal psychology (sometimes referred to as Western psychology meeting Eastern mysticism), as developed through theorists such as Ken Wilber and Jorge Ferrer. The major advances in psychoanalytic theory can be subsumed under the banner of *object-relations theory*, the beginnings of which started in the second period but which came to fruition, as far as being applied to religion, in the third. Object-relations theorizes that developmental period *before* that of the oedipal (i.e., the *pre-Oedipal* or "developmental line" of *narcissism*). Like ego psychology, it too was more apt to allow for the positive, adaptive function of religion in the lives of individuals and society. Even more, we will find that some of these post-Freudian psychoanalytic theorists went so far as to legitimate a religious dimension to the personality. We will address in detail such advances in the later chapters of this book, illustrating their application to religion and their link with yet divergence from Freud.[17]

---

[17] For a more expansive treatment of the developments and figures in the second and third periods, see Parsons, "Psychology of Religion."

THE MULTIPLE PROJECTS: PSYCHOLOGY "AND" RELIGION, PSYCHOLOGY "OF" RELIGION, PSYCHOLOGY "AS" RELIGION, PSYCHOLOGY "IN DIALOGUE WITH" RELIGION

There is a second, related grid that we will find helpful in our treatment of Freud, psychoanalysis, and religion. Even if not named as such at the time, retrospectively speaking, each of the eras of the psychology *and* religion movement contain the gradual emergence and development of several projects or enterprises that punctuate its landscape. Those projects are as follows: the familiar psychology *of* religion; psychology *as* religion (or better, *psycho-spirituality)*; two major dialogical projects, the *psychology-theology dialogue* and the *psychology-comparativist dialogue*; and the rich interdisciplinary conjunction between psychology and its sister social sciences (i.e., sociology and anthropology). Given the multiple projects that have animated the relation between psychology and religion, the field is better captured by, as we proposed earlier, the designation psychology *and* religion (hence our use of the term "psychology and religion movement"). Using the conjunctive *and* has distinct advantages: it is *comprehensive*, in that it acknowledges that dialogue, diversity, and multiple projects have come to characterize the often contested terrain that marks the intersection between the psychological and the religious; and *neutral*, in that it accommodates the fact that its many varying participants (e.g., scholars, practitioners, religious professionals) situated in their diverse social settings (e.g., the university, the clinic, the seminary, the church/mosque/temple/monastery) champion different, and sometimes opposed, intellectual agendas. This broad designation, then, would encompass all of the projects: the psychology of religion, *psycho-spirituality*, and the various dialogical projects. One last qualification is needed, namely, that the boundaries of the various projects (which should rightfully be framed as separate and distinct) are porous enough so that *in practice* they (like a Venn diagram) sometimes encroach upon each other's academic territory (as we will see in the chapters ahead).[18]

To unpack these projects and enterprises in more detail, the usual way to describe the relation between psychology and religion emphasizes the preposition *of*. The project known as the psychology of religion, then,

---

[18] Further detail of the projects can be found in Parsons, "The Psychology of Religion: An Overview." For an encyclopedic summary of those working in the psychology of religion project, see David Wulff, *Psychology of Religion: Classic and Contemporary*, 2nd ed. (New York: John Wiley and Sons, 1997).

assumes a specific psychological model or method (which, of course, could be of various kinds), a series of cultural phenomena (which is to say, "religion"), and a one-way relationship between the two: psychological models provide the lens through which one deciphers the meaning of religious ideation and practice (the central aim of the "hermeneutical" [i.e., interpretative] task). In a general sense one could say that all those using psychological models of any kind to interpret religion are engaged in the psychology of religion. Certainly, the originative theorists (especially and paradigmatically Freud) who were writing during the initial period of the relation between psychology and religion (1880–1944) are almost always framed as having practiced the psychology of religion. How does this project work? If you look into your dark garage with a flashlight, depending on the shape of the lens (usually a circle, but imagine that it could also be a triangle or a square), you will see the contents of the garage etched out in the shape of your lens. In this analogy the lens is the specific psychological model you are employing, while the content of your garage is "religion." Psychology sheds light on religion, but only in relation to the nature of the model (or "shape of the lens") involved. What this usually means, at least for psychologists *of* religion, is that the various elements of the human imagination, the expression of which is invariably shaped by culture, personal biography, and psychophysiological determinants, will be present in every religious narrative. In this sense, religion is akin to a cultural "movie." The (dis)contents of one's psyche are projected onto the cultural "screen" in the disguised and distorted form known as "religion," only to be retranslated and reinterpreted in light of theories about its proper source (i.e., the human imagination). In the case of Freud's psychology of religion, the projector responsible for the religious movie seen by the audience on the cultural screen will always follow the laws of his theory. Whether dealing with the origins, rituals, or everyday religiosity of the "common-man," Freud will see elements of the structural model, developmental considerations, parents, and Oedipus everywhere.

In order to illustrate this, let's take a fairly recent film (*Teeth*, 2007) and a corresponding Hindu scriptural text (from the *Kalika Purana*). *Teeth* is a story about a teenage woman, part of a Christian abstinence group, beginning to explore her sexuality and romantic life. Unfortunately, she is subjected to unwanted, aggressive male sexual advances. At a crucial juncture in the film she realizes that she has an amazing power: the ability to sever the penis in the act of sexual intercourse. The movie, then, deals with themes revolving around misogyny and female empowerment. Specifically with respect to severing the penis, the theme is universal and well represented. It is none other than the theme of *vagina dentata* (the "toothed" vagina). Speaking psychologically, the reason one finds this so widely represented is due to another well-worn universal theme: the fact of male castration anxiety. The relevance of the movie becomes apparent in that it illustrates how religion is, in a very real sense, just like a movie. Take the following passage from the *Kalika Purana*:

> During a battle between the gods and the demons, Sukra, the guru of the demons, was able to revive all the demons that were slain. Siva knew that Sukra could not be killed because he was a Brahmin, and so he resolved to throw Sukra into the vagina of a woman. From Siva's third eye there appeared a horrible woman with flowing hair, a great belly, pendulous breasts, thighs like plantain tree trunks, and a mouth like a great cavern. There were teeth and eyes in her womb. Siva said to her, "Keep the evil guru of the demons in your womb while I kill Jalandhara [the chief of the demon army], and then release him!" She ran after Sukra and grabbed him, stripped him of his clothes and embraced him. She held him fast in her womb, laughed and vanished with him.[19]

Are we to assume that Siva's creation "really" had teeth in her vagina? Are we not wiser to think that it is a human-based creation – one that, given the above narrative, can be interpreted as expressing male castration anxiety? And, if so, might we look for developmental reasons that might exacerbate this anxiety? Might we also conclude that this anxiety is *projected* onto the grand cultural metanarratives found in religious traditions? Finally, if we are to take this perspective as the preferred one, then how does such a conclusion factor into the ultimate truth claims found within religion? Do the latter, as religious framings would have it, come from some divine *ontos* (which is to say, an eternal, unchanging, divine realm) or from the human mind? If not, then what might psychologists, sociologists, and political theorists say about the efficacy of presenting serious questions needing sustained reflection in a language of *ontos* and *thou shalts* that all too often, in this case and many others, serve to defend and keep intact a labile male narcissism? What we have here is a religious text where the psychoanalyst can say we "create" narratives, myths about gods in *our* image. If we expand this one case to apply to religion in general, we can say that its various narratives are but instances, albeit transformed and symbolically rendered, of the contents of the human

---

[19] Sudhir Kakar, *The Inner World* (New York: Oxford University Press, 1979), 92.

imagination at work – an imagination that is determined, at least in part, by developmental factors.

To prefigure a bit of what will be detailed in the chapters ahead, the general problem with the "psychology of" approach is that of *reductionism*. All too often Freudian interpretations of religion, which certainly have some merit to them, are left unqualified and, as a result, are taken to apply to the entire "territory" of the "what" of religion. But from the perspective of those in religious traditions, Freudian maps, however helpful they may be, are limited and do not account for the farther reaches of religious territory. We will come back to this point again and again, each time with ever more sophisticated degrees of analysis. For now, we can say that some of the other projects within the psychology *and* religion movement understand this critique and endeavor to go beyond it. While agreeing that one's faith trajectory and religious products are invariably complicated by the developmental baggage we bring along for the ride, they (see below) are also interested in articulating a "More" on the "farther side" of the Freudian unconscious. In other words, they find a need to expand on the map of the human imagination bequeathed to us by the psychoanalytic founder.

A good example of the latter lies in that project we have referred to as *psycho-spirituality*. The latter is paradigmatically represented in the work of Carl Jung (first period), Abraham Maslow (1908–1970), the founder of humanistic psychology (in the second period), and those figures that dot the landscape of transpersonal psychology (in the third). These psychological theories do not only interpret religion (hence participating in their "psychology of" function) but also intentionally offer themselves as a secular substitute for it. When this happens, we have an example of psychology that acts "like" a religion. Not so much psychology *of* religion but psychology *as* religion or, better, a *psycho-spirituality*. Indeed, many contemporaries find their existential needs for meaning and wholeness met by such psycho-spiritual analyses of human suffering and their prescriptive solutions. While psychoanalysis has always been characterized as being antithetical to such a project, a fact that stems from a deep theoretical rift that developed between Freud and Jung, it is the case that subsequent psychoanalytic formulations in the second and third periods have come much closer to Jung and psycho-spirituality than Freud's classic reductive psychoanalytic models. We will call such innovative and "spiritual" psychoanalytic models *transformational*, being content at this point to merely introduce the term in anticipation of further detailing it in the chapters ahead.

There are yet other projects that constitute the relation between psychology and religion. Historically, there have been many instances of psychological models, in performing their psychology of religion task, receiving not only interest but also a firm response from the religious tradition in question. In other words, what we have here are what can be called *dialogical* projects. The most famous of these is the *psychology-theology dialogue*, now often referred to as *practical theology* and *pastoral psychology*, which started for all intents and purposes (as far as psychoanalysis is concerned) with Freud's long relationship and correspondence with the Swiss pastor and lay analyst Oskar Pfister (in the first period), instantiated in a socio-structural sense in the second period by notable figures such as the theologian Paul Tillich and the philosopher Paul Ricoeur, then growing more intellectually sophisticated through diverse figures (e.g., Don Browning, James Fowler) in the third period. More recently, there has been a rekindling of the *psychology-comparativist dialogue*, comprised of the interaction between psychology and non-Western religions, which started with Freud's debate with the French novelist Romain Rolland over the famous "oceanic feeling" and his correspondence with the aforementioned Indian analyst Girindrasekhar Bose (1886–1953) and with the Japanese analyst Heisaku Kosawa (1897–1968). In the second and third periods that project became more significant with advances in psychoanalytic theory, the cultural diffusion of Eastern religions, and a new clinical base seeking to integrate psychoanalytic techniques with spiritual ones (e.g., yoga, meditation). As we will see, these "dialogical" projects have spurred a broad interdisciplinary conversation culminating in an expansion of the scope of psychoanalytic methodology.

Contrary to the more reductive movie analogy we linked to the psychology of religion, in which religion is "nothing but" the projected elements of the human imagination, the above *dialogical* projects are better framed with respect to an astronomical metaphor. Take as an example seeing a bright star on a clear night. Let's say that the star represents the light of the divine, whatever you may consider that to be. If you were a theologian or a religious believer of any kind, you would insist that the light "is": the evidence given to the physical eye is enough to confirm its reality. Theology might go even further to hypothesize about the nature of that star: how big it is, in what galaxy it is, how hot it is, and so on. Psychologists participating in the various dialogical projects may or may not think the star exists, but they are willing to contribute to the religious task of deepening and clarifying the relation to the light by showing how it is refracted by the Earth's atmosphere and by the perspective of the observer (which is to say, by the very human developmental and cultural "baggage" we carry along for the ride). Once understood and clarified, the believer's relation to the light is shorn, to the extent possible, of that baggage.

Because the above two dialogical projects invariably engage social and cultural issues and debates, they extend to a third dialogical project, namely, the intersection between psychoanalysis and its sister social sciences (anthropology and sociology). The latter have proved invaluable in questioning a central psychoanalytic claim, namely, that it offers objective, "value-neutral" and universal conclusions about human nature. They are useful antidotes to such claims for they articulate arguments that ask us to unmask and reflect on what they see as implicit cultural assumptions baked into psychological theory. In other words, they ask: Are psychological models, because they implicitly reflect social conditions and cultural values, better described as *ethno*psychologies? And, if so, what remains of their status as universal and value-neutral? For example, when Freud posits that the Oedipus complex is a universal, core nuclear conflict underlying development and neurosis, was he simply taking a local psychological conflict and inappropriately claiming it to apply to all humans in any culture and in any era? Might there be other "nuclear complexes" that are ginned up by other developmental trajectories set in alternate cultural systems? Indeed, such perspectives often go much further by exposing implicit gender and racial coding, unexamined epistemological stances with respect to foundational concepts like the "self," the "body," "reality," and, importantly, the nature and aim of any healing system. We will find such perspectives compelling in critiquing Freud's views on religion and, as a consequence, essential for revisions found in later psychoanalytic theorizing.

Finally, in a book about psychoanalysis and religion it is incumbent upon the scholar of religion to note that while for many what defines and constitutes "religion" may be assumed and therefore not always questioned, the fact is that the term has been the subject of intense debate for quite some time. We know the term is Western in origin, its etymology being derived from the Latin *religio*, the meaning of which has been debated, ranging from the definition of "to bind, connect" to wider meanings pointing to individual social obligations of multiple sorts to a more distinctly religious framing limited to monastic life and its vows. Only gradually did it come to also designate ritual acts, myths, belief systems, and the various churchly accoutrements familiar to the contemporary person. What becomes clear through tracing its history is this: to a large extent, perhaps even a determinative one, scholars of religion have done more to "invent" the term than anyone else.[20]

How does the above impact the assessment of psychoanalytic theories of religion? On the one hand, we will agree to the everyday use of the term "religion" in a conversational, colloquial sense. Most people have a general idea of what it means, and it seems overly exhausting to deny that common agreement. On the other hand, one cannot ignore the fact that within the halls of academia it is equally common to dispute that there exits any self-evident understanding of its definition. Indeed, there are notable figures who have uncovered the term's hidden assumptions, fought for its qualification, offered substitutions, even called for its dismissal. While we will not wade deeply into such thorny debates, we will, in taking a portable lesson from them, underscore the fact that Freud and his heirs, in applying psychoanalysis to religion, entered into what can be called the "definitional debate." Our major concern will be how *they* came to define religion and how it served to mark yet qualify their interpretative contributions. To take an example, for Freud the only deserving definition was what he called "the common man's" understanding of religion – an understanding that was Western, assumed institutionalized patriarchal forms of sociocultural power, and whose normative expression was centered in the monotheistic "mighty personality" of an exalted Father-God. He went on to disparage a "higher" form of religion as found, for example, in philosophical and theological literature. Indeed, in his *Future of an Illusion* he defiantly chastised those "philosophers" who tried to "stretch the meaning of words" to the point that words like "God" and "religious" ceased to bear any resemblance to the Being worshipped by the "common man." As one might expect, his most important correspondents, being representatives of the dialogical projects, not only critiqued his framing of religion but offered quite different definitional strategies. What is even more interesting is that psychoanalysts after Freud expanded his narrow definition, in part due to the critiques offered in the dialogical projects. If one is to fully understand Freud and also religion, then, the problem of definitional strategies must

---

[20] One would not be wrong in saying that debates concerning the definitional problem are as old as the field itself. Historical markers can be found in W. C. Smith, *The Meaning and End of Religion* (Minneapolis, MN: Fortress Press, 1991 [1962]); J. Z. Smith, *Imagining Religion* (Chicago: University of Chicago Press, 1988); Russell T. McCutcheon, *Studying Religion* (New York: Routledge, 2018).

be of some concern. Becoming aware of the assumptions any theoretical model has about what constitutes religion allows one to more effectively ascertain the limits of that theory while enabling their fair and judicious application.

REFLEXIVE, DIALOGICAL, INCLUSIVE

The above framing of the relation between psychology and religion in terms of its three eras, multiple projects, and definitional strategies is useful in that it serves to contextualize Freud and the evolution of the psychoanalytic theory of religion. Further, as we shall see in the chapters ahead, it will offer a way to clearly understand critiques of Freud and psychoanalysis that are both *internal* (that come from within the psychoanalytic tradition) and *external* (that come from other disciplines). By running Freud's contribution through this framing of the field and its projects we will not only arrive at the best understanding of what Freud actually said but also, by slowly chipping away at him from diverse psychoanalytic and non-psychoanalytic perspectives, provide cautionary tales here, modify his positions there, all the while showing how he and subsequent revisions in the psychoanalytic theory of religion have been fruitfully integrated into a broader, more productive interpretative framework. To be sure, a straightforward use of classic Freudian theory is not without its relevance. At the same time, if left there, the contribution of psychoanalysis to the academic study of religion will be both limited and marginalized. A revised psychoanalytic theory of religion, taking into account the history of critique and dialogue, is designed precisely to advance the scope and relevance of psychoanalysis to the study of religion.

Telescoping the argument to come, what we will champion in these pages is an abstract formula for the use of a revised psychoanalytic theory of religion. That formula can be summed up as follows: *reflexive, dialogical, inclusive*. *Reflexive* is a term often found in sociological and anthropological literature and, while admitting of varying definitions, will be used in this study to denote the hidden cultural biases that may be apparent in the supposed value-neutral, scientific formulations of psychoanalytic theory. As mentioned in the previous section, a classic example is the universalizing of the Oedipus complex, which may be a universal *possibility* but not a universal *actuality* (and thus dependent on cultural, socioeconomic, and familial conditions for its "actualization"). In the chapters ahead, we will broaden this to include multiple aspects of psychoanalytic theory, ranging from the essentialism involved with Freud's theorizing about the development of femininity to racial coding to normative aims of therapy. Reflexivity necessarily implies a dialogical relation with sociology and anthropology, the awareness of the "ethno" dimension of psychoanalysis, and overcoming the pitfalls of colonialism and orientalism when applying theory to other cultures.

Dialogical refers to engagement with the "other" social sciences and to proponents of the *psychology-theology* and *psychology-comparativist* dialogues. Often intersecting with the above-mentioned "reflexive" cautionary tales, we will find a host of themes engaged in such dialogues, ranging from alternate conceptions of the body and the human mind to introspective techniques and strategies for defining religion. The term *dialogical*, then, signifies that multiple partners (e.g., textologists [those who specialize in the translation and contextualization of scriptures], philosophers, theologians, social scientists, and comparativists) sit at the table. To be sure, multiple dialogues with multiple partners was initiated and thus authorized by Freud himself. He read, conversed with, and was influenced by a host of social scientific, humanistic, and even theological writers in presenting and then reflecting further on his varied analyses of religion. While it is true that not all of his conversations with his dialogical partners progressed very far, he set the stage, even if at times only in germinal form, for later, more fruitful advances. All too often Freud "on religion" is presented in a methodological vacuum, so that once Oedipus is presented the task is done. On the contrary, given the history of interdisciplinary influence on applied psychoanalysis and the advances it has wrought, it is more fruitful to think of the psychoanalytic theory of religion as interdisciplinary from the start. What we will find is that many dialogical counters to Freud were picked up by later psychoanalysts and wired into new theoretical investigations of religion.

Finally, *inclusive* refers to the need to acknowledge the spectrum of models found in the evolution of psychoanalytic theories of religion. That spectrum can be reduced to three basic approaches: the *classic-reductive*, the *adaptive*, and the *transformational*. Freud is usually identified with only the classic-reductive. His contribution lay in reducing religion to the projection of developmentally determined aspects of the human imagination, showing its regressive, childish, even pathological character, and analyzing how its socio-structural manifestations could enable tribalism, prejudice, moral turpitude, fear, and guilt. At the same time, as many have rightly pointed out, one finds Freud in his case histories and cultural works admitting that there may be some *adaptive* value in religion as well. While we will note such formulations in the pages ahead, it will also become clear that the adaptive school is more fully embraced and given theoretical foundation in second and third period developments within psychoanalysis. Finally, we have already introduced the term *transformational* to denote those later psychoanalytic formulations that acknowledge a deeper, spiritual dimension to human beings. To be sure, this was not something that Freud himself articulated in his writings. Nevertheless, looking back over his works, his correspondences, and the dialogical projects, we will find what can be referred to as "openings" in his theory that have been seized on as the germs for the more detailed formulations found in later transformational psychoanalytic theory. Indeed, part of our task will be to isolate and unpack the classic-reductive formulations, adaptive strands, and transformational openings in Freud's work in order to show how they are developed in post-Freudian psychoanalytic theorizing about religion. Our tripartite division, then, will serve as a kind of rhetorical bridge, promoting continuity even in the face of real differences between Freud and his psychoanalytic heirs.

While not named as such in the existing literature, the shift to a *reflexive, dialogical, inclusive* psychoanalytic theory of religion has been well under way for some time. This will become very evident in some of the theoretical advances and their application to religious phenomena adduced in the later chapters of this book. But such a shift needs to be not only named but also needs an organizational strategy and directive. It is those aims that our formula is designed to facilitate. The process of detailing our formula will be enabled by the use of the terms "cautionary tales" and "portable lessons." The former is a literary term that, while in some sense being a more aesthetically pleasing way of saying "critique," goes further to warn of the dangers involved in applying psychoanalysis to religion without taking account of the sage advice offered by multiple disciplinary perspectives. Moreover, it does not necessarily negate the use of unqualified Freudian models. Depending on the case, sometimes a purely "psychology of" approach, even one following Oedipal reductionism, is warranted. Portable lessons, in our usage of the term, are linked to cautionary tales in that once articulated, the latter can result in revisions in theory and the capacity to make the most judicious, informed use of psychoanalytic models. For example, aside from Oedipal models, one may learn how a particular religious phenomenon may require an adaptive or transformational approach, or even all three, aided by dialogue and reflexivity. It is useful to have multiple psychoanalytic models in one's tool kit for the investigation of religious phenomena, to know how and when to use a specific model, and to be able to accurately assess the latter's benefits and limits.

THE CHAPTERS TO COME: A BRIEF TOUR

In order to read Freud on religion deeply and with some sympathy, it helps to have knowledge of his biography and developmental past. Chapter 1, "Why Freud Wrote on Religion," will sift through his early life and college years, focusing on significant intellectual and sociocultural influences, his relation to Judaism and Christianity, and the developmental roots of what have been called his "Rome neurosis" and "Hannibal complex," both of which impacted his relation to religion. It will also survey Freud's use of an array of literary themes and dream associations, many of which found meaningful expression in his works on religion.

Chapters 2–6 are devoted to a close reading of Freud's seminal texts on religion and the subsequent critiques leveled at his varied analyses. Why is this necessary? Despite all that has been written about Freud's psychology of religion, some of which is quite insightful, there are still too many errors concerning precisely what he said about religion. In addition to significant omissions, one often finds a lack of articulating the critiques of his position and the integration of them into later psychoanalytic theories of religion. As a result, it is all too often the case that the status quo reigns. Given this, in order to convey the importance of psychoanalysis as a method for interpreting religion, one must start at the beginning with Freud, then progress through the multidisciplinary external and later internal psychoanalytic critiques. Such a strategy will enable the process of knowing what of Freud to keep, what to discard, and what to revise.

We begin our process in Chapters 2 and 3, where we will focus on two of his central works on religion, *Totem and Taboo* and *Moses and Monotheism*. These two works will be framed as "bookends," being the first and last of Freud's monographs on religion. Although written decades apart, they are linked by important psychoanalytic postulates, especially the modification of Freud's theory of the unconscious to include a phylogenetic dimension. We will proceed by presenting the core elements of Freud's arguments in each book, carefully unpacking each with respect to the relevant aspects of Freud's clinical theory. Once the core arguments have been exposed, constructive criticism of this aspect of Freud's theorizing about religion will be introduced from noted works written in the "projects" (especially the dialogue with the other social sciences) within the psychology and religion movement. This process will cement the need and value of especially the *reflexive* dimension of our formula while preparing the ground for how later psychoanalytic theory offers resources for repairing the more troubling efforts of Freud.

Chapters 4 and 5 will present Freud's best-known texts on religion: *Future of an Illusion* and *Civilization and Its Discontents*. In order to clarify Freud's position in these works, opportunities will arise to discuss several earlier, smaller, but important and cultural texts; brief portions of other, relevant theoretical works; and case-history material. Along the way, signature aspects of the theological response to Freud's works (as found in the *psychology-theology dialogue*), feminist critiques, sociological perspectives (e.g., Freud's "decline" position with regard to secularization), perspectives from the academic study of religion (concerning his restriction of the definition of religion to that of the "common man"), later psychoanalytic critiques, and observations concerning Freud's normativity and philosophical tendencies will be presented. These two chapters, then, will highlight especially the importance of the *dialogical* dimension of our formula.

The vast majority of Freud's cultural works focused on Western religious traditions. Yet one can tease out other, less evident textual strands that engaged a wider spectrum of non-Western religious traditions, mysticism and spirituality. Chapter 6, "Freud and Eastern Religions," speaks to this dimension of his interpretative forays. After exploring Freud's views, we will turn to his correspondence with three pivotal figures: Romain Rolland, the Indian analyst Girindrasekhar Bose, and the Japanese analyst Heisaku Kosawa, all of whom were significant for laying down theoretical parameters for advancing the *psychology-comparativist* dialogue. We will end with a summary treatment of advances in the latter enterprise.

Once we have fully explored what Freud wrote about religion and the various critiques that have been leveled against him, we are in a position to look at innovations in the post-Freudian psychoanalytic interpretation of religion. Chapter 7, "Psychoanalysis and Religion beyond Freud," will look at significant developments in the psychoanalytic theory of religion in the second and third periods. Our conceptual bridge to these later developments will be the tripartite division of classic-reductive, adaptive, and transformational psychoanalytic models. This chapter, then, highlights the *inclusive* dimension of our formula. It will begin by linking such developments with Freud's twin conceptualizations of the ego (ego as "mechanism" and as the pre-oedipal "self"), moving on to show how such conceptions led to advances in ego psychology and object-relations theory and how, in the latter, one begins to see the articulation of a generic, religious dimension (the transformational) to the human personality. We will include a close examination of the most important figures in this progression and their use by subsequent scholars and analysts.

The above discussion will result, by way of a series of cautionary tales and portable lessons, in the establishment of a new psychoanalytic tool kit. What remains is the need to illustrate how such advances might be utilized in the analysis of religious phenomena. Chapter 8, "Revisions and Applications," cements what we have achieved by offering two psychobiographical case histories, one culled from the west (St. Augustine) and the other from the east (Sri Ramakrishna), each designed to address related but different applications of a *reflexive, dialogical, inclusive* psychoanalytic theory of religion.

Finally, in the concluding chapter, "Psychoanalytic Spirituality," we will return full circle to the notion that we live in an age of the "triumph of the therapeutic" and that Freud's understanding of self and society has morphed, as the poet W. H. Auden said, into "a whole climate of opinion / Under whom we conduct our different lives." In contrast to the previous chapters, the focus of which was on the application of psychoanalytic theories to religion, we will shift our gaze to the cultural consequences of psychoanalytic modes of thought. In so doing, we will turn to sociological and anthropological studies, their entry into the definitional problem concerning how to define religion, and how such perspectives illuminate the role of psychoanalysis in creating not only our therapeutic culture but also, if in an indirect, unintended sense, and certainly against the wishes of its founder, a nontraditional, post-institutional, psychoanalytically informed "spirituality."

I

Why Freud Wrote on Religion

Most psychologists are perfectly content to focus on their clinical sessions and theory-building and don't feel the additional need to write numerous books on the dynamics of religion. But Freud engaged in both tasks. On the one hand, he had a full day of seeing patients, finding time to write dozens of volumes devoted to original theoretical formulations (his *metapsychology*), complete with detailed case histories. This aspect of his oeuvre (his *clinical works*) has rightly dominated over a century of criticism and subsequent modifications of his theories. Freud's professional life was, after all, that of a medical doctor, psychologist, and scientist. Not only did he frame himself in exactly those terms but he also characterized psychoanalysis as a science born of empirical data and research. His heroes were men like Charles Darwin and the physiologist Ernst Brücke (the latter his teacher at the University of Vienna), and he modeled his theories in a way that later led to him being dubbed a "biologist of the mind."[1] Freud thought that psychoanalysis, like any scientific theory, should be falsified with the advent of new data, as indeed it was even during his own lifespan.

On the other hand, Freud penned additional works dedicated to analyzing religion (*applied psychoanalysis*, expressed in that part of Freud's oeuvre dubbed his *cultural works*). This is especially head-scratching in that Freud openly referred to himself as a "godless Jew" and atheist. Given this, one is faced with multiple questions. What was Freud's relationship to religion, and what motivated him to write so much about

---

[1] See Frank Sulloway, *Freud, Biologist of the Mind: Beyond the Psychoanalytic Legend* (Cambridge, MA: Harvard University Press, 1992 [1979]).

religion? What were the seminal relationships, intellectual influences, and cultural events that shaped his understanding of religion? Were there any developmental determinants that played a role in how he engaged religion?

Linked to this last point is the interesting fact that Freud, during the course of his own psychoanalytic "self-analysis," uncovered an array of dream associations, significant life events, and literary themes that he associated with religion, weaving such themes into his cultural works. In other words, while Freud may well have been a biologist of the mind, he was also a widely read humanist possessed with a certain literary genius. Indeed, Freud was a master rhetorician who, in 1930, won a noted literature award, the Goethe Prize. Even a cursory glance at any of his works (both clinical and cultural) reveals an astounding array of excerpts from poems, novels, philosophers, even sacred texts. Freud was clear he thought that certain philosophers and artists, the latter existing at the margins of culture, had unusual access to the unconscious and a unique ability to represent unconscious processes through narratives, myths, and symbols. He went so far as to intimate that the pillars on which psychoanalysis rested were prefigured by such "intuitive psychologists," admitting he had to be prepared to relinquish any claim to priority in the many instances in which psychoanalytic investigation had done nothing more than confirm the truths that poets and philosophers had recognized by intuition. So it is that throughout his works one can find Freud citing, for example, the poet Schiller and the pre-Socratic philosopher Empedocles as prefiguring instinct theory; the strong relationship between the ideas of Shakespeare, Schopenhauer, and Nietzsche and those of psychoanalysis; and the use of philosophical metaphors (notably, Plato's chariot) to explain the psychoanalytic view of the psyche. It is unfortunate that the way in which Freud constructed his narratives is often hidden as a result of faulty (English) translations. The original German edition was filled with humanistic terms that have been limited or "medicalized" and so, for all intents and purposes, omitted (as with his liberal use of *das Seele* or "the soul," perhaps because such words were not "scientific" enough) or changed from "experience-near" to "experience-distant" (e.g., *Ich* or the "I" to "ego"; *Über-Ich* or the "over-I" to "super-ego").[2]

---

[2] See Bruno Bettelheim, *Freud and Man's Soul* (New York: Vintage, 1983).

At the very least, this emphasis on the "humanistic" Freud is important in that it reveals intellectual influences beyond that of medicine and science while offering alternative ways of how to "read Freud."[3] But we may additionally ask whether the inclusion of specific humanistic figures and the various writings, plays, and poems with which he chose to adorn his works on religion conveys a deeper meaning that reveals how he sought to contrast psychoanalytic and religious modes of thinking. Freud's own legacy authorizes us to go even further, to inquire whether we might find in such allusions clues to Freud's biographical and developmental past and their complicity in both fermenting and illuminating the motivations behind his interest in writing about religion.

This chapter will investigate such vital observations and the questions they provoke by initially concentrating on his relation to religion in his early years, then segueing to his years as a student in Vienna, his self-analysis, and insight into his developmental past. To be sure, there have been numerous studies from a variety of perspectives that can be found detailing Freud's life, his relations with others, his studies and intellectual influences, even what his personal dreams revealed about his inner life.[4] Our presentation will be far more selective, being tailored to select those elements that have a direct bearing on his relation to and interpretation of religion. It will prepare us, in the chapters ahead, for spying the presence of rich autobiographical material and literary allusions in his writings on religion. Further, it will lead us to the roots of what has been called his "Rome neurosis" and "Hannibal fantasy," both of which were formed in relation to Judaism and Christianity and both of which help to explain the developmental contributions to his interest in writing about religion. It will also begin the process of illuminating his answer to the "problem" of religion as found, among other places, in his use of humanistic texts to introduce what can be called the "psychoanalytic motto" ("Where id was, there ego shall be"), especially revealing when linked to Freud's remark to his friend and colleague, the Protestant pastor Oskar Pfister, that his aim in analyzing religion was to create a social space for a *lay* curers of soul.

---

[3] See *Translating Freud*, ed. D. Ornston Jr. (New Haven, CT: Yale University Press, 1992).
[4] See D. Anzieu, *Freud's Self-Analysis* (London: Hogarth Press and the Institute of Psychoanalysis, 1986); A. Grinstein, *Sigmund Freud's Dreams* (New York: International Universities Press, 1980).

FROM FREIBERG TO VIENNA: THE EARLY YEARS

Sigismund Schlomo Freud was born on May 6, 1856, in Freiberg, Moravia (now Pribor, Czechoslovakia). His father Jacob (1815–1896) was a wool merchant, while his mother Amalia (1835–1930) was twenty years his junior. In order to secure a better economic future, Jacob moved the family in 1860 to Vienna where Freud stayed until 1938, then being forced to emigrate to London by the Nazi threat.[5] The psychoanalytic myth is that Freud's family was essentially secularized and bent on socializing the young Sigismund into a world where assimilation into European culture was a major aim. Jacob had loosened his ties to his Chasidic Jewish past and Amelia to her Jewish Orthodoxy; German was spoken in the household; and while some of the major Jewish holidays (Passover and Purim) were celebrated, simple observances such as dietary laws and the Sabbath were all but ignored. In sum, as the myth has it, Freud ended up godless yet ethical, bequeathing a science of the mind to aid in establishing a better civilization.[6] To be sure, in the final analysis Freud would proclaim his atheism; hold to a liberal, humanistic, ethical understanding of Judaism; and valorize universal human principles and, of course, science. At the same time, subsequent scholarly work has weaved a more complex (if at times contested) portrait of his early religious upbringing and relation to both Judaism and Christianity.[7]

We know that Sigismund's early interest in Judaism was precipitated by his father, who gave him a Bible with an inscription in Hebrew: "It was in the 7th year of your age that the spirit of God began to move you to

---

[5] The standard biographies of Freud are those of Ernest Jones, *The Life and Work of Sigmund Freud*, 3 vols. (New York: Basic Books, 1953–1957); Peter Gay, *Freud: A Life for Our Time* (New York: W. W. Norton, 1988); and, more recently, Joel Whitebook, *Freud: An Intellectual Biography* (Cambridge: Cambridge University Press, 2017).

[6] Dennis B. Klein, *Jewish Origins of the Psychoanalytic Movement* (Chicago: University of Chicago Press, 1981), 42.

[7] The question of Freud's complex relation to Judaism has been the subject of scrutiny for some time. For a summary of earlier entries, see Justin Miller, "Interpretations of Freud's Jewishness 1924–1974," *Journal of the History of Behavioral Sciences* 17 (1981): 357–374. A discussion of the merits and problems of many of these earlier attempts can be found in Klein, *Jewish Origins*, xi–xvii, and, more recently, in Sandor Gilman, *Freud, Race, and Gender* (Princeton, NJ: Princeton University Press, 1993). Among those who have entered the fray, albeit without agreement, are Peter Gay, Emmanuel Rice, William McGrath, Carl Schorske, Yosef Yerushalmi, and Richard Bernstein (all cited below and in Chapter 3).

learning."[8] Even so, there is no indication that Jacob foisted in the young Sigismund a specifically religious investment in Judaism. "Sigmund" Freud (he changed his name at the age of twenty-two) reaffirmed this, noting how his reading of the Bible was the forerunner for his later widespread humanistic curiosity. He would later state in a letter to the editor of the Jewish Press Centre in Zurich: "I have always had a strong feeling of solidarity with my fellow-people, and have always encouraged it in my children as well. We have all remained in the Jewish denomination."[9] Yet in that very same letter he would also state: "I can say that I stand apart from the Jewish religion as from all other religions: that is to say, they are of great significance to me as a subject of scientific interest, but I have no part in them emotionally."[10]

The ties between his family's Judaism and humanism continued into Sigismund's adolescence. From 1865 to 1873 Freud attended the Leopoldstädter Gymnasium in Vienna (akin to an American preparatory school for the intellectually gifted), ranking first in his class every year (with the exception of but one semester).[11] It was there that he studied with Samuel Hammerschlag, whom he credited with continuing his love for the humanities, ethics, and a liberal take on Judaism while authorizing him to repudiate the ritualistic and metaphysical doctrines of Judaism.[12] Indeed, a humanistic rendering of Judaism was fit for Jews who wished to assimilate into the emerging politically liberal atmosphere of Vienna. Such an atmosphere was a means to Jewish emancipation, and, generally speaking, Jews were very patriotic during that era. A general refrain was that sectarian and religious differences could be overcome through the advocacy of the enlightenment ideals of reason, equality, and the search for universal truths. Given this, it is understandable that Freud became interested in a career in law and, beyond that, politics.[13] The family never tired of repeating the prophecy, offered by a strolling poet while the family was eating in one of Vienna's parks, that the young Freud would one day be a cabinet minister.[14] It may well be that Freud's changing of his name from Sigismund (a name that at the time prompted

---

[8] Gay, *Freud: A Life for Our Time*, 12. Freud later bequeathed that bible to his son Ernst (see E. Rice, *Freud and Moses: The Long Journey Home* [Albany: State University Press of New York, 1990], 29).
[9] Rice, *Freud and Moses*, 41.   [10] Ibid.
[11] W. McGrath, *Freud's Discovery of Psychoanalysis: The Politics of Hysteria* (Ithaca, NY: Cornell University Press, 1986), 59.
[12] For the curriculum of the school, see Rice, *Freud and Moses*, 48ff.
[13] C. Schorske, *Fin-de-Siècle Vienna* (New York: Vintage, 1981), 189.   [14] Ibid.

anti-Semitic jokes) to Sigmund was in part due to his desire to assimilate and to appear less Jewish.[15]

During these important adolescent years, then, Freud was socialized into a Judaism that was humanistic but not overtly religious. Indeed, despite his rejection of religious ritual and metaphysics, aided through men like his father and Hammerschlag, he came to honor the humanistic ideals of Judaism, even identifying with biblical figures, of which Moses and Joseph were particularly prominent in his life and thought. Joseph, the great Jewish dream interpreter of the Bible, modeled that Jew who, living in Egyptian culture, aspired to and achieved assimilation despite persecution, while Moses, the paradigm of morality, came to further represent the defiant rejection of oppressive authority in the striving for social justice and freedom.[16] These identifications made their appearance in several of his clinical and applied works, coming to serve him in good stead as he entered on his career path.

DEVELOPMENTAL CONSIDERATIONS

Of course, Freud later came to understand the pivotal developmental influence that his parents came to have on his life and thought. It is hardly surprising, for example, that in the process of discovering the Oedipus complex during his self-analysis one finds him confessing that he uncovered the infantile memory of accidently seeing his mother in the nude (*matrem nudam*, as he put it) during a train journey – a sight he thought "awakened" his libido.[17] Similarly, he had multiple reminiscences about his father, including crucial dream associations that he linked to religion and his Hannibal fantasy (which we will simply note at this time, further unpacking it below). There were others he touted as having a direct bearing on his applied writings on religion, foremost among whom was his childhood nursemaid. The latter, whom Freud referred to as his "second mother," was Catholic (Freiberg being essentially Catholic, with only about 130 of the roughly 4,500 inhabitants being Jews) and tutored him, as he put it, in all things sexual and religious.[18] The nanny took him to the local churches, and, as Freud's

---

[15] See Klein, *Jewish Origins*, 46, 49.
[16] McGrath, *Freud's Discovery of Psychoanalysis*, 21; 31–32.
[17] See his October 3, 1897, letter to his friend and colleague Wilhelm Fliess in S. Freud, *The Origins of Psychoanalysis: Letters to Wilhelm Fliess*, ed. M. Bonaparte (New York: Basic Books, 1954).
[18] Gay, *Freud: A Life for Our Time*, 7.

mother recounted, "when [he] got home, [he] would preach and tell us what God Almighty does."[19] Unfortunately, just before Freud's third birthday his nursemaid was found guilty of theft, summarily dismissed, and never returned. Freud mourned her loss, reminisced about his ambivalent relationship to her in his self-analysis, and came to think there was a direct link between this nanny and Catholicism. As a result, scholars have pondered the ways in which she formed a decisive developmental influence on his later ambivalent relation to Catholicism and, we can add, to the city of Rome. Indeed, it is with the nanny that we begin to touch on a pivotal developmental root of his fabled Rome neurosis (which, as with his Hannibal fantasy, we will simply note, returning to it below).

Another pivotal relationship that Freud reveals was to his nephew John. It may seem odd to refer to the young Sigismund actually having a nephew but such was the case, for Jacob had two sons from a previous marriage of which one (Emanuel) had a son (John) a scant year older than Sigismund. The two became playmates, engaged in unruly and pugnacious behavior, and actively conspired in what Freud later called their "misdeeds." He further came to understand that his relationship with John laid down the pattern for many for his later relationships with men such as Joseph Breuer (with whom he collaborated to investigate hysteria) and Carl Jung (the initial designated heir of psychoanalysis). Such relationships, Freud came to believe, were composed of not only the expected fraternal competition and exploration of sexuality but also a fraternal solidarity, a "brother band," held together by the joint aim of overthrowing paternal authority and their institutions.[20] Needless to say, one of those social institutions would be traditional forms of religion. As we shall see, Freud sought multiple other conspirators, both within and outside psychoanalysis, to aid him in that task.

FREUD, ROME, AND HANNIBAL

Freud's interest in law, politics, and assimilation continued into his student years at the University of Vienna, which he entered in 1873. Notably, from 1873 to 1878 he was a member of the Leseverein der

---

[19] Ibid.
[20] This line of thought is best detailed in McGrath, *Freud's Discovery of Psychoanalysis*, and in his "Freud as Hannibal: The Politics of the Brother Band," *Central European History* 7 (1974): 31–57.

deutschen Studenten, a political student group that advocated German nationalistic themes.[21] By 1881 he had received an M.D., going on to study that neurotic disease dubbed "hysteria" at the Salpêtrière in Paris with Jean-Martin Charcot. In 1895 he published, with his older colleague Joseph Breuer, his first psychoanalytic study (*Studies on Hysteria*) and then, in 1900, his most famous work, *The Interpretation of Dreams*. During his years at the university and early professional life, then, there was a shift from his more cultural and political interests to settling on a career in science and medicine. That shift was hardly total, as Freud would later apply his newfound theories of the mind to cultural interests and social institutions such as religion until his death in 1939.

The reasons for this shift are complex, as is the case for any young man's career choices during this formative phase of the life cycle. Indeed, a fair amount of ink has been spent detailing the influence of Freud's teachers, course curricula, and introduction to various scientific theories on his gradual turn to science, medicine, and, eventually, the creation of psychoanalysis. Certainly, there was a kind of "medical materialism" all its own that informed the halls at the university. Freud's curriculum was inhabited by men such as the physiologist Ernst Brücke (of whom Freud said was "the greatest authority that worked upon me"[22]), Theodor Meynert (the brain anatomist), and the internist Hermann Nothnagel, all of who imbued upon Freud a positivistic, materialistic orientation and the need to proclaim but one God only: that of *Logos* (Reason). Even as early as 1874, in just his second year at college, Freud was able to confidently write to a friend that he was a "godless medical man and an empiricist."[23] To add to this stew, Freud was aware of and applauded the general trend toward secularization in early twentieth-century Europe. He was, in sociological terms, a "decline theorist," meaning that he thought religion was losing the battle against science and would soon be extinct as a viable social institution. Later, Freud went on to think this was an emerging crisis for Western civilization and that steps had to be taken to offset the coming social dislocation. Those steps, as we shall see in Chapter 4, formed a crucial part of his argument in *Future of an Illusion*.

In addition to intellectual and developmental factors, we can add that certain shifts in the sociopolitical landscape played a role on Freud's emerging thought. Like most Jews of his era, Freud aspired to assimilate

---

[21] See McGrath, *Freud's Discovery of Psychoanalysis*, 97ff.
[22] P. Gay, *A Godless Jew* (New Haven, CT: Yale University Press, 1987), 61.
[23] Ibid., 38.

into what was a politically liberal atmosphere in Vienna. However, during the 1870s anti-Semitism began to rear its ugly head. The Leseverein der deutschen Studenten became fractured, as the racist German nationalist students in the group began to see their fellow Jewish members as enemies.[24] Freud later reflected how the anti-Semitic atmosphere made him so uncomfortable that he considered himself no longer a German, and by the time he received his degree from the University of Vienna, he had entirely given up hopes for Jewish assimilation. Jews were being pilloried as a group in newspapers, the theater, politics, and religion, and Freud wrote to his fiancée Martha Bernays of "riots and anti-Semitic demonstrations."[25] The slow growth of the Viennese Christian Socialist Party throughout the 1890s culminated in the election of Karl Lueger, who campaigned on an explicitly anti-Semitic platform, as mayor of Vienna. Even worse, Freud saw Catholic ("Roman") complicity in his election. Freud later reaffirmed his disillusionment to the Nobel laureate Romain Rolland when he wrote that his hopes for the Christian love command, or "love extended to all mankind," were rendered but an "illusion" in the face of such anti-Semitism.[26] In his 1930 cultural work *Civilization and Its Discontents* Freud spoke directly to prejudice and tribalism in his reference to what he called "the narcissism of minor differences" and religious renderings of the love command, offering a psychoanalytic analysis of their "unpsychological" nature, the harm done to culture, and what psychoanalysis had to offer as a prescription. We will explore these at length in the chapters to come. For now, it will suffice it to note that his analysis was born of the existential reality of being the recipient of such hate.

To this end, a window into how this new sociopolitical reality impacted Freud's psyche can be seen in a pivotal dream of 1897 dubbed the "uncle with the yellow beard" (analyzed in 1900 in his *Interpretation of Dreams*). Early in 1897 a friendly mentor had proposed Freud for a professorship at the University of Vienna, at that time perceived to carry with it a veritable godlike status (Freud was but a *Privat-dozent*, equivalent to being a "lecturer," the lowest faculty rank). Freud knew that cultural anti-Semitism had invaded the halls of academia. By 1894, only two of the fifty-three Jews teaching at the university had reached the rank

---

[24] Klein, *Jewish Origins*, 54.
[25] Gay, *Freud: A Life for Our Time*, 16; Klein, *Jewish Origins*, 11, 54.
[26] See William B. Parsons, *The Enigma of the Oceanic Feeling* (New York: Oxford University Press, 1999), 23ff.

of professor. Moreover, two of Freud's colleagues had recently been put up for that title and been denied, a fact that Freud chalked up to what he politely called "denominational considerations."[27]

It was in this atmosphere that Freud had the following dream: "My friend R. was my uncle. I had a great feeling of affection for him. I saw before me his face, somewhat changed. It was as though it had been drawn out lengthways. A yellow beard that surrounded it stood out especially clearly."[28] On the face of it this dream looks to be nonsense and, quite frankly, meaningless. But in the hands of Freud's understanding of dreams, it achieves a much deeper message. Freud held that the *manifest* dream (the description or recounting of a dream you have on waking) is but the *disguised* version of repressed *latent dream wishes* lurking in the unconscious. Such wishes, because of the dynamic nature of the unconscious, seek expression. But they are often forbidden, because of their transgressive content. We have already seen that the unconscious expresses itself in many ways (e.g., slips of the tongue, symptomatic acts, neuroses). The conditions of sleep lead to a diminishing of the forces that repress the transgressive wishes of the unconscious. They are allowed to be expressed as dreams but only at a cost. The repression barrier (which Freud once compared to a tollbooth) transform the latent unconscious wishes into a manifest dream by distorting and disguising them. This process Freud called the *dreamwork* (the elements of which are displacement, condensation, considerations of representation, and secondary revision). The net effect of the dreamwork is that, for all intents and purposes, the true meaning (which is to say, the nature of the latent wishes) of a dream is hidden. The antidote, as one might expect, is to engage in analysis, which means free-associating to the various elements of the dream with the aim of uncovering the forbidden latent wishes.[29]

Without going through the labor of recounting Freud's lengthy analysis of his dream we can cut to the chase and reveal exactly the nature of the forbidden latent dream wishes. First and foremost, Freud found that the operative wishes were that his two colleagues were denied promotion not because of being Jewish but because one was a simpleton and the other a criminal.[30] Beyond that were wishes that he could have the political power to eliminate any and all rivals and promote himself to a

---

[27] Freud, *The Interpretation of Dreams*, S.E. 4: 170ff.   [28] Ibid., 171ff.
[29] The clearest explanation of the dreamwork is in Freud's shorter work *On Dreams*, S.E. 5: 629–722.
[30] McGrath, *Freud's Discovery of Psychoanalysis*, 177.

professorship. As any psychologically informed, honest university teacher who has vied for "tenure" knows, such a dream is not unusual. But, in Freud's case, it reveals the deep extent to which the sociopolitical surround had invaded the deepest recesses of his psyche.[31]

Another series of dreams Freud had during this time not only reveal the impact of the sociopolitical atmosphere and its anti-Semitism but also link both to religion, and do so in a way that connects such forces to the developmental portrait we sketched in the previous section. This series of dreams all had in common the city of Rome and Freud's failure to get to it (at least in the "manifest" dreams proper), and eventuated in what have been called his Rome neurosis and Hannibal fantasy.[32] During the course of his self-analysis Freud came to see that he equated certain cities with various neuroses, of which Rome was the most central. Between 1895 and 1898 he traveled to Italy and longed for but felt inhibited about visiting Rome. He once wrote to his friend Wilhelm Fleiss that his relation to and longing for Rome was "deeply neurotic."[33] He further revealed that he had different psychological reactions to different "Romes." For example, he linked ancient Rome, of which he was enamored, to European high culture and intellectual pursuits (he specifically referenced the eighteenth-century archaeologist and art historian Joachim Winckelmann). On successfully analyzing his Rome dreams and finally visiting the great city in 1901, he said of this "first" Rome: "I contemplated ancient Rome undisturbed (I could have worshipped the humble and mutilated remnant of the Temple of Minerva near the forum of Nerva)."[34] But if Freud loved ancient Rome, he could not stand medieval, Catholic Rome (the "second" Rome): "I found I could not freely enjoy the second Rome; I was disturbed by its meaning, and, being incapable of putting out of my mind my own misery and all the other misery which I know to exist, I found almost intolerable the lie of the salvation of mankind which rears its head so proudly to heaven."[35] This was Karl Lueger's Rome, the seat of anti-Semitism, hatred, and tribalism. It was this Rome that needed to be defeated.

Going back to our earlier discussion of Freud's nanny, some opine that Freud reacted to the loss of this nursemaid with feelings of

---

[31] Schorske, *Fin-de-Siècle Vienna*, 187.
[32] The dreams themselves are catalogued in Freud's *Interpretation of Dreams* but fully analyzed in light of their sociopolitical context and developmental infrastructure in the studies by Schorske and McGrath.
[33] See Freud's letter to Fleiss in *The Origins of Psychoanalysis*, 236.   [34] Ibid., 335–336.
[35] Ibid.

disappointment and betrayal and that those feelings, alongside his initial attachment to and deep affection for her (his "second mother"), became associated with both his attraction to and yet disappointment with Catholic Christianity and, as a result, his ambivalent feelings toward Rome. In other words, the "good" nanny was linked with Winckelmann's Rome – the first, ancient Rome that represented a true extension of love for all humankind, a sense of maternal connection, and the possibility of social assimilation. The "bad" nanny, on other hand, which had abandoned Freud and led to disillusionment and feelings of betrayal, was linked to the "second" Rome and its complicity in anti-Semitism. This, then, would be the deepest developmental root of his antipathy toward and suspicion of Christianity.[36]

Be this as it may, such echoes of the developmental past would not have been exponentially magnified were it not for actual sociopolitical events. Such events led to the Rome dreams, and in analyzing them Freud came across a set of associations that revealed another layer in which he linked anti-Semitism, politics, and Christianity: the Hannibal fantasy. Freud revealed that the dreams led to a memory of when, as a boy, his father Jacob had recounted a story about walking down the street and having his new fur hat (perhaps a Jewish *streimal*) knocked off his head by a Christian who, adding insult to injury, said "Jew! Get off the pavement!"[37] The intent of the father was to affirm to his son how political liberalism had changed things for the better. That is, anti-Semitism was openly practiced when Jacob was a young man, but the new liberal sociopolitical atmosphere of Vienna bore promise. Unfortunately, this moral entirely bypassed the young Freud (being only around ten years old). What Sigismund recalled was only the "unheroic conduct" of his father. Endeavoring to replace the story with one more befitting of his budding sense of masculine narcissism, Freud conjured up a satisfying alternative in fantasy: "I contrasted this situation with another which fitted my feelings better: the scene in which Hannibal's father, Hamilcar Barca, made his boy swear before the household altar to take vengeance on the Romans. Ever since that time Hannibal has had a place in my fantasies."[38] Like Freud, Hannibal had been "fated not to see Rome" and "symbolized the conflict between the tenacity of Jewry and

---

[36] Schorske, *Fin-de-Siècle Vienna*, 192–193.
[37] Gay, *Freud: A Life for Our Time*, 12. The details of Jacob's hat are famously inscribed in the pages of his *Interpretation of Dreams* (see S.E. 4).
[38] See Freud, *Interpretation of Dreams*, 230.

the organization of the Catholic church."³⁹ Freud's identification with Hannibal was both "pledge and project" and, as project, both "political and filial": "he defined his oedipal stance in such a way as to overcome his father by realizing the liberal creed his father professed but had failed to defend. Freud/Hannibal as 'Semitic general' would avenge his feeble father against Rome, a Rome that symbolized 'the organization of the Catholic Church' and the Habsburg regime that supported it."⁴⁰ Later in life, when Freud the father was presented with anti-Semitic taunts while with *his* sons, he "routed a gang of about ten men ... by charging furiously at them with his walking stick."⁴¹ Only a complete failure of the psychoanalytic imagination would think this had nothing to do with his memory of Jacob's hat and Hannibal.

THE REDEMPTIVE MISSION OF PSYCHOANALYSIS

Freud's Rome neurosis and Hannibal fantasy, then, were the developmental core motivating Freud's psychoanalytic unmasking of Catholic anti-Semitism as well as certain forms of clerical, authoritarian, and monarchical power. Indeed, some have argued that Freud's cultural works were aimed, at least in part, in deconstructing this kind of religious and sociopolitical authoritarianism.⁴² That thought is important, and bears a bit more development. How exactly is it that the cultural works can be linked to what can be called the "redemptive" mission of psychoanalysis? And did Judaism have any role in that mission?

During his university days it was becoming evident to Freud that a career in law and politics was not in the offing. What replaced his interest in the latter was a career in medicine and then, eventually, psychoanalysis. In finally resigning himself to the futility of his aspirations for assimilation, Freud retreated to "the only free realm" left to him, namely, "the inner life of the psyche."⁴³ Politics may have been a dead end but psychoanalysis might still be a means to conquer those malignant social forces and institutions (like religion) that impeded social justice while providing a basis for establishing a new social whole. Psychoanalysis could accomplish such an aim by offering theories about the inner realm and creating a social space (which is to say, the clinical space) that would

---

³⁹ Ibid., 229.   ⁴⁰ Schorske, *Fin-de-Siècle Vienna*, 191.
⁴¹ Gay, *Freud: A Life for Our Time*, 28.
⁴² McGrath and Schorske in particular have articulated this line of thought.
⁴³ Klein, *Jewish Origins*, 14.

function as an actual praxis. By enabling the task of introspection, instinctual renunciation, insight, and sublimation, human beings could be "re-formed" and an alternate route for cultural change could be manifested: transformed people transform culture.[44] As one perceptive commentator put it: "Freud, the most political of adolescents, turned in the wake of his political disillusionment to the philosophical, scientific realm to express his radical impulses."[45]

The road to actualizing this mission was filled with obstacles. Freud needed the sympathy of multiple like-minded colleagues as well as social institutions to support the furthering of his cause. Here again the many resources of Judaism came to the rescue, the first of which was B'nai B'rith. The latter was essentially a Jewish service organization devoted to the ongoing support and protection of Jews in society. In early twentieth-century Vienna it took the form of fraternal lodges where Jews could meet and, as in Freud's case, offer a sounding board for developing academic work. Freud was a member from 1897 to 1902, years in which (not so coincidentally) Karl Lueger, the founder of the Austrian Christian Social Party, was mayor of Vienna. If Freud felt ostracized by the academic culture at the University of Vienna, then the reverse can be said for his many lectures at the lodge. It can be fairly stated that the lodge became the primary academic forum for his evolving ideas, ranging from his emerging theories about neuroses to his understanding of dreams. Importantly, the lodge did not valorize "religious" Judaism per se as much as the humanistic and enlightenment themes of unity, humanity, and friendship. The lodge, in highlighting their role as part of a redemptive humanistic mission designed to counter the intolerant, racist, inhumane culture germinating in Vienna, strongly endorsed the notions of ethical reform, repairing the fractured social whole, and the universality of humankind.[46] This mission, then, was appropriated by Freud in a specifically psycho-analytic way. As Jacqueline Rose once put it, Freud "adopted universalism as a specifically Jewish dream of freedom and justice which it was the task of Jews in general, and psychoanalysis in particular, to disseminate across the globe ... it was the task of Jewish *particularity* to *universalize* itself."[47]

As Freud gained confidence and created intellectual links to like-minded colleagues, his participation in B'nai B'rith began to decline. In

---

[44] See ibid., 32, 142.   [45] McGrath, *Freud's Discovery of Psychoanalysis*, 109.
[46] See Klein, *Jewish Origins*, 75–87.
[47] In E. Said, *Freud and the Non-European* (London: Verso, 2003), 72.

its stead he founded, starting in 1902, what became known as the "psychoanalytic circle," the first social form of the later "psychoanalytic movement." It is hardly an accident that all seventeen of its members from 1902 to 1906 were Jewish. Yet despite the support and intellectual nourishment he had received from his Jewish friends and colleagues, Freud was concerned that psychoanalysis might be seen as a "Jewish science" and a "Jewish national affair." Surely, this was at least part of the reason that Freud sought ties to the wider world of European psychology, finally deciding on a gentile, Carl Jung (the son of a Protestant minister), as heir to the psychoanalytic throne. As he once said to his fellow psychoanalysts about appointing Jung: "It is absolutely essential that I should form ties in the world of general science"; "Jews must be content with the modest role of preparing the ground"; and "Only [Jung's] appearance has saved psychoanalysis from becoming a Jewish national concern."[48] Even here, however, one hears the echo of Freud's allegiance to the Jewish humanistic redemptive mission. So it is that he said to Jung, his heir apparent: "If I am Moses, then you are Joshua and will take possession of the promised land of psychiatry, which I shall be only able to glimpse from afar."[49] The political overtones are unmistakable when, in 1907, he would ask Jung if he had any contacts who might be used to get the German Kaiser Wilhelm interested in psychoanalysis.[50] Indeed, whether it was Jung or, as we shall see, the Protestant lay analyst Oskar Pfister, the noble laureate Romain Rolland, the Indian analyst Girindrasekhar Bose, or the Japanese analyst Heisaku Kosawa, Freud was always on the lookout for new members of the "band of brothers" who could globally disseminate psychoanalysis.

If B'nai B'rith was essential to fermenting Freud's emerging theories, then another resource within Judaism was equally responsible for instigating creativity, self-cohesion, and the continuance of the psychoanalytic redemptive mission in Freud's world. Using contemporary psychoanalytic terminology, that resource can be referred to as cultural "self-objects" (a psychoanalytic term signifying culturally and religiously valued figures offered for idealization, identification, and nurturance), of which the figure of Moses was central. Freud's complex relationship to Moses will occupy us in Chapter 3, where we will look in detail at his last book,

---

[48] See Klein, *Jewish Origins*, 94; Gay, *A Godless Jew*, 120, chapter 3.
[49] Klein, *Jewish Origins*, 94.
[50] See Freud's letter to Jung of August 18, 1907, in *The Freud–Jung Letters*, ed. W. McGuire (Princeton, NJ: Princeton University Press, 1974).

Moses and Monotheism (1939). For our discussion here, we can turn to a revealing, earlier essay titled "The Moses of Michelangelo."

Freud wrote the essay (initially published anonymously in December 1913) shortly after Jung had abdicated his role as heir and defected from the movement.[51] To make things worse, World War I loomed on the horizon, threatening not only the integrity of the psychoanalytic movement but the very existence of Europe. In other words, Freud was subject to the most intense personal strain imaginable. In this state he was motivated to travel to Rome, of all places, to the site of Michelangelo's statue (which adorned the tomb of Pope Julius II), there to sit "for three lonely weeks."[52] In and of itself, Freud's travel to Rome to see Michelangelo's Moses in such circumstances speaks volumes about the influence of Judaism on his psyche. As he once stated: "No piece of statuary has ever made a stronger impact on me than this."[53]

The statue itself depicts a seated Moses, his right hand protecting the famed stone tablets and his left resting on his lap. It is based on chapter 34 of Exodus where Moses, having received the tablets from God, descends from the mountain only to encounter the Israelites, now engaged in idol worship and dancing around the Golden Calf. Infuriated, Moses cast down the tablets, breaking them asunder. Exactly what Michelangelo had in mind in trying to capture this story has been debated.[54] For his part Freud came to the conclusion that Michelangelo caught Moses while he was possessed by fury but before he actually broke the tablets. Why? Because in the midst of the fracturing of his community and in a state of outrage, he could now frame Moses as countering temptation by controlling his anger and, as a result, preserving the tablets. As Freud put it: "In this way he [Michelangelo] has added something new and more than human to the figure of Moses; so that the giant frame with its tremendous physical power becomes only a concrete expression of the highest mental achievement that is possible in a man, that of struggling successfully

---

[51] For the essay itself, see S.E. 13: 210–236. For exactly why Freud did not append his name to his own essay, see Ernst Simon, "Sigmund Freud the Jew," in *Leo Baeck Institute Yearbook* 2 (1957): 302–305; Moshe Halevi Spero, "Self-Effacement and Self-Inscription: Reconsidering Freud's Anonymous 'Moses of Michelangelo,'" *Psychoanalysis and Contemporary Thought* 24 (2002): 359–462.

[52] Rice, *Freud and Moses*, 124. In keeping with our narrative, Peter Homans has observed that Freud's interpretation of Moses contained a veiled reproach against Julius II, who advocated for a Christian theocracy. See Peter Homans, *The Ability to Mourn* (Chicago: University of Chicago Press, 1989), 50.

[53] See S.E. 13: 213.   [54] Rice, *Freud and Moses*, 125.

against an inward passion for the sake of a cause to which he has devoted himself."⁵⁵ It bears repeating that for Freud the Moses of Michelangelo fit his own personal situation. He too was faced with apostates (e.g., Jung), the fracturing of his movement, and a world in crisis. Finally, Freud went home, there to write furiously, producing several essays (dubbed the "metapsychological papers") which defined the basic tenets of the psychoanalytic view of the psyche. Like Moses, who had preserved what God had bequeathed him, Freud's metapsychological papers were his gift to culture, his "psychoanalytic tablets."⁵⁶

In sum, then, Freud may not have been a religious Jew, but he did find personal sustenance and creative nourishment in Jewish cultural self-objects like Moses. The latter, in the form of Michelangelo's Moses, had a particular meaning for him as a result of his upbringing, the immediate exigencies of his sociocultural surround, and his dedication to the redemptive mission of psychoanalysis.

FREUD'S ANSWER TO RELIGION

Returning to intellectual influences on Freud during his days at the University of Vienna, it is common for those who have spent considerable time in university social spaces to name a significant book, teacher, or course that radically changed their worldview. The American psychoanalyst Erik Erikson, noting that college is usually attended during late adolescence, referred to that stage of the life cycle as one in which one's personal identity and development of a worldview begin to take shape. Sociologically speaking, universities, which Erikson dubbed *moratoriums*, allocate the time and space to ferment such valuable psychological changes. One is exposed to a variety of new ideas, people, modes of expressing sexuality, and career options, which, through experimentation and reflection, help to facilitate significant life choices. In the above we saw how the college-age Freud, exposed to the emerging science of his day, not only decided on a career in medicine but reinforced a specific approach to religion and, indeed, his status as an atheist.

Added to that list were the humanistic texts from the Western philosophical and literary past. As we have seen, this included a long list from

---

⁵⁵ Ibid., 127.
⁵⁶ Freud planned a series of a dozen essays he called *Zur Vorbereitung einer Metapsychologie* (Preliminaries to a Metapsychology) in 1914–1915, right after his paper on Moses. While many were written, only five of them remain.

Plato and Empedocles to Shakespeare and Goethe. One could further include the likes of Kant, Schopenhauer, Nietzsche, and a range of anthropological and sociological theorists, all of whom influenced Freud and many of whom we shall see again in the chapters ahead.[57] For now, in narrowing our purview to Freud's take on religion, we can focus on a single thinker who was to suggest an approach that profoundly affected his later cultural works: the German philosopher Ludwig Feuerbach (1804–1872). To be sure, in avowing his atheism Freud had occasion to cite numerous figures of the enlightenment and Western humanistic past that he had read, fashioning himself to be following in their godless footsteps (e.g., Voltaire, Diderot, Lessing, to name but a few). However, Feuerbach held a special place of honor. In a letter to a friend during his student years, Freud said of Feuerbach: "Among all the philosophers I worship and admire this man the most."[58] His book *The Essence of Christianity* (1841), read by Freud as a student and found in his library in London at the end of his life, endeavored to translate the "metaphysical" doctrines of Christianity into human "anthropology" (a term that, in Christian theological discourse, refers not to the "social science" of that name but to the understanding of the human personality and, as such, is conducive to psychology). Feuerbach stated that "theology is not treated as a mystical pragmatology as in Christian mythology, nor as ontology, as in speculative philosophy of religion, but rather as psychic pathology."[59] Since Feuerbach also thought that the dogmas of Christianity were but wishes ("religion is the dream of the wakened consciousness; the dream is the key to the secrets of religion"[60]), some have rightfully suggested that Freud's later view, so forcefully stated in his *Future of an Illusion*, was influenced by his reading of Feuerbach. Indeed, it is hard not to see the connection when faced with Feuerbach's contention that the effect of humankind's critical reason, when aimed at religion, amounted to nothing less than "the destruction of an illusion – an illusion ... whose effect on mankind ... is utterly pernicious."[61]

In Freud's hands, this meant that both religion and politics could be understood as but an "epiphenomenal manifestation of psychic forces."[62]

---

[57] For a reasoned analysis of philosophical influences (especially Kant, Schopenhauer, and Nietzsche) on Freud's work and his place in the philosophical tradition, see Alfred I. Tauber, *Freud, the Reluctant Philosopher* (Princeton, NJ: Princeton University Press, 2010). We will see how Freud engaged other social scientific views on religion especially in Chapter 2.
[58] Gay, *A Godless Jew*, 53. [59] McGrath, *Freud's Discovery of Psychoanalysis*, 106.
[60] Ibid. [61] Gay, *A Godless Jew*, 55. [62] Schorske, *Fin-de-Siècle Vienna*, 183.

Worse, Freud knew that many of our social institutions were simply "unpsychological." Rather than facilitating transformation and unity, they fomented neuroses, tribalism, moral hypocrisy, dis-ease, and a stunting of the intellect. Following in the steps of Feuerbach, Freud came to see that foremost among these institutions were those created by religion. But while Freud followed Feuerbach's injunction to translate "metaphysics" into "anthropology," what Feuerbach lacked was a scientific model of the human personality. It was the "developmental infrastructure" of belief, then, that Freud later added, thus nuancing the seminal insight of Feuerbach.

THE PSYCHOANALYTIC MOTTO RECONSIDERED

Offering a methodological position on the true source of religion can go only so far. It needs, as a supplement, a *praxis*, in the form of a clinical space, to exponentially expand its existential effect. Along these lines the Freudian emphasis on transforming the human personality, religion, and culture at large found expression in the most famous of his clinical one-liners: the psychoanalytic motto of "Where id was, there ego shall be." The motto occurs in his *New Introductory Lectures on Psychoanalysis* (1933):

> It is easy to imagine, too, that certain mystical practices may succeed in upsetting the normal relations between the different regions of the mind, so that, for instance, perception may be able to grasp happenings in the depths of the ego and in the id which were otherwise inaccessible to it. It may safely be doubted, however, whether this road will lead us to the ultimate truth from which salvation is to be expected. Nevertheless it may be admitted that the therapeutic efforts of psychoanalysis have chosen a similar line of approach. Its intention is, indeed, to strengthen the ego, to make it more independent of the super ego, to widen its field of perception and enlarge its organization, so that it can appropriate fresh portions of the id. Where id was, there ego shall be. It is a work of culture – not unlike the draining of the Zuider Zee.[63]

On the face of it, the motto seems quite straightforward. Yet here is where learning to "read" Freud becomes important. Understood in the broader context of the paragraph as a whole, the motto reveals Freud's

---

[63] See Freud, "The Dissection of the Psychical Personality," in S.E. 22: 57–80. For an extended discussion of the psychoanalytic motto, see Parsons, *The Enigma of the Oceanic Feeling*, 79–80.

deep humanism, thorough command of the written word, and devotion to a humanistic, redemptive psychoanalysis.

To show this, we can begin by unpacking Freud's reference to the Zuider Zee. One of Freud's more perceptive commentators, the psychoanalyst Bruno Bettelheim, has pointed out that although the draining of the Zuider Zee was a technical achievement, Freud chose to refer to it not in terms of the German word *Urbarmachung*, which is (as Freud knew) the proper German term to denote the reclamation of land for agriculture, but as *Kulturarbeit*, which can be translated as "the labor to achieve culture." He adds that Freud's choice of this metaphor is significant. It recalls something close to Freud's heart: the story of Goethe's *Faust*. The essence of the latter consists in Faust's renouncing his more youthful and grandiose attempts at harnessing the "meaning of the universe" in favor of the more limited goal of the "reclamation" of land from the sea – a task aimed at creating a working community beneficial to himself and humankind. Read from this perspective, the psychoanalytic motto is best understood as pointing to how analysis leads to a kind of "reclaiming" of "the soul." And the latter is simply the practical and attainable task of helping the ego in its attempt to mediate between the power of unconscious urges and the realities of the external world. What psychoanalysis strove for was insight, renunciation, sublimation, structure building. Psychoanalysis was that interpretive and cultural science that endeavored to make people more civilized and civilization more human.[64]

The religious reference of the above becomes even more evident when viewed in light of Freud's deliberate rendering of the grammatical structure of the motto. In the German original the motto reads "*Wo Es war, soll Ich werden.*" Missing from the *Es* and *Ich* (both of which are capitalized in the German) are the definite articles (i.e., *das* or "the"). Rhetorically, this has the effect of elevating *Es* and *Ich* into archetypes. The use of the German verb *werden* (to become) and *soll* (must, shall be) now become tinged with a definite and deliberate religious meaning. The motto recalls the creation imagery ("becoming") of Genesis and the imperative language of Exodus. What "should" and "must" be the case, as a command, is that the Ego replace, fill in, "reclaim" the unconscious. Where before there was ocean, now there is land. Where before there was murkiness of desire, now "should be" the structure of ego. By intentionally using the grammar of religious language, and intentionally referring

---

[64] See Bettelheim, *Freud and Man's Soul*, 61–64.

to Faust, Genesis, and Exodus, Freud was juxtaposing the contrasting agendas of psychoanalysis and religion. Psychoanalysis was that science of the human personality that would replace religion. This sentiment, as we shall see in the chapters ahead, was hardly confined to the psychoanalytic motto. Indeed, it forms the very essence of his argument throughout his works on religion. What Freud aimed at was nothing less than the establishment of a secular cure of souls.

Freud reaffirmed this psychoanalytic answer to religion in a letter to the Protestant pastor Oskar Pfister (1873–1965). Interestingly enough, the two were very good friends, Pfister often visiting Freud's household, writing to him often, and even becoming a "lay" analyst (the very first "pastoral" psychologist).[65] Soon after the publication of his *Future of an Illusion*, Freud wrote to Pfister that his aim was not only to hasten the total deconstruction of religious institutions but also to insert in their stead a veritable secular cure of souls (namely, psychoanalysis). This new institution would be manned not by priests but by "a profession of *lay* curers of souls."[66] Freud thought that the latter would do what religion could not: transform and educate the instincts in a manner that would create a more tolerant social whole. And, of course, they would be guided by the command: *Wo Es war, soll Ich werden.*

A few conclusions, then, can be drawn from our discussion. Freud was a humanist and atheist influenced by a number of theories mediated to him through his stints at the gymnasium and the University of Vienna. At the same time, he had a certain allegiance to and fondness for the ideas and figures linked to his Jewish upbringing. Freud may not have been a fan of the more strictly "religious" dimensions of Judaism, but its cultural self-objects and institutions served what psychologists call an "adaptive" function. This came to the fore when Freud was faced with the realities of the sociopolitical atmosphere of his day. When faced with an anti-Semitic academic atmosphere, it was the B'nai B'rith that came to the rescue. When faced with the disintegration of his personal and professional life, it was the figure of Moses that gave him sustenance, confidence, and purpose. When Catholicism seemed to betray its foundational ethic to love the Other, it was the identification with Hannibal and the redemptive

---

[65] Pfister had published articles on psychoanalytically informed pastoral care as early as 1908 and visited Freud as early as 1909, establishing himself as a Freud family favorite and trusted advisor (see Gay, *A Godless Jew*, 75ff., on how their relationship evolved).

[66] See Freud's letter to Pfister of November 25, 1928, in S. Freud and Oskar Pfister, *Psychoanalysis and Faith: The Letters of Sigmund Freud and Oskar Pfister.*

mission of psychoanalysis that spurred on something akin to a Mosaic prophetic self-consciousness, albeit one psychoanalytically and humanistically conceived. In sum, through investigating the relevant developmental, intellectual, and sociopolitical forces, we are beginning to get a handle on why Freud wrote about religion.

2

Totem and Taboo

The Origin of Religion

The first association that comes to mind when one thinks of Freud on religion is predictable: Oedipus. And, famously, Freudian interpretations are usually linked to his most well-known and controversial work on the subject: *Future of an Illusion* (1927). That work, as well as his others on religion, is connected by a general methodological statement found in his *The Psychopathology of Everyday Life* (1901):

> I believe that a large part of the mythological view of the world, which extends a long way into the most modern religions, *is nothing but psychology projected into the modern world*. The obscure recognition of psychical factors and relations in the unconscious is mirrored ... in the construction of a *supernatural reality*, which is destined to be changed back once more by science into the *psychology of the unconscious*. One could venture to explain in this way the myths of paradise and the fall of man, of God, of good and evil, of immortality, and so on, and to transform *metaphysics* into *metapsychology*.[1]

Freud was invested in translating abstract, experience-distant "metaphysics" into the more existentially accessible, experience-near dimensions of human experience. Psychoanalysis did this by providing a "function" (projection) tied to a "developmental infrastructure" (the interplay between id, ego, and super-ego as they are determined by the stages of childhood development) to any metaphysical abstraction. In other words, as noted in the introductory chapter, religion is not from the hand of the divine but the very human projection of complex developmental issues and unconscious wishes. One can subsume all of Freud's

---

[1] Freud, *The Psychopathology of Everyday Life*, S.E. 6: 258–259.

varied analyses of the expressions of religion (be they myths, symbols, scripture, faith, conversion, mysticism, etc.) under this general methodological umbrella.

That being said, one must be careful not to let this foundational statement overshadow the fact that Freud wrote numerous essays and books about religion and that his various analyses were far reaching, at times going beyond a simple recourse to the oedipal triangle. In fact, Freud's writings on religion were strewn throughout his works, being found as early as a small paper on ritual acts in 1907 (and even earlier if one counts selective passages in works not directly devoted to religion, in various letters, and in offhand comments) and extending to his death in 1939.[2] Taking this rather substantial commentary on religion into account, and given that Freud's analyses on religion were rich, varied, and engaged a wide spectrum of issues, it would be wise to work through his many contributions deliberately with an eye to context as well as to continuity and development of his thought. It is true that this approach demands a certain labor and attention to detail. However, if one wishes to gain accurate knowledge of the totality of Freud's approach to religion, then there is no other choice.

Keeping these points in mind, our journey can be initiated with Freud's first book-length work devoted to religion, *Totem and Taboo* (1913). In a fortunate twist of aesthetic synchronicity, it also happens to be about "the beginning," namely, the origins of religion. In the next chapter we will move on to address his *Moses and Monotheism*, which not only is his last (1939) book on religion, but also has the virtue of continuity in that Freud, deliberately coming back to themes and analyses offered in *Totem and Taboo*, extended his ideas about how religion developed historically out of what he conceived to be its origins. These two major works, being Freud's first and last and linked by the common issues and themes they address, can be framed as the "bookends" of Freud on religion.

TOTEM AND TABOO: THE ARGUMENT

The four essays that constitute *Totem and Taboo* were originally published separately in the psychoanalytic journal *Imago* during the years 1912–1913. Freud linked the essays by subsuming them under the same general heading: "Some Points of Agreement between the Mental Lives of

---

[2] For a survey of Freud's earliest comments on religion, see R. Rainey, *Freud as Student of Religion* (Atlanta, GA: Scholar's Press, 1975), chapter 6.

Savages and Neurotics." They were then jointly published under the title *Totem and Taboo*, with the aforementioned heading now becoming the subtitle of the book. Freud's psychoanalytic approach is evident from that subtitle: there is something about the way the mind works in neurotics that is the key to primitive religion (indeed, to all religion). Each essay offers different but related reflections on various aspects of this problem.[3]

A few general observations can prepare us for the analysis to come. First, the book focuses on what Freud thought was the first historical form of a "pre" religion ("totemism") and the first societal set of laws and morals (subsumed under the rubric of "taboo"). Freud claimed that totemism eventually morphed into "religion" (by which he meant the added notion of "God" and its linked, complex institutional framework). Additionally, he was convinced that history had shown that cultural forms continued to evolve and that science would soon be replacing religion altogether. In other words, he was firmly convinced of the sociological reality of "secularization" (defined generally as the gradual cultural marginalization of religious ideas and institutions and their waning ability to command idealization and allegiance). In these essays he was bent on explaining the historical origin of religion as well as society and morality, further offering some cursory thoughts on the reason behind its historical development but leaving an analysis of its contemporary form and what he thought was its inevitable decline for later studies (issues we will investigate in the chapters ahead).

Second, during this era the social sciences (psychology, anthropology, sociology) as a whole were jointly emerging. Freud was not shy about first relying on, then taking on, these new disciplinary comers. He is willing to "readily confess" that it was Wilhelm Wundt, a prominent psychologist of his day, and Jung, the author of that emerging threat to Freud's psychoanalysis that he eventually called a "collective unconscious," which provided what Freud called the "first stimulus" for his essays. Indeed, Freud goes on to say that he aims to provide a "methodological contrast" to such competitors.[4] Wundt's problem, from Freud's perspective, was that he never articulated or championed a "depth" dimension to psychology. In other words, his was a non-psychoanalytic psychology.

---

[3] As with all of Freud's works, James Strachey's editorial introduction to *Totem and Taboo* in the *Standard Edition*, vol. 13, provides a detailed overview of the stages of publication. See also E. Wallace, *Freud and Anthropology* (New York: International Universities Press, 1983).

[4] Freud, *Totem and Taboo*, S.E. 13: xiii–xiv.

These essays reveal Freud's upending Wundt's arguments by showing how the notion of the unconscious provides superior explanatory power when trying to decipher the riddle of totemism and its taboos.[5] As for Jung, as we will explicate in detail in the pages ahead, Freud corrected the latter's mistakes by arguing for the primacy of Oedipus and a phylogenetically based "collective" mind that countered the need for Jung's formulation of a collective unconscious populated by archetypes.[6]

Freud was similarly invested in showing the need for psychoanalytic ways of thinking about the researches of the other social sciences. The Société d'Anthropologie de Paris had been founded in 1859 and the German Anthropological Society in 1869 (E. B. Tylor, the father of Anglo-American anthropology, received his initial appointment at Oxford in 1884), while the first department of sociology had been founded by Emile Durkheim at the University of Bordeaux in 1895. Indeed, Tylor, Durkheim, and a host of anthropologists dot the landscape of *Totem and Taboo*. His own work, says Freud, seeks "to bridge the gap" between such disciplines, noting that "cooperation between them could not fail to be of benefit to research."[7] Freud's first work on religion, then, is clearly meant to address interdisciplinary concerns. Since most of the literature he dealt with was about primitive religion and hence siphoned through the anthropological literature of his day, it would be reasonable to call *Totem and Taboo* the very first work in "psychoanalytic anthropology." How well he did that is open to question. Indeed, there was more than a little blowback from his anthropological and sociological colleagues.[8] With respect to our

---

[5] Wilhelm Wundt (1832–1920), the acknowledged founder of experimental psychology, can be rightly framed alongside Freud, James, and Jung as the fourth great figure of the "first period" (1880–1944) of the emerging "psychology and religion movement." While not having the name recognition of the other three men, Wundt founded the first psychological laboratory in 1879 at the University of Leipzig, bequeathing to later generations a psychophysical approach to human experience and consciousness that stressed the importance of analysis and the classification of data. His legacy is responsible for introducing questionnaires, interviews, and a statistical approach to the psychology of religion.

[6] As detailed later in this chapter, Freud countered Jung with his own psychoanalytic version of something close to a "collective mind." In acknowledging the latter's existence, albeit in a psychoanalytically specific way, Freud was saying to Jung that there is but one (and only one) "universal archetype" that exists, its name is Oedipus, and its origin is historical and due to the trauma of the primal deed and its aftermath.

[7] Freud, *Totem and Taboo*, S.E. 13: xiii–xiv.

[8] Wallace, in his *Freud and Anthropology*, chapter 1, has surveyed the salient texts that comprise Freud's interest in anthropology well before he wrote *Totem and Taboo*. He makes the important point that Freud's emerging metapsychology was influenced by his readings in the anthropological literature (p. 3).

comments in the Introduction, it's as if Freud were inviting a debate over what we called the need for psychoanalysis to have a "reflexive" dimension. As we shall see, Freud's position fared poorly in the exchange.

This book also represents the first psychoanalytic investigation into the comparative (cross-cultural) study of religion. Most understand *Totem and Taboo* as centered on the origins and development of Western religion. Yet, in relying on anthropological literature that looked at Australian aborigines, the so-called primitive cultures of the distant past, and developments such as matriarchal religions, Freud framed his conclusions as universal and thus determinative of all religious expressions. Again, as in the case of those working in the other social sciences, Freud's works have elicited more than a little consternation from those who study the comparative study of religions.

The Origins of Religion, Morality, and Society

The fourth essay of the volume ("The Return of Totemism in Childhood"), which Freud (as well as his subsequent interpreters) thought was the most successful of the volume, is singularly marked by what can rightly be termed the ambitious, grandiose nature of his project: nothing less than the historical and psychological origins of religion, morality, and society.

Freud begins by reviewing the reigning anthropological literature of his day on primitive societies (particularly the aboriginal tribes of Australia). His summary characterization of these "primitives" is pejorative: their mental life is archaic and instinctual, their level of cultural development simple, their worship of higher beings (relative to those found in contemporary religious forms) lacking, and their manner of maintaining social order rudimentary. What dominated their lives was a religio-social system called totemism (a term that, like "animism" and "exogamy," is a Western anthropological construct) understood by anthropologists of his day as being a universal phenomenon that all cultures pass through, a primitive phase of human development and civilization. While we will only note this now and go into detail later, in such characterizations Freud was depending on certain "evolutionary" anthropological theorists who, even in his own era, were being castigated for their errors and Eurocentric biases.[9]

---

[9] See, for example, Wallace, *Freud and Anthropology*; C. Brickman, *Aboriginal Populations in the Mind* (New York: Columbia University Press, 2003).

Sifting through the anthropological literature, Freud then presents a selective summary of totemism. First, the totem is a class of assorted material objects (usually animal) that are revered and worshipped, understood to be the ancestor and father of the clan, who protected the clan, whom the members of the clan identified with (often through dressing up in the guise of the totem), and who should not be killed (except on those few sacred occasions dubbed the "totem meal" when it is permissible in a ceremony to kill the totem and eat it). While the latter characterizes its "religious" dimension, Freud, again relying on the anthropological literature of his time, appends to that its "social" dimension, consisting of a set of laws or "taboos" of which exogamy (the taboo against incest) was primary. Although religion in the "high" sense of the worship of higher beings and an elaborate institutional structure is not to be found, Freud is willing to speak of totemism and exogamy as a form of "pre-religion" that, if analyzed closely, might provide clues as to the nature of later, more developed "traditional religion" in general.[10]

Given this, Freud asks: How did this primitive community in its religious and social dimensions come to be? While Freud applauds the literature on the subject, he insists that what they did not see, and which psychoanalysis supplies, is the contributing factors of the psycho-sexual developmental scheme in tandem with the dynamics of the structural model. It is here that Freud thought psychoanalysis could contribute to a "dialogue" with its sister social sciences.

In embarking on this mission Freud stresses the clinical data. One could say that Freud thought that the secrets of humanity and history, diverse cultures and religion, could be unveiled through the analysis of patients in a consulting room in fin-de-siècle Vienna. Specifically, he adduces psychoanalytic analyses of children and their "animal phobias." Freud had just written (in 1909) a case history on "little Hans" and his horse phobia (titled "Analysis of a Phobia in a Five-Year-Old Boy"[11]). Drawing on similar psychoanalytic case histories from his colleagues, he made the argument that when one analyzes the spectrum of behavior exhibited by children toward animals of various kinds (ranging from simple fear to more complex, conflicted attitudes), one finds that they all have a singular source: the child's father. In other words, the child has

---

[10] Here Freud was following in the footsteps of his counterpart Emile Durkheim, who employed a similar strategy, sociologically conceived, in *The Elementary Forms of Religious Life* (New York: Free Press, 1995 [1912]).

[11] Freud's case of "little Hans" can be found in S.E. 10: 3–152.

displaced the range of emotions and conflicted attitudes found in the Oedipus complex from the father to the "totem" animal. If human nature is universal, then the singular clue to what the totem really is, and how it came to be, has been found: the totem is nothing but a substitute father.

One suspects that Freud, privy to clinical data and possessed of the notion that there was a universal human nature, was convinced that he knew the true origin of totemism before he embarked upon writing *Totem and Taboo*. As he said to his psychoanalytic colleague Ernst Jones: "I already know the results; my instinct tells me that."[12] Nevertheless, in the spirit of interdisciplinary conversation, he presented a full range of social scientific theorizing on totemism, yet was careful to selectively choose and combine those elements of the various arguments that would tally with, if not support and be enhanced by, the depth psychoanalytic perspective he would provide. Briefly put, he adopts Darwin's assertion that before the existence of any society there were roving groups of primal humans consisting of a feared and envied primal father, his wife (or wives) and sons, some of whom were castrated or driven out by the fearsome father; J. J. Atkinson's theory that the primal horde came to an end when the brothers banded together and killed the primal father out of jealousy, competition, and envy; and Robertson Smith's suggestion that totemism, now conceived of as a kind of "brother clan," was punctuated by ceremonies in which prohibitions were lifted and the totemic animal was killed and eaten ("the totem meal"). Insisting that the explanation for the origin of totemism needed to be at once "a historical and a psychological one" and that it "should tell us under what conditions this peculiar institution developed and to what psychic needs in men it has given expression,"[13] Freud then presents his psychoanalytic version of the origin of totemism, beginning with the "acting out" of the oedipal wish to kill the father:

> One day the brothers who had been driven out came together, killed and devoured their father and so made an end of the patriarchal horde. United, they had the courage to do and succeeded in doing what would have been impossible for them individually.... The violent primal father had doubtless been the feared and envied model of each one of the company of brothers; and in the act of devouring him they accomplished their identification with him, and each one of them acquired a portion of his strength. The totem meal, which is perhaps mankind's earliest festival, would thus be a repetition and a commemoration of this memorable and criminal deed.[14]

---

[12] Wallace, *Freud and Anthropology*, 57. [13] Freud, *Totem and Taboo*, S.E. 13: 108.
[14] Ibid., 141–142.

Thus, Freud finds the murder of the primal father to be the true historical event (later mythologized in Western, monotheistic scripture but in a disguised, displaced form with nary a trace of its actual source) that gave rise to the feeling (as well as the doctrine) of the "original sin" lurking in us all. So it is that he says (by way of once again running a crucial biblical text through one of his favorite tragic plays, Goethe's *Faust*): "in the beginning was the Deed."[15]

Psychoanalytic logic would predict that the acting-out of the hostility toward the father would result in guilt and remorse. Thus, the socio-religious institution known as totemism is also a kind of memory or monument born of remorse for the great deed:

> Totemic religion arose from the filial sense of guilt.... They thus created out of their filial sense of guilt the two fundamental taboos of totemism, which for that very reason inevitably corresponded to the two repressed wishes of the Oedipus complex.... The totemic system was, as it were, a covenant with their father, in which he promised them everything that a childish imagination may expect from a father – protection, care, and indulgence – while on their side they undertook to respect his life.... Society was now based on complicity in the common crime; religion was based on the sense of guilt and the remorse attaching to it; while morality was based partly on the exigencies of this society and partly on the penance demanded by the sense of guilt.[16]

There are implications of the above Freudian "origin myth" that are important in that they link with his later monographs on religion. The first is that while Freud speaks of "conscience" and "morality" throughout *Totem and Taboo* he had not yet formally named and introduced his famous concept of the super-ego. However, retrospectively speaking, what Freud was doing in *Totem and Taboo* was speaking about the historical and psychological origin of *both* the individual and cultural super-ego. Unconscious ambivalence, evident in the Oedipus complex, eventuated in the "acting-out" of the murder of the primal father and, in reaction, the establishment of laws, prohibitions, society, and religion. This means that the very first set of laws (taboos) were born *not* of detached critical reason and the production of a calculated blueprint for communal life, as if early brilliant philosophers somehow stepped to the fore, but in reaction to the unconscious and its "drives" (*triebe*). Freud did not think that "ethics," understood in the contemporary cultural form as a reasoned philosophical/theological discipline, was present at the origins of civilization. Rather, the earliest form of morality, namely, taboos,

---

[15] Ibid., 161.   [16] Ibid., 145, 143, 144, 146.

which for Freud were the precursors to the later, more developed laws, rules, and regulations of society, were based in the dynamics of psychological functioning, of which the unconscious played the starring role. This idea served as the basis for his critique of Kant's famous categorical imperative, which, as he indicates in the preface of *Totem and Taboo*, mistakenly valorized the prestige of the conscious mind. As we will expand in later chapters, Freud went so far as to say that modern ethical postulates and cultural commands had a depth (unconscious) dimension and meaning. This is particularly true with respect to religious commands, which, however noble in their abstract form, were often mendacious, being ruled in their actual implementation and practice by unconscious content and desire.

In later works Freud articulated how one's own personal super-ego is formed developmentally as the result of the mediation of values from both the parental unit and the "cultural" super-ego behind them. Culture "gets into" the individual psyche through the formation of the super-ego. If the very first manifestation of the cultural super-ego was that socio-religious system called totemism, then its later iteration is nothing less than modern notions of God and the more familiar, traditional accouterments of traditional religion. As an important aside, this indicates that Freud did not think that religion was always but a useless illusion. On the contrary, in both *Totem and Taboo* and his later works, Freud thought it had served a historically valuable and necessary function by helping to ensure, through the control of human aggression, the continued survival of civilization. This underlines the point that Freud's view of the interaction between individuals and society was one that highlighted essential conflict. The origins of society, morality, and religion were born of ambivalence and violence, and because humans are possessed of innate, powerful, and ineradicable aggressive instincts, they are perpetually at odds with social rules, regulations, and institutions. Humans are, as he would later say, "enemies" of civilization. We do not "by nature" or spontaneously renounce instinctual urges and strain to adapt to the rules and regulations of civilization. The neurotics, who as a group have the most difficulty with such renunciations, may be prime examples, but they merely expose a deep trait lying within the species as a whole. Civilization, then, exists in some sense to counter the natural, instinctual urges of human beings. It needs, as it were, weapons to combat the natural human tendency to upset the social order. In his later works Freud will carry this argument forward into ever more expanding detail by articulating what he calls the "mental" assets of civilization, of which religion was primary. This is an instance of what we called the "adaptive" psychoanalytic view of religion – one carried forward yet again in his *Future of an Illusion*. The problem, aside from the many psychological critiques he had about this regressive form of adaptation, is that Freud came to think that the ability of religion to offset aggressiveness was waning, and he gave specific reasons as to why he thought that to be the case while arguing for a substitute (i.e., psychoanalysis) to counter the coming social dislocation (we will pick up the threads of that part of his argument in Chapter 4).

From Totemism to Christianity: The Historical Development of Religion

The fourth essay is also the source of another important aspect of Freud's early investigation of religion, namely, its historical development after totemism. To be sure, his ruminations on this topic were brief, cursory, and lacking in the kind of nuance and detail one might expect of any historical account that spans centuries. Even so, one finds Freud offering thoughts on the dynamics involved in the development of matriarchal religion, monotheisms (notably Christianity), and a few crucial religious concepts, rituals, and doctrines. In order to fully grasp his hypothetical scenario, one must engage, alongside his conclusions about the primal crime and the subsequent origins of religion, morality, and society, two additional postulates: a Freudian rendition of "mass psychology" and a uniquely psychoanalytic view of time and history.[17]

Initially, psychoanalytic views of time and history are best illustrated with respect to individual development. As we saw in the previous chapter, in an ideal sense a male goes through phases of sexual development (oral, anal, phallic, latency) culminating in mature, healthy sexual object-relations in which the Oedipus complex is successfully navigated. The developmental (historical) directionality here is for the most part linear and hence "like an arrow." In the case of neurotics, an alternate trajectory is found. Characteristic of their developmental trajectory are regressions and fixations, which can indicate a movement backward. Neurotics, as Freud once said, suffer from "reminiscences," by which he meant the past (e.g., traumas). In the worst-case scenario, one cannot free oneself from

---

[17] See P. Rieff, "The Meaning of History and Religion in Freud's Thought," in *Psychoanalysis and History*, ed. B. Mazlish (Englewood Cliffs, NJ: Prentice Hall, 1963), 3–41.

the pull of the past, leading to the repetition of unhealthy behavior. In this case neurotics are thus framed as subject to the endless repetition of what Freud called "the return of the repressed." This, then, would be the psychoanalytic version of the "circular" view of time and history. There is never anything new, only the repetition of the old. Of course, this is where psychoanalysis steps in. The aim is to revisit the past, but in a way so that it is transformed into a move forward. We "spiral" out of our past, growing out of repetitive behavior and into mature, healthy forms of being and relating.

In *Totem and Taboo* Freud went on to speculate about not simply individual development but also the development of groups or masses of people (and therefore entire cultures as well). He held that the latter were subject to similar dynamics. To make this move from singular individuals to entire groups Freud needed to offer an extension of psychoanalytic theory: the concept of a "collective mind." Freud affirms this when he states, "I have taken the basis of my whole position the existence of a collective mind, in which mental processes occur just as they do in the mind of an individual."[18] The dynamics of groups of peoples (which is to say, of societies) was framed as a singular living organism modeled after the development of individuals.

In Freud's view, the promotion of something like a collective mind means that the human species universally shares certain historical traumas (such as the primal deed). There is an "archaic heritage" that "comprises not only dispositions but also subject-matter – memory-traces of the experience of earlier generations."[19] While Freud understands that the notion of a collective mind is problematic, he also thinks that it can be in part answered "by the inheritance of psychical dispositions."[20] The reference has been taken to be to the theories of the biologist Jean-Baptiste Lamarck (1744–1829), who had earlier posited the inheritance of acquired characteristics (the modern-day theoretical version being that of transgenerational epigenetics). The acceptance of the transmission of such inherited vestiges constitutes the psychoanalytic solution to the problem of social psychology. With the notion of a collective mind, states Freud, "we have bridged the gulf between individual and group psychology: we can deal with peoples as we do with an individual neurotic."[21]

---

[18] Freud, *Totem and Taboo*, S.E. 13: 157.
[19] Freud, *Moses and Monotheism*, S.E. 23: 99.
[20] Freud, *Totem and Taboo*, S.E. 13: 158.
[21] Freud, *Moses and Monotheism*, S.E. 23: 100.

The practical implication of this hypothesis is that every single human being suffers from the dim guilt of the primal deed (i.e., Freud's version of "original sin"). Even more, that trauma continues to exert pressure on history, social institutions, morality, and religion. In effect, the phylogenetic dynamics of Oedipus becomes the driver of history. "The Deed" started society, morality, and religion, and continues to exert its influence, much like a collective "return of the repressed."

One can, then, speak of something like a "phylogenetic" dimension to the unconscious: a communal, species-wide, deep dimension of the unconscious formed out of past, species-wide traumatic historical events that is dynamic and that shapes history and cultural forms. It exists in addition to the more unique historical events that influence singular individuals (i.e., "ontogeny"). If this is so, then how do the "phylogenetic" and "ontogenetic" dimensions to the unconscious interact in the individual? In fact, Freud found such alternate dimensions to be of real use in explaining what he saw as gaps in the clinical setting. For example, in certain case histories Freud was perplexed by an overly aggressive, condemning super-ego or excessive castration anxiety preponderating over against what one would expect from the actual life events of the patient. But the notion of what Freud dubbed "primal fantasies," directly linked to our collective phylogenic past, took care of that clinical problem:

Primal phantasies ... are a phylogenetic endowment. In them the individual reaches beyond his own experience into primaeval experience at points where his own experience becomes too rudimentary. It seems to me quite possible that all the things that are told to us to-day in analysis as phantasy – the seduction of children, the inflaming of sexual excitement by observing parental intercourse, the threat of castration (or rather castration itself) – were once real occurrences in the primaeval times of the human family, and that children in their phantasies are simply filling in the gaps in individual truth with prehistoric truth.[22]

The key phrase here is "beyond his own experience." Freud is saying that one needs the influence of the phylogenetic "deep past" to supplement the usual psychoanalytic focus on the more usual "developmental past" (ontogeny) to account for the clinical data of neuroses. The lines laid down by the inheritance of the phylogenetic unconscious pattern the

---

[22] Freud, *Introductory Lectures on Psychoanalysis*, S.E. 16: 358–377. One wonders if, aside from countering Jung, another reason for Freud's adherence to phylogenesis was the controversy over the famous "seduction theory": the notion of "primal fantasies" allowed him to keep the notion of actual seduction and trauma, now relegated to the primal past.

experiences of the individual; the lines of imagination and fantasy were literally determined by events of the deep archaic past.[23]

Now that we have surveyed the basics of Freud's theory of the collective mind and its dynamics, as well as his notions of time and history (arrow/circle/spiral), we are prepared to fully understand his conception of how religions developed. As a result of the influence of the collective mind, Freud is willing to say that all subsequent developments in religion exist in relation to the primal deed: they "are reactions to the same great event with which civilization began" and "attempts at solving the same problem" (which is to say, the shared guilt and psychic upheaval initiated by the primal deed).[24] The strength and power (as well as the promise of protection and guidance) of the primal father, collectively forgotten, buried, and repressed, seeks a "return." There is a natural gradient, then, toward monotheism and patriarchy, not necessarily because they are more rational or "better" structures but because "as a group" we are unconsciously determined to follow the dynamic designs of the inherited, collective, "phylogenetic unconscious." This may explain the fact that Freud has little to say about the emergence of matriarchal social structures and the tradition of mother goddesses. He does suggest that they likely preceded patriarchies and male-gendered monotheisms. However, being but inadequate and partial returns of the repressed, they were destined to eventually give way to them.[25]

Freud does not detail the precise development from totemism to institutional religion. He passes off the development of the "concept" of God as coming "from some unknown source."[26] But Freud does lay out the general dynamic sequence: primal deed, remorse/guilt, the creation of totemism as a form of the return of the repressed, the eventual morphing of a "father-animal" to an idealized "Father-God" (the totem being "the *first* form of father-surrogate" and the idea of God "a later one").[27] This will allow Freud to state in *Totem and Taboo* (and elaborate later in his *Future of an Illusion*) that psychoanalysis teaches us a singular point: the conception of God found in any individual is "formed in the likeness of his father, that his personal relation to God depends on his relation to his father in the flesh and oscillates and changes along with that relation, and

---

[23] Freud's use of the "collective mind" also required his acceptance of the "recapitulation theory," popularized by the zoologist and anatomist Ernst Haeckel, that "ontogeny recapitulates phylogeny" (i.e., "the biogenetic law").

[24] Freud, *Totem and Taboo*, S.E. 13: 145.   [25] Ibid., 144, 149.

[26] Ibid., 147. See also Freud, *Moses and Monotheism*, S.E. 23: 133.

[27] Freud, *Totem and Taboo*, S.E. 13: 148.

that at bottom God is nothing other than an exalted father."[28] This means that the individual's image of God is both phylogenetically and ontogenetically determined. As Freud later (1923) went on to say, in speaking of a case history: "the ideational image belonging to his childhood is preserved and becomes merged with the inherited memory-traces of the primal father to form the individual's idea of God."[29]

Specifically with respect to Christianity, Freud had something to say about the origin and popularity of that tradition as well. The attempt to solve the problem of the rebelliousness of the sons and their guilt over the primal deed becomes the basis for what Freud characterized as the "solution" of a "son" religion. Jesus, as son, represents the "band of brothers" and their collective guilt. His sacrifice (crucifixion) is the redemptive act that atoned for our collective guilt. This differs from how Christian theology frames Christ's sacrifice, and so Freud insists that such theological overlay is but misleading, displaced, mythological rationalizations of actual historical events and the return of the collective phylogenetic repressed (i.e., the primal crime). The popularity of Christianity lies precisely in that we all dimly feel that collective guilt and dimly understand the need for atonement. The death of a representative member of the band of brothers, then, has a special appeal to the needs of our collective phylogenetic guilt. If original sin is bound up with the primal murder and the crucifixion understood to be atonement for collective guilt, then the ritual of communion becomes a later transformation of the totem meal (one "eats" the flesh and blood of God). Freud then interjects an interesting twist: while Christ "saved" the band of brothers from the guilt of original sin (primal parricide), so too did he accomplish the "other" side of ambivalence, the wish to entirely displace the father: a father-religion was replaced by a son-religion. This narrative, thought Freud, in unconsciously appealing to multiple phylogenetic and ontogenetic fantasies, explained the great popularity of Christianity.

The Evolution of Culture

There is another context within which one must view Freud's sweeping claims as to the development of religion. That context is this: Freud bought into a view, widely shared by the early anthropologists he diligently read and utilized, that there was a socio-evolutionary thrust to

---

[28] Ibid., 147.   [29] Freud, "A Seventeenth-Century Demonological Neurosis," S.E. 19: 85.

human history, civilization, and the development of religions. But Freud did the anthropologists one better by suggesting that there was a correlation between "the development of men's view of the universe and the stages of an individual's libidinal development."[30] Specifically, he postulated the progression of religion from a pre-religious phase (e.g., animism) to an institutional one (religion proper) to a post-religious phase (science). In this progression, "[t]he animistic phase would correspond to narcissism both chronologically and in its content; the religious phase would correspond to the stage of object-choice of which the characteristic is the child's attachment to his parents; while the scientific phase would have an exact counterpart in the stage at which an individual has reached maturity, has renounced the pleasure principle [and] adjusted himself to reality."[31] This evolutionary frame sets up the later argument in *Moses and Monotheism* where, in seizing on Moses as heralding an evolutionary cultural advance, Freud links the Mosaic prohibition on images with the renunciation of id-based instinctual desire, the advance in ethical maturity, and intellectuality (i.e., the rise of the ego and reality testing). It did so by favoring memories, reflection, and deduction over the inevitable illusions of sense-perception and developmental determinants. It also sets up similar arguments in *Future of an Illusion* and *Civilization and Its Discontents* where Freud again rehearses the evolutionary view in an attempt to frame psychoanalysis, as a form of science, as the logical heir to a declining monotheism.

In other works, Freud supplemented this evolutionary drift of history by detailing a few of its more modern developments (colloquially referred to as the "three blows theory"). Freud claimed that in the last few centuries humans had suffered from three basic blows to our "species narcissism" and that all three blows were directly defended against by the representatives of traditional religion. The first was with Copernicus and Galileo, who, to the consternation of Catholicism and the Pope, posited that the earth is not the center of the universe (heliocentrism). The second was with Darwin, who, to the chagrin of the religious imagination (as in the later Scopes trial), posited an evolutionary theory that claimed humans are descended from apes. The third, thought Freud, was due to psychoanalysis, which taught that we are not masters even in our own home (which is to say, the discovery of the unconscious upset the enlightenment notion of the "prestige of consciousness"). Freud hoped that this

---

[30] Freud, *Totem and Taboo*, S.E. 13: 90.   [31] Ibid.

"disillusionment" of the religious imagination and species narcissism would eventually lead to the embracement of psychoanalysis as a means to transform instinct and a mature adaptive response to reality.[32]

The Nature of Religious Worldviews

The above evolutionary schema is helpful in that it informs two other, interrelated aspects of Freud's arguments that, while unfurled in *Totem and Taboo*, are also important for future psychoanalytic studies of religion. Those arguments are (1) the structural notion of religion as a "cultural dream" (which underlies his critique of religious worldviews) and (2) the introduction of a "pre-oedipal" dimension to religious worldviews (which are given greater sophistication in later object-relational theories of religion). Both arguments are born in Freud's discussion of animism in the third essay (titled "Animism, Magic and the Omnipotence of Thoughts").

In once again following the anthropological literature of his day, Freud defined animism as "the doctrine of souls" and, in its wider sense, "the doctrine of spiritual beings in general."[33] He further characterized it as an early attempt to construct a working worldview (what he later referred to as a *Weltanschauung*): animism was "the first complete theory of the universe."[34] Indeed, any "religion" (or in this case pre-religion) offered such a commanding, all-encompassing theory about the nature of humans and the cosmos. The animistic worldview was one in which all things, animate as well as inanimate, were infused with consciousness, spirits, and souls. Such forces became the causal nexus around which one's life and fate revolved. As one might imagine, some kind of relationship with them was of paramount importance. In order to control, influence, or adapt to this animistic reality, primitives invented a general set of operating practices that anthropologists subsumed under the broad heading of magic (which Freud referred to as "the earliest fore-runner of the technology of to-day"[35]). For example, if one had enemies, one way to harm or defeat them would be to create an effigy. Harming the effigy would then

---

[32] Freud, *Introductory Lectures on Psychoanalysis*, S.E. 16: 285. To take this logic even further, one can only wonder what Freud would say, if he were alive today, about the confirmed existence of exoplanets and the psychological blow to our species narcissism that would be dealt humanity in the event of proof of other, more technologically advanced, extraterrestrial civilizations (a "fourth blow" as it were).
[33] Freud, *Totem and Taboo*, S.E. 13:75.   [34] Ibid., 94.
[35] Freud, *New Introductory Lectures*, S.E. 22: 166–167.

result in a like harm to the living person in question. Or if rain was needed for crops, one might resort to "playing at rain" (e.g., various rituals that consisted of scattering water). Such practices, then, were conceived of having a causal relation to and effect on the external world.

Freud thought this worldview was both primitive and a magnificent illusion. Animism and its pre-technological system of magic paled in comparison to scientific experimentation. Primitives did not think to engage in the slower, more laborious series of tasks involved in finding universal laws through empirical experimentation. They opted for a more regressive (i.e., infantile) solution, namely, the belief in the "omnipotence of thoughts." Magical practices, according to Freud, confused imagination with reality, operating on a principle in which an ideal connection was substituted for a real one. Mistaking an ideal for a real connection simply means that one is convinced that reality corresponds to what one may be thinking or wishing. There is a one-to-one correspondence between what goes on in the inner world of one's mind and what happens (as an effect) in external reality. Psychologically speaking, then, the animating principle behind the belief in the efficacy of magic is the wish.[36]

To better understand the psychological logic behind the primitive animistic worldview, Freud once again relies on his method of correlating the mental life of savages and neurotics. Citing case history material, he relates how, especially in obsessional neurotics, one regularly finds this kind of "superstitious" mode of thought. For example, the neurotic might relate a life episode in the clinical setting in which they are thinking of a person and then, as if by magic, they appear around the corner. Or they might for no good reason be impelled to inquire about the health of an acquaintance they hadn't seen in years, only to find that person had just died – a seeming coincidence explained by the neurotic as the causal result of being sent a telepathic message. Freud observes that in such cases the neurotic thinks that the world revolves around them and their thoughts. In other words, just like the primitive, the neurotic is basing their understanding of how the world works on the principle of the "omnipotence of thoughts."

Freud then traces the origin of this primitive, superstitious way of thinking about the world (i.e., the omnipotence of thoughts and magical thinking) to the "narcissistic" (a descriptive and not necessarily pejorative clinical term) or "pre-oedipal" developmental phase. In this phase, the

---

[36] Freud, *Totem and Taboo*, S.E. 13: 83.

infant, in a dyadic relationship with the parent (usually the mother), feels merged with that (parental) "Other." When one has a particular need or desire in that early developmental stage the mother "magically" appears to satiate it. For example, if one is hungry, the mother's breast "appears," leading to a kind of unconscious assumption about the workings of external reality (namely, that there is a one-to-one correspondence between a wish and an effect in the world "out there"). Psychologically speaking, of course, this is a primitive form of thinking that is not always surmounted, as is evinced in neurotics and, more problematically, raised to the status of a working logic in the animistic worldview. But it also appears (as vestige) in later religious forms, a paradigmatic instance being the "magical" power of language as found in Genesis: "Let there be Light!"[37]

Emphasizing the importance of "the wish," Freud goes on to compare the construction of the animistic worldview to the mechanisms that produce a nightly dream (i.e., what we detailed earlier as the "dreamwork"). He suggests that wishes (the "latent" dream thoughts of nightly dreams) are a major part of the animistic worldview and how, in evoking the notion of "secondary revision" (another mechanism of the dreamwork whose function consists in presenting a seemingly unified, connected, intelligible whole out of an otherwise nonsensical, disparate, irrational dream), animism as an operative "complete system" (i.e., worldview) is made to "make sense" or hold together despite its logical faults and often irrational elements. In other words, it is here that we find the beginning of Freud's view that any religious worldview, including modern ones, operate "like a dream" (and here recall our earlier discussion that Feuerbach once referred to religion as the "dream of waking consciousness"). In his brief summary of dream theory titled *On Dreams* (1901), Freud prefigured this line of thought. There, by way of drawing parallels between individual dreams, the dreamwork, and religion, he notes that "dream symbolism extends far beyond dreams," being found in "fairy tales, myths, and legends" and, as a result of this fact, it "enables us to trace the intimate connections between dreams and these latter productions."[38]

Placing this analysis in the context of Freud's views on the evolution of culture (in the previous section), animism relies on the logic of the omnipotence of thoughts and corresponds to the developmental phase

---

[37] Freud, *New Introductory Lectures*, S.E. 22: 166–167.
[38] Freud, *On Dreams*, S.E. 5: 629–722.

of narcissism. But cultural evolution gave rise to an advance: traditional forms of institutional religion (e.g., monotheism). Developmentally speaking, it harkens to that phase of giving up at least a part of one's narcissism by more fully acknowledging the existence of the Other (one's parents, of whom the father is primary), an attachment to them, and the need to secure their favor for protection and sustenance. It moves, then, from narcissism to the oedipal phase of development. Even here, however, we have but another "worldview" that, while an advance, suffers from the same fate as all worldviews. In his later essay "The Question of a *Weltanschauung*" (1933), Freud comes back to this, defining a *Weltanschauung* as an imaginative construction aimed at solving the problems of existence based on one overriding hypothesis. But that, thinks Freud, is bound to fail, demonstrably contains illusions, and, while perhaps serving an adaptive function by assuaging personal and cultural anxiety, does so at the cost of inhibiting the intellect and the progress of the search for truth. Only with the advent of science, framed as the third major advance beyond animism and religion, do we get the notion of a world constituted by law-like regularities that exist outside our control. This acknowledgment, which Freud compares to adult maturity, demands a certain renunciation of self (narcissism), a kind of methodological humility, and the injunction to slowly adapt oneself to that world through empirical observation, the collection of data, experimentation, theory building, and the continual falsification of such theories. Such tasks are often difficult, and the accumulation of knowledge proceeds slowly and generationally, but that is the actual lot of humans. It requires, in the emotional sense, the ability to tolerate ambiguity and the will to truth, knowing that such a task will never be realized in a given life span, hence being relegated to subsequent generations. Importantly, Freud claims that science does not create or promote a *Weltanschauung* in the sense in which he defined it. More to the point, he claims that psychoanalysis is in the service of science. Its law is the pursuit of empirical data, experimentation, verification, and falsification.

TOTEM AND TABOO: CRITIQUES

One might reject multiple elements of Freud's theorizing yet still find portable lessons for use as part of one's academic tool kit. Among the latter is the notion of religious worldviews functioning as a cultural dream (or what we earlier referred to as religion as a "movie"), the latter engaging both oedipal and pre-oedipal components. So too can one count among the portable lessons Freud's emerging (if not explicitly stated) notion of a cultural super-ego, its psychological dynamics, and (as he would later detail) the latter's complicity in fomenting religious mendacity, racism, misogyny, and tribalism (which is to say, unexamined unconscious content). That said, history has not been kind to Freud's myth of the origins and development of religion. Disciplinary perspectives outside psychoanalysis were quick to level decisive critiques, growing in number and sophistication through subsequent decades. Interestingly enough, those within psychoanalysis have also ceased to defend the totality of Freud's position. In fact, there is close to what could be called a "professional disavowal" of Freud's theorizing on the origins and development of religion.

Suspicious Sources

Freud never engaged in actual anthropological research but drew on a group of anthropological theorists (e.g., E. B. Tylor, Sir James Frazer, Robertson Smith, J. J. Atkinson, Herbert Spencer) labeled the "armchair titans," signifying their lack of personal ethnographic work and questionable reliance on data supplied by missionaries, travelers, and others on the ground. Certain conclusions that Freud lifted from his preferred anthropologists were found to be invalid. For example, while the term "totemism," despite being a Western colonialist construct, was admitted to having existed in some form in some cultures, it was disputed that it was a unitary phenomenon with stable characteristics, while debates swirled over the very aspects Freud assumed as being probable or true. The latter included the framing of totemism as being the earliest form of religion, as universal, as necessarily linked with exogamy and the prohibition against killing. Commentators also cast doubt on the actual existence of the totem meal, and skepticism abounded concerning the reality, much less the universality, of the primal horde and the enactment of patricide (the primal deed). In short, just about everything Freud depended on to make his argument was cast into abeyance even in this early "first" period of the psychology and religion movement. Freud's theory of origins was beginning to disintegrate, sharing in the same fate as the anthropologists he depended on – sources that, as one pundit put it, "had been rejected by the anthropological profession before *Totem and Taboo* reached it."[39] Freud knew of the critiques of this early group of

---

[39] Wallace, *Freud and Anthropology*, 113.

anthropologists, not the least confirmation being that he not only met one of its chief architects, the anthropologist Franz Boas (who started the first American program in anthropology at Columbia University in 1896), but also sat in on a critical lecture he gave entitled "Psychological Problems in Anthropology" at Clark University (when Freud visited there in 1909). Freud summarily dismissed such criticisms, rationalizing that he was not an anthropologist but a psychoanalyst and, as such, "had a right to take out of ethnological literature what I might need for the work of analysis."[40] For evident reasons, that response has, historically speaking, fallen flat.

Baseless Biology

Freud also promoted the view that humanity, as a collective, was possessed of an "archaic heritage," a phylogenetically inculcated oedipal dynamic. Here we must turn from anthropological sources to biology. Freud's perplexing adherence to phylogenesis and the biogenic law ("ontogeny recapitulates phylogeny") was roundly dismissed.[41] Lamarck's thesis had been disputed as early as the 1880s by the biologist August Weismann, while Ernst Haeckel's recapitulation theory was discredited with the emergence of genetics as the reigning theory of transmission.[42] It was concluded that physical and cultural characteristics acquired during the course of a lifetime could not be genetically transmitted. Freud's attempt to counter Jung by situating Oedipus as a foundational "universal archetype," hence the driver of all religious formations, was in jeopardy. His unwillingness to give up phylogenesis became problematic for his fledgling movement. As Ernest Jones, one of Freud's earliest and closest of allies, politely put it: "It is not easy to account for the fixity with which Freud held this opinion and the determination with which he ignored all the biological evidence to the contrary."[43] Applying Freud's own psychoanalytic method against him, one could venture to explain his irrational and stubborn insistence as due in part to his earnest wish to offset the threat of Jung's emerging psychology (i.e., his framing of the "collective unconscious") and in part to his desire to reconfigure and hence validate the essence of his formerly abandoned seduction theory (i.e., Freud's notion of "primal fantasies"). In that case *Totem and Taboo* can be framed as a kind of conceptual trash-heap useful for

---

[40] Ibid., 177–178.   [41] See Brickman, *Aboriginal Populations in the Mind*, 65ff.
[42] Ibid., 64.   [43] Jones, *Life and Work of Sigmund Freud*, vol. 3: 313.

ameliorating the tensions that marred psychoanalytic theory and threats to its academic hegemony. In any event, given the analysis offered in this and the preceding section, our portable lesson is this: one can no longer hold to Freud's theory of origins or his misguided view of how religions developed historically. Oedipus is not the root and key to human civilization, religion and morality; the nineteenth-century socio-evolutionary thesis and its implications do not hold; matriarchal religions stand in their own right; and there is no "phylogenetic unconscious" that is dynamic and the determining factor in manifesting cultural forms favoring patriarchy and monotheism.

Structural Suitability

Despite the above, one could attempt to rescue (as indicated in the first paragraph of our "critique" section) certain architectural elements of Freud's theory for application to religion. In fact, despite numerous criticisms, certain anthropologists of Freud's day were generally sympathetic to the structural model (id/ego/super-ego), the existence of defense mechanisms (e.g., repression, sublimation, projection), and the notion of a sexual developmental line (libido theory). It is significant that more than one anthropologist (e.g., Alfred Kroeber, Geza Roheim) enrolled in psychoanalytic institutes. This has carried forward into the "second" and "third" periods, where one finds even the most lauded of sociologists and anthropologists engaging psychoanalytic theory (e.g., Talcott Parsons, Philip Rieff, Clifford Geertz, Victor Tuner, Gananath Obeyesekere), even if some prefer to use more sophisticated developments in psychoanalytic theory (e.g., ego psychology, object-relations theory). Today, one can even speak of the subdisciplines of "psychoanalytic sociology" and "psychoanalytic anthropology."[44] At the same time, many of these same theorists have advocated for what we have called a reflexive element with respect to multiple psychoanalytic theoretical postulates (e.g., developmental lines, defense mechanisms, the structural model, psycho-social conceptions of the life-cycle, gender and race, normative views of health, of the instinctual energies of the body, and epistemological assumptions

---

[44] The list is long, but aside from the comprehensive summary offered by Wallace in his *Freud and Anthropology*, representative studies include F. Weinstein and G. Platt, *Psychoanalytic Sociology* (Baltimore: Johns Hopkins University Press, 1973); G. Obeyesekere, *The Work of Culture* (Chicago: University of Chicago Press, 1990); and P. Homans, *The Ability to Mourn* (Chicago: University of Chicago Press, 1989).

about the nature of self and reality). While a comprehensive summary of such critiques is beyond the parameters of our present discussion (although we will come back to address other reflexive elements in later chapters), our point can be made by cataloging a few important, historically central challenges to Freud's theory in each of the three periods of the psychology and religion movement that advise the turn to reflexivity.

Developmental Differences

While most working in contemporary psychoanalysis are more than willing to discard phylogenesis and Freud's myth of origins and development, a further round of critiques requires a different revision of psychoanalytic theory. One could argue that even if one shears away the notion of the phylogenetic unconscious, there is a debate over prioritizing psychology over against the other social sciences (as Freud clearly did). For example, even without resorting to phylogenesis, psychoanalysis still held to the universality and primacy of the Oedipus complex. So it is that the noted anthropologist Bronislaw Malinowski, through ethnographic research, felt compelled to empirically document that certain cultures did not evince the Oedipal triangle.[45] Indeed, as we shall detail in Chapter 6, two of Freud's non-Western psychoanalytic correspondents, the Hindu Girindrasekhar Bose and the Buddhist Heisaku Kosawa, both of whom were instrumental in founding psychoanalytic institutes in India and Japan, respectively, also argued that different kinds of "complexes" not named Oedipus were found in their clinics. As expected, Freud politely brushed their arguments to the side.

In the "second" period of the psychology and religion movement, the debate over universality and attendant cultural issues achieved a new level of reflexive sophistication. The anthropologist Ann Parsons (daughter of Talcott), following Malinowski's lead, again confirmed the existence of multiple complexes. However, unlike Malinowski, Parsons offered a way in which the "dialogue" between psychoanalysis and the other social sciences could proceed in a more nuanced, reasonable manner. Parsons argued for keeping Freud's "structural" model, along with its notion of biologically driven sexual and aggressive instincts and developmental stages, but then allowing for ethnographic research to determine how the cultural "collective representations" (a Durkheimian concept) of

---

[45] B. Malinowski, *Sex and Repression in Savage Society* (London: Forgotten Books, 2012 [1927]).

gender as well as the relationships within nuclear and extended family life could determine object choice, the aims of instinctual satisfaction, and thus the culturally relative nature of a given psychological complex. In other words, Freud had cavalierly collapsed culture and individual psychology, not allowing a space for culture to intervene in which "objects" might be the target of sexual and aggressive impulses. For Freud the "biological" father and the "sociological" father were always one and the same. Oedipus, inside us all, simply ruled the cultural day (in part because, aside from the familiar "ontogenic" developmental vicissitudes, the primal deed and phylogenesis had laid down the oedipal gradient for fantasized sexual and aggressive activity). But Parsons reasoned that different cultures, because of different family arrangements and culturally specific constructions of gender, led to alternate complexes aside from the oedipal.[46]

In the "third" period of the psychology and religion movement, such critiques have led to several new lines of inquiry: could it be that the Oedipus complex is better framed as a universal possibility but not a universal actuality, that it might be actualized only given a certain family and cultural configuration? If so, is Freud best cast as a psychologically gifted ethnographer of his culture who, unfortunately, went to great lengths to universalize (and then "ground" historically in *Totem and Taboo*) a local sociohistorical finding with only a narrow, selected sample size? Should psychoanalytic models be reformed and adapted to each and every new culture? While the answers to such questions admitted of some variance, the understanding that psychoanalysis needed to engage its sister social sciences as equal partners was widespread both within and outside the discipline. By this third period some psychoanalysts and sociologists pointed to how cultural and family shifts even in Western cultures had led to a new clinical database, evincing new kinds of mental dysfunction not named Oedipus, which necessitated new theorizing about the human psyche. This new sociocultural reality and its clinical data (analysands with new forms of neuroses) became the basis for the need to formulate new forms of psychoanalytic theory and technique (e.g., ego psychology, object-relations theory) – revised psychoanalytic forms that many later social scientists came to prefer over classic Freudianism. Even so, these new revisions do not wholly negate oedipal theory but, rather,

---

[46] Ann Parsons, "Is the Oedipus Complex Universal?," in *Man and His Culture: Psychoanalytic Anthropology after Totem and Taboo*, ed. W. Muensterberger (New York: Taplinger, 1970), 331–384.

relativize it by asking us to do the work of culture in order to see Freud's relevance and applicability. Another portable lesson for the psychoanalytic theory of religion, then, is as follows: there are many cultural phenomena and religious forms, some (but not all) of which can be fruitfully analyzed with the Freudian oedipal tool kit, others being better suited for investigation by later revisions in psychoanalytic theory evincing reflexivity (which we will attend to in later chapters of this volume).

Ethno-psychological Elements

The history of cautionary tales did not stop with considerations of development and the universality of the Oedipus complex. Some, like the noted sociologist Talcott Parsons, argued that Freud got the relation of the structural model to culture wrong. Culture not only "gets into" the mind through the super-ego, as Freud claimed, but also gets into the ego (the "what" of reality is mediated by culture) and the id (culture "patterns" the expression of aggressive/sexual impulses through the mother–infant relationship). Others argued that culture shapes the length and importance of each developmental phase and noted that different cultures valorize different "defense mechanisms" as well as facilitate different forms of neuroses.[47]

A related series of critiques was centered on the assumed, normative (best read as "culturally coded") views of race and gender found in *Totem and Taboo*. We have seen that the anthropological literature Freud drew on also advocated a socio-evolutionary perspective on the nature and history of human civilizations. By the time Freud was writing *Totem and Taboo*, their general perspective on civilization had been thoroughly critiqued and, to a large extent, discredited. Indeed, the ethnocentrism baked into the supposedly value-neutral and scientific postulates of evolutionary "stages" and "hierarchies" complete with value-laden notions of race, ethnicity, and "the primitive" had been firmly exposed and dismantled. The subsequent anthropological rejection of socio-evolutionism avowed that there was no progression from barbarism to

---

[47] See, for example, T. Parsons, *Social Structure and Personality* (New York: Simon and Schuster, 2007 [1964]), and S. Kakar, *The Inner World* (New York: Oxford University Press, 1979). Along these lines, as a theoretical "opening" for our valorization of dialogue and reflexivity, Freud once wrote that "every neurosis has a purpose: *it is directed toward certain persons* and would disappear at once on a South Sea island or in a similar situation for *there would no longer be a reason for it*" (Wallace, *Freud and Anthropology*, 185).

civilization, no biological variations between races, no "higher or lower" in civilization, and more: "all men are totally civilized."[48] This is important in that Freud's adoption of sociocultural evolution and its framings of the primitive invariably led to the charge that psychoanalysis, when framed as a value-neutral science, actually had built into it coded views of gender and race. If one marries Lamarck and anthropological socio-evolutionism with psychoanalytic concepts like regression, fixation, primitivity, and developmental stages, and both under the banner of assuming white, patriarchal, European civilization as being the highest evolved standard (as did Freud), then one is in danger of unjustly framing "the Other" as less individuated, moral, intelligent, and prone to "primary process" functioning. Moreover, this "Other" can take multiple forms: women, people of color, and religious traditions. If Freud was guilty of this, then there may exist "ethno" dimensions in psychoanalytic theory that need to be reflexively recognized and discarded.[49] This is one of the central portable lessons of our use of the term "reflexivity."

To unpack the above assertion a bit more, the Freudian equation of primitives with children, neurotics, and women, implicit in *Totem and Taboo* and overt in his later work, suggested that inherent in the latter group was the lesser capacity for being individuated and civilized compared with their white, male counterparts. This had consequences for the psychoanalytic clinical encounter. Indeed, people of color, as is evinced in psychoanalytic case histories in the prestigious journal *Psychoanalytic Quarterly* in 1914 (and here the authors, following Freud, assumed the biogenic law in which individual development recapitulates "the history of the race"), were framed as less individuated, more prone to regression, psychosis, and primary process thought, and lacking in ego-strength.[50]

---

[48] The phrase was uttered by Franz Boas. See Brickman, *Aboriginal Populations in the Mind*, 65.

[49] The notion that psychoanalysis has an "ethno" dimension is correlated to those studies that see psychoanalysis less as a potentially revolutionary praxis than one which, through suggestion and even brainwashing, resocializes the analysand in problematic ways. For setting the question and a spirited discussion, see Brickman, *Aboriginal Populations in the Mind*, 178–198. Our use of the term *reflexivity*, then, extends to the need to take into account this body of literature.

[50] Ibid., 87ff. There has been a growing literature on how to perform reflexive applied psychoanalysis with regard to race. Franz Fanon's *Black Skin, White Masks* (New York: Grove Press, 2008 [1952]) was, of course, the classic original work in this field, as is the more contemporary work by Brickman. For more contemporary representative studies, see, for example, E. Abel, "Race, Class, and Psychoanalysis? Opening Questions," in *Conflicts in Feminism*, ed. Marianne Hirsch and Evelyn Fox Keller (New York:

Indeed, during this same era, it is unfortunate that two of the original members of the Indian psychoanalytic society, Owen Berkeley-Hill and Claude Dagmar Daly, were British army officers who, in using psychoanalysis as a vehicle of cultural oppression and British colonialism, portrayed Indians as infantile and inferior.[51] Daly, for example, wrote that "in the Hindu one finds a psychology that differs considerably from the European, its equivalent with us being found in pathological cases."[52] Fittingly, Salman Akhtar (a contemporary Indian-American psychoanalyst) refers to this as "a racist countertransference."[53] Indeed, Freud had further extended his view of "what is primitive" to what he assumed was the norm in primitive societies, namely, collective social organizations. The latter would lead to a lack of individuation and hence to a more regressive position with respect to others and a realistic apprehension of the world around us. In this stereotypical psychological portrait, then, there is both a "colonialist" element and a racial subtext in early psychoanalytic theory and practice.

Totem and Taboo did not specifically articulate a theoretical position with respect to female development. However, given that *Totem and Taboo* is primarily a male affair in which "the primitive" plays a starring role, Freud's later written reflections on female development have been linked by scholars to his views on primitives. To this end, it is noteworthy that Freud's reference to women's sexuality as being a "dark continent" is the same term used by the colonial explorer Henry Morton Stanley in his framing of Africa.[54] To be sure, it is an established consensus within contemporary psychoanalysis that Freud's essays on women were both pejorative and shot through with the cultural norms of his day (an unabashed patriarchy). Having summarized what Freud said about women's development in the introductory chapter, we can proceed to feminist responses that, most forcefully instituted by Simone de Beauvoir's *The Second Sex* as early as 1949 (and continues to this day), were both logical and determinative. In a general sense, the early critiques observed, as had the anthropological critique of the universality of Oedipus in *Totem and Taboo*, that Freud had failed to appreciate the

---

Routledge, 1990), 184–204, and J. Lorand, *The Fetish Revisited: Marx, Freud, and the Gods Black People Make* (Durham, NC: Duke University Press, 2018).

[51] S. Aktar and P. Tummala-Narra, "Psychoanalysis in India," in *Freud along the Ganges*, ed. S. Aktar (New Delhi: Stanza, 2008), 11–12.

[52] Ibid. [53] Ibid., 13.

[54] See R. Khanna, *Dark Continents: Psychoanalysis and Colonialism* (Durham, NC: Duke University Press, 2003).

influence of culture on psychological development. Once again, he had collapsed culture and psychological development, thereby not allowing space for culture to be a partner in determining how, in this case, women develop. For example, given a culturally hegemonic structural patriarchy that forecloses social opportunities for women, one may find clinical examples of penis envy where the penis is understood as a symbol for male prestige, power, and life options. But in alternate cultural configurations one might find very different types of clinical data as well as "complexes" (e.g., clitoris envy and male pregnancy fantasies). What Freud did was to assume that the meaning of being male and female in all cultures is invariant and essential. This has led scholars to conclude that Freud's theories had an "ethno-psychological" dimension in that it contains unexamined values and assumptions inherent in its cultural surround (in this case, a particular normalized construction of gender) that, in turn, create the psycho-social soil for a certain gender identity.

Fortunately, not all using psychoanalytic theory still subscribe to Freud's mistakes. As a portable lesson, a robust body of literature exists that affords a corrective to the cautionary tales we have elaborated – a corrective that seeks to revise, without wholly abandoning, psychoanalytic methodology. For example, Diane Jonte-Pace, in summarizing the history of critiques emanating from both feminist and critical race studies, suggests that they can be framed as falling into three basic groupings: critical, inclusive, and analytic.[55] Critical theorists tend to dismiss Freud altogether; inclusivists tend to move from Freud to other, less overtly racist/misogynist psychologies; and analytic theorists (initiated by Franz Fanon's *Black Skin, White Masks* and Juliet Mitchell's *Psychoanalysis and Feminism*) not only advocate for cultural reflexivity and the reformation of "ethno" assumptions within psychoanalytic theory but also, in recalling that one dominant narrative within Freud's theory accentuates

---

[55] See the following works of D. Jonte-Pace: "Analysts, Critics, and Inclusivists: Feminist Voices in the Psychology of Religion," in *Religion and Psychology: Mapping the Terrain*, ed. D. Jonte-Pace and W. B. Parsons (New York: Routledge, 2001), 129–148; "Psychoanalysis, Colonialism, and Modernity: Reflections on Brickman's *Aboriginal Populations in the Mind*," *Religious Studies Review* 32, no. 1 (2006): 1–4; and *Speaking the Unspeakable* (Berkeley: University of California Press, 2001). For a partial list of further representative studies on how psychoanalysis can reflexively engage constructions of sexuality and gender, see J. Mitchell, *Psychoanalysis and Feminism* (New York: Basic Books, 2000 [1974]); Nancy Chodorow, *The Reproduction of Mothering* (Berkeley: University of California Press, 1978); and J. Hamman, "The Reproduction of the Hypermasculine Male: Select Subaltern Views," *Pastoral Psychology* 66 (2017): 799–818.

its socially critical if not revolutionary praxis (as we emphasized in Chapter 1), promote this culturally self-reflexive form of psychoanalysis as practically useful. They do so by showing how psychoanalysis can illumine the way in which cultures manifest and maintain their unequal gendered hierarchies and racist elements. Rather than reproducing social norms, a reflexive psychoanalysis can illumine, challenge, and deconstruct them. Properly revised, "applied" psychoanalysis is all the more helpful in analyzing the implicit assumptions concerning race and gender in religious narratives and practices. It is the analytic school, then, that not only best represents our use of the term "reflexivity" but also tallies with, indeed extends, Freud's intent to see psychoanalysis as a socially liberative tool.

In this regard it is important to recall that Freud's own formulations changed throughout his life as new clinical data warranted. The cultural theorists within this analytic school, following the logic of including new data as part of the reformulation of theory, are simply actualizing such a directive. They point to a general portable lesson: that when one uses psychoanalytic methodology to analyze religious phenomena, it is better to do so in dialogue with the perspectives offered by its sister social sciences and culture theorists. Through such dialogue its models are reformed and clarified, reductionism and orientalism (i.e., the employment of stereotypical narratives designed to maintain Western colonial power) mitigated, "ethno" elements made transparent, and manifest errors avoided.

In the chapters ahead, particularly with respect to responses found in the dialogical enterprises within the psychology and religion movement, we will see other reflexive moves, linked especially to the emergence of transformational theory, which address the implicit cultural assumptions regarding "self," "reality," and even a few central psychoanalytic framings (e.g., instinct theory, the structural model) within classic Freudian psychology. To be sure, while our above narrative is offered at a "meta" and "experience-distant" level, our illustrations (especially in Chapter 8) will serve to translate abstract formula into practical application. For now, we rest content with having presented a series of cautionary tales and portable lessons that will serve as a foundation for that later discussion and application.

3

Freud's *Moses*

The Advent of Monotheism

When one first opens the pages of *Moses and Monotheism* one is struck by Freud's employment of a curious organizational strategy. The volume consists of three independent essays with the third having two sections, the first of which has two prefaces and the second introduced by a "summary." Given Freud's sterling reputation as a prose writer, such disorganization is at first perplexing. The prefaces explain why this might be the case. Faced with old age and cancer (the book was published in 1939, the year of his death), the rise of fascism in Germany, the fear of persecution, and subsequent forced move from Vienna to London (in 1938), Freud was doubtful the book would ever be finished, much less see the public light of day. Indeed, with some hesitation he decided to publish the first two essays independently ("Moses an Egyptian," "If Moses Was an Egyptian ...") in the psychoanalytic journal *Imago* in 1937, thinking that would be the end of it. The third essay ("Moses, His People, and Monotheistic Religion"), which deals more provocatively with the identity of Moses and origins of monotheism, was deemed too sensitive to publish. The rise of Nazism in conjunction with the risk of offending both Jews and Christians was too great a risk not only to Freud but also to the profession of psychoanalysis and its many adherents, analysts, and friends.[1] However, once safely situated in London, Freud had a change of heart and, apologizing for the many repetitions and

---

[1] Yosef Yerushalmi provides a detailed sociohistorical context for Freud's concerns in chapter 2 of his *Freud's Moses: Judaism Terminable and Interminable* (New Haven, CT: Yale University Press, 1991).

organizational problems, decided to include the previously published essays along with the new, third essay in a single volume.

Freud's stated intent in the book (in being "scientific" and "objective," as he put it) was to argue the following: how psychoanalysis, following the lines laid down in *Totem and Taboo*, could expose the dynamics involved in the continued historical development of religion, ascertain the factors involved in the creation of Jewish monotheism and identity, and illumine the reasons behind the resiliency of the Jewish people and tradition. To be sure, Freud understood that his analysis would not be well received in theological quarters.[2] He begins the book by saying that denying "a people of the man whom they take pride in as the greatest of their sons"[3] was not a task he undertook lightheartedly. But he goes on to say that more important was the search for the facts. No consideration, he says, will "induce us to put the truth aside in favor of ... national interests."[4]

MOSES AND MONOTHEISM: THE ARGUMENT

Freud's argument can be properly unpacked with respect to several leading themes: (1) Moses was an Egyptian; (2) Moses created the Jews and gave them monotheism; (3) the Jews murdered Moses in a reenactment of the primal deed, leaving monotheism behind; and (4) the return of the phylogenetic repressed led the Jews to once again accept monotheism, which morphed after and alongside Judaism into Christianity and Islam (with Freud offering a brief aside to the religions of "the east"). In making his argument, Freud, as with *Totem and Taboo*, availed himself of the relevant academic literature of his day, most specifically works penned by historians and biblical scholars. Once again, then, we have an attempt at dialogue even if, as with *Totem and Taboo*, history has deemed Freud's theories to be highly problematic.

Moses Was an Egyptian

The first, short essay is designed to offer evidence for one fact: Moses was an Egyptian (both culturally and biologically). The standard biblical narrative of the creation of Jewish identity goes back to the book of Genesis; to Abraham (for all intents and purposes the patriarch and

---

[2] Ibid., 113. [3] Freud, *Moses and Monotheism*, S.E. 23: 7. [4] Ibid.

biological progenitor of the Jewish people) and his sons. Yet Freud says not a word about that "pre-history" of Judaism, preferring instead to focus on the deciding factor of the man Moses. The biblical narrative of Moses in Exodus portrays him as a Jew born of the tribe of Levi who, when the pharaoh ordered all male Jewish children drowned, was fortunate enough to have his mother send him down the river in a small basket, there to be picked up by the Pharaoh's daughter, who raised him as her own son. Freud, however, argues to the contrary. In the first essay of the book, he begins by accepting the historical scholarship of J. H. Breasted and Eduard Meyer, who argued that the name "Moses" is of Egyptian origin. Mixing in psychoanalytic interpretations of "hero myths," Freud concludes that it is probable that "Moses was an Egyptian ... whom the legend was designed to turn into a Jew."[5] He goes on to suggest that Moses was a nobleman, perhaps the governor of a border province where he came into contact with Semitic tribes.[6]

Modern scholarship has accepted only one of Freud's conclusions: the name "Moses" is indeed Egyptian (although Moses himself was a Hebrew who was raised in Egypt).[7] Freud was aware that his conclusions were merely the first of a series contrary to tradition and, in some instances, scholarly consensus. The most charitable way to take his claims here (as elsewhere in the book) is to note that Freud played with the idea of naming the book *The Man Moses, an Historical Novel* and that the second essay is titled "If Moses Was an Egyptian ...." Both titles ask us to suspend judgment in order to openly receive an argument best framed in terms of an "as if" story.

Moses Created the Jews and Gave Them Monotheism

Freud goes on to claim that not only was Moses an Egyptian nobleman but, further, he literally formed the Jews as a group ("it was this one man Moses who created the Jews"[8]), bequeathing them monotheism and the attendant rite of circumcision (understood as a group identity marker). Freud's argument here has two parts: historical and psychological.

Drawing on the historical studies of his day, Freud observes that well before Moses Egyptian culture valorized polytheism, replete with

---

[5] Ibid., 15. [6] Ibid., 60–61.
[7] See, for example, W. W. Meissner, *Psychoanalysis and Religious Experience* (New Haven, CT: Yale University Press, 1984), 118.
[8] Freud, *Moses and Monotheism*, S.E. 23: 106.

narratives about death and the afterlife (as evinced in the narratives around the god Osiris).⁹ The change from polytheism to monotheism was implemented by Pharaoh Amenhotep IV (who later changed his name to Ikhnaton), who expunged all traces of Egyptian polytheism in favor of a strict monotheism based on the sun god Aton. Significantly, this was the world's first monotheism: exclusive (there is only one God) and immaterial (prohibiting all images), marginalizing magical and mythical elements, disdaining ceremonials and sacrifices, enforcing circumcision, and valorizing the more abstract ideals of ethics, justice, and truth. It was this religion, argues Freud, that the Egyptian nobleman Moses was socialized into and accepted as his own. When Amenhotep/Ikhnaton died and subsequent social shifts undermined Aton monotheism, Moses left Egypt, taking with him the Jewish inhabitants of his province. As their leader, he avowed that they were his "chosen people," bequeathing them monotheism.

Having presented his preferred historical narrative, Freud then turns to psychoanalysis. Why did the Jews accept Moses and monotheism? Part of the reason may be simply developmental, namely, Moses was a father-figure and protector. However, given that this was the first appearance of "true" monotheism, Freud argued that a deeper, phylogenetic explanation was needed. Recall that Freud, in *Totem and Taboo*, had suggested that the return of the (phylogenetic) repressed would eventually lead to patriarchy and a true monotheism (by which he meant the return of the primal father). Moses and the one and only God "behind him," then, was nothing less than the external event that awakened the dynamic power of the phylogenetic unconscious. As Freud put it, what Moses brought was not so much a novelty as it was "the revival of an experience in the primeval ages of the human family which had long vanished from men's conscious memory."¹⁰ With Moses the memory of the primal father came alive:

The first effect of meeting the being who had so long been missed and longed for was overwhelming and was like the traditional description of the law-giving from Mount Sinai. Admiration, awe and thankfulness for having found grace in his eyes – the religion of Moses knew none but these positive feelings towards the

---

[9] The scholarship Freud cites is J. H. Breasted, *A History of Egypt* (London: Charles Scribner's Sons, 1906) and *The Dawn of Conscience* (London: Charles Scribner's Sons, 1934); Arthur Weigall, *The Life and Times of Ikhnaton* (London: Thornton Butterworth, 1910); and A. Erman, *Die Ägyptische Religion* (Berlin: G. Reimer, 1905).

[10] Freud, *Moses and Monotheism*, S.E. 23: 129.

father-god. The conviction of his irresistibility, the submission to his will, could not have been more unquestioning in the helpless and intimidated son of the father of the horde.... A rapture of devotion to God was thus the first reaction to the return of the great father.[11]

Freud adds that such intense awe and admiration, being feelings beyond the normal range of the personal unconscious, required a correspondingly altered state: "only religious ecstasy can bring them back."[12] In other words, what is uncovered in that altered state known as religious ecstasy is the contents of not only the personal unconscious but more, that of the universal memory-traces that define the content of our phylogenetically transmitted archaic heritage. Similarly, another distinguishing aspect of Judaism, the rite of circumcision, added to the activation of such dim archaic memories. The phylogenetically buried memory of the castration enacted by the primal father was now rendered just palatable enough by circumcision, psychoanalytically understood as a symbolic castration. These factors led to the willingness of the Jews to submit to the authority of Moses, God, and, behind them, the primal father. Indeed, for Freud the emergence of monotheism, by eliciting the power of the phylogenic repressed, had an obsessive quality about it: it had to be believed. As such, it operated in a way reminiscent of the *credo quia absurdum*: logical objections to it were powerless.[13]

We will attend to what happened (according to Freud) after that pivotal event. But first we must pause to consider some relevant psychological observations Freud made as to the historical importance of this first appearance of monotheism and how it signified a turning point in the evolution of human history. Recalling our discussion in the last chapter, central to his argument is the Mosaic prohibition on images – a prohibition he linked to the renunciation of the immediate gratification of id-based instinctual desire and the growth in ethical maturity (super-ego functioning) and intellectuality (the rise of the ego and reality testing). This "progress in spirituality," as Freud calls it, favored memories, reflection, and deduction over the inevitable illusions of sense-perception.[14] The fruits of such advances as mediated through generations were a stepping-stone to the next cultural advance: the rise of science. In essence, then, Freud inserted Moses and the prohibition against images as part of the evolutionary view of culture he had held since *Totem and Taboo*.

---

[11] Ibid., 133–134. [12] Ibid., 134. [13] Ibid., 85. [14] Ibid., 111ff.

Next, in signaling that religion had some therapeutically beneficial effects, Freud went on to speak of how this "progress in spirituality" had another, adaptive consequence for Jews: the increase in self-esteem. Freud held that the Mosaic proclamation that the Jews were his (and God's) "chosen people" had psychological value insofar as it could not have but helped raise their self-esteem (which, clinically speaking, is a positive, adaptive narcissistic phenomenon). Freud believed that this was "the only instance of its sort in the history of human religions" of such a phenomenon.[15] Indeed, he affirms that it was this special form of self-esteem that enabled the Jews to continue their tradition despite centuries of persecution. Moreover, an increase in self-esteem was furthered by the growth in intellectuality and ethics in two senses: as a result of the accomplishment felt by renouncing and sublimating the need for immediate instinctual gratification and as a result of the acclaim accompanying the cultural products that invariably issue from the exercise of one's reason and imagination.

At the same time, Freud argues that correlated with Jewish self-esteem and cultural impact was an increase in anti-Semitism. He acknowledges that there were non-psychoanalytic reasons, indeed, sociological ones, for such hate: the Jews were foreigners, minorities, and had distinguishing ethnic and racial marks. But additionally, in going back to his ruminations on the Jews being God's chosen people, Freud suggests that it instigated jealousy not only in the normal "ontogenic" sense (narcissism and tribalism) but also in the "phylogenic" sense: it ignited that kernel of "archaic" historical truth in which certain "sons" were favored by the godlike primal father.

The Jews Murdered Moses

Returning to Freud's preferred historical narrative, there was one major blip in the continuity of tradition: the murder of Moses and the subsequent abandonment of monotheism. Freud's reconstruction of that narrative was based on the scholarship of the historian and biblical scholar Ernst Sellin, who, starting in 1922, claimed that his reading of the Book of Hosea suggested that Moses had been murdered. While this thesis was for many quite dubious, it fit perfectly with Freud's stress on the power of the

---

[15] Ibid., 45.

return of the phylogenetic repressed.[16] We have already seen that Moses awakened the grandeur of the primal father (the acceptance of Moses was the "re-establishment of the primal father in his historic rights"[17]) and that the monotheistic prohibition against images and the stress on justice and truth were advances. But the strength of the phylogenetic unconscious overwhelmed reason and morality, and a historical moment of phylogenetically driven "acting out" against the "father" (Moses and behind him the primal father) occurred. Predictably, the return of the (phylogenetic) repressed led to the repetition of the primal deed. In sum, Freud thought that he had corroborated Sellin's thesis by bringing in psychoanalytically framed phylogenetic factors.

Further Developments in Monotheism

After the murder of Moses, the Jews abandoned monotheism. Once again following the researches of Eduard Meyer, Freud narrates a history that has the Jews wandering in the wilderness for generations, engaging other wandering Jewish tribes (the Midianites in particular), eventually idealizing yet another Moses (the "Midianite Moses") who introduced them to a new God: Yahweh (the volcano God), described by Freud as "uncanny" and "bloodthirsty."[18] In other words, departing from the normative understanding of the biblical narrative, Freud posits that there were two Moses and two religions. However, as time passed, several factors served to bring the Jews back to the Egyptian Moses and his monotheism: an oral tradition that kept the memory of the latter alive, the prophetic tradition, and, most importantly, the increase in guilt and longing fueled by the buried memory of the murder of Moses (and behind him the primal father). Freud defends his acceptance of this revisionist narrative by claiming that the biblical narrative had been "distorted by the influence of powerful tendentious purposes and embellished by the products of poetic invention."[19]

This line of argument adds to the factors that Freud emphasized as necessary for the continuance of the Jewish tradition. He understood that heightened self-esteem and certain sociological factors (written and oral traditions, the prophetic lineage) were in some measure responsible for the continuation of a tradition. But once again, he also returned to the

---

[16] Yerushalmi provides a critical look at Sellin and Freud's appropriation of his thought in chapter 2 of his *Freud's Moses*.
[17] Freud, *Moses and Monotheism*, S.E. 23: 86.   [18] Ibid., 34.   [19] Ibid., 41.

factor of the phylogenetic unconscious. In the pages of *Moses and Monotheism* Freud observes how the latter was instrumental to his modeling of "mass psychology." The development of groups of peoples functions like that of a single individual. Groups, like individuals, follow the familiar psychoanalytic sequence: early trauma, defense, latency, outbreak of neurosis, partial return of the repressed.[20]

Freud then turns his attention to other religious traditions. Commensurate with his earlier attempts in *Totem and Taboo*, Freud echoed how the return of the phylogenetic repressed played a crucial role in the subsequent monotheisms (Christianity and Islam) and in what he called the "apparently rationalistic religions of the East."[21] In some sense Judaism had set the stage for Christianity in that the murder of Moses created the expectation that a "Messiah" would return. Freud observes that for Christians the expectation of a Messiah became projected onto the figure of Jesus. The subsequent genius of St. Paul was to theologically ground a "son" religion, thus admitting to the "original sin" within us all and, as a consequence, our dim appreciation of the need to sacrifice the leader of the band of brothers. Herein lies yet another phylogenetic reason for anti-Semitism. The claim that the Jews (and indeed all of us) killed God has a core historical truth to it. The Christians, however, at least admitted it, offered up a "son" for sacrifice, and hence were purified. Freud, then, drew a direct connection between the primal deed, the creation of totemism, the murder of Moses, the expectation of the Messiah, and the birth of a "son religion." While the murder of the son was an advance (in that people intuitively knew that a member of the "brother band" had to be sacrificed), there was also, relative to Judaism, some regression that accompanied Christianity: the affirmation of magical, mystical, and superstitious elements, the valorization of ceremonials and rituals, and a retarding of intellectuality and freedom of thought.[22]

Islam (the "Mohammedan religion," as Freud calls it), is deemed an "abbreviated repetition" of Judaism. Freud suggests that Muhammed originally intended to accept Judaism "in full for himself and his people" but that its development was stunted in that Muhammed never suffered the fate of Moses.[23] The rationalistic religions of the East, on the other

---

[20] Ibid., 80.   [21] Ibid., 93.   [22] Ibid., 86ff.
[23] Freud said little about Islam, but there is a growing psychoanalytic literature concerning it. See, for example, O. El Shakry, *The Arabic Freud* (Princeton, NJ: Princeton University Press, 2017); *The Crescent and the Couch*, ed. S. Akhtar (New York: Jason Aronson,

hand, Freud framed as "ancestor cults" and, as such, stopped short "at an early stage of the reconstruction of the past."[24] To be sure, such comments were cursory at best. Freud apologized for his lack of detail and for concentrating on mostly one case (i.e., Judaism) "from the copious phenomenology of religions" in part because he lacked the "expert knowledge" necessary to "complete the enquiry."[25] On that point, at least, contemporary scholars of the history of religions would concur.

MOSES AND MONOTHEISM: CRITIQUES

Perhaps the philosopher Paul Ricoeur said it best when he stated that Freud's *Moses* "contains an impressive number of hazardous hypotheses."[26] Interestingly enough, despite the many factual errors and dubious assertions that run throughout this last of Freud's books, it has commanded a good deal of insightful commentary. We can subsume this secondary literature, along with our own additions to it, under two basic headings: (1) Freud's *Moses* and its contributions to the psychoanalytic study of religion and (2) Freud, Judaism, and identity.

Freud's Moses *and Its Contributions to the Psychoanalytic Study of Religion*

Within a scant few years historians and biblical scholars had vented at the sheer number of Freud's numerous historical mistakes and dependence on outdated and questionable sources.[27] As we have seen, "Moses" may be an Egyptian name, but there is no evidence that he was anything but a Hebrew. Additionally, Freud's portrait of the Egyptian Pharaoh Akhenaten as a reformer who instituted monotheism is an error, as is the notion that ethics was at its core.[28] The latter did not offer "ethical discipline in the formation of character" and evinced "no interest in social justice or the welfare of society."[29] There is, then, "no basis for a

---

2008); J. Jones, *Blood That Cries Out from the Earth* (New York: Oxford University Press, 2008); E. Said, *Freud and the Non-European* (New York: Verso, 2003); and F. Benslama, *Psychoanalysis and the Challenge of Islam* (Minneapolis: University of Minnesota Press, 2009).

[24] Freud, *Moses and Monotheism*, S.E. 23: 92–93.   [25] Ibid., 92.
[26] Ricoeur, *Freud and Philosophy*, 245.
[27] See, for example, W. F. Albright's classic work *From the Stone Age to Christianity* (Baltimore: Johns Hopkins University Press, 1946), 166–167, 194–196.
[28] See Rice, *Freud and Moses*, 139.   [29] Ibid., 139–140.

conclusion that Akhenaten's Atonism was the inspiration for Mosaic monotheism."[30] The postulation of "two Moseses" (Egyptian and Midianite) remains unsubstantiated, and Ernst Sellin, the scholar Freud depended on for his thesis that Moses was murdered, came to doubt, if not formally retract, his own hypothesis (to which Freud predictably responded: "it might be true all the same"[31]). Later, in the "third period" of the psychology and religion movement, W. W. Meissner, himself a psychoanalyst and Jesuit, and by way of summarizing the findings of contemporary biblical scholarship, concluded: "Freud was able to advance an ingenious reconstruction on the basis of a historical account that has so altered in the intervening years that it is no longer tenable."[32] Finally, as we have endeavored to point out, Freud's entry into the comparative study of religion (as he himself admits) was cursory and uninformed. Freud may have been convinced he had the keys that unveiled a historical reality that was, in his view, so badly distorted by the more accepted narratives as found in the Bible. Contemporary historical and biblical scholarship, however, clearly beg to differ.

While little can be said to resurrect and defend Freud's argument, there are in fact portable lessons that can be mined from his work. This mining is most profitable if one siphons and reconstitutes Freud's central arguments concerning the psychological determinants of monotheism and continuance of Jewish identity and self-esteem through the lens of the later, more sophisticated theoretical developments and concepts within object-relations theory. While a fuller treatment of the latter will be offered in Chapter 7, the limited use of a few of its central concepts here will prove to be of value. In effect, what we will see is that Freud had all the right observations but, lacking a sophisticated understanding of the dynamics of the pre-oedipal and the developmental line of narcissism, his explanatory thesis (the recourse to phylogenesis) missed the mark.

To wit: Freud did not dismiss the power of purely cultural factors in the continuance of Judaism: the forceful narratives of prophets, oral and written testimonies, ritual ceremonies, religious education. What perplexed him was the overwhelming response to the "great man" (Moses) that seemingly went beyond cultural determinants and the return of a tradition after the Jews murdered Moses. Continuing the thesis advocated in *Totem and Taboo*, Freud thought only a phylogenetic explanation sufficed. It was the return of the phylogenetic unconscious, the "archaic

---

[30] Ibid., 141.   [31] Ibid., 149.
[32] See Meissner, *Psychoanalysis and Religious Experience*, 108ff.

heritage" that was inherited and comprised "not only dispositions but subject matter – memory traces of the experience of earlier generations" that was the determining, operative factor. In going beyond culture, Freud stated that this factor was independent of "direct communication and of the influence of education."[33]

As with *Totem and Taboo*, such a hypothesis was again refuted in its "strong" sense where dispositions, vestiges, and memory traces are inherited. The dubious nature of Freud's thesis was most artfully (and politely) put by the historian Yosef Yerushalmi: "Certum, quia absurdum est (Certainly, because it is absurd)."[34] The initial generation of psychoanalysts both of and after Freud's generation (e.g., Ernest Jones, Heinz Hartmann) similarly abandoned the strong Lamarckian thesis. More recently, scholars such as Robert Paul and Jan Assmann have attempted to reframe the reasons for the continuance of tradition by offering anthropological and sociohistorical theses to supplant Freud's recourse to phylogenesis.[35] But here an opportunity arises to address a lingering lacuna from our treatment of this problem in the last chapter, namely: Do supplementary resources exist within psychoanalysis that rescue Freud's line of thought without having to rely on a phylogenetic hypothesis?

The answer, as we have suggested, lies in the theoretical developments offered by psychoanalytic object-relations theory. There are essentially two parts to this argument. First, recall that one of Freud's concerns in *Totem and Taboo* was to undermine Jung's growing threat by offering a psychoanalytic counter to his notion of a collective unconscious populated by archetypes. Object-relations refutes Jung by acknowledging the veracity of his clinical observations but disputing his theoretical framing of the clinical data. Jung correctly saw in his patients a new kind of "transference": not the standard Freudian transferences (where a regressed patient may project sexual and oedipal issues onto the analyst) but what later object-relation theorists came to realize were pre-oedipal or

---

[33] Freud, *Moses and Monotheism*, S.E. 23: 99.
[34] Yerushalmi, *Freud's Moses*, 30–31. Yerushalmi and R. Bernstein, in *Freud and the Legacy of Moses* (Cambridge: Cambridge University Press, 1998), have engaged in a spirited debate about "strong" (which they both reject) versus "weak" (which Bernstein entertains) versions of phylogenesis. The turn to object-relations theory obviates the need for that debate.
[35] See R. Paul, *Moses and Civilization* (New Haven, CT: Yale University Press, 1996), and J. Assmann, *Moses the Egyptian* (Cambridge, MA: Harvard University Press, 1998). While not undertaken in these pages, an object-relational approach that undercuts the need for phylogenesis is well situated to be in dialogue with Assmann's cultural approach and could supplement Paul's nuanced cultural-oedipal thesis.

narcissistic transferences. Jung called such instances "inflation" where the patient would, for example, see the analyst as God or, alternately, themself as God, further attributing such transferences to the power of archetypical material. Object-relations theorists such as Heinz Kohut later reframed the same Jungian transferences as instances of the emergence of early, untransformed narcissistic structures called the "grandiose self" (I am great and powerful) and "idealized parent imago" (the parent is great and powerful). But these structures stemmed not from a "collective unconscious" and its archetypes but from the pre-oedipal developmental period where, in order to maintain a sense of personal cohesiveness and equilibrium in the face of the demands of external reality, the child balloons their own ego (as when the child states: "I am Superman") or merges with a source of power and protection (the parent or God). Indeed, object-relations later came to reframe Jung's developmental notion of "individuation" as constituting the developmental line of narcissism. In other words, Jung had the right clinical observations but the wrong theory.[36]

This line of argument helps to rectify Freud's phylogenetic hypothesis in the following way. Simply put, object-relational theorizing about the narcissistic line of development obviates the need for a phylogenetic thesis. To unpack this, we can move to the second phase of our argument. Like Jung, Freud's psychoanalytic version of a "collective mind" was misguided. Yet, again like Jung, the psychological observations he made with respect to Moses and Judaism fit seamlessly with the innovative concepts offered by object-relations theory. For example, Freud thinks the archaic heritage, awakened and brought to life in the altered state of religious ecstasy, is needed to account for the unambiguously "positive feelings" of "admiration, awe, and gratitude" relative to the figure of Moses. Object-relations would say that one need not go back into the distant past or speak of an archaic heritage so much as an earlier developmental phase: the pre-oedipal or narcissistic, where idealization is extreme, where one's will completely submits to the idealized other (as the Jews did with Moses) even over against the objections of logical reason. Along these same lines Freud refers to how Moses presented to the Jews a "more grandiose idea of their God," with which, through belief, one

---

[36] For literature that attempts to read Jung as an object-relations theorist, see P. Homans, *Jung in Context* (Chicago: University of Chicago Press, 1989); M. Jacoby, *Individuation and Narcissism* (New York: Routledge, 1990); and A. Samuels, *Jung and the Post-Jungians* (New York: Routledge, 1986).

could take "part in his greatness," resulting in an increase in self-esteem and the move to intellectuality and morality. This fits hand-in-glove with Kohut's "idealized parent imago" that eventually transforms more archaic narcissistic mergers into the more mature psychological structure of realistic self-esteem through love, concern, and what Kohut calls "mirroring" (i.e., "you are special"; "I love you"; "you are chosen"). The godlike idealization of Moses, then, along with the self-esteem and tenacity it generates, is now seen as dependent on the narcissistic developmental themes they successfully address. The identity and continuity of tradition is also accounted for in that the continued valorization of religious figures (what object-relational theorists call cultural self-objects), which serves to uphold their status as worthy objects for idealization, spans the generational gap. In this context recall once again how Michelangelo's Moses, in its psychoanalytically adaptive and object-relational framing as a cultural self-object, afforded Freud narcissistic sustenance and stability during a time of personal upheaval. These considerations suggest that Freud had the psychological observations right but unfortunately resorted to a dubious theory emphasizing phylogenesis, in part because he wished to counter Jung and in part because he did not have a developed clinical or theoretical understanding of the pre-oedipal period. Promptly corrected with respect to object-relations theory, Freud's views on the continuance of tradition can be rescued and applied, as a portable lesson, to other similar dynamics in religious traditions. Indeed, this same relational phenomenon, involving as it does deep, archaic forms of idealization, has been noticed in modern-day religious figures with respect to another "great man," namely, the "guru," the therapeutic dimension of which has been psychoanalytically interpreted as due to the latter's ability to elicit and address narcissistic deficits (we will come back to this very example in Chapter 7).

Freud, Judaism, and Identity

In a related but different take on Freud's *Moses*, some have seen its worth primarily as one more chapter in his ongoing struggle with his Jewish identity. Freud wrote to Lou Andreas-Salomé that the figure of Moses "haunted" him, and we have already seen how much time and energy Freud devoted to an analysis of Michelangelo's statue of Moses at a crucial juncture in his personal and professional life.[37] Speaking to this,

---

[37] Rice, *Freud and Moses*, 124.

Meissner has noted that any applied "cultural" work, particularly that of a psychoanalyst, reflects "the dynamic configurations and conflicts embedded in the individual's personality structure" and that in this regard "Freud is no exception."[38] Subsequent eminent psychoanalysts such as Erik Erikson, Sudhir Kakar, and Heinz Kohut followed suit, similarly writing on idealized religious heroes that engaged their personal religious proclivities (Martin Luther, Vivekananda, and Dag Hammarskjöld, respectively). Of course, *Moses and Monotheism* was hardly a hagiography. To the contrary, the Moses Freud ended up with was a far cry from any traditional Jewish theological perspective (as one critic put it, Freud rendered "a whole people illegitimate"[39]). At the same time, Freud was in some sense drawn to Judaism and its figures, if not in a typically religious way. So it is that one can ask: How could Freud, by way of critically engaging his tradition, reconstitute Judaism in a manner that accorded with his psyche? To put it another way: What conclusion did Freud reach concerning the nature of that "essence" of Judaism he could abide by? In a very real sense, this discussion is an extension of our earlier survey (in Chapter 1) of Freud's relation to Judaism.

The question of what constituted the essence of Judaism had been directly broached by Freud in the "Preface to the Hebrew Translation" of *Totem and Taboo* (a preface added in 1930; the actual translation was not published until 1939). Addressing the "reader" of the Hebrew translation, Freud answers the question of what is left of being a Jew if one rejects (as he had) all ceremonial and "nationalist ideals" by stating: "A very great deal, and probably its very essence," going on to affirm that "unprejudiced science cannot remain a stranger to the spirit of the new Jewry."[40] The conjunction of the "essence" of Judaism with science appears to be a good fit with the socio-evolutionism that animates both *Totem and Taboo* and *Moses and Monotheism* as well as the crucial role Freud thought Moses, Judaism, and monotheism played in that evolution. Recall from Chapter 1 that in his little essay on Michelangelo's Moses Freud had framed the statue as "a concrete expression of the highest mental achievement that is possible in a man, that of struggling successfully against an inward passion for the sake of a cause to which he has devoted himself."[41] This accords with Freud's assertion in *Moses and Monotheism* that the prohibition against images led to instinctual

---

[38] Meissner, *Psychoanalysis and Religious Experience*, vii; Rice, *Freud and Moses*, 128.
[39] M. Hewitt, *Freud on Religion* (Durham, UK: Acumen, 2014), 64.
[40] Freud, *Totem and Taboo*, S.E. 13: xv.   [41] Rice, *Freud and Moses*, 127.

renunciation, reflection, intellectuality, and the growth in morality. Along these lines it is significant that when Freud had an opportunity to present selections of his book to a waiting public in England, he (because of ill health) directed his daughter Anna (a famous psychoanalyst in her own right) to read only the chapter entitled "The Progress in Spirituality" (the German is "Geistigkeit"), which heralded the consequences of the Mosaic prohibition on images and the subsequent triumph of abstract reason over the more dubious knowledge garnered through the senses.[42]

In *Totem and Taboo* Freud had also spoken of a cultural evolution from animism/totemism to monotheism to science. As we noted above, the prohibition in images becomes a crucial juncture in the historical progression to science. And, as we have suggested (and will detail further in the next chapter), Freud completes the cycle by framing psychoanalysis as a scientific "secular cure of souls" and "universal" moral regimen designed to keep civilization whole. Freud is the secular Moses who has bequeathed to us a non-religious yet universal moral regimen (his "tablets") through which humans can learn to renounce and then sublimate baser instincts in the service of what he would later refer to as the power of Eros (the human need for civilization and unity). While Moses, monotheism, and Judaism played a central role in this "redemptive" process, psychoanalysis was not a religion but a science – a historically necessary humanistic substitute. Again, in *Future of an Illusion*, Freud, in an effort to show the historical necessity of replacing religion with a secular cure of souls, identified himself (albeit rhetorically) with St. Boniface.[43] Boniface had chopped down the sacred tree of the Saxons (read "religion") without any divine retribution. Freud was similarly offering to replace religion with a secular cure of souls, and he assured us that no punishment would be forthcoming. Rather, psychoanalysis, as the heir to monotheism and commensurate with science, would maintain the social whole in the face of secularization.

---

[42] For the context of Anna Freud's talk, see Yerushalmi, *Freud's Moses*, 51.
[43] See Freud, *Future of an Illusion*, chapter 8.

4

Future of an Illusion

The Secular Cure of Souls

If *Totem and Taboo* and *Moses and Monotheism* can be framed as "the bookends" (being the first and last of Freud's works on religion), then *Future of an Illusion* and *Civilization and Its Discontents* can be called "the twins." Written a scant three years apart (1927 and 1930, respectively), they form the essential core, the most widely known and influential of Freud's varied analyses of religion. While the two works are joined by central themes that continue to preoccupy Freud's ruminations on the relation between the individual, civilization, religion, and the historical process, they also evince a striking disparity in tone. *Future of an Illusion* exudes an enlightenment agenda, valorizing the power of reason, the efficacy of psychoanalytic modes of personal transformation, and the eventual victory of humanism, science, and tolerance. *Civilization and Its Discontents*, on the other hand, prescient in what was to come (namely, World War II), is more pessimistic, warning of the ascendancy of the darker forces of human nature, the "unpsychological" structures of social institutions, and the growing uneasiness of humans in civilization. In this chapter we will focus on *Future of an Illusion*, leaving our treatment of *Civilization and Its Discontents* for Chapter 5.

FUTURE OF AN ILLUSION: THE ARGUMENT

In *Future of an illusion* Freud remarks that he is not concerned with the origins and development of religion, as was the case with *Totem and Taboo*, but with what he refers to as "the finished body of religious ideas as it is transmitted by civilization to the individual," further clarifying the latter as consisting of "present-day white Christian" institutional religion.[1] With respect to this form of religion, Freud offers two distinct arguments: the *epistemological* argument (exemplified in the second word of the title: "Illusion") and the *sociohistorical* argument (aptly indicated by the first word of the title: "Future").

Most commentators emphasize Freud's epistemological critique of religion. Put briefly, in the latter Freud directed his readers to see how contemporary religion, as a worldview, was based on developmental factors, emphasizing (as he had with dreams) the role of childish wishes. Psychologically speaking, religion was a form of illusion that catered to a person's sense of helplessness, the existential need for protection, care, guidance, and justice. While *Totem and Taboo* was focused on origins (the enactment of and reaction to the primal deed as informed by the dynamics of the Oedipus complex), *Future of an Illusion* focused on what Freud terms the *manifest* motives (i.e., helplessness and the need for the father). The sociohistorical argument, on the other hand, is evident from the very first paragraph of the work. There Freud observes that when one has lived in a culture for an extended period of time, it is natural to seek "what its origins were and along what path it has developed."[2] Once again, the reference is to *Totem and Taboo*. But then he goes on to say that "one sometimes also feels tempted to take a glance in the other direction and to ask what further fate lies before it and what transformations it is destined to undergo."[3] In other words, here Freud is more intent on what he frames in the book as the coming demise of religion, its cultural consequences, and the role psychoanalysis is destined to play in that mix. It is the sociohistorical argument that provides not only the broad context for the epistemological critique but also the urgency and power that pervades the book as a whole. That said, the two strands of argument are not mutually exclusive, being inexorably interrelated and crisscrossing throughout the course of the book.

The Epistemological Argument: "Illusion" and the Classic-Reductive Model

Freud's epistemological argument is summed up in a pithy paragraph that opens chapter 6 of his work. There Freud states, quite simply, that religious ideas "are illusions, fulfillments of the oldest, strongest and most

---

[1] Freud, *Future of an Illusion*, S.E. 21: 24, 20.   [2] Ibid., 5.   [3] Ibid.

urgent wishes of mankind."[4] In detailing the "manifest" motive, he goes on to state:

[T]he terrifying impression of helplessness in childhood aroused the need for protection – for protection through love – which was provided by the father; and the recognition that this helplessness lasts throughout life made it necessary to cling to the existence of the father, but this time a more powerful one. Thus the benevolent rule of a divine Providence allays our fear of the dangers of life; the establishment of a moral world-order ensures the fulfillment of the demands of justice, which have so often remained unfulfilled in human civilization; and the prolongation of earthly existence in a future life provides the local and temporal framework in which these wish-fulfilments shall take place. Answers to the riddles that tempt the curiosity of man, such as how the universe began or what the relation is between body and mind, are developed in conformity with the underlying assumptions of this system. It is also an enormous relief to the individual psyche if the conflicts of its childhood arising from the father-complex – conflicts which it has never wholly overcome – are removed from it and brought to a solution which is universally accepted.[5]

Freud has a specific, psychoanalytic rendering in mind when he uses the term "illusion." He does not, as some may think, equate illusion with outright error and falsehood. According to Freud it is possible, however unlikely, that God actually exists. It is also possible, however unlikely, that a Messiah will come and found a golden age. It is the high degree of unlikeliness that leads Freud to wonder less about their possible truth and more about the motivation of those who believe in what he thinks is clear nonsense. His answer is that they believe due to the power of certain wishes: for protection (from natural as well as human forces), consolation, justice, and simple answers to the big questions. In turn, such motivations follow a psychological gradient born of childhood helplessness, a time in which one's anxieties were assuaged by the presence of the earthly father.

Civilization, then, offers religious ideas as one of many options for navigating the exigencies of life. But in choosing that option one performs a regressive act, and hence a childish solution, to the universal and very human problem of adaptation to an often harsh and challenging reality. It is important to note that Freud does not altogether deny that belief can be psychologically comforting or that civilization as a social entity has not historically benefited from religion. Rather, the question is: At what cost? Freud thinks religious ideas and institutions cater to baser, primitive needs while stunting the intellect. Is one's sense of self-esteem and identity

---

[4] Ibid., 30.   [5] Ibid.

challenged by the exigencies of life? Well, then, religion offers a means (prayer) through which one can feel relatively confident in changing reality and fate. Are the demands of civilization, which enjoin one to renounce certain wishes, and perceived injustices stemming from fate and others, weighing on the soul? Well, then, religion offers a prescription, the confession of faith, that will admit one to heaven while sending one's enemies to eternal suffering. Does the intellect and one's curiosity demand the answer to what Freud referred to as the "riddles of the universe"? Well, then, there is a historical litany of religious intellectuals, basing their thought on revealed scripture and tradition, who provide ready, ultimate answers. Indeed, it is particularly the latter that irks Freud the most. He suggests that certain religious ideas are so improbable that they move, as if on a sliding scale, from "illusions" to "delusions." As he put it, when the degree of unlikeliness of religious ideas is such that they are "so incompatible with everything we have laboriously discovered about the reality of the world," then it is best to "compare them ... to delusions."[6] Freud is adamant that "many brilliant intellects" have broken down as a result of the conflict between reason and a commanding super-ego formed out of religious tenets. The latter often wins due to it being buttressed by the power of an idealized tradition and the memory of parental love, which enjoins obedience through the fear of the loss of that love.[7] At the same time, Freud is also aware that, historically speaking, some of those brilliant intellects have broken through the psychological sway of such forces to exercise disinterested curiosity. He pointedly notes that, even in overcoming the internal obstacle of super-ego channeled obedience, such brilliant intellects have been subject to an additional hurdle: social repression, condemnation, and imprisonment. Freud finds historical examples of the latter in what we in Chapter 2 called the "three blows" theory: heliocentrism versus geocentrism (Galileo, Copernicus); evolution versus creationism (the famous Scopes monkey trial); and his own postulation of psychoanalysis and the unconscious (belief as illusion). In each case, it was institutional religion, in defense of labile narcissism, that led the charge against the advance of science.

Freud thought that there was a better alternative than the recourse to religion and belief. He articulated that option with respect to what the Dutch writer Multatuli framed as the "twin" gods of Logos (Reason) and Ananke (Necessity) – gods that valorized the empirical findings of science

---

[6] Ibid., 31.   [7] Ibid., 27.

and a psychoanalytically informed, mature adaptation to reality. Such mature individuals lived without the crutch of religious illusions, were capable of successfully adapting to the demands of civilization through sublimation, had healthy super-egos, and lacked debilitating forms of neuroses. In effect, Freud was offering a normative ideal of the healthy mature person, which he contrasted to the strategy employed (i.e., "regressive adaptation") by the believer.

Religion and the Adaptive Model

The foregoing affirms what most identify Freud with: the pejorative classic-reductive school of psychoanalysis. In other words, religion and belief is "nothing but" a projection in the service of those who are developmentally challenged. However, widening Freud's analysis to include his clinical case histories and other smaller papers on religion, one finds evidence of a more positive strain, what we have called the adaptive, that also merits consideration. For example, in his famous case history of the "wolf man," Freud observes how religious narratives and symbols afforded his young patient the psychological opportunity to adapt to culture's demands:

[I]t may be said that in the present case religion achieved all the aims for the sake of which it is included in the education of the individual. It put a restraint on his sexual impulses by affording them a sublimation and a safe mooring; it lowered the importance of his family relationships and, thus, protected him from the threat of isolation by giving him access to the great community of mankind. The untamed and fear-ridden child became social, well-behaved, and amenable to education.[8]

Again, in his often-overlooked analysis of the "demonological possession" (the religious way of thinking about neuroses) of the seventeenth-century painter Christoph Haizmann, Freud showed how the latter's neurotic melancholy, based in his ambivalent relation to his father, was nonetheless therapeutically "worked through" by means of the accoutrements of the Church. The latter included therapeutic intervention by idealized, empathic church functionaries (priests) who elicited and addressed Haizmann's conflicts through a deft, ritualistic use of the "cultural containers" of God (the "good" father) and Satan (the "bad" father). It also included offering Haizmann an eventual home in a holy

---

[8] See S.E. 17:114–115.

order, which, by enjoining him to live a life of asceticism, resulted in a stay of his melancholy.⁹

These examples suggest that Freud was aware of, and not wholly antithetical to, forms of religious psychotherapy. Indeed, in an earlier paper titled "On Psychotherapy" (1905) he admits that religious forms of psychotherapy have healing potential. He states that psychotherapy, of which psychoanalysis is a specified form, "is in no way a modern method of treatment" but "the most ancient form of therapy in medicine," going on to say that "there are many ways and means of practicing psychotherapy. All that lead to recovery are good."¹⁰ In distinguishing specifically psychoanalytic modes of therapy from the spectrum of others, Freud plays on Leonardo da Vinci's distinction between *per via di porre* (the application of a substance onto a canvas, as exemplified in painting) and *per via di levare* (the uncovering and chipping away at a surface to reveal the art within, as with sculpture). Freud equated the former with "suggestive-supportive" types of therapy, the latter with the analytic, uncovering techniques used by psychoanalysis. At its best, religious forms of therapy, framed as instances of the directive, value-laden form of the suggestive-supportive type, work by monitoring and containing the unconscious in an "experience-distant" fashion through public symbols and narratives. When illness occurs, religious therapies work by manipulating unconscious content skillfully through the empathic mediating presence of idealized religious functionaries, various forms of introspection (e.g., prayer, contemplation) and the reintegration of the anomic individual into a greater, supportive social community and its preferred worldview. Freud noted that the two types of therapy could be combined, that psychoanalysis was an "impartial tool which both priest and layman can use in the service of the sufferer," and that psychoanalysis could be "extraordinarily helpful" in "pastoral work." The latter observations, which Freud offered in a letter to the lay analyst and minister Oskar

---

⁹ Freud, "A Seventeenth Century Demonological Neurosis," S.E.: 19: 69–108. Freud's adaptive analysis was given greater psychoanalytic sophistication in Erikson's analysis of Luther in his *Young Man Luther* (New York: W. W. Norton, 1958). In other words, one can draw a historical line between Freud's more cursory analysis of Haizmann and the monastery and Erikson's more sophisticated analysis, due to advances in ego psychology, of the impact of the monastery and church practices on Luther. For more cases of the suggestive-supportive type in India, see Sudhir Kakar, *Shamans, Mystics, and Doctors* (New York: Alfred A. Knopf, 1982).

¹⁰ Freud, "On Psychotherapy," S.E. 7: 257–270. See also Kakar, *Shamans, Mystics, and Doctors*, 275ff.

Pfister, indicates that Freud lent a qualified approval to what later came to be fully institutionalized as pastoral psychology.[11]

At the same time, it must be emphasized that, even given Freud's admission of the adaptive potential of religious forms of therapy, he cautioned that they, as opposed to psychoanalysis, could not effect a permanent cure. The reason, he says, is that they conceal the play of unconscious forces. In other words, they cannot eventuate in the more lasting "education" of the unconscious and its instincts. It does not, per the psychoanalytic motto, replace the id with ego. While religious forms of therapy may well lead to a happier life that is adaptive, it does so on the basis of offering illusions that signify the continued presence and influence of infantilism. In so doing, they leave themselves open to the charge of enabling a pernicious "return of the repressed." More problematically, there is the possibility that religious forms of therapeutic intervention might, in pushing a specific value-laden, "suggestive" worldview, fail to empathically connect with the uniqueness and deepest core of the individual, preferring to enforce a form of "higher" religious repression (think, for example, of religious counseling services devoted to "curing" members of the LGBTQ community). While Freud did not specifically comment on the latter instance, so familiar to the contemporary Western person, it is not hard to predict what he would say. If one needed confirmation, then one could turn to his response (in 1935) to the American mother who requested he cure her gay son. Freud reminded her that many famous, creative men of the past were homosexual; that it was "nothing to be ashamed of, no vice, no degradation"; that "it cannot be classified as an illness"; and that it was "a great injustice to persecute homosexuality as a crime – and a cruelty, too."[12]

A Case History of Conversion

The above considerations serve to inform Freud's analysis of a case of conversion. The latter was the focus of his short paper *A Religious Experience* (1928), penned mere weeks after the publication of *Future of an Illusion*.[13] The paper recounts how an American physician, responding to an interview in which Freud discussed his book and restated his atheism, wrote Freud to offer a testimony of faith. In it he

---

[11] See Freud and Pfister, *Psychoanalysis and Faith*, 17.
[12] "A Letter from Freud," *The American Journal of Psychiatry* (1951): 786–787.
[13] The essay is found in S.E. 21: 167–172.

described an event that led to his crisis of faith, then to a deconversion of sorts, and, subsequently, due to a specific series of events, a reconversion to Christianity. Setting the stage for his narrative, he admitted to Freud that his attitude toward Christian doctrines had been one of ambivalence, and as a result, he had been in and out of the Church. Then came "the event." While "passing through the dissecting room" at "the University of X," his gaze fell on a "sweet-faced dear old woman" who had died and was being carried to a dissecting table. It made such an indelible impression on him that it occurred to him to finally doubt the existence of God, the implication being that a supreme being in his goodness would never allow such an event to occur. While not a part of the letter to Freud, one can remark that this, theologically speaking, is an instance of the problem of "theodicy" (the problem of evil and its theological explanation and defense). In other words, the event that caused the doctor so much consternation was a case of the classic saying: "Why do bad things happen to good people?" As a result, on arriving home, the doctor decided to stop going to church (i.e., he "deconverted"). But then the doctor had second thoughts and, on reconsideration, decided he would allow God to show him the error of his ways. Sure enough, "God made it clear to my soul that the Bible was His word, that the teachings about Jesus Christ were true, and that Jesus was our only hope."[14] It was this process of reconsideration, punctuated by unspecified, multiple "infallible proofs" (as he called them), that led to a reconversion. Theologically speaking, this last series of events are instances of grace. God bequeathed to the doctor his love, manifested initially in terms of reflection and reconsideration and then as a full-blown return to the Church. The doctor then begged Freud "as a brother physician" to take heed in the hope that "God will reveal the *truth* to your soul."[15] Theologically speaking, this would be an instance of agape: loving the neighbor in the hope that they will see the Light. Freud politely responded that God "had not done so much for me" and that, given his age, he would undoubtedly die "an infidel Jew." The physician assured him that "being a Jew was not an obstacle" and that he would pray for him. Freud ends the summary by noting wryly: "I am still awaiting the outcome of this intercession."[16]

The psychoanalytic version of this "deconversion and reconversion" theme differs considerably from its theological counterpart, the latter employing the notions of theodicy, conversion, grace, and agape.

---

[14] Ibid., 169.   [15] Ibid., 170.   [16] Ibid.

The key lies in the instigating event: the sweet-faced dear old woman. For Freud the latter unconsciously recalls nothing less than the mother, and the violence done to her by God reflects but a string of memories of paternal abuse reaching all the way back to the dim memory of the primal scene where, according to Freud, the little boy, inadvertently hearing groans coming from the parents making love, comes to the conclusion that the father is attacking the mother. In other words, the physician's cursory theological meanderings on the existence of evil are, at least in this particular case, but a misdirection, being a disguised and displaced narrative ruled by the dynamics of oedipal conflict. Psychoanalytic logic would further suggest that the doctor, who unquestionably had seen cadavers before, must have been unusually psychologically ripe on this particular day to react as he did. That ripeness, the logic would say, was due to what must have been ongoing conflict in his own love life (possibly manifested in a dream the night before). The colloquial way of putting this latter observation is that the doctor "woke up on the wrong side of the bed" (due to romantic conflicts and perhaps a repressed dream that continued to influence his mood). To be sure, absent free associations and therapeutic intervention, we cannot ascertain the specific details. However, that some such life turmoil predisposed the doctor to such a reaction on this particular day (as opposed to all the other times he saw cadavers) is, psychoanalytically speaking, all but certain.

Moving on, the next step, deconversion and ceasing to believe in God, is but a displaced version of killing the father: "his desire to destroy his father could become conscious as doubt in the existence of God."[17] The next phase, "reconsideration," reflects the influence of other aspects of the

---

[17] Ibid., 171. With respect to the *psychology-theology dialogue*, theologians may find solace in at least one passage in this little paper that can be described as an "opening" for dialogue. In analyzing the religiously contained oedipal fantasy found in his correspondent's reaction to the sight of the sweet old woman, Freud remarks that his analysis is enabled by the fact that "his ideas of 'father' and 'God' had not yet become widely separate" (171). The meaning and implication of such a separation is not readily apparent, and it is a stretch to think that Freud sought to legitimate a "religious" meaning of God that stranscended developmental determinants. Nevertheless, the notion of a separation provides an opening for theologians wishing to articulate a Jamesian "More" beyond developmental considerations. Similarly, they might link this passage to one in *Totem and Taboo* where Freud, by way of discussing the origin of religion and the eventual morphing of the totem into the concept of God, admits that while the psychoanalytic contribution (the oedipal factor) must loom large, one must not "overlook the complexity of the phenomenon under review" (157, n. 2); that his own analysis must proceed "without prejudice to any other sources or meanings of the concept of God, upon which psychoanalysis can throw no light" (147).

Oedipus complex: the continued identification with and love of the father, the continued need for safety and protection, and the fear of castration and guilt. Clearly, it was those unconscious factors and not "grace" that won out, the result being reconversion. Along these lines one can offer an educated guess that the many "infallible proofs," while remaining unnamed by the physician, must have had an oedipal resonance. His subsequent act of proselytizing was motivated by continued (if unconscious) ambivalence, which was assuaged by converting those (like Freud) who personified and thus represented his now repressed hostile feelings. Converting Freud, then, was but one way to eliminate (i.e., continue to repress) the unconscious hostility toward the father. This could theoretically go on forever: as long as nonbelievers exist, they must be converted lest one's own ambivalence and unconscious hostility erupt back into consciousness. This explains why some might feel a bit of unease when confronted by proselytizing believers (i.e., one viscerally feels their hostility, even when presented as agape).

Certain conclusions can be culled from the above. Most evidently, religious ideation functioned to monitor and contain what amounts to an oedipal crisis. The doctor, conflicted as a result of what we hypothesized to be a recent romantic tension and, as a result, whose unconscious was ready to be activated, reacted to a common event (seeing the cadaver) in an uncommon way (reacting as he did). He then played out the unconscious oedipal dynamic with respect to a culture that offered him a set of symbols, figures, and narratives that enabled him, in a displaced and experience-distant manner, to engage and resolve his momentary conflict. In this sense, one could say that religion, by wearing the unconscious "on the outside" in the form of symbols and narratives, "contained" unruly instincts and provided an adaptive function.

At the same time, for Freud such a resolution would not be the preferred mode of adaptation or of monitoring and containing the unconscious. There is a difference between realistic, mature forms of adaptation and regressive, defensive ones. Recall that Freud thought religious forms of therapy, of which conversion is an element, are subject to the return of the repressed. Recall again that the physician had a history of ambivalence toward the Church. One suspects that this particular instance of deconversion and reconversion was not his first, nor would it be his last. By theologically reframing his oedipal crisis in terms of the concepts of theodicy, grace, and the need to proselytize, the physician is complicit in a misdirection and "higher" form of repression that kept him (and any believer) ignorant of the determining forces of conversion. Moreover, there are potentially dangerous social ramifications of religious forms of containing and monitoring the unconscious. In this regard, recall how the doctor, after his reconversion, offered to pray for Freud's conversion. However politely the doctor framed that offer, and however rationalized it may have been through the notions of charity and agape, it is at least implicitly a form of violence considering the history of Christian anti-Semitism and that Freud, while a declared atheist, was still a Jew. Individually speaking, if the physician had been successful in his attempt to convert Freud, it would have served the purpose of helping offset the return of his ambivalence (which is, as just stated, what the doctor by admission habitually suffered from and, as psychoanalysis would predict, would be subject to in the future). However, if, under certain social conditions, the need to convert is extended from one person to a group (the "Other" in all its forms), overt violence may well be manifested. In other words, it is not a large leap from an individual's displaced unconscious ambivalence to group tribalism and racism. As we will see in the next chapter, Freud came back to theorize more about this important theme in *Civilization and Its Discontents* with respect to, of all things, the Christian love command.

The Sociohistorical Argument: "The Future"

We have seen that Freud indicates that religious forms of suggestive-supportive therapy could potentially have adaptive value, although he certainly preferred psychoanalytic therapy for a host of reasons. Freud held out a similar view of the sociohistorical function of religion throughout the course of human civilization. "Religion," he writes, "has clearly performed great services for human civilization. It has contributed much towards the taming of the asocial instincts.... It has ruled human society for many thousands of years and has time to show what it can achieve."[18] On the other hand, Freud offers a counter thesis. Whatever adaptive function religion has historically implemented, it has "not succeeded in making the majority of mankind happy, in comforting them, in reconciling them to life and in making them into vehicles of civilization."[19] More importantly, Freud thought we were at what he called a "turning point" in history where religion was no longer capable of being functional for either individuals or civilization. If so, then what are the cultural

---

[18] Freud, *Future of an Illusion*, S.E. 21: 37.   [19] Ibid.

consequences? In answering this, we will find that there is something akin to a prophetic call to arms contained in *Future of an Illusion*. As with his epistemological take on religion, Freud's sociohistorical arguments consist of several stages, summarized below in interlocking sections.

The Material and Mental Assets of Civilization

In preparing his argument, Freud first turns to a specific characterization of civilization and the place of religion within it. The usefulness of civilization lies in two related functions: *material* (economic) and *mental* (i.e., psychological). The former provides the needed mastery and control of nature and the accumulation and distribution of wealth; the latter consists of rules, regulations, and various cultural institutions designed to offset asocial tendencies. Some of the theorists in the former group included not only sociologists and economists in general but, while remaining unnamed, Karl Marx in particular. Freud goes so far as to reference "the great experiment in civilization that is now in progress in the vast country that stretches between Europe and Asia," which posited that the solution to asocial instincts lay in the proper distribution of wealth.[20] Marx was convinced that human nature was pliable and, given the right economic and social conditions (i.e., communism), humans could live cooperatively and peacefully. As a counter (as elsewhere in his works where he takes on Marx by name), Freud observes that antisocial and destructive tendencies are universal and ineradicable. "Every individual," says Freud, "is virtually an enemy of civilization."[21] Marx was wrong because he did not understand the power of unconscious aggression and man's antisocial nature. His view of the human personality, being uniformed as it was by clinical data, led to a naïve, simplistic solution such as communism. So it is that here, as elsewhere in his works where Freud challenges Marx, civilization is cast as needing to find other ways aside from the material to foster coercion and the renunciation of instinct.

As a result, *Future of an Illusion* moves quickly from the material to the mental, being concerned with the tools civilization has in its inventory to offset man's natural, antisocial, aggressive instincts. Aside from the general recourse to rules and regulations, and before centering his analysis on religion, Freud mentions cultural ideals as mediated through idealized

---

[20] Ibid., 9.   [21] Ibid., 6.

public figures as effective ways in which civilization gets humans to comply with its forced renunciations. Think, for example, of President John F. Kennedy's memorable line: "Ask not what your country can do for you – ask what you can do for your country." Delivered by a valued authority figure (and hence, in psychoanalytic terms, an instance of the authorizing power of an idealized "cultural super-ego"), such a line was used to promote the internalizations of the American ethos and the injunction to act accordingly. Renunciation of self for the whole, otherwise felt as a burden, is greatly lessened, if not positively countered, by the narcissistic satisfaction gained in identifying with a country that is framed as better than others, even chosen by God. This cursory example is portable and can be generalized to include any valued ideal and all idealized personalities in the cultural arena.

Art, by which Freud meant literature, theater, and visual media such as photography, painting, and sculpture, which we can modernize to include films, television, and social media, also serves the aims of civilization by authorizing the free play of fantasy activity. The unconscious driver of all of the latter examples is unrequited sexual and aggressive wishes. In this sense, the cultural function of art, through individual participation, is to fulfill those wishes that have to be renounced (due to culture) or remain unfulfilled (due to the exigencies of life). To bring this home, the next time one feels a need to see a certain type of movie, one may inquire about the nature of unconscious forces at work. For example, let's take the most storied figure in the Marvel Universe: Spiderman. Psychoanalytically speaking, the "origin story" of Spidey is revealing. A nerdy teenage budding scientist (Peter Parker), often bullied and shunned, is bitten by a radioactive spider, only to find that he, as a result of the bite, has gained newfound powers: super strength, the ability to crawl on walls, a tingling spider sense, and the ability to produce a sticky, web-like substance. It is not far-fetched to see the connection between the latter and the additional muscle mass, height, growth, and ability to produce a sticky substance that is associated with male pubescence. It's hardly an accident that, in a recent installment of the series in which Peter gets a new suit, he offers that "it's a bit tight in the old web-shooters." Even more, in this fantasy Oedipus plays the starring role. Peter Parker becomes Spiderman on that fateful day when he intentionally lets a robber escape, only later to find that the robber went on to kill his father substitute (Uncle Ben). Devastated with sorrow, regret, and guilt (feelings that indicate an unconscious identification with the robber's act and hence patricidal urges), Peter (at the behest of his super-ego) vows to spend his life fighting crime, complete with a new persona, a costume, and, above all, the need to keep his "real identity" secret. The latter, now read as pointing to oedipal crime and guilt, becomes the determining factor that constantly interferes in his relationships with women: Aunt May, Betty Brandt, Mary Jane Watson, and Gwen Stacey. Indeed, the creators of Spiderman (Stan Lee, Jack Kirby, Steve Ditko) found a way to portray the plight of male adolescence in an imaginative enough way to elicit the allegiance of male unconscious contents in an experience-distant manner. By identifying with Spidey we literally act out an oedipal crisis and its resolution, even if momentarily.

Freud went on to opine that, at the collective level, art promotes shared group experiences, feelings of group identification, and narcissistic satisfaction in being part of nationalistic achievements. Certainly, Freud's argument is portable, and one can extend it to address any number of cultural institutions and products that function to offset aggressive and sexual drives: organized sports, work (a profession of any kind), and love arrangements. But in this book Freud was only tangentially concerned with exploring the varieties of such cultural functions. His main focus was the interplay between civilization and what he conceived to be its major "mental asset," namely, religion.

Religion versus Art

One can make a direct correlation between the expressions of the artistic imagination (like Spiderman) and that of religion in the following sense: just like movies and television shows, the vast panoply of religious narratives embodies a host of developmental themes, anxieties, and needs tailored to a waiting populace. There seems to be a religious "movie" for every unconscious wish and identity need. In the case of Spiderman, psychoanalysts would say that its immense popularity shows the continued prevalence in Western culture of conflicted, oedipally based developmental lines. Indeed, the adaptive value of a movie like *Spiderman* is not unlike that of the conversion experience of the American physician as detailed above. But there is an important distinction between art and religion that, for Freud, rested on how culture framed the latter's source of authority and moral function.

Recall the discussion in the introductory chapter about how psychoanalysis treats religion as a movie. In going to the theater, if the movie is a good one, you get lost in its narrative line. You forget yourself, all your troubles, and instead enter into the alternate reality the movie is weaving. If the movie is convincing, you come away feeling edified, entertained, re-created. But you would not go so far as to say that the movie was "real." The movie actually came from a film housed in a projector at the back of the movie theater. There is no reality "on the other side" of the screen. In other words, unlike religion, art does not make ontological claims about the nature of "reality," and its function is not to create or assert a particular worldview. Many artists exist at the margins of culture, seeming to have what Freud called an intuitive access to the unconscious and the talent to portray those processes in a symbolic manner. In this sense, artistic expressions are cultural products of what we can call the "individuating imagination," defined as acts of the imagination that express the contents of the unconscious in symbolically transformed ways for the purpose of individual and collective growth. At its best, art is edifying, providing occasions for introspection, reflection, wisdom, and so, in psychological terms, individuation (defined as the growth and flowering of one's unique individuality). Along these lines recall that Freud thought the great poets and philosophers arrived at similar conclusions about the mind as did psychoanalysis, albeit expressed in experience-distant, artful ways. Indeed, this is one of the reasons he cites so often from the works of Plato, Empedocles, Goethe, Schiller, and Shakespeare, from *Oedipus Rex*, *Hamlet*, and *Faust*. Rather than reinforcing social norms, artistic products more often than not challenge them and (especially) censorship, valorizing creativity; individual expression; experimentation with social roles, gender, and sexual identity; and even what constitutes reality.

For Freud religion is also an act of the imagination. But while psychoanalysts treat the latter as a kind of cultural dream or movie that embodies developmental themes, those who have allegiance to institutional religion beg to differ. Societies always frame the epistemological status of religion and its institutional accouterments as sacred and rooted in a divine ground. To put it slightly differently, in taking a cue from the sociological theorist Peter Berger, the human tendency to externalize the expressions of the human imagination, an important result of which is the establishment of an ordered and meaningful worldview (or *nomos*, as he calls it), attains not only an objective reality over and against us but also, in the hands of religion, one that is framed as sacred (the *nomos* becomes a *cosmos*). The net effect is a form of misdirection: the more precarious and humanly constructed nature of the *nomos* is hidden by the attempt to anchor it in an unchanging, authoritative divine ground.[22] For Freud, it is that very framing that serves to actualize its specific psychological function and dynamics vis-à-vis the individual. Those functions included fostering acts of repression, feelings of guilt and fear, tribalism, racism, and the stunting of the intellect. Expressions of the religious imagination are not, as with art, occasions for individuation but function to repress its free play. What concerned Freud, then, is the institutional, epistemological co-opting of the expressions of the imagination and its implications when internalized and held fast by the power of the dynamics that accrue between the id, ego, and super-ego.

The "Universal Obsessional Neurosis": Religion, Rituals, and the Cultural Super-Ego

For Freud one of the main ways in which religions co-opt the imagination is by subsuming it as part the content of the cultural super-ego. In a nonreligious sense, recall how in the above we made mention of the power of idealized national figures (such as JFK) and their social function as instances of the cultural super-ego. In that sense, Freud thought the formation of the super-ego, both individual and cultural, was an absolutely necessary condition for the continued existence of human civilization. To this end, Freud, in the initial pages of *Future of an Illusion*, remarks on the value of the cultural and individual super-ego in no uncertain terms:

It is in keeping with the course of human development that external coercion gradually becomes internalized; for a special mental agency, man's super-ego, takes it over and includes it among its commandments. Every child presents this process of transformation to us; only by that means does it become a moral and social being. Such a strengthening of the super-ego is a most previous cultural asset in the psychological field. Those in whom it has taken place are turned from being opponents of civilization into being its vehicles.[23]

In this broad context Freud was willing to say that religion, which supplies the content of the cultural super-ego, had served an "adaptive"

---

[22] See Peter Berger, *Sacred Canopy* (New York: Anchor Books, 1990 [1967]). Here is one of those places that a true dialogue between psychoanalysis and sociological thought would bear fruit. Berger's threefold dialectical process of world-construction (i.e., externalization, objectification, and internalization) lacks psychoanalytic depth yet is ripe for Freudian concepts like idealization and internalization, particularly with respect to the formation and continued influence of the cultural and individual super-ego.

[23] Freud, *Future of an Illusion*, S.E. 21: 11.

purpose, at least in a phase-appropriate historical sense. It had, up until Freud's era, protected civilization from man's innate aggressive, antisocial impulses, albeit with some psychologically problematic consequences. Recall that Freud, in *Totem and Taboo*, had posited the totem animal as the first cultural super-ego in everything but the name. That figure, later morphed into "God," was the beginning of society's use of religion to offset man's natural aggression toward civilization. It is here that the meaning of his view, found in *Future of an Illusion*, of religion as a "universal obsessional neurosis" becomes apparent. In *Totem and Taboo* Freud had linked obsessional neurosis to mankind's earliest set of taboos. There, in drawing an equation between the instinctual endowment of primitives and that of neurotics (he speaks of the latter as having "inherited an archaic constitution as an atavistic vestige," as exhibiting the "aboriginal population" in our mind, and as suffering from "taboo sickness"[24]), Freud observes that both primitives and neurotics need additional measures to help the ego defend against unusually strong sexual and aggressive antisocial instincts: "taboos" (in the case of primitives) and, later, obsessive "rituals" and "ceremonials" (in the case of neurotics). In *Future of an Illusion*, Freud carries this essential logic further. Invoking an earlier essay he had penned (titled "Obsessive Acts and Religious Practices" [1907]), which spoke more directly to how religion in contemporary culture offsets antisocial tendencies, he called attention to how public, universal religious rituals ("prescriptions, performances, restrictions, and arrangements") were analogous to the more idiosyncratic, private rituals of obsessive neurotics.[25] In the case of public religious rituals, Freud emphasized how they served to counter egoistic, antisocial tendencies to the extent that devout believers, by participating in a universal obsessional neuroses, could be spared the task of having to construct a personal, individual one. In other words, the cultural function of religious rituals is that they serve to internalize and re-memorialize the renunciatory values of civilization as found in the cultural super-ego. To abrogate the latter is, developmentally and unconsciously speaking, tantamount to breaking the love bond with the idealized parental unit. They were the ones who, through the process of idealization and internalization, originally mediated a set of moral rules and behavior by virtue of a universal, public set of values (invariably, if generically, informed by religion) existing "behind them" in the general cultural atmosphere.

---

[24] Freud, *Totem and Taboo*, S.E. 13: 26, 66.
[25] See Freud, "Obsessive Acts and Religious Practices," S.E. 9: 115–128.

In this way, civilization could invoke control not only on the conscious level but also by means of the more powerful developmental and unconscious one.

The problem was that religion had served to keep civilization intact at a cost. The internalization of the cultural super-ego and religious rituals (which serve to cement the "memory" of the dictates of the individual and cultural super-ego) invariably resulted in masochism, the heightening of fear and guilt, the stunting of the intellect, and enhanced social tensions and dis-ease. It is at this juncture that Freud adds an important sociohistorical qualification. He was convinced of a new, crucial historical development that would undermine the ability of civilization to use religion in its present form, thus rendering it functionally useless as a means to offset human aggression. That development is the decline of religion or, put in sociological terms, the fact of *secularization*. Indeed, it is Freud's adherence to the reality of secularization that adds a certain urgency and prophetic flavor to his sociohistorical argument.

The Consequences of Secularization

Regurgitating the argument laid down in *Totem and Taboo*, Freud starts his focus on the decline of religion by reiterating how civilization evinces a socio-evolutionary thrust from a pre-religious phase (animism, totemism) dominated by narcissistic (pre-Oedipal) concerns to an oedipally based institutional one ("traditional" religion proper) to a more mature, adult post-religious phase (science). Again referencing *Totem and Taboo*, Freud remarks that "we find ourselves at this very juncture in the middle of that phase of development"; that religion can be understood as a needed, functional, historically appropriate "universal obsessional neurosis"; but that "a turning-away from religion" is the inevitable future.[26] This is Freud's simple way of declaring that he is a "decline theorist"; that secularization was a fact. As such, psychoanalysis, as a secular cure of souls, is the logical heir to religion.

Freud was not a sociologist, nor did he offer empirical proof or theoretical defense of his belief in secularization. Indeed, what he does say by way of offering reasons for the decline of religion are noteworthy in their brevity. Principally, he says that it is the rise of science that has occasioned the disillusionment with religious tenets and worldviews.

---

[26] Freud, *Future of an Illusion*, S.E 21: 42–43.

While admitting that the latter is "perhaps not the only reason," he stresses how "criticism" and "the scientific spirit" has "whittled away the evidential value of religious documents," while "natural science has shown up the errors in them."[27] He was convinced that, in this process of growth, "there is no stopping."[28]

The decline theory of religion now baldly stated, Freud raises the specter of a coming doom. In so doing, his argument proceeds by way of distinguishing three basic social types. The first, which plays an outlier in the argument of the book, is that of the "true believer." This type is bound to their religious tradition "by certain ties of affection," by which Freud means a socialization process mediated by the family (parental) unit and the formation of the super-ego. Such ties are emotionally strong, being unconsciously determined, hence not subject to alteration by the arguments of reason or the sociological process of secularization. They will not, as Freud remarks, "be led astray from his faith by these or any similar arguments."[29] Such believers, whom Freud thought to be in the minority, are not his concern, for regardless of the slow decline of religion they will behave in a civilized fashion, albeit with the concomitant increase in fear and guilt along with a general stunting of the intellect. His major concern, a group of nominal believers he thought to be in the majority, he termed "the masses." The latter, standing in contrast to the true believers, are characterized in wholly unflattering terms: they are "lazy and unintelligent; they have no love for instinctual renunciation ... [and] are not spontaneously fond of work"; they "have not enjoyed any personal education" and, because of their long hours of exhausting labor, do not take interest in artistic pursuits.[30] Oppressed and uneducated, such people obey the precepts of religion only out of fear and coercion. They have not sublimated their instincts yet, dangerously, stand ready to give up their religious façade, letting their passions overrule their reason. The third social type he refers to as "brainworkers" and the "vehicles of civilization." Possessed of a healthy super-ego and capable of sublimating and educating their instincts through reasoned discourse, civilization has "little to fear" from them, for in them "the replacement of religious motives for civilized behavior by other, secular motives would proceed unobtrusively."[31] In the text, this social type is

---

[27] Ibid., 38.   [28] Ibid.
[29] Ibid., 47. See also P. Rieff, *Freud: The Mind of the Moralist* (Chicago: University of Chicago Press, 1959), chapter 8.
[30] Freud, *Future of an Illusion*, S.E. 21: 7, 13.   [31] Ibid., 39.

represented by the interlocuter, inserted by Freud as a rhetorical foil at the beginning of chapter 4. Freud portrays this type as having sympathies to religion yet also open to psychoanalysis. Freud thought such types could help his effort to gain social legitimacy for his secular cure of souls (namely, psychoanalysis). This logic can be found throughout Freud's written correspondence. He once asked Jung before the latter's abdication whether he knew someone in the office of the then Kaiser of Germany who could help disseminate psychoanalysis. Indeed, his correspondence with professional authorities from India to Japan to the United States is replete with such aims and requests.

Freud held that the real danger to civilization lay in the oppressed masses of nominal believers precisely due to the inevitable process of secularization. And so it is that we come, at the very end of Chapter 7 in the current book, to the definitive paragraph of his sociohistorical argument. Targeting the masses, Freud comments that as long as they do not hear of the findings of science and the reality of secularization, "all is well." The problem lies in the fact that they will inevitably do so, "even if this piece of writing of mine is not published."[32] The net effect will be nothing short of catastrophic. The masses are "ready to accept the results of scientific thinking, but without the change having taken place in them which scientific thinking brings about in people."[33] In other words, incapable or unwilling to educate or sublimate their instincts, and now bereft of the one thing, religion, which served to keep their antisocial instincts at bay, they will turn against the prohibitions, rules, and regulations that keep civilization intact. Freud ends the paragraph with a challenge: "either these dangerous masses must be held down most severely and kept most carefully away from any chance of intellectual awakening, or else the relationship between civilization and religion must undergo a fundamental revision."[34]

Freud's Solution

Freud went on to offer some details as to this "fundamental revision." His agenda was twofold: (1) on the individual level to educate and sublimate the instincts, strengthen the ego, shore up the super-ego, and make as many people as possible "vehicles" of civilization; (2) on the social-structural level to create new institutions that would replace religion in

[32] Ibid. [33] Ibid. [34] Ibid.

a manner commensurate with the aim of keeping civilization whole while fulfilling the psychological needs of the human populace. In both cases Freud was, at least in this work, notably optimistic, banking on the power of human reason and progressive nature of cultural evolution.

With regard to individuals, Freud counted on generational change. On the one hand, Freud admits that "a certain percentage of mankind ... will always remain asocial."[35] On the other, and opposed to previous centuries, contemporary generations had the benefit of a new tradition, that of science, which bequeathed a new knowledge base complete with modes of inquiry that valorized the explanatory power of reason guided by experimentation, empirical verification, and falsification. As a result, Freud opined that we are at that juncture in history where we can "replace the effects of repression" with "the results of rational operation of the intellect."[36] He observes how "new generations, who have been brought up in kindness and taught to have a high opinion of reason," would be more willing to accept rational reasons for following the precepts and renunciations of civilization as opposed to the fear and guilt-driven myths of religion.[37] New generations will "be ready for its sake to make the sacrifices as regards work and instinctual satisfaction" and will "be able to do without coercion."[38] It is this rendering of the power of reason that led Freud to be "optimistic about the future of mankind."[39]

Freud then attempted to put some meat on the bones of such high-minded and agreeable aims by offering social structural changes that might facilitate their actualization. Cautioning that the demise of religion, while inevitable, will not occur "by force and at a single blow," Freud focuses on two interrelated social structural changes, both addressing the educational system of his day and aimed at strengthening the intellect. The first critique took aim at the religiously driven repressive educational norms he thought led to a retardation of sexual development. Such education not only heightened repression and neurosis but also inhibited the mature development of a curious, inquiring, and critical intellect. Freud conjoins to this a second point that targeted premature religious influence, meaning that children were socialized into a religious worldview well before they were interested in or even capable of considering their existential relevance and intellectual worth. The net effect was that later, when the child's intellect awakened, religious tenets were, as a result

---

[35] Ibid., 9.   [36] Ibid., 44.   [37] Ibid., 8.   [38] Ibid.   [39] Ibid., 53.

of emotional bonds, unconscious forces, and cultural norms, that much harder to challenge.[40]

Another structural change is the insertion of psychoanalysis as a means to educate and sublimate the instincts, thus helping people to realistically adapt to the exigencies of life. This aim, implicit throughout *Future of an Illusion*, became explicit in Freud's letters to the Protestant pastor Oskar Pfister. There Freud revealed the "secret link" between *Future of an Illusion* and an earlier book he wrote on the importance of having lay analysts. The latter was written to protect psychoanalysis from being governed solely by the medical profession, while *Future of an Illusion* was written to protect psychoanalysis from the church. So it is that Freud stated to Pfister: "I should like to hand it over to a profession of *lay* curers of souls who ... should not be priests."[41] Recall in this regard our earlier analysis (in Chapter 1) of the grammatical structure of the "psychoanalytic motto," and Freud's rhetorically elegant way of contrasting the aims of religion and psychoanalysis. Siphoned through the analysis presented here, we now see that the psychoanalytic motto was similarly affirming the need for the creation of a social space (the clinical setting) that would, for all intents and purposes, (eventually) replace religion and priests yet serve a similar, indeed better, adaptive function vis-à-vis the continued advancement of civilization. If civilization had depended on religion to defend against the hostility of the masses, and if religion was on the decline and unable to fulfill its cultural function, then a psychoanalytic secular cure of souls was the needed antidote. It would not be wrong to say that what Freud was after was a change in the cultural super-ego: a "triumph of the therapeutic," which valorized psychoanalysis, now understood as a moral science that enjoined one to inwardness, self-knowledge, renunciation, sublimation, and increased empathy.

FUTURE OF AN ILLUSION: CRITIQUES

There is an abundance of scholarly commentary on *Future of an Illusion*. The diversity can be organized with respect to the following rubrics: (1) the definitional problem with respect to his use of the term "religion," (2) responses from those in the psychology–theology dialogue, (3) social scientific objections to his adherence to the reality of secularization and his threefold social typology, (4) observations from feminist and race

---

[40] Ibid., 46ff.   [41] See *Psychoanalysis and Faith*, 126.

theorists concerning his continued lack of reflexivity, and (5) psychoanalytic critiques seeking a wider view of developmental lines and the inclusion of adaptive and transformational models. Each of these rubrics houses not only cautionary tales but also portable lessons that we can carry forward in the pursuit of a revised psychoanalytic tool kit.

The Definitional Problem: Beyond the "Common-Man's" Religion

Our survey of Freud's thought in *Totem and Taboo* and *Moses and Monotheism* has made clear that, with but a few qualifications, Freud's interests were focused on Western religious traditions, assumed institutionalized patriarchal forms of sociocultural power, and normative expressions centered on the monotheistic "mighty personality" of an exalted Father-God. Freud further qualified this as pertaining to the understanding of religion found in the "common man":

> In my *Future of an Illusion* I was concerned much less with the deepest sources of the religious feeling than with what the common man understands by his religion – with the system of doctrines and promises which on the one hand explains to him the riddles of this world with enviable completeness, and, on the other, assures him that a careful Providence will watch over his life and will compensate him in a future existence for any frustration he suffers here. The common man cannot imagine this Providence otherwise than in the figure of an enormously exalted father. Only such a being can understand the needs of the children of men and be softened by their prayers and placated by the signs of their remorse.[42]

For Freud the above was the only deserving definition of religion. He went so far as to defiantly chastise those "philosophers" who tried to "stretch the meaning of words" to the point that words such as "God" and "religious" ceased to bear any resemblance to the Being worshipped by the common man. He was well aware of more sophisticated philosophical and theological attempts to "rescue" this common man's religion by replacing what he called the "mighty personality of religious doctrines" with "an impersonal, shadowy and abstract principle."[43] Such attempts, thought Freud, ran the risk of stretching "the meaning of words until they retain scarcely anything of their original sense."[44] Abstract renderings of the divine are not a "higher, purer concept of God" so much as an "insubstantial shadow" of the exalted Father God.

---

[42] Freud, *Civilization and Its Discontents*, S.E. 21:74; *Future of an Illusion*, S.E. 21: 30–31.
[43] Ibid.   [44] Freud, *Future of an Illusion*, S.E. 21: 32.

The common man's religion was "the only religion which ought to bear that name."[45]

We do not have to speculate, then, as to how Freud entered what we have called the "definitional debate" over religion. He is very clear about where he stands. The question is how to evaluate Freud's strategy. With respect to those working in the discipline of religious studies as a whole, Freud's position raises multiple concerns if taken to apply to the entire territory of the "what" of religion. Even a cursory survey of the history of method spanning theological, philosophical, and social scientific approaches reveals that there are multiple and often contested ways of defining religion. For example, take the definitional strategy of Emile Durkheim, whose works Freud read and cited and who, like Freud, developed his definition out of his study on totemism (i.e., his classic work *The Elementary Forms of Religious Life*). In analyzing early totemic societies, Durkheim came to a conclusion quite different from that of Freud, defining religion as a "unified system of beliefs and practices relative to sacred things, that is to say, things set apart and forbidden – beliefs and practices which unite into one single moral community called a Church, all those who adhere to them."[46] Being a sociologist, what was important to Durkheim was group functioning. Religion was a projection not so much of the individual but of the group. Religion was a way of expressing group sentiments and functioned to establish group identity and solidarity. In fact, one could say that any group finds a way to express itself through symbols, myths, and narratives – a fact that has led some in the Durkheimian tradition to see religion in ways that are nontraditional, even noninstitutional. Take, for example, the phenomenon of "civil religion" in which a nation (e.g., the United States) takes on qualities of a "religion." It has its set of founders and saints (presidents and moral leaders), scriptures (the Constitution, Bill of Rights), laws and ethics (Supreme Court), the sacred spaces of churches and monuments (the White House, Statue of Liberty), symbols (the eagle, the flag), sacred days (July 4, Memorial Day), and rituals (pledge to the flag, juror oaths). One could extend this to apply to sports teams, universities, and political parties (note that many have insignia or "totems" like elephants, donkeys, birds, bears, to designate their "group").

---

[45] Freud, *Civilization and Its Discontents*, S.E. 21:74.
[46] E. Durkheim, *The Elementary Forms of Religious Life* (New York: Free Press, 1995 [1912]), 62.

One could also cite Freud's two major competitors in the first period of the psychology and religion movement: William James and Carl Jung. In valorizing the mystical element within religion, Jung offers that "by the term 'religion' I do not mean a creed," adding that creeds, and indeed all forms of religious doctrine, are but "codified and dogmatized forms of original religious experience."[47] What, then, is his definition of "original religious experience"? Here Jung followed the lead of Rudolph Otto, a noted theologian and comparative scholar of religion of his era, who framed such matters in terms of the experience of the "numinosum," by which he meant a direct, mystical encounter with the divine described as mysterious, nonrational, "wholly Other," awesome, frightening, and fascinating ("mysterium tremendum et fascinans").[48] This fit Jung's own psychological model of religion well, for experiences of "tremendum et fascinans" were precisely those that characterized the encounter with the collective unconscious and its archetypes. William James, on the other hand, in acknowledging that the term "religion" is contested, offered in his *Varieties of Religious Experience* that religion would be defined "arbitrarily" as the following: "the feelings, acts, and experiences of individual men in their solitude, so far as they apprehend themselves to stand in relation to whatever they may consider the divine."[49] This generic, individually based definition, which some see as having Protestant overtones (the tradition James grew up in), admits that "theology, philosophy, and ecclesiastical organizations secondarily grow" out of the experiential relation to the divine.[50] For James, the deepest heart of religious experience lay in mystical states of consciousness, the defining marks of which were passivity, noesis (direct knowledge of the divine), transiency, and ineffability. Closer to Jung than Freud, there is still a variance of the "circumscription of the topic," as James liked to call it, which, like Freud and Jung, fit his preferred notion of the dynamics of the subconscious quite well (i.e., the tidal flat metaphor we adduced in the introductory chapter).

One could go on to speak of the later, multiple, and contrasting attempts in diverse disciplines to define religion. For example: the theologian Paul Tillich's definition of faith as "ultimate concern," the

---

[47] C. Jung, *Psychology and Religion* (New Haven, CT: Yale University Press, 1977 [1938]), 4–6.
[48] Ibid.
[49] W. James, *The Varieties of Religious Experience* (New York: Modern Library, 1929 [1902]), 31–32.
[50] Ibid.

anthropologist Clifford Geertz's injunction to ethnographic "thick description" and elaborate definition of religion as a cultural system, and Anthony Pinn, who, drawing attention to the history of American structural racism, offers a nonessentialist definition of African American religion as "a quest for complex subjectivity" – one that is ever-evolving, draws from multiple religious traditions, and aims at the need to make sense of injustice and suffering.[51] But the point has been established enough to offer the following portable lesson: properly qualified, there is a place for Freud's definition of religion as well as his model for interpreting it. There may be some for whom the oedipally based common man's religion is an approximate fit, and one can admit to the general observation that, regardless of how one defines religion, any faith journey carries with it the "baggage" of some form of developmental determinism. At the same time, if by "religion" we mean a cultural phenomenon that admits of being empirically wider, more culturally complex, and theologically informed than that addressed by Freud, then at the very least a certain interdisciplinary dialogue is needed, if only to see where Freud's interpretative efforts are of value and where they fall flat.

Dialogical Responses: Psychology and Theology

A good deal of such interdisciplinary dialogue has taken place through the auspices of those working within the psychology–theology dialogue. While here we must be selective in our examples (for we cannot address the responses of each and every one of the figures that populate the psychology–theology dialogue throughout the three periods), we can still isolate the major strategies they collectively used in their counters to Freud. The essential, linked structural strategies are three: (1) an alternate definition of religion; (2) debates over the precise framing of the human personality, which, in taking into account Freud's structural model, might add enough nuance to enable the possibility for a faith journey that transcends developmental determinants (this is the category of "theological anthropology"); and (3) a corresponding non–oedipally based understanding of the Divine. These three structural strategies are further nuanced by a few central

---

[51] See P. Tillich, *The Dynamics of Faith* (New York: Harper, 2009 [1956]); C. Geertz, *The Interpretation of Cultures* (New York: Basic Books, 1973); and A. Pinn, *Terror and Triumph* (Minneapolis, MN: Fortress, 2003).

framings of the dialogical nature of the relationship between psychoanalysis and theology, of which we can isolate four: (1) correlation, (2) dialectic, (3) stage approaches, and (4) transference. The consequences are logical to predict: if one offers a different definitional strategy that is linked to an expanded view of the person and a framing of God that transcends the determinants of the earthly father, then one can arrive at a view of the faith journey that, as we stated in the introductory chapter, is better suited to the "star" metaphor than the "movie" metaphor. These strategies and modes of dialogue are not mutually exclusive and can be found in many of the most prominent responses to Freud.

A few notable examples will suffice to illustrate the above points. The beginning of the psychology-theology dialogue can be traced to Freud's long relationship with Oskar Pfister. When Freud wrote *Future of an Illusion* he sent a copy to Pfister, who responded with a short essay entitled "The Illusion of a Future," the paradigmatic work in the "first period" of the psychology–theology dialogue.[52] With respect to the definitional problem, Pfister's logic was that one might accept Freud's analysis of religion only if one confines his reductive treatment to an equally reductive definition of religion (i.e., the common man's religion). He agreed to a certain extent with Freud's adoption of Feuerbach's thesis, which treated religion "as a dream"; that "ideas of God and the beyond are often painted with colours from a wish-palette"; and, on a personal level, how he found in his own faith journey "the features of my father, of various pastors ... and behind them the direction of hatred." On the other hand, he considered it "wrong to squeeze all rejections of religion into a wish-schema."[53] If one defines religion more widely, projected oedipal elements are only one part of a total quilt of one's representation of the divine. While Pfister shared Freud's allegiance to the "god" Logos, he offered his own conception of the divine as "one which, based on the first chapter of the Gospel of St. John, I regard as divine wisdom and love."[54] Thus Pfister can say: "It is a great shame that Freud neglects the very highest expressions of religion" and, further (in a letter to Freud), that "our difference derives chiefly from the fact that you grew up in proximity to

---

[52] O. Pfister, "The Illusion of the Future: A Friendly Disagreement with Prof. Sigmund Freud," *International Journal of Psychoanalysis* 74 (1993): 557–579.
[53] Ibid., 563.   [54] Ibid., 578.

pathological forms of religion and regard these as 'religion', while I had the good fortune of being able to turn to a free form of religion which to you seems to be an emptying of Christianity of its content, while I regard it as the core and substance of religion."[55] By "free form," it should be noted, Pfister meant liberal Protestantism, the figures of which punctuate his essay to Freud.

Pfister's definitional strategy of religion evoked the linked one of reframing Freud's understanding of the person (i.e., theological anthropology). Again, Pfister understood that if one accepts Freud's pairing of religion with the dynamics of the structural model, then one might conclude that his analysis of religion is reasonable. But if one switches up the understanding of personhood, the latter further correlated with a "higher" conception of the divine, then one can embrace Freud yet also go beyond him to articulate a faith journey that is only partially determined by developmental considerations. Pfister offered the figure of Jesus as well as selected figures in Protestant theology as illustrations of his point. For example, Pfister claimed that Jesus' ideas of "the father" were "completely cleansed of the dross of oedipal attachment ... [and] heteronomy."[56] The "religion" Jesus advocated, then, corresponded to a view of human nature described as an "ideal-realism" and based on "a magnificent, intuitive anthropology and cosmology."[57] As a result, Pfister framed Jesus as championing what could retrospectively be called a pastoral form of psychoanalysis. Pfister claimed that Jesus handled "transference" in a way that "deserved the admiration of all Freud's pupils," dissolving the oedipal complex and raising the individual to a higher moral plane.[58] He could do so, claimed Pfister, because unlike the common man's religion, Jesus valorized "coercion-free individualism" and aimed at a higher form of love in which "everything egotistical disappears."[59]

The basic structural elements laid down by Pfister are portable, being found in more sophisticated responses (the actual content of which varies) in the second and third periods of the psychology–theology dialogue. For example, Paul Tillich, widely considered to be the postwar intellectual architect of pastoral psychology, offered a series of linked terms ("ultimate concern," the "God above God," the correlational method) that integrated yet transcended Freud's contributions by engaging the definitional problem, a revised anthropology, and a new conception of faith

---

[55] Ibid., 562; Freud and Pfister, *Psychoanalysis and Faith*, 122. [56] Ibid., 561.
[57] Ibid., 564. [58] Ibid., 562. [59] Ibid., 564.

and God.⁶⁰ Tillich's project turned on what he called the "correlational method," a term utilized to define the relation between psychology and theology. Tillich was convinced that what he called man's "estranged state" (i.e., original sin) was best described by the secular investigations of modern psychology and could expose the disordered nature of one's "ultimate concern" (faith journey). For example, Tillich agreed with Pfister that Freud offered the tool kit to decipher the origins of what he called the "heteronomous" conception of God, the latter framed as the product of projection and Oedipus. And again like Pfister, Tillich thought that holding to this conception of God was simply bad theology. It needed to be transcended, for it held fast to the subject/object dichotomy and the emotional bondage of Oedipus and the super-ego. How, then, might one arrive a deeper conception of God, one that redefined religion as being "more" than the common man's religion? Tillich responded by offering a sophisticated, psychologically informed, theological anthropology. Tillich noted that Freud's structural model did not take into account realistic anxiety, defined as consisting of the ineradicable anxieties concerning fate and death (dubbed "ontic"), guilt and condemnation (dubbed "moral"), and emptiness and meaninglessness (dubbed "spiritual"). Tillich thought that existential psychology was much better at cataloguing this latter dimension of the "estranged" state (i.e., original sin) of humans. In effect, Tillich superimposed on Freud's id/ego/super-ego model the existential psychologist's insistence on these forms of realistic, structural, and unavoidable anxieties. The problem, thought Tillich, was that there were times when the reality of death, condemnation, and meaninglessness was so great that one was overwhelmed and could no longer affirm oneself. In other words, while both psychoanalysis and existentialism were very good at describing the "estranged" state of humans, they failed to offer the kinds of healing solutions that fully met the challenge of such anxieties. It is here that the correlational method and Christianity came to the fore. Psychology described the estranged state and its predicament, but the existential questions the latter gave rise to could be answered only by a liberal Protestant form of Christianity (hence the correlation of terms).

In articulating such answers Tillich notes that what Freud and the existentialists did not see was that we, as humans, are "in relation" to

---

⁶⁰ Tillich's response to the psychologists can be found in his *The Courage to Be* (New Haven, CT: Yale University Press, 1952) and *The Meaning of Health* (Berkeley: North Atlantic Press, 1984 [1961]).

something deeper, which he called the "ground of Being" (a theological/philosophical framing of the divine). In other words, over against both psychoanalysis and existentialism, he attached an explicit religious dimension to the human personality. How this works in a life with respect to overcoming the structural anxieties lies in the portrait of Jesus' anguished cry on the cross: "Why has thou forsaken me?" This cry reveals the very human side of Jesus beset by the structural anxieties. Jesus, in effect, models the deepest form of our human predicament. In overcoming those anxieties, Jesus also models the acceptance yet transcendence of the basic anxieties and the fullness of the courage to "affirm" oneself despite the realities of existence. This portrait of the cry of Jesus necessitated a move to an "ultimate concern," which, being distinguished from the common man's belief, was defined with respect to what Tillich called "absolute faith" – a faith that was directed toward "the God above God," framed as transcending Freud's oedipally based heteronomous God in that it was "nondual" and so beyond the subject–object relation. That is the God who appears when the self crumbles, giving one the capacity to affirm oneself even in the face of total despair.

While Pfister and Tillich were the two major figures of the psychology–theology dialogue in the first and second period, respectively, their portable strategies were followed by multiple others. Staying in the second period, the additional notable response was that of the philosopher of religion Paul Ricoeur, who championed a *dialectical* approach based on the "hermeneutical method," defined as any method designed to ascertain the existential meaning behind a text, symbol, or narrative. In this context Freud was framed as having practiced a "hermeneutics of suspicion," in which a simple, unreflective faith, dubbed by Ricoeur a "first naiveté," was determined in part or whole by the dynamics of the unconscious. In this sense, religious symbols and narratives functioned more like symptoms, and their meaning was found in the regressive archaeological excavations of psychoanalysis. Like Tillich, Ricoeur was convinced that there existed a regressive *arche* (i.e., unconscious determinants) of religion that consisted of childish motivations and that any true faith journey could not afford to neglect Freud's analysis. Believers must take heed to acknowledge Freud's *arche* and work through the developmental determinants of faith. However, once clarified by this inner work, one can arrive at a "second naiveté" where religious symbols and narratives could catapult the believer into new terrains of inwardness and health. Religion could mediate a teleology, a wisdom that pointed to the "More," to the numinous and sacred. Religious symbols, in this sense, were not merely "symptoms" but transformational conduits to the divine. The mature believer, in other words, was a psychoanalytically aware individual engaged in the continual *dialectical* process of relating *arche* (Freud) to the *telos* of religion.[61]

More briefly, in the third period one sees the new attempt to make the psychoanalytic category of *transference* central to the dialogical project. This is exemplified by Peter Homans when he attempted to chart a middle course between Freud and Protestant theologians and their use of terms like transcendence, immanence, and Tillich's "God above God." Rather than resorting to such theological terms, Homans offered a different path: once one has become aware in the clinical analytic session of developmental determinants of the faith journey, one can then turn to linked psychological phenomenon such as reverie, fantasy activity, and the production of iconic images. It is through the adaptive potential of the latter, now seen as correlated not simply with the unconscious but with deeper psycho-religious resources, that one can become aware of new possibilities for moving beyond developmental determinants.[62] James Jones, a psychoanalyst and theologian bent on establishing a relational theology, also seized on transference by defining religion as a relationship with God dubbed as "the affective bond with the sacred."[63] Such a relationship, in Jones's view, "enacts and reenacts the transferential patterns present throughout a person's life," which may signify not only regressed fixations but also adaptive potential.[64] He then leaves space for imagination and fantasy freed from developmental determinants so that religion, in its various forms, can speak to ultimate issues of meaning (purpose, death, forgiveness, religious experience). In the third period one also finds the instantiation of a *stage* approach, or "faith developmental theory." Exemplified in the work of James Fowler, a hierarchy of stages was posited by combining psychoanalysis with moral developmental theory and cognitive developmental ones to show how the progression of mature faith transcended developmental determinants.[65] While the

---

[61] This summary is drawn from Ricoeur's classic work, *Freud and Philosophy*.

[62] P. Homans, *Theology after Freud* (New York: Bobbs-Merrill, 1970).

[63] J. Jones, *Contemporary Psychoanalysis and Religion* (New Haven, CT: Yale University Press, 1993), 65. See also Pamela Cooper-White, *Shared Wisdom* (New York: Augsburg, 2004). For articles championing the psychology-theology dialogue, see the journal *Pastoral Psychology*.

[64] Ibid., 65.

[65] J. Fowler, *Stages of Faith* (New York: Harper, 1995 [1979]). For a survey of some of the Jewish responses, see Gay, *A Godless Jew*, and for a notable Catholic response, H. Küng, *Freud and the Problem of God* (New Haven, CT: Yale University Press, 1990).

focus on *transference* and *stages* obviously differs, the proponents of both follow their predecessors, embracing yet countering Freud by way of offering alternate definitional strategies, psycho-religious portraits of the person (theological anthropology), and conceptions of the divine.

This truncated survey, then, illustrates some major strategies employed during the course of the psychology–theology dialogue at work. It is fair to say, in pointing to the establishment of the institution of pastoral psychology and its continued presence in churches, universities, and hospitals, that what began with Freud and Pfister has changed the religious landscape in ways that have expanded well beyond the two men's initial friendship and correspondence. For our purposes, we will see in the chapters ahead how their cautionary tales have been integrated as part of a revised psychoanalytic tool kit and, as a result, a wider purview of the psychoanalytic theory of religion.

Sociological Responses: Decline or Persistence?

Freud's sociohistorical argument in *Future of an Illusion* was not lost on the "other" social sciences. Most pertinent are the faults sociologists have found with his division of society into three distinct social types (the masses, true believers, and brainworkers). While the latter was useful as a rhetorical ploy that advanced Freud's argument, there is no social theorist who would, empirically speaking, empirically defend such a simple division or the cursory way in which Freud characterized each of the three social types.[66] Even more glaring is Freud's insistence on a strong version of the "decline" theory of religion (secularization). As multiple social scientists have noted, any assessment of the reality of secularization is inexorably linked with how one defines religion.[67] Many proponents of the decline theory define religion as Western, institutional, and implicitly Christian, and secularization framed as due to numerous causes: pluralism, modernity, class stratification, separation of church and state, democracy, privatization, and the rise of individualism. Granting this definitional strategy of what constitutes "religion" and

---

[66] For an early statement, see Rieff, *Freud: The Mind of the Moralist*, chapter 8.

[67] As the anthropologist Mary Douglas once put it, any debate over the reality of secularization "due to modernization" is entirely dependent on one's "chosen definition of religion" (see M. Douglas, "The Effects of Modernization on Religious Change," in *Religion and America: Spiritual Life in a Secular Age*, ed. M. Douglas and S. Tipton [Boston: Beacon Press, 1982], 30). Other prominent social theorists (e.g., Thomas Luckmann, Courtney Bender, Linda Woodhead) have made similar points.

"secularization," there may be some truth to the reality of religious decline (paradigmatically articulated by Peter Berger in his classic work *The Sacred Canopy*). However, even here the decline is local, not total, and history has seen reversals, again paradigmatically stated by Peter Berger, who, having once sided with the decline theorists, later admitted that he had been mistaken.[68]

Going further, if one changes up one's definition of religion to include unchurched, noninstitutional cultural expressions, paradigmatically seen in the rapid contemporary growth of those who profess to be "nones," "New Age," or "spiritual but not religious," one sees not only the "persistence" of religion and spirituality but its growth.[69] Those in the "persistence" camp can be illustrated once again with respect to two of Freud "first period" competitors, Emile Durkheim and Carl Jung. As unpacked in greater detail earlier, Durkheim defined religion as composed of symbols, narratives, rituals, and "collective representations" that were projections of whole groups of peoples, ranging from traditional organized religion to group representations not often identified as part of traditional, institutional religion. So defined, "religious" expressions will exist as long as one finds any collectivity. We also saw that Jung adopted a different definitional strategy than Freud by positing a religiously toned collective unconscious populated by archetypes that continuously seek expression. This lends itself to a persistence theory in that if a culturally valorized set of religious narratives, symbols, and myths become dysfunctional, then the collective unconscious would naturally spew forth substitutes (as with, for example, the emergence of UFO religions, which Jung took to be expressions of the wholeness linked with self-archetypes, in mid-twentieth-century Western cultures).

While Durkheim and Jung exemplify but two contrarian positions available in Freud's era, many prominent social theorists in the second and third period followed suit.[70] Without further laboring to present the totality of such views, and acknowledging that the many social scientific studies also evince debates over how to use the terms "secularization" and

---

[68] See Berger, *The Sacred Canopy*. For his retraction, see www.christiancentury.org/article/2012-03/protestantism-and-quest-certainty.

[69] See, for example, *Being Spiritual but Not Religious: Past, Present, Futures*, ed. William B. Parsons (New York: Routledge, 2018); E. Drescher, *Choosing Our Religion: The Spiritual Lives of America's Nones* (New York: Oxford University Press, 2016).

[70] For a good overview of theories of secularization, see D. Pollack's summary in Oxford Bibliographies: www.oxfordbibliographies.com/view/document/obo-9780199756384/obo-9780199756384-0073.xml.

"religion," there is nothing in the general flow of their conclusions to corroborate Freud's prediction that religion would entirely disappear (in fact, just the opposite).[71] This does not mean that his program for creating a social space for psychoanalysis has failed (again, just the opposite) or that psychoanalysis, as a secular cure of souls, is not an advance for civilization. Indeed, to a certain extent Freud was successful: not only has psychoanalysis become a legitimate secular cure of souls, it has made its way well past the clinic to universities, to the arts, and even to political systems, there to be used as a tool for investigation, interpretation, and an aid in the project of social structural change and individual transformation. In other words, one can still use Freud and his advocacy of a secular cure of souls without endorsing his simple conclusions regarding secularization and social typology.

Reflexivity: Feminist and Race Critiques

Feminists and race theorists have seen *Future of an Illusion* marred by the same lack of reflexivity found in *Totem and Taboo*. As in the latter, Freud continued his evolutionary views of comparative human societies in which "contemporary" religion (now described with the unfortunate choice of words as "our present day white Christian civilization") is seen as bearing a "fatal resemblance to the mental products of primitive peoples," thereby again drawing an analogy between the regressed, childish neurotic believer (the common man) and "the primitive."[72] In other words, we can observe the presence of an unnecessary linkage that signifies racial coding. Similarly, feminists have noted how Freud's view of gender has crept into his analysis of the regressed, childish

---

[71] It is true that, as stated above, if one restricts the term "religion" to western forms of Christianity, then one can make an argument for decline (see www.pewforum.org/2019/10/17/in-u-s-decline-of-christianity-continues-at-rapid-pace). But there is similar evidence that Christianity is growing in the Southern Hemisphere, while Islam is predicted to continue to grow globally (see www.pewforum.org/2015/04/02/religious-projections-2010-2050; www.theatlantic.com/magazine/archive/2002/09/christianitys-new-center/303077; www.pewresearch.org/fact-tank/2017/04/06/why-muslims-are-the-worlds-fastest-growing-religious-group). If one shifts one's definitional strategy to include those of "unchurched" traditions, such as those who claim to be "spiritual but not religious," then one also finds growth (see www.pewresearch.org/fact-tank/2017/09/06/more-americans-now-say-theyre-spiritual-but-not-religious). Finally, if one defines "religion" following Durkheim and Jung, then religion will continue to exist regardless of its institutional expression; see, e.g., Gary Laderman, *Sacred Matters* (New York: New Press, 2010).

[72] Brickman, *Aboriginal Populations in the Mind*, 46.

believer. In contrast to the common man, Freud posits the normative ideal of the mature, "post-religious" brainworker who subscribes to the gods of reason (Logos, now read as science) and brute necessity (Ananke, the fact of the natural, amoral world of cause and effect). This person is characterized as without illusions, having accomplished the feat of the total renunciation of any religious belief, capable of introspection and sublimation, having a healthy super-ego, and individuated. But critical feminist theory has noted that this portrait tallies with his views of the ideal, mature male, while his characterization of the believer is more like his view of femininity: "both believers and women share common psychical characteristics: a weak super-ego, a poorly developed sense of morality, a restricted intellect, opposition to cultural advance, insufficient respect for reality, *Ananke* and *Logos*."[73] Freud depends on masculinity as the universal norm and ideal, while his analysis assumed a patricentric, patriarchal culture and a form of religion situated within it. Indeed, such critiques go further to note that such gender coding seems to have influenced Freud's evaluation of not simply the common man and that of "primitive" religion but also Judaism and Christianity. As we saw in our discussion of Freud's *Moses*, it is not Christianity but only the Mosaic (and male) stress on renunciation and intellectuality that Freud hails as part of the evolutionary move from animism/totemism through Christianity (as universal obsessional neurosis) to a world guided by science and those without illusions. There is evidence, then, to note a link between Freud's positing of a hierarchy of religions and his views on gender and race.[74]

To be sure, such cautionary tales do not abrogate his many insights or the proper application of his models so much as ask us to perform the needed reflexive acts to unburden psychoanalytic models of unnecessary linkages for proper use. Along these lines, some feminist and critical race approaches (what we referred to in Chapter 2 as the "analytic school"), while discarding Freud's essentialism with regard to gender, race, and the primitive, reframe his analysis as profitable if taken to be a deconstructive

---

[73] Ibid., 123.
[74] A series of feminist critiques specifically aimed at Freud's *Future of an Illusion* can be found in J. Van Herik, *Freud on Femininity and Faith* (Berkeley: University of California Press, 1982), and J. Kristeva, *In the Beginning Was Love: Psychoanalysis and Faith*, trans. A. Goldhammer (New York: Columbia University Press, 1989. See also K. Bingaman, *Freud and Faith* (Albany: State University of New York Press, 2003), and J. Jones, *Religion and Psychology in Transition: Psychoanalysis, Feminism, and Theology* (New Haven, CT: Yale University Press, 1996).

act that illuminates the structure of patriarchal culture and its religious forms. In this sense, psychoanalysis can be more fruitfully used in the service of cultural change.

Psychoanalytic Critiques: Developmental Considerations and Inclusivity

While it is correct to say that Freud generally held to a classic-reductive view of religion that centered on the determinants of Oedipus, we have seen a few outliers: his qualified concession that religion could be adaptive and that it engaged other developmental factors. As summarized in Chapter 2, prominent among the latter was his view that animism emerged from the pre-oedipal developmental stage. As we will see in the next two chapters, Freud was to come back to this in *Civilization and Its Discontents*, where he analyzed the famous "oceanic feeling" as well as the allure of the Christian love command as issuing from the stage of primary narcissism (in which the infant feels at one with the mother). In fact, one finds evidence in *Future of an Illusion* of the developmental contribution of the dyadic mother–child relationship. Most notably, he states that the narcissistic needs for security and for protection from hunger and anxiety are originally met by the mother, not the father. In his presentation Freud notes that the mother is the infant's original object-choice and first love object. He refers to this bond as being that of the "anaclitic" (strongly dependent) attachment type.[75] For Freud, the function of the mother is then later replaced by the more powerful father, hence paving the way for the emphasis on Oedipus. Later psychoanalysts, however, have found more merit in Freud's passing reference to early object-relations and attachment. Prominent among the latter group is John Bowlby (1907–1990), the founder of an offshoot of object-relations theory called "attachment theory."

Attachment theory relies on a biosocial system in infants that seeks attachments to caregivers in the service of an adaptive need to ward off danger, isolation, and anxiety in favor of a felt sense of security, vitality, management of emotions, and ability to calmly explore the environment. The fact that its basis lies in the dyadic mother–infant relationship obviates the primacy of the instinctual basis of Freud's oedipally based structural model. Bowlby thought that the early dynamics of the mother–infant dyad helped determine whether the later, mature individual could

---

[75] Freud, *Future of an Illusion*, S.E. 21: 23–24.

establish the ideal of secure relationships or whether such relationships were prone to anxiety, ambivalence, disorganization, and even complete avoidance. This theoretical structure was subsequently taken up by theorists such as Lee Kirkpatrick and Marsha Hewitt to supplement Freud's focus on Oedipus in *Future of an Illusion*. In their view, the primary function of religion is not characterized so much by the dynamics of Oedipus as it is by the dynamics of attachment. From the attachment theory perspective, humans need to feel securely attached to powerful others and a divine Other to offset feelings of loneliness, loss, and depression; to assuage fear and anxiety; and to manage the inevitable exigencies life brings.[76] In other words, these formulations allow for a pre-oedipally based adaptive view of religion.

In the chapters to come we will find that multiple psychoanalytic figures had occasion to theorize further on pre-oedipal developmental lines as being complicit in religion, functioning in both classic-reductive and adaptive ways. For now, we can, in reaffirming that even Freud noted that developmental factors not named Oedipus were complicit in the cultural "movie" called religion, offer a portable lesson that summarizes Freud's multiple takes on religion. The latter can take the form of a summary formula as follows: *religion consists of narratives, figures, myths, and symbols, mediated through functionaries, scriptures, and rituals, which are transformed, disguised projections of unconscious contents, rooted in a spectrum of developmental lines and available to everyone on the public "cultural screen." Every psychic conflict, anxiety, and wish is represented in a form experience-distant, universal, and general enough to engage a vast array of psychological discontents. The very generality of religious narratives affords each individual the opportunity to personalize a myth, symbol, or figure to fit their unique needs.*

Our formula is not designed to establish an essentialist view of religion. Rather, it is offered as a way-station, a preliminary placeholder designed to summarize Freud's multiple takes on religion to this point. Psychoanalytically speaking, it highlights how religious narratives, myths, and symbols embody, albeit in a disguised and transformed way, a host of developmental themes, anxieties, and needs that include not only oedipal issues but potentially a much wider range of developmentally based psychological issues. As one psychoanalytic commentator recently put

---

[76] See L. Kirkpatrick, "An Attachment-Theory Approach to the Psychology of Religion," *The International Journal for the Psychology of Religion* 2, no. 1 (1992): 3–28; M. Hewitt, *Freud on Religion* (Durham, UK: Acumen, 2014).

it, as far as religion is concerned, "There is a god for every psychic season, a myth for every hidden wish and a legend for every concealed anxiety."[77] In other words, religious narratives are like "wearing the unconscious on the outside," being "cultural containers" for unconscious wishes and projections. Religious ideation is, unlike an individual dream, public and general, available to all. But they are also private and individual in the sense that we engage them in ways that address the uniqueness of our own personal developmental history.[78] God the Father and the Virgin Mary are general enough public symbols capable of eliciting each person's unique, individual relation with their earthly parents and significant others. This means that fifty different believers, if analyzed, would be found to have fifty different takes on what otherwise appears to be a uniform public symbol. Like the dreamwork, the deeper meaning of our private relation to the public symbols and narratives is often complex, ruled by dynamics of the unconscious, and must be interpreted in the clinical social space.

The thesis offered in *Future of an Illusion*, which emphasizes the Oedipal dimension of such projections, their relation to the earthly father, the role played by wishes, and the generally pejorative (i.e., regressive, defensive, childish) value judgment attached to believers, would fit in this formula. But so do Freud's reflections on the possible pre-oedipal contributions to religion and the possible adaptive, therapeutic function of religion as found in his case histories and shorter essays. As stated above, what we will see in the chapters ahead is that Freud's cursory observations on the pre-oedipal and adaptive functions of religion became the seeds for their full flowering in the later theories of ego psychologists and object-relations theorists. Indeed, even transformational ways of thinking about the human personality, best represented above in responses from those in the psychology–theology dialogue, will similarly become authorized in the theories of later psychoanalysts. All fit seamlessly into our summary formula, which is flexible enough to be in the service of either the "movie" or "star" metaphor. Telescoping to the chapters ahead, we can say that this presentation of our "summary formula," being preliminary in nature, will find its more sophisticated incarnation as an evolving Winnicottian "God-representation," the details to which we will attend in Chapter 7.

---

[77] Kakar, *Shamans, Mystics and Doctors*, 272.
[78] See G. Obeyesekere, *The Work of Culture* (Chicago: University of Chicago Press, 1990).

5

Civilization and Its Discontents

The *Unbehagen* of Religion

Freud's final choice for naming what many consider to be his most famous cultural work is quite revealing. The preliminary title was *Das Unglück in der Kultur*, which translates best as "The Unhappiness in Civilization." *Unglück* was then replaced by *Unbehagen*, which is hard to find an English equivalent for and, unfortunately, was eventually translated as "Discontents." A better rendering would have been discomfort, unease, dissatisfaction, or the French word *malaise*. Even so, what Freud really meant by *Unbehagen* becomes clear only as his argument unfolds. Humans are dissatisfied and uneasy in civilization for the same reasons we have already seen: our innate aggressive instinct makes us asocial. But Freud adds a corollary to this: our dissatisfaction is increased by what he called the "unpsychological" proceedings of society, particularly its commands and institutions, of which religion stands at the forefront. Psychoanalysis is the therapeutic intervention that contributes to lessening not only (through active therapy) the unease in individuals but also (through the applied analysis of "cultural pathology") the additional unease created by social institutions. Continuing the agenda initiated in *Future of an Illusion*, then, Freud was not only offering means to transform individuals but also advocating for social-structural change. The important, further details of what he meant by that, keeping in mind its relation to his previous work, is the task to which we now turn.

FREUD, ROMAIN ROLLAND, AND OCEANIC FEELINGS

Freud begins *Civilization and Its Discontents* with a narrative that, at first glance, seems to be a bit odd and out of kilter with the rest of the book. In the initial paragraph he refers to a letter he received from what he calls a "great man" (who he names in a footnote as Romain Rolland), one of the "exceptional few" who eschewed "false standards of measurement" such as wealth and power and knew what was of "true value" in life.[1] Now forgotten by most, Rolland was a popular figure in European circles around the time of World War I. A professor of musicology at the prestigious Sorbonne, he won the Nobel Prize for literature in 1915, gaining additional fame through his book *Above the Battle*, a series of essays during World War I that attempted to broker peace through reasoned dialogue and humanitarianism. He continued his role as the "conscience of Europe" (as he was dubbed) after the war, warning against the rise of anti-Semitism and fascism. Like many, Freud admired him, establishing a correspondence that began in 1923 and lasted until his death. Indeed, in one of his earliest letters to Rolland one can see the high esteem with which Freud held him. He writes: "Unforgettable man, to have soared to such heights of humanity through so much hardship and suffering! I revered you as an artist and apostle of love for mankind many years before I saw you."[2] In return, Rolland said he was one of the very first in France to appreciate Freud's writings, that Freud was the "Christopher Columbus of a new continent of the spirit" who had inspired his life and thought.[3] As we have seen before, Freud liked to share his work with those whom he considered to be the "brainworkers" and "cultural elite," not the least reason being to help disseminate psychoanalysis and his critique of religion. We need not be surprised, then, to learn that when *Future of an Illusion* came out, Freud immediately sent a copy to Rolland (as he had to Pfister). Rolland returned the favor just as quickly by writing a letter (dated December 5, 1927). Thus began the famous debate over "oceanic" feelings, which played out in the first chapter of *Civilization and Its Discontents*.

In his letter Rolland offered that he "entirely agreed" with what he thought to be a "just" analysis of the "common man's" religion, stating that "with a calm good sense, and in a moderate tone, it pulls off the blindfolding bandage of the eternal adolescents, which we all are, whose amphibian spirit floats between the illusion of yesterday and ... the illusion of tomorrow."[4] But Rolland was not through, offering a counter to Freud's reductionistic treatment of religion. Freud, thought Rolland, had missed out on the true source of religions everywhere. In other words,

---

[1] Freud, *Civilization and Its Discontents*, S.E. 21: 64.
[2] Parsons, *Enigma of the Oceanic Feeling*, 172.   [3] Ibid., 170.   [4] Ibid., 173–174.

like Pfister, Rolland was playing with the "definitional problem" that plagues all those who enter into this domain. This origin, stated Rolland, consisted in a mystical "sensation of "eternity," a feeling of something limitless, unbounded – as it were, "oceanic." The problem was that the oceanic feeling, despite being the "true subterranean source" of religion, was not only "collected" and "seized" by Churches and religious systems but also "dried up by them" to the point that "it is inside the Churches" that the oceanic feeling is "least available."[5] Rolland, who was abreast of the major figures in the psychology and religion movement of his day, made it clear to Freud that he thought the oceanic feeling was amenable to psychological analysis, further enjoining Freud to engage in a mutual effort to investigate the mystical oceanic.

The term "mysticism," like that of "religion," has been subject to debates over its proper meaning and definition.[6] What can be said for now is that there exists a canonical received view as to its definition and interpretation within psychoanalytic circles. First, as regards to the "what" of mysticism, the psychoanalytic understanding follows that of William James in his *Varieties of Religious Experience*. Freud was aware of the latter, seminal work, having visited (as we have seen) with James and others at the 1909 conference at Clark University. In that work, which offers dozens of descriptions of mystical experience from multiple religions, James laid down a few central characteristics – noesis, passivity, ineffability, and transiency – that he saw as the defining "marks" of mysticism and mystical texts. One could certainly add a fifth mark, as James is candid in his view that *unity* is similarly a defining core characteristic of mysticism:

This overcoming of all the usual barriers between the individual and the Absolute is the great mystic achievement. In mystic states we both become one with the Absolute and we become aware of our oneness. This is the everlasting and triumphant mystical tradition, hardly altered by differences of clime or creed. In Hinduism, in Neoplatonism, in Sufism, in Christian mysticism, in Whitmanism, we find the same recurring note, so that there is about mystical utterances an eternal unanimity which ought to make a critic stop and think, and which brings it about that the mystical classics have, as has been said, neither birthday nor native

---

[5] Ibid.
[6] For a comprehensive summary of the definition and debates over the term "mysticism," see William B. Parsons, "Mysticism: An Overview," in *Oxford Research Encyclopedia of Religion*, ed. John Barton (2019), https://oxfordre.com/religion/view/10.1093/acrefore/9780199340378.001.0001/acrefore-9780199340378-e-55.

land. Perpetually telling of the unity of man with God, their speech antedates languages, and they do not grow old.[7]

James's equation of mystical experience with episodic feelings of unity was definitive enough that it has become the conceptual lens through which those within psychoanalysis have understood the oceanic feeling. Indeed, it is fair to say that the canonical psychoanalytic understanding of mysticism is as follows: (1) Rolland's oceanic feeling is a paradigmatic illustration of the transient, ineffable mystical experience of unity, and (2) the oceanic feeling is virtually identical with "mysticism everywhere" (a form of perennialism or the "common core" theory of mysticism).

Linked to this definition of mysticism is Freud's interpretation. The latter, based on the defining characteristics of the oceanic feeling as that of unity and limitlessness, is traced to an early, pre-oedipal phase of development (i.e., "primary narcissism"), where the infant's ego, still merged with the mother, was marked by such unitive, limitless feelings of eternity. In other words, the basis of all mystical experience was empirical and developmental, and having a mystical experience was a "regression" to the "memory" of the unitive ego-feeling of primary narcissism. The varieties of descriptions of mystical experience found in religious texts reflect religio-cultural overlays and variations of an empirically based, universal developmental stage. Additionally, sensing a challenge to his oedipal analysis of the common man's religion, Freud opined that oceanic feelings, based on the Mother, did not displace the true origin of religion, the latter based on the culturally superior role of the Father and the wish for guidance and protection. Freud thought that mystical experiences, perhaps neutral in and of themselves, could be used defensively, as a kind of soothing antidote to the horrors and exigencies of the external world and to regain lost feelings of omnipotence and immortality. Later studies would amend Freud by noting that such regressions could also be framed as having an adaptive value, being a way to restore feelings of connection and trust.

This general portrait of the psychoanalytic theory of mysticism, still operative among many psychoanalytic researchers, has been subject in more recent literature to a series of cautionary tales and, as a result, prescriptions for portable lessons that not only seek a revised psychoanalytic theory of mysticism but also offer a critical revision of the accuracy of the canonical "received view" (i.e., what Freud really said about

---

[7] James, *The Varieties of Religious Experience*, 410.

mysticism). To that discussion we will return in the next chapter. For now, we can emphasize the following point: faced with a "religious" phenomenon that did not fit that of the common man, Freud once again had to resort to a non-oedipal, indeed pre-oedipal, interpretative strategy.

THE GENERAL FRAME: EROS AND THANATOS

In some sense Rolland was a "silent interlocuter" behind the text, a brainworker who enabled Freud to address counters to his argument in *Future of an Illusion*. Having dismissed Rolland, Freud could turn to the new argument found in the pages of *Civilization and Its Discontents*. It is fortunate that Freud offers us a few passages throughout the work where he links what will be his coming arguments contra religion with those articulated in *Totem and Taboo* and *Future of an Illusion*. For example, Freud once again affirms his thesis of the primal deed as his "origin myth" of the beginning of human civilization. The "primordial ambivalence" that ruled the son's relation to the father eventuated in the "acting out" of aggression in the primal deed. The latter, in turn, led to totemism and the first laws (taboos). The innate asocial, aggressive instincts were thus kept at bay, and, through time, civilization adopted more sophisticated means (i.e., laws, commands, religious institutions) for protecting the unity and growth of the human populace. So, too, in rehashing once again his secularization thesis, does Freud affirm that civilization was in the middle of a phase in which religion, which had served its purpose as the "universal obsessional neurosis" of mankind, was being replaced: "it is to be supposed that a turning-away from religion is bound to occur with the fatal inevitability of a process of growth, and that we find ourselves at this very juncture in the middle of that phase of development."[8]

What is new is the general frame that provides the context for his further observations on religion. Foremost among the details of that frame is Freud's use of the conflict between Eros and Thanatos. He took the idea from the pre-Socratic philosopher Empedocles, who had posited an eternal, primordial, and cyclic relation between the two "heavenly powers" (Love and Strife in Empedocles' terminology). In making this "mythology" his own, Freud gave the two powers a uniquely psychoanalytic rendering. Freud defined Eros as that tendency "whose purpose is to combine single human individuals, and after that families, then races,

---

[8] Freud, *Future of an Illusion*, S.E. 21: 43.

peoples and nations, into one great unity, the unity of mankind."[9] While not naming the term as such, recall that in *Future of an Illusion* Freud had articulated the various means (which is to say, its "mental assets") through which civilization facilitated the tendency toward unity (e.g., how the idealization of and identification with great men and leaders might occasion the renunciation of instinct and asocial tendencies). In *Civilization and Its Discontents* Freud goes on to add a few more to his previous list. For example, he affirms the positive effect of what he calls "aim-inhibited" love, defined as the binding force animating friendship, families, local group activities, and the group/tribal valorization of certain ideas and values.[10] So, too, does Freud think culture has a lot to say about the transformation of certain instinctual aims into what he terms "character traits." For example, the eroticism that animates the "anal stage" of development, obsessed as it is with the excretory organs and its products, is transformed into the traits of parsimony, order, and cleanliness, all crucial to the proper functioning of civilization.[11] Aligned with this is the cultural injunction to work (e.g., to have a profession, a career). Work offers the option of "displacing a large amount of libidinal components, whether narcissistic, aggressive or even erotic on to professional work."[12] Indeed, in many ways Freud thought that the compulsion to work, however odious it may be for some, was a foundation of communal life. In all this Freud thought what was being valorized was "the urge towards union with others in the community" – an urge he termed "altruistic."[13]

Alongside the instinct to preserve the self and join it to others in ever greater unities is Thanatos, defined as that "contrary instinct seeking to dissolve those units and to bring them back to their primaeval, inorganic state."[14] If Eros is in the service of civilization, then Thanatos, whose derivative and main representative in every individual is our innate aggressive instinct, opposes this program of civilization. The process of civilization, then, presents "the struggle between Eros and Death, between the instinct of life and the instinct of destruction, as it works itself out in the human species."[15] While Freud hoped for the best outcome in the war between the heavenly powers, a certain pessimism pervades *Civilization and Its Discontents*. With World War II on the horizon, one can see how the more optimistic, enlightenment view of the power of reason (and Eros) found in *Future of an Illusion* was giving way, in *Civilization and Its Discontents*, to a mood of apprehension and anxiety. Freud rightly

---

[9] Freud, *Civilization and Its Discontents*, S.E. 21: 122. [10] Ibid., 108ff.
[11] Ibid., 97ff. [12] Ibid., 80. [13] Ibid., 140. [14] Ibid., 118–119. [15] Ibid., 122.

saw that Thanatos was on the ascendancy. Indeed, in one of his most dire assessments of the human species, he once wrote to Lou Andreas-Salomé that humanity was "organically unfitted" for civilization: "We have to abdicate, and the Great Unknown ... will sometime repeat such an experiment with another race."[16]

THE *UNBEHAGEN* OF RELIGIOUS DOCTRINES

Thrown into the tension between Eros and Thanatos is another factor, namely, the happiness of individuals. Freud locates what he calls the "program" of the latter in the fabled "pleasure principle," which, as we have seen, characterizes the dynamic drives of the unconscious. Of course, Freud went to great pains to show that one cannot simply actualize the desires of one's id. One's own mental constitution (the structural model), in tandem with the external conditions and prohibitions foisted on one by virtue of living with others in civilization, amounts to the need to articulate strategies for gaining happiness. While Freud's reflections on this essential theme range widely to address numerous topics (e.g., science, history, technology), he comes back to religion time and again throughout the work, even if his reflections are more sporadic, less orderly and detailed than one might wish. Freud asks: In what ways is religion in the service of Eros or Thanatos? What advice does religion offer to make us happy? Do such suggestions actually work? If not, why not, and what are the negative repercussions of following such advice? How might psychoanalysis be used to analyze the shortcomings of religion, with respect to both individuals and social structures, while advising a better course?

Central to his attempt to answer such questions, and building on his previous works, Freud adds new layers to his analysis of the dynamics of the religious cultural super-ego. The latter, constituted in the psyche through the idealization and internalization of the parental unit, the culture "behind them," and subsequent respected and idealized others, is one of the mental assets through which civilization checks aggressive, asocial instincts. Its content (i.e., ideals, commands, doctrines), re-memorialized through rituals, is in large measure informed by the creative products of that historical string of idealized religious figures that constitute a "tradition" and are enforced by idealized father-figures

---

[16] Jones, *The Life and Work of Sigmund Freud*, 2: 177.

(priests, prophets) who, more often than not, cannot be challenged. What is problematic is that the content of the cultural super-ego is structured in such a way that it does not take into account the clinical data and facts concerning the actual mental constitution of human beings. As Freud puts it, his project targets "the unpsychological proceedings of the cultural super-ego."[17]

In a general sense, most pivotal among the negative psychological consequences of the religious super-ego is the increase in guilt. For Freud the latter is the most important problem in the development of civilization and may well "reach heights that the individual finds hard to tolerate."[18] Indeed, left without any psychoanalytic intervention, the consequences of the religious super-ego will continue to subject humans to increasing guilt. Why is this the case? The answer revolves around Freud's psychoanalytic understanding of the nature of guilt. For Freud, when one's unacknowledged and unexamined aggressive instincts are redirected through the cultural and individual super-ego and its unpsychological commands on the unwitting and helpless ego, it is felt as "guilt," now understood as aggression turned back on the self. Religion, then, may in some measure, as Freud had argued in *Future of an Illusion*, help the program of Eros, but only at the cost of an increase in guilt. The solution is an applied psychoanalytic analysis of the unpsychological nature of religious institutions, doctrines, and commands. At the very least, that would lessen the severity of a harsh cultural and individual super-ego, lessen guilt, and give individuals a greater chance to freely actualize their unique quest for happiness.

Becoming more specific, Freud expands on his analysis to look at the consequences of the unpsychological proceedings of religious commands and doctrines. In following his oedipal analysis of the monotheistic worldview in *Future of an Illusion*, he comes back to a singular point: there exists a "developmental infrastructure" to even the highest commands, ideals, and doctrines promoted by the religio-cultural super-ego. Any doctrine or command that does not take this infrastructure into account invariably runs the risk of creating heightened guilt and unease. Most notable among his various analyses is that which targets the Christian love command. At its face, it appears to be in the service of Eros, being one of the mental assets of civilization designed to counter aggressive, antisocial instincts toward civilization and the "other" in all of its forms.

---

[17] Freud, *Civilization and Its Discontents*, S.E. 21: 143.   [18] Ibid., 133.

However, in its unqualified, extreme form, which insists that one love universally, Freud thought it to be unpsychological and impossible to fulfill. Why? Because it is based on the assumption that our ego has unlimited mastery over the id. If more is demanded (in this case, to love universally) than one is capable of producing, then there will be psychological consequences: "revolt will be produced in him or a neurosis, or he will be made unhappy."[19] Freud went further to attribute the origin of this extreme framing of the love command to developmental factors, specifically those issuing from the pre-oedipal phase. The command to love universally compels because it caters to the nostalgic pull of – in fact, is the developmental residue of – a time when love was abundant and one did not distinguish between objects (namely, the pre-oedipal developmental phase of union with the mother). One is enjoined to love everyone as oneself because it recalls an ideal time when in fact that was the case. This analysis highlights two interrelated points. First, Freud is once again resorting to a pre-oedipal, not oedipal, analysis. This adds to the list of those non-oedipal analyses that mark his psychology of religion. Second, he is showing how a command, which in reality is ruled at least in part by a developmental (pre-oedipal) infrastructure, is taken up by the cultural super-ego and, through a form of projection and misdirection, idealized as issuing from an unchanging divine reality, then internalized, there to create guilt and *Unbehagen*. The solution is to shear such commands of their developmental pull and, by subjecting them to rational discourse, offer a better, revised version that can be implemented in a psychologically responsible way. As we will detail in the last section, "*Civilization and Its Discontents*: Critiques," Freud in fact did just that. In other words, his analysis was not only deconstructive but also constructive.

Freud's analysis becomes even more pointed, sociological, and culturally relevant when he links the love command to what he calls the "narcissism of minor differences." In asking us to "love universally," the love command fails to take into account the displaced aggression that such an unrealizable command invariably occasions. It is always possible, says Freud, to bind a certain number of people into a group through love. But this also leads to a form of tribalism in which other groups of people, namely, the "out" group, are left to receive the various expressions of their aggressiveness. Freud notes that when St. Paul "posited universal love between men as the foundation of his Christian community, extreme

---

[19] Ibid., 143.

intolerance on the part of Christendom towards those who remained outside it became the inevitable consequence."[20] Indeed (and here one cannot fail to recall Freud's university days in Vienna, the ascendancy of Karl Lueger, and the impact on him of the general anti-Semitic atmosphere), he wryly notes that "the Jewish people, scattered everywhere, have rendered the most useful services to the civilizations of the countries that have been their hosts."[21] Along these lines, continues Freud, it is hardly an accident that "the dream of a Germanic world-dominion called for antisemitism as its complement."[22]

The psychological dynamic of the "narcissism of minor differences" is portable, applying to everything from the strife between Catholics and Protestants (notably in Great Britain and Ireland in the later part of the twentieth century) and the Sunni and Shia (e.g., in Saudi Arabia and Iran respectively) to early twenty-first-century American anti-immigration sentiment. Indeed, one could also extend the portable lesson to apply to cousin theological doctrines, most dramatically that of predestination as linked to the various formulations concerning the end-time. For Freud, predestination is but a theological rationalization of tribalism, of "being chosen," hence catering to narcissistic needs for love, mirroring, and acceptance. In turn, the latter is susceptible to forms of tribal violence, of which the doctrine of an apocalyptic divine judgment is an extreme form. What is pathological for Freud is that such doctrines are nothing more than imaginative creations, rationalized fantasies, as it were, of developmental themes, needs, and conflicts. The frightful next step is when they are co-opted by religion and used to justify social actions, an analysis worth considering given their status as doctrinal mainstays in religious traditions as seemingly opposite as those of radical terrorists (e.g., ISIL) and certain Christian members of American political parties, both "tribes" of which continue to impact contemporary world politics. The danger, for Freud, is that when we fail to see that we ourselves create such doctrines (through developmentally based imaginative activity), further rationalizing and objectifying them through religious institutions, we then become open to use them as justifications to enact violence. In other words, warning of the primitivity of the human species, Freud was signifying the ways in which institutional religion was complicit in helping developmental factors (i.e., pathological narcissism) win out over reason,

---

[20] Ibid., 114. [21] Ibid. [22] Ibid., 115.

Eros, even the survival of the species (which is to say, religion "in the service of" Thanatos).

To be clear, the lesson here is not that Freud thought all religious commands were devoid of value. Indeed, as mentioned above (and which we will fully unpack below), Freud offered a revised version of the love command based on rational considerations: he was keen on noting not only the "developmental infrastructure" of even seemingly high and noble theological formulations but also how such forces undermined any attempt to fully actualize their lofty aims. We earlier saw that in *Totem and Taboo* Freud, referencing Kant, had warned of this feature of human beings.[23] Later, in a subsequent, additional rejoinder to Kant and his grand ethical law (i.e., the "categorial imperative"), he noted that while it is noble to think that Kant's moral law "couples the conscience within us with the starry Heavens" and that a "pious man might well be tempted to honour these two things as the masterpieces of creation," in actual point of fact many have little or even no conscience or sense of justice.[24] As Freud put it: "God has done an uneven and careless piece of work."[25] What he means is that such ethical laws all too often neglect the developmental origins and determinants of the super-ego (i.e., one's "conscience"), and how a faulty super-ego affects, even perverts, the noble implementation of ethical principles and legal rulings. Again, here Freud was speaking from personal experience. While the potential mendacity of religious commands had been indelibly imprinted on him as a Jew at the University of Vienna, it was reinforced during World War I. In his little paper "The Disillusionment of War" (1915), he observed the general disillusionment that occurred for many when they realized how even the most cultured individuals and those in power seemed incapable of acting in a civilized manner. They were, in Freud's terms, "cultural hypocrites," by which he meant those who, seemingly abiding by noble commands, actually used the latter in the service of untransformed, selfish, and base instinctual drives. Mendacity, lying, sheer barbarism, unbridled lust for power, and censorship ruled the day. Certainly, such lessons are conveyable and can be seen in all eras and political systems. As a counter, applied psychoanalysis provides the kind of moral education and social structural change needed to expose and reform the developmentally challenged.[26]

---

[23] Freud, *Totem and Taboo*, S.E. 21: xiv
[24] Freud, *New Introductory Lectures on Psychoanalysis*, S.E. 22: 61.   [25] Ibid.
[26] Freud, "The Disillusionment of the War," in S.E. 14: 275–289.

THE *UNBEHAGEN* OF RELIGION AND SEX

Turning to another consequence of religious prescriptions for happiness, Freud seizes on religious teachings regarding sexuality. As laid down in his *Totem and Taboo*, Freud was convinced that sexuality, in the form of the dynamics of Oedipus, was at the root of the civilization, religion, and morality. From its beginnings, then, religion and the cultural super-ego aimed at monitoring and regulating sexuality. Indeed, recall that one of the very first laws of civilization (i.e., the taboo of exogamy) aimed at forbidding the most fervent sexual wish of the unconscious, namely, incest (a law that, while in the service of Eros by enabling the "greater unity" outside the family, Freud also referred to in *Civilization and Its Discontents* as "perhaps the most drastic mutilation which man's erotic life has in all time experienced").[27] Of course, with the development of civilization, the restrictions of sexual life became much more pervasive. At times Freud speaks highly of such efforts of civilization. For example, as indicated earlier in this chapter, how aim-inhibited love, paradigmatically manifested in the bonds of friendship, helped to create and sustain ever greater unities of peoples. But what about religious proclamations concerning genital sexuality? Freud put forth that the Judeo-Christian tradition valorized the unchanging, divinely inspired norm of heterosexual monogamy. This was not necessarily a problem, for it jibed well with Freud's adherence to the Darwinian propagation of the species. On the other hand, like all aspects of the cultural super-ego, it was unpsychological in that it did not take into account the diversity of individual sexual impulses. Clinical data revealed that the sexual impulses and aims of human beings did not always fit under the normative banner of heterosexual monogamy. As Freud put it, the requirement "that there shall be a single kind of sexual life for everyone, disregards the dissimilarities, whether innate or acquired, in the sexual constitution of human beings; it cuts off a fair number of them from sexual enjoyment, and so becomes the course of serious injustice."[28] In this regard recall how Freud, when asked by a mother to "cure" her gay son, responded that homosexuality was "nothing to be ashamed of, no vice, no degradation"; that "it cannot be classified as an illness"; and that it was "a great injustice to persecute homosexuality as a crime – and a cruelty, too."[29] Freud's solution was predictably consistent: the cultural super-ego must be changed in ways

---

[27] Freud, *Civilization and Its Discontents*, S.E. 21: 104.   [28] Ibid.
[29] See "A Letter from Freud," 786–787.

that accord with the actual psychological constitution of individuals – a fact that has come to pass in no small measure due to the social authority of a clinical space (i.e., psychoanalysis) that has legitimated the expression of alternate sexualities.

Although Freud stressed how the binding prison of a harsh super-ego increased the ability of the religious cultural super-ego to command allegiance, he also offered that the dynamic nature of instinctual life was such that non-normative sexualities inevitably leaked through, expressing themselves in ways that were tacitly acknowledged and allowed by culture at large. For example, with regard to religion, he noted that monasticism could be a refuge for those who had other than heterosexual aims. Freud did not go on to address in any detail the multiple other ways diverse gender identifications and sexual aims (e.g., asceticism/celibacy, cross-dressing, eunuchs, divine androgyny, polymorphous encounters) have been expressed, if not legitimated, within the history of religions (although the logic of his thought allows for educated guesses). That said, we will find in the chapters ahead how subsequent developments in *reflexive, dialogical, inclusive* psychoanalytic theory have sought to engage at least some of this diversity of expression. For now, we can emphasize how Freud's analysis reaffirms the lesson that there exists an unpsychological dimension to religious commands concerning sexuality, which, once subject to psychoanalytic inquiry, can lead to reformation and social structural change.

PSYCHOANALYTIC VERSUS RELIGIOUS PROGRAMS FOR LIFE

One also finds in the pages of *Civilization and Its Discontents* Freud's normative suggestions, strategies, and prescriptions to navigate the lifecycle with the aim of best ensuring happiness. To a certain extent such suggestions stem from his foundational psychoanalytic principle (which we earlier articulated) in which the purpose of life is set by the pleasure principle modified in accord with the reality principle. In his view, suffering was apparent in three interrelated domains: as coming from (1) the physical constitution of the body, (2) the demands put on one by external reality, and (3) the way in which civilization mediated relations between people. Since such suffering was always complicated by the structural dynamics that obtained between the id, ego, and super-ego, humans as a group were fated to continually manage strategies for achieving happiness. Indeed, every person "must find out for himself in what particular fashion he can be saved."³⁰

The latter indicates that Freud clearly left room for individual choice in matters of solution to the problem of happiness. As we have already seen, he chimed in as to the contribution psychoanalysis might offer in expanding the freedom to choose. Nuancing this further, herein lies the foundation of one of the more famous maxims often associated with Freud, namely, that therapy moves the individual from the suffering of "neurotic misery" to the "common unhappiness" inherent to all in everyday life. Psychoanalytic therapy, while not offering salvation, could at least mitigate suffering to the extent that individuals might be freed up enough to find the best strategy for happiness in a way that suits their unique needs. Further, along such lines Freud thought that the best technique for happiness, again enabled through therapy, is to be able to find appropriate work (e.g., a career or its equivalent, which we have seen served to monitor and sublimate sexual, aggressive, and narcissistic needs) as well as appropriate love arrangements ("to love and be loved," as Freud put it). The German saying "lieben und arbeiten" ("to love and to work") has functioned as a short maxim of Freud's view as to the best strategy for navigating the vicissitudes of life.³¹

Of course, religion also offers strategies and prescriptions to navigate the life-cycle and best ensure happiness. It is Freud's normative conception of the best way to happiness, informed by what psychoanalysis teaches us about the person, which became the basis for his reflections and evaluation on those religious teachings that offered (in his view) less satisfying alternatives. For example, Freud points to a saintly path, represented by the Christian monk St. Francis, whose solution to the problem of happiness amounted to that of loving all. For Freud, such saints, by "displacing what they mainly value from being loved on to loving," are able to bring about "a state of evenly suspended, steadfast, affectionate feeling."³² The cost for Freud is the complete excising of genital love: its stormy agitations, fears, and anxieties. While Freud is not wholly disavowing the strategy for happiness adopted by St. Francis, it is clearly not the option he would advise or personally adopt. Indeed, in once again

---

³⁰ Freud, *Civilization and Its Discontents*, S.E. 21: 83.
³¹ This was not formally stated by Freud but rather later by the ego psychologist Erik Erikson, who used it to sum up Freud's view of health. Nevertheless, it has attained the status of a pithy maxim.
³² Freud, *Civilization and Its Discontents*, S.E. 21: 102.

resorting to a non-oedipal interpretation, he thought that such a strategy stemmed from the pre-oedipal period where love was abundant and universal. Such a universal type of love had the same problem as that of the dictates of the love command: it forfeited its value by not discriminating between objects (which is to say, not all people are worthy of love). Freud also attacked the "solution" found in Hinduism, specifically that of yoga, which he refers to as "the wisdom of the East." Freud suggests that the path of the ascetic/hermit, in adopting the strategy of voluntary isolation, does in fact avoid suffering. However, in conjunction with the technique of yoga, such worldly wisdom ends up enjoining one to adapt to life by "killing off the instincts."[33] For Freud, that solution is in the service of Thanatos and the death instinct. While it may well be a viable solution to suffering, it leads to a form of quiescent happiness that succeeds by sacrificing much of what many call life.

THE THERAPEUTIC CULTURAL SUPER-EGO

So far, we have seen Freud engaging in his usual deconstruction of the cultural super-ego. We have also suggested that there is a constructive counterpart. Recall from the last chapter how Freud wished to establish a social space for a psychoanalytic secular cure of souls, one that would serve to educate the instincts and replace the moral function of an outdated, declining Western religious tradition. In the waning pages of *Civilization and Its Discontents* he comes back to this theme in a slightly different and sociologically suggestive way. He again affirms, in noting the development of civilization can be compared to that of a person, that we are growing out of that phase of civilization defined by the universal obsessional neurosis known as religion into a more secularized, scientific phase. Then, in an extension of his thought, Freud remarks that in every epoch the cultural super-ego is composed of, among other things, the echoes and residues of the personality and creative intellectual products of great men. While Freud warns against anybody that might hold him up as a secular prophet (over against, one might argue, evidence to the contrary), there is no question that he magnified the existential reach of his theory by instantiating a clinical social space (his "church," so to speak) to affect culture at large. At the very least, one could say that Freud's project was to change the cultural super-ego from a religious to a

---

[33] Ibid., 79.

therapeutic register. One could further observe that he succeeded in that psychoanalysis has become a part of our everyday life to the point of suffusing our cultural soup with its concepts, norms, and freedoms. In that sense, there has been a "triumph of the therapeutic" that has indeed changed the structure and content of our cultural super-ego. In pointing to this structural change one can speak of an important aspect of the constructive nature of his project. The nature and dynamics of this process, as well as the intended and unintended consequences of Freud's ideas, are worth considering, particularly as they continue to change our religious landscape. We will return to this topic in the concluding chapter.

CIVILIZATION AND ITS DISCONTENTS: CRITIQUES

In addition to the various cautionary tales summarized at the end of the preceding chapter on *Future of an Illusion*, we can add an important group of scholarly critiques that fall under our rubric of reflexivity. As mentioned at the beginning of this chapter, many have noted that there is a philosophical flavor to *Civilization and Its Discontents*. Taken further, some have suggested that Freud went beyond the more objective, neutral stance he thought endemic to scientific discourse to offer normative solutions to the problem of happiness and living in civilization. For example, one could, as suggested above, venture to frame the popular saying of transforming "neurotic misery" into "common unhappiness" and the maxim of "lieben und arbeiten" (to love and to work) as normative conceptions of health and aims of Freudian psychoanalytic therapy. As we shall see, subsequent revisions in psychoanalytic models, notably those of Erik Erikson, Heinz Kohut, and Sudhir Kakar, offer quite different ideals of health and transformation. This is not to render moot lessons such as acknowledging the developmental infrastructure of religious worldviews, doctrines, and commands but to note, in accord with our stress on reflexivity, that Freud, even in being informed by psychoanalytic models and data, was going beyond that data to offer normative philosophical reflections on the problem of happiness.

Cautionary tales along similar lines can be found strewn throughout critical scholarship on *Civilization and Its Discontents*. For example, Lee Yearly and Don Browning have seized on what Freud called the "heavenly powers" (i.e., his "mythology" of Eros and Thanatos), which he admitted to be modeled on the Western pre-Socratic philosopher Empedocles, as metaphors that capture life's meaning and purpose as well as the nature of the world, cosmos, and historical process.[34] They offer this as evidence that there are implicit "ethnoreligious" elements, clearly Western and cultural, smuggled into Freud's use of psychoanalytic theory. Similarly, one could say that Freud offered normative visions for living ethically. This is best illustrated in his comments on an extreme version of the Christian love command. We have seen Freud's unveiling of what he thought was the developmental infrastructure of such a command, and noted that the portable lesson is that all forms of religious commands may indeed have such an infrastructure. But we also suggested, without going into detail, that he offered, along this deconstructive psychoanalytic "hermeneutics of suspicion," a corresponding constructive move that went beyond psychoanalysis to offer a rational, philosophical position. In now detailing that position we can point to how Freud argued that one might love the other if they represent high ideals that are worthy, for one would share in their joy and sadness as if it were one's own. What he railed against was loving a stranger who not only might be hostile to one but also wishes one emotional or physical harm. That would be a disservice to those one does in fact love, for it would fail to distinguish the moral worth of people and perhaps authorize, if not justify, the asocial behavior of the "enemies" of civilization. As Wallwork has pointed out, Freud's stance is close to a Jewish form of other-regard based on the principles of respect and fair reciprocity.[35] So, for example, Freud is willing to say that if the stranger embodies one's ideals then, yes, one can love them, that if the neighbor "behaves differently, if he shows me consideration and forbearance as a stranger, I am ready to treat him in the same way."[36] Again, reciprocity is indicated when Freud says the following: "If this grandiose commandment had run 'Love thy neighbor as they neighbor loves thee,' I should not take exception to it."[37]

These various critiques, which unearth normative views of health and healing, ethics and the moral life, even metaphysical metaphors concerning "heavenly powers," alert us to what social scientists and culture theorists caution us to be reflective about, namely, how the application of psychological models may entail unexamined assumptions that betray

---

[34] D. Browning, *Religious Thought and the Modern Psychologies* (Philadelphia: Fortress Press, 1987), and Lee Yearly, "Freud as Critic and Creator of Cosmogonies and Their Ethics," in *Cosmogony and Ethical Order*, ed. R. Lovin and F. Reynolds (Chicago: University of Chicago Press, 1985), 381–413.
[35] E. Wallwork, *Psychoanalysis and Ethics* (New Haven, CT: Yale University Press, 1991).
[36] Freud, *Civilization and Its Discontents*, S.E. 21: 110.   [37] Ibid.

the presence of ethnopsychological values. Freud admitted as much when he stated that his own attempts at "applied psychoanalysis" did not form any part of psychoanalytic theory or psychoanalysis "in general" but only his individual proclivities, that there existed other "excellent" psychoanalysts who did not necessarily share his views on religion, and that his analysis should not deter them from using the "nonpartisan" method of analysis for arguing opposed views.[38] In other words, one can use his psychology, properly qualified, without buying into his normative philosophical views.

---

[38] See Freud and Pfister, *Psychoanalysis and Faith*, 117.

6

Freud and Eastern Religions

It is common fare to think that Freud reflected mainly on Judaism and Christianity, leaving Eastern religions in the lurch. Part of this is attributable to the fact that in Freud's era relatively little was known of Buddhism and Hinduism. Before 1880, which is to say, the beginning of the psychology and religion movement, the engagement with Eastern religions in Europe and North America was sporadic and piecemeal, informed primarily through the auspices of missionaries, business enterprises, travel, and trade. By the time the psychology of religion was establishing itself as an intellectual discipline, the gradual dissemination of Eastern religions in the West was only just beginning. With respect to academia, chairs in Oriental studies and comparative religion at Ivy League schools and European institutions (including the University of Vienna where Freud studied and taught) were newly minted, giving rise to an initial generation of scholars (e.g., Rudolph Otto, Friedrich Heiler, Max Müller) and the introduction of the first accessible translations (notably, the classic Sacred Books of the East series). On the wider cultural scale, Eastern religious ideas were beginning to be disseminated through the auspices of philosophers and poets (e.g., Nietzsche, Emerson, the Theosophical movement) and visits from Eastern holy men (e.g., Vivekananda, Yogananda), the latter initiated by the World's Parliament of Religions in Chicago (1893). In the United States one finds for the first time the establishment of institutions for meditative techniques aided by a social base of Asian immigrants (approximately one million strong). The exemplars of Hinduism and Buddhism, as well as their Western sympathizers, were eager to frame Eastern religions as commensurate with the scientific enterprise.[1]

This "oriental renaissance," as Raymond Schwab once called it, was not entirely lost on those writing in the psychology and religion movement.[2] Even Freud's written corpus indicates that he was familiar, if but in a cursory way, with many Eastern texts, gods, goddesses, and contemporary adepts (e.g., *The Upanishads*, *Bhagavad Gita*, and various Buddhist sutras; Kali and Vishnu; Ramakrishna, Vivekananda, Tagore, and Gandhi). Indeed, if one looks closely at his corpus, one finds that Freud reflected a bit more on those traditions than is usually acknowledged. One could complain that his works contain but a handful of what appear to be a series of unconnected passages and obscure footnotes about Eastern religions. However, when the latter are contextualized with respect to Freud's various correspondences with representatives of such traditions, one finds a cohesive narrative that indicates that Freud's engagement with Eastern religions was more substantial and important than usually acknowledged.[3]

THE OCEANIC FEELING REVISITED

While Freud's ruminations on Eastern religions can be found scattered throughout his corpus, the logical place to start is by revisiting the first chapter of *Civilization and Its Discontents*. This is not simply because in that chapter Freud refers to Eastern mystical practices by name but also because his correspondent, Romain Rolland, was a disillusioned Catholic who linked his oceanic feeling to Eastern religions. In his letter of December 5, 1927, to Freud, Rolland cited as evidence of the oceanic feeling his upcoming biographies of two Hindu saints, Ramakrishna and Vivekananda (which, on publication, he sent to Freud as a gift). One could say, then, that this chapter can be framed as the *locus classicus* not

---

[1] William B. Parsons, "Themes and Debates in the Psychology–Comparativist Dialogue," in *Religion and Psychology: Mapping the Terrain*, ed. D. Jonte-Pace and William B. Parsons (New York: Routledge, 2001), 229–253.
[2] Ibid.
[3] Ibid. See also William B. Parsons, "Freud's Encounter with Hinduism," in *Vishnu on Freud's Desk*, ed. T. G. Vaidyanathan and J. Kripal (Delhi: Oxford University Press, 1999), 41–80; William B. Parsons, "Psychoanalysis Meets Buddhism," in *Changing the Scientific Study of Religion: Beyond Freud?*, ed. J. Belzen (New York: Springer, 2009), 179–210.

only of the psychoanalytic interpretation of mysticism, but also of the psychology–comparativist dialogue as well.[4]

We saw in the preceding chapter that the canonical view of the psychoanalytic theory of mysticism emphasized four points: (1) that Rolland's oceanic feeling was an instance of the Jamesian transient mystical experience of unity, (2) that the oceanic feeling was identical to all mysticism(s) east and west (a form of perennialism), (3) that Freud's interpretation was developmental and empirical, tracing the origin of such feelings of eternity and unity as the regression to the pre-oedipal developmental phase of primary narcissism, and (4) that oceanic feelings could be used defensively (consolation, protection) or adaptively (trust, connectivity). It is certainly consistent with psychoanalytic theory to render transient mystical experience of unity with such an interpretative model, as is illustrated in multiple psychoanalytic studies after Freud.[5] Indeed, we can again affirm, as we did in the preceding chapter, that the canonical view, still operative within many psychoanalytic circles, emphasizes this definitional strategy ("mysticism" as transient unitive experience) as well as this interpretative model (regression to primary narcissism). That said, we also stated in the preceding chapter that the canonical view misrepresents Freud's understanding and interpretation of the oceanic feeling, displays a general ignorance of the complexity of phenomena subsumed under the rubric of "mysticism," and, as a result, renders both the canonical psychoanalytic definitional strategy and interpretative bias problematic. Telescoping the detailed argument to come, we can say that Freud understood the oceanic feeling not as a transient experience but as an enduring state, and while he did use pre-oedipal theory to interpret it, he offered a second, quite different model for mystical experience proper. The unpacking of this line of investigation will lead us once again to a reconsideration, as a cautionary tale, of what is meant by the term "mysticism" as well as the articulation of certain portable lessons that can be integrated as part of the tool kit available to a reflexive, dialogical, inclusive psychoanalytic theory of religion.

DECONSTRUCTING THE CANONICAL VIEW

Freud's interpretation of the oceanic feeling was based on Rolland's description in his letter of December 5, 1927. The latter, then, comprises

---

[4] See the discussion in Parsons, *Enigma of the Oceanic Feeling*, chapters 1–4.
[5] Ibid., chapter 6.

the "case" presented to Freud for interpretation. How did Rolland characterize the oceanic feeling? First, proceeding autobiographically, Rolland insisted that it was a "constant state," not a transient experience. As he put it in his letter to Freud, "I myself am familiar with this sensation"; it was a "prolonged feeling" and "constant state (like a sheet of water which I feel flushing under the bark)."[6] Importantly, Freud himself understood it as such. By way of summarizing Rolland's letter in *Civilization and Its Discontents*, Freud notes that the oceanic feeling consists in a "peculiar feeling, which he himself is never without."[7] Being an educated man and university professor well read in the classics, Freud knew what the familiar transient mystical experience was and, as consequence, that Rolland's oceanic feeling could not be classified under that heading. Indeed, Freud evinces true perplexity as regards this state-like phenomenon, declaring that it left him "no peace," that its analysis had caused him "no small difficulty" because of its "intangible quantities."[8]

There is no indication that Freud was familiar enough with the variety of mystical phenomena to know that permanent mystical states have been catalogued within religious traditions. Indeed, herein lies a cautionary tale: reading "mysticism" through the lens of William James's *The Varieties of Religious Experience* can mislead. The portable lesson is that a dialogue with theologians, comparativists, and scholars of religion is the antidote. They have long noted the existence of permanent mystical states, as is evinced in the Hindu Sri Ramana Maharshi, who speaks of the prolonged feeling of the oceanic (as distinguished from the transient feeling of the oceanic, usually designated with the unqualified term *samadhi*) when describing the advanced mystical form known as *sahaja samadhi* (a qualified form of *samadhi*), and St. Teresa of Avila, who distinguished between transient unitive experiences (in mansion 5 of her mystical text *Interior Castle*) and the apex of the spiritual life (described in mansion 7) of the *spiritual marriage*, where the Holy Trinity resides permanently and continuously in the depths of the soul.[9] This is not to claim that there is an exact equivalence between Rolland's oceanic feeling and those states described by St. Teresa and Sri Ramana Maharshi. Rather, it is to point out that the notion of a mystical state is not an

---

[6] Ibid., 173–174.   [7] Ibid., 39.   [8] Ibid., 38, 44.
[9] See A. Osborne, *Ramana Maharshi and the Path of Self-Knowledge* (New York: Samuel Weiser, 1973), and St. Teresa of Avila, *The Interior Castle*, trans. K. Kavanaugh and O. Rodriguez (New York: Paulist Press, 1979).

anomaly and that there exist many such states catalogued in mystical literature.

What, then, about the canonical view that Freud's analysis emphasized the regression hypothesis? That too is misleading. If one looks back at Freud's interpretation, he did not emphasize the "regressive" hypothesis, as if what he was interpreting was an "episodic" mystical experience. Rather, Freud emphasized a "preservation" model in which the early ego feeling of unity and limitlessness found in primary narcissism could be preserved (as Freud thought in the case of Rolland) alongside the more "sharply demarcated" ego feeling of adulthood. In other words, what Freud endeavored to explain was the fact that Rolland was "never without" the oceanic feeling.

In starting his analysis, Freud seized on its central ideational content: the indissoluble bond of being one with the external world as whole. As an interesting aside, and in accordance with our narrative in Chapter 1 of why Freud wrote about religion, Freud's association to this indissoluble bond was to Christian Grabbe's play *Hannibal* where, as Freud recounts it, Rolland meant "the same thing as the consolation offered by an original and somewhat eccentric dramatist to his hero who is facing a self-inflicted death: 'We cannot fall out of this world.'"[10] It should be said that this association was not lost on Freud. It was not so much a "free association" as a deliberate, rhetorical addition to the text. It demonstrates anew the analytic self-awareness and literary sophistication which is littered throughout his works. Faced with a religious datum that challenged his oedipal model for religion, Freud felt it incumbent to offer a psychoanalytic response. Once again, Freud was Hannibal, whose father had sworn him to an oath to overcome religion, this time a mystical one. Indeed, one can hear echoes of the unitive, maternal matrix that characterized his relationship with the Catholic nanny of his childhood and, behind that, the city of Rome, with all it meant to him.

Moving to his actual interpretation, Freud began by reflecting on what was for him uncharted territory: the empirical, pre-oedipal developmental origin of such religious feelings. He notes that in the developmental stage of primary narcissism, the infant's sense of self and the world is more unitary than that of the adult: "An infant at the breast does not as yet distinguish his ego from the external world as the source of the sensations flowing in upon him. He gradually learns to do so, in response to various

---

[10] Parsons, *Enigma of the Oceanic Feeling*, 40–41.

promptings ... originally the ego includes everything, later it separates off an external world for itself."[11] He then goes on to conclude that adult ego-feelings are but a "shrunken residue" of an original all-embracing feeling and that there may exist many people in whose mental life this primary ego-feeling has persisted. If so, it "would exist in them side by side with the narrower and more sharply demarcated ego-feeling of maturity, like a kind of counterpart to it. In that case, the ideational content appropriate to it would be precisely those of limitlessness and of a bond with the universe – the same ideas with which my friend elucidated the 'oceanic feeling.'"[12]

Freud went on to say that while in and of itself Rolland's oceanic feeling was neutral, being akin to a developmental residue or psychological appendix, it could be taken up by the Churches and framed in such a way as to cater to defensive modes of adapting to reality, even to rekindle the memory of archaic, pre-oedipal forms of omnipotence and grandiosity. Here, as elsewhere in *Civilization and its Discontents*, Freud's comments reveal his concern with how the "unpsychological" proceedings of religious institutions (in this case, mystical theology) create *Unbehagen* in culture.

As to the question of whether Freud's analysis was correct, we may adduce yet another set of cautionary tales. More recent studies have shown that, perhaps as a result of the limited nature of Freud's correspondence with Rolland, he was unaware of crucial aspects of Rolland's oceanic feeling that preclude it from being what Freud framed it as: an essentially aesthetic, benign, developmental appendix. What, then, were those crucial aspects? Based on a reconstruction of the totality of Rolland's mystical life (of which Freud was unaware) as found in his journals, autobiography, letters, and written corpus, it has been argued that the oceanic feeling was not merely aesthetic and neutral (a psychological appendix) "preserved" from primary narcissism, but a therapeutic and existential achievement, the denouement of a psycho-religious process that involved introspection, renunciation, insight, and transformation.[13] This makes sense, given that other mystical states (such as the ones cited above in Sri Maharshi and St. Teresa) similarly frame their respective achievements as advanced phenomena in the mystical path requiring a long existential and ethical process. These observations suggest not only that did Freud get the "case" wrong but that his classic

---

[11] Freud, *Civilization and Its Discontents*, S.E. 21: 66–67.   [12] Ibid.
[13] See Parsons, *Enigma of the Oceanic Feeling*, chapter 5.

psychoanalytic model was insufficient to account for its existential and ethical dimensions. Later developments in psychoanalytic theory have noticed this and, with the advent of transformational models, have attempted to correct Freud's deficiencies. We will return to this in the following chapter.

FREUD, MYSTICAL PRACTICES, AND TRANSIENT MYSTICAL EXPERIENCES

Freud's interpretation of the oceanic feeling emphasized its state-like character. However, there are other texts in his corpus that reveal him offering a different model for the interpretation of the more familiar Jamesian transient mystical experiences. The fact that Freud was generally aware of the latter and its characteristic of being transient is abundantly clear in his *Future of an Illusion*. In chapter 5 of that work, in the midst of a discussion where Freud rebukes what he calls the "desperate efforts" of philosophers to defend the legitimacy of institutional religion, he turns to the thought of the early Church Father Tertullian. Freud notes that doctrines such as Tertullian's *credo quia absurdum* suggest the argument that religious doctrines are "outside the jurisdiction of reason" and "must be felt inwardly" as an "experience which bears witness to that truth."[14] In countering this argument, Freud goes on to say:

what is one to do about the many people who do not have this rare experience? One may require every man to use the gift of reason which he possesses, but one cannot erect, on the basis of a motive that exists only for a very few, an obligation that shall apply to everyone. If one man has gained an unshakable conviction of the true reality of religious doctrines from a state of ecstasy which has deeply moved him, of what significance is that to others?[15]

Freud's discussion evokes what William James called the *noetic* dimension (knowledge gained by a special kind of intuition) of mystical experience (indicated where Freud speaks of "the truth of religious doctrines" as dependent on a "state of ecstasy"). Moreover, he does not engage in an interpretation of mystical experiences so much as offers a rationalization of his own position by suggesting that religious states of ecstasy are far too rare and inaccessible to empirical, scientific verification to serve as the basis for the defense of institutional religion. One can also note that the

---

[14] Freud, *Future of an Illusion*, S.E. 21: 28.   [15] Ibid.

passage is littered with rhetorical questions that give one the impression that Freud is not denying that such altered states have some adaptive value for what he refers to as the "very few." His aim is less about the interpretation of mysticism and more about defending his view of the "common man's" religion.

Freud came back to the problem of transient mystical experience in the concluding paragraphs of the first chapter of *Civilization and Its Discontents*. To put those paragraphs into proper context, recall that Freud had sent Rolland *Future of an Illusion* in late 1927 and Rolland had responded by December 5 of that year. Then, two years later, Freud wrote to Rolland (in a letter of July 14, 1929) asking him permission to cite his letter "in a new work" that "lies before me still uncompleted" in which he mentions the oceanic feeling (an unmistakable reference to *Civilization and Its Discontents*). Rolland (in a letter of July 17, 1929) responded in the affirmative, adding that he was "much honored to learn that the letter I wrote to you at the end of 1927 has prompted new researches" and that he was now close to publishing his "long studies on the Hindu mind." The latter, he said, examined "the ritualistic and multi-secular physiology which is codified in treatises on yoga." Freud responded three days later, exclaiming "my best thanks for your permission!" and, as an aside, "I cannot imagine reading all the literature which, according to your letter, you have studied. And yet it is easier for you than for us to read the human soul!"[16]

So it is that Freud, at the end of the first chapter of *Civilization and Its Discontents*, turned away from the state-like oceanic feeling to address the relation between mystical practices and episodic mystical experience. In so doing, he refers to a "another friend of mine" who had "encyclopaedic knowledge" and had assured him that through the "practices of Yoga" and by "fixing the attention on bodily functions and by peculiar methods of breathing" that one could evoke "sensations and coenaesthesias in oneself, which he regards as regressions to primordial states of mind." Freud goes on to state how it "would not be hard to find connections here with a number of obscure modifications of mental life, such as traces and ecstasies."[17] Freud distinguishes this second mystical

---

[16] See the letters between Rolland and Freud as found in the appendix of Parsons, *Enigma of the Oceanic Feeling*.

[17] Freud, *Civilization and Its Discontents*, S.E. 21: 72–73. While Freud's analysis of the episodic mystical experiences was inspired by Rolland, the "another friend" may well have been Frederick Eckstein, brother of Freud's patient Emma, who was a Sanskritist (see Masson, *The Assault on Truth*, 233ff.).

phenomenon from the state-like oceanic feeling, emphasizing the regression hypothesis rather than his earlier preservation model. Significantly, instead of carrying this new model forward, Freud draws back, simply stating, "But I am moved to exclaim in the words of Schiller's diver: 'Let him rejoice who breathes up here in the roseate light!'"

What can we make of this recourse to Schiller? This question is important, for perhaps it contains, if in poetic form, the hidden substance of his new model for interpreting mystical experience proper. Along these lines, we need to be reminded of Freud's rhetorical genius, how he was awarded the Goethe Prize for literature, and how the humanistic writings of the past found their way into a majority of his written corpus. The reference to Schiller needs to be analyzed to unearth its reference. One need not look too far, for Schiller's poem "Der Taucher" ("The Diver") combines oedipal with oceanic imagery. Briefly summarized, this short, one-stanza poem depicts the plight of a young page who accompanies a king and his retinue to a cliff overlooking a swirling whirlpool, described in the poem as an "ocean womb" that "boils and hisses ... a gaping chasm ... leading down to the depths of hell."[18] The king throws a goblet into the whirlpool, challenging anyone in his party to retrieve it, offering his blessing and crown in return. The page is the only one to step up to the challenge, diving into the feared whirlpool, miraculously emerging from its depths and exclaiming:

> Long life to the King! Let him rejoice
> Who breathes up here in the roseate light!
> For below all is fearful, of moment sad;
> Let not man to tempt the immortals e'er try,
> Let him never desire the things to see
> That with terror and night they veil graciously.

Filled with amazement and curiosity, the king asks the page to dive a second time to bring more word of the fearful depths contained in the whirlpool. With the additional promise of the king's daughter's hand in marriage, the page obliges, only never to return.

One does not have to read Freud's mind to see why he chose this poem. There was always a discernible psychoanalytic logic behind his inclusion of the writings of poets, novelists, and philosophers, and Schiller's "Diver" is no exception. In this case, it is clear that the latter is a metaphor for the psychoanalytic task. One "dives" into the whirlpool

---

[18] Parsons, *Enigma of the Oceanic Feeling*, 44ff.

of the unconscious, a whirlpool inhabited by powerful and dangerous forces. Moreover, the theme of Schiller's "Diver" is oedipal: the page embarks on his dive to receive the favor of the king, his daughter's hand, and eventually his crown, hence displacing the king himself. The poem, then, casts the "mystical" diver as performing an inner exploration quite like the one psychoanalysis enjoins one to undertake.

Given that throughout his works Freud's citation of poets had an internal logic and consistency, it is even more to the point that his appeal to Schiller's "Diver" in the context of Hindu mystical practices was not confined to the first chapter of *Civilization and Its Discontents*. In 1904, Freud had opportunity to counsel a student named Bruno Goetz (later a noted poet), from the University of Vienna. Goetz had been studying with the Indologist and Sanskrit scholar Leopold von Schroeder, known for his critical editions of Hindu scriptures as well as more historical and comparative work. Indeed, as mentioned at the outset of this chapter, Freud's era was one in which Eastern religious thought was just beginning to make its way westward into universities, and von Schroeder was one of but a handful of scholars who took a sustained, scholarly interest in Eastern scriptures and practices. Goetz had become especially interested in the *Bhagavad Gita*, relating to Freud how taken he was with its insight and profundity. In a series of letters recounting his meetings with Freud, Goetz recalls how he cautioned him about the depths of the inner dive catalogued by the "Hindu philosophers." Freud told him "to take care, young man take care" for, while it was right to be enthusiastic about such matters, one should "keep that cool head" lest one go mad:

> If... one without the aid of a clear intellect you become immersed in the world of the *Bhagavad Gita*, where nothing seems constant and everything melts into everything else, then you are suddenly confronted by nothingness.... Do you know what that means? And yet this nothingness is simply a European misconception.... Or, if misunderstood, it is madness.... What do these European would-be mystics know about the profundity of the East? They rave on, but they know nothing. And then they are surprised when they lose their heads and are not infrequently driven out of their minds.[19]

The two references to Europe indicate that Freud was aware of the substantial debates over the meaning of "nirvana" (in which von Schroder participated) that occupied scholars of the comparative study

---

[19] Ibid., 48.

of mysticism in the later nineteenth and early twentieth centuries.[20] Freud then went on to speak about Hindu scriptures:

The *Bhagavad Gita* is a great and powerful poem with awful depths. "And still it lay beneath me hidden deep in purple darkness there," says Schiller's diver, who never returns from his second brave attempt.... The Hindu Nirvana is not nothingness, it is that which transcends all contradictions ... the ultimate in superhuman understanding, an ice-cold, all-comprehending yet scarcely comprehensible insight.[21]

Once again we see Freud alluding to Schiller's "Diver" in characterizing the depths that mystical techniques could induce. Importantly, while the poem has a tragic ending, Freud's characterization of the "Hindu divers" indicates that the mystic, unlike the page, succeed in avoiding madness while gaining the "ice-cold, all-comprehending yet scarcely comprehensible insight." What we have here is a young Freud (recall this is 1904) who is in the process of reading his own emerging view of the psyche and its dynamics back into the wisdom contained in an honored classic text. The Hindu philosophers dimly saw and existentially grappled with what Freud was more clearly able to articulate as being the hazards of the unconscious, the conflicts of Oedipus, and the insights of psychoanalytic therapy. There is no evidence to indicate that Freud was endorsing the ontological views of Eastern religions; rather, he was reinterpreting their seminal insights through the lens of his emerging theory: nirvana was simply a culturally variant way of formulating the truths discovered and articulated by psychoanalysis, and the Hindu philosophers and "divers," it seems, had gone so far as to gain deep insights into the unconscious.

To reaffirm the above, recall our earlier analysis of the "psychoanalytic motto" (the full text of which we quoted in Chapter 1 and runs: "Where Id was, there Ego shall be"). In this text, which we can now add was written in 1931 and clearly meant as another response to Rolland, Freud states: "It is easy to imagine ... that certain mystical practices may succeed in upsetting the normal relations between the different regions of the mind, so that for instance, perception may be able to grasp happenings in the depths of the ego and in the id which were otherwise inaccessible to it." While he goes on to say that "[i]t may safely be doubted ... whether this road will lead us to the ultimate truths from

---

[20] See Guy Welbon, *The Western Interpreters of the Buddhist Nirvana* (Chicago: University of Chicago Press, 1968).
[21] Parsons, *Enigma of the Oceanic Feeling*, 48.

which salvation is to be expected," he also admits "that the therapeutic efforts of psychoanalysis have chosen a similar line of approach." In other words, Freud is once again drawing an equation between mystical techniques like yoga and psychoanalytic therapy. Freud admits that mystical practices, like psychoanalytic ones, help one dive into the depths of the unconscious, there to grasp the hidden, complex dynamics of the life of the unconscious. Where he draws the line is the further religious claim that such techniques help one access the "ultimate truths" that lead to "salvation." In other words, at best mystical practices can be in the service of gaining knowledge about unconscious contents and, properly interpreted within the therapeutic situation, could be healing and adaptive.

In sum, then, in the pages of *Civilization and Its Discontents* we have Freud presenting two different mystical phenomena (the state-like oceanic feeling and the transient mystical experience), offering two different models (preservation of primary narcissism and regressive insight into the unconscious) for their respective interpretation.

The *Unbehagen* of Eastern Religious Doctrines

There is another, neglected text in his correspondence with Rolland that deserves mention: his short, 1936 "open letter" (as he referred to it) to Rolland, written on the occasion of Rolland's sixtieth birthday and titled "A Disturbance of Memory on the Acropolis."[22] The paper is framed by Freud as a self-analytic session designed to explain the reason behind what he called a "feeling of derealization," one that led to a falsification of memory. The disturbance took place in 1904 during an annual trip he took with his brother Alexander. They had been planning to visit Corfu, a Greek Island, by way of the Italian port of Trieste. However, upon arriving in Trieste they were advised, due to inclement weather, to visit Athens instead. This option, says Freud, opened up the possible fulfilment of a long-standing wish to visit the Acropolis – a site that was obviously rife with symbolism – although he was depressed about the feasibility of accomplishing the trip. When they finally did make it to Athens, Freud, standing amid the ruins of the Acropolis, was astonished and moved to say: "So all this really does exist, just as we learnt at school!" He goes on to say that his utterance involved a "splitting of the ego" between the "person" who made the remark and the "person" who took cognizance

---

[22] Freud, "A Disturbance of Memory on the Acropolis," S.E. 22: 239–248.

of the remark. Whereas the first person was astonished at the existence of the Acropolis, the second person was astonished that the existence of the Acropolis was ever in doubt. Freud reasons that such a disturbance indicates he had a "feeling of derealization," which could be expressed as follows: "what I see here is not real."

Since the small paper is framed as an exercise in self-analysis, Freud then went on to inquire as to what psychological forces were responsible for the derealization and, before that, his depressed mood on learning he had an opportunity to go to Athens. Emphasizing the oedipal, Freud argued that his consternation was tied to the wish to "do better" than his father – a form of oedipal victory and success that invariably brought feelings of guilt:

> But here we come across the solution to the little problem of why it was that already at Trieste we interfered with our enjoyment of the voyage to Athens. It must be that a sense of guilt was attached to the satisfaction of having got so far: there was something about it that was wrong, that was from the earliest times forbidden.... It seems as though the essence of success were to have gotten further than one's father, and as though to excel one's father were something still forbidden.[23]

At Trieste, the fulfillment of the wish to go to Athens was only a possibility, leading to depression due to oedipal conflict. But once on the Acropolis, that possibility was turned into actuality: the wish was fulfilled. This unconscious wish was so powerful and forbidden that the ego had to resort to a new defense to ward off guilt, namely, derealization: "what I see here is not real."

What, one may ask, does this have to do with Rolland and Hinduism? By this point in time (1936) Rolland had sent him biographies of the two saints, Ramakrishna and Vivekananda (published in 1930). Freud knew that central tenets of Hinduism included maya ("the world is an illusion") and reincarnation. As in *Civilization and Its Discontents* Freud was interested in finding out the "developmental infrastructure" of such doctrines. It was, then, feelings of derealization that were the basis of maya – feelings that could be evoked though intense meditational activity, then misinterpreted by Hinduism as pertaining to the nature of reality. Along these lines it is relevant that in this "open letter" Freud also cast suspicion on reincarnation by stating that the phenomenon of déjà vu was "explained" by a "naively mystical and unpsychological attempt" to see it

---

[23] Ibid., 247.

as "evidence of a former existence of our mental self."[24] In other words, the true psychological core behind the (mistaken) doctrine of reincarnation was déjà vu. Finally, while Freud did not say so explicitly, one could extend his logic to posit a linked psychological phenomenon, the feeling of depersonalization (summarily put, the defensive thought "I am not real"), as the true psychological core of the (mistaken) mystical doctrine of the illusory nature of the "self," best represented in the Buddhist doctrine of "anatta" (no-self).

Freud offered two other important observations that merit our attention. First, while Freud wrote even less about Buddhism than Hinduism, the little he did say has cast a lasting shadow on the psychoanalytic dialogue with Buddhism. Specifically, an almost off-the-cuff remark, in which Freud equated Thanatos with the "nirvana principle" (in his famous work *Beyond the Pleasure Principle* [1920]), has come to represent what is taken to be his rather disparaging view of Buddhism. By this Freud meant that while part of our instinctual constitution strives to make ever greater unities with others (i.e., Eros), its warring counterpart (Thanatos) is that which strives to reduce psychic tension and limit growth and complexity by compulsively repeating patterns of behavior and regressively actualizing an earlier inorganic state (i.e., death). Second, recalling our discussion in the last chapter, the existential implication of this view becomes evident when, while commenting in *Civilization and Its Discontents* on the "programs for life" (i.e., ways of fulfilling happiness) as found in religious traditions, he mentions "the wisdom of the East." Freud goes on to suggest that, with respect to the latter, the path of the hermit is one option, in that it adopts the plan of voluntary isolation in order to avoid suffering. In this sense, the worldly wisdom of the East prescribes that one "kill off the instincts," which, of course, is reminiscent of the death instinct. Needless to say, this was not Freud's stated preference (i.e., "to work and to love"). This is crucial, for while Freud was willing to say that Eastern introspective practices could lead to insights into the unconscious, he was also alerting the reader that such insights, if taken under the banner of religious ideology (the cultural super-ego), might prescribe taking those insights in the service of a "program for life" whose aims were at odds with the more rational aims of psychoanalysis.

---

[24] Parsons, *Enigma of the Oceanic Feeling*, 83.

Linking back to the lessons offered in *Civilization and It Discontents*, then, one could say that the above indicates that Freud was doing for Eastern religions what he did for Western ones. Religious traditions that utilized doctrines like maya, anatta, and reincarnation were examples of the "unpsychological proceedings" of the (religious) cultural super-ego. And, as with Western religions, Freud offered a corrective concerning their doctrines: a developmental infrastructure and "basement theology" that revealed their true psychological origins (e.g., derealization, depersonalization, Thanatos) while offering a better solution: a secular cure of souls designed to heighten the ability to love and work.

FREUD'S TURN TO THE EAST: CRITIQUES

Freud's observations on Eastern religions have evoked a series of notable scholarly responses. Their diversity can be organized with respect to the following rubrics: (1) the definitional problem with respect to the use of the term "mysticism," (2) responses from those in the first period of the psychology–comparativist dialogue, (3) reflexive critiques, and (4) responses from those in the second and third periods of the psychology–comparativist dialogue. Each of these rubrics houses not only cautionary tales but also lessons that we can carry forward in the pursuit of a revised psychoanalytic tool kit.

The Definitional Problem: "Mysticism"

In previous chapters we noted how Freud entered into the definitional debate over the "what" of religion. We can now add that both he and Rolland entered into a subset of that debate: the meaning of the term "mysticism." While in a colloquial, everyday sense its referent may be readily apparent, even unquestioned, in academia things are different: there is no one agreed-on definition of the term that adequately captures the multiple, diverse phenomena that have been termed "mystical." Given this, where should we locate the Freud–Rolland debate over the meaning of the oceanic feeling? To ascertain that, one must proceed historically and genealogically.

The origin of the term "mysticism" starts with the Greek mystery religions where "mystikos," derived from the verb *muo* (to close), lacked any direct reference to the transcendent, referring only to the hidden or secret elements of ritualistic activities. It was later picked up by the early Church Fathers, becoming an adjective ("mystical theology" and "mystical contemplation"), which found its meaning and definition with respect to three interrelated contexts: biblical, liturgical, and spiritual. Implicit in such terms was the notion that mystical experience brought one into contact with a transcendent reality. However, it is important to note that such experiences could be accessed only through the auspices of Church and tradition, a total religious matrix. Adding even more complexity, modern comparativists argue that one cannot assume that the Christian version of mysticism is the "same" as the mystical element in other religious traditions, as if the Buddhist nirvana, the Hindu moksha, and the Muslim fana are exact equivalents. Each religious tradition defines its aims and understanding of the self with respect to its own terminology and within a total religious matrix, and one cannot simply dispense with such contextualization without risk of mischaracterizing the phenomena (the "case," so to speak) under investigation.[25]

Where, then, does the oceanic feeling fit in this frame? As Michel de Certeau has catalogued, it was not until the sixteenth and seventeenth centuries that one finds the emergence of mysticism as a noun (*la mystique*), but now altered: mysticism is framed as a subjective "experience" divorced from Church and tradition and the view of the divine as "God" was replaced by the generic term "the Absolute," now framed "as an obscure, universal dimension of man, perceived or experienced as a reality [*un réel*] hidden beneath a diversity of institutions, religions, and doctrines."[26] Mysticism became democratized, now conceived of as an innate part of human equipment, subject to investigation and interpretation from a psychological perspective, and associated with a laundry list of generic terms (e.g., peak experiences, joy, bliss, transcendence of space and time, sense of immortality). William James, Carl Jung, and Rolland were all operating with this notion of "mysticism." Indeed, de Certeau himself confirms this by calling attention to what he calls a "significant debate": that between none other than Rolland and Freud over the nature of the "oceanic feeling." It is here, thinks de Certeau, that Rolland's efforts to secure a "mystical psychoanalysis" mark the historical trend toward a noninstitutional form of mysticism and (psycho)spirituality.

---

[25] See William B. Parsons, ed., *Teaching Mysticism* (New York: Oxford University Press, 2011).

[26] M. de Certeau, "Mysticism," *Diacritics* 22 (1992): 11–25.

This is further corroborated by Rolland's letter of December 5, 1927, to Freud. He insinuated that the oceanic feeling was independent of, even prior to, Churches and their accoutrements, to the extent that, as he put it, "it is inside the Churches (whichever they may be) that true 'religious' sentiment is least available."

In our terminology, then, Rolland's entry into the psychology–comparativist dialogue shaded into his advocacy of the development of the psychoanalytic transformational school, which, we can now add, is akin to a psychoanalytic version of psycho-spirituality. This trend has come to fruition for many in contemporary culture who use psychological formulations for the purposes of organizing, monitoring, and expressing the need for wholeness, numinous experiences, and individuation. Such systems (which include psycho-spiritualities like those of Carl Jung, Abraham Maslow, and transpersonal psychology) have enabled those who seek a modern, unchurched, nontraditional way of mapping religious proclivities. It would be accurate to say that psychological forms of "modern" mysticism and spirituality (i.e., psycho-spiritualties), in their status as noninstitutional and unchurched, are deracinated cultural products of classic, traditional mysticism ("mystical theologies"). They seek the "juice" of peak experiences (to use Maslow's phrase) without what they consider to be the often mendacious accoutrements invariably advocated by church and tradition.

The problem is that Rolland, arguing from his own experience, posited his oceanic feeling, in its widest sense, as essentially equivalent to "mysticism everywhere." Yet even within the "tradition" of psycho-spirituality one gets different versions of the perennial "core" of mysticism. If one goes by the framings offered by the various theorists in this tradition, one cannot say that their versions of the mystical core are equivalent: Rolland's oceanic feeling, Jung's Self archetype, and Maslow' peak experiences are descriptively different and, as a result, indicate quite different cores. Given this, the matter is then further complicated if one extends any particular psycho-spiritual form of mysticism to be "the same" as that found in Buddhism, Hinduism, and indeed all mysticism. To this point, even in his own day Rolland's easy link between his own mysticism and "mysticism everywhere" had its detractors. For example, Yogi Sri Krishnaprem, an advocate of Bengali Vaishnavism (a theistic Hindu tradition), objected to Rolland's vague, generic "oceanic feeling" as perennial core. The latter, he said, was really a "vague Wordsworthian Spirit divine which rolls though all things," and that while "the ocean may be a great thing," it was not the same as, much less equivalent to, "the infinitely more maddening sense-destroying beauty of Sri Krishna" as bequeathed to "the living experience of the [theistic] mystics."[27]

The above cautionary tales suggest that one should de-link Rolland's "mysticism" from other forms as framed in diverse religious traditions. In other words, Freud's analysis pertains to a single case history, that of Rolland, itself being in the "tradition" of psycho-spirituality and thus not equivalent to the numerous and multiple varieties of Hindu mysticism or, for that matter, to "mysticism everywhere." To buttress this line of thought, the contemporary academic study of mysticism has thoroughly debunked perennialism. In its place stands what has been called "constructivism" or "contextualism," which, by virtue of compelling epistemological and textual critiques, amounts to a "plea for differences," where mystical experiences, states, and their associated contemplative techniques are posited as different not only degree but also in kind.[28] Making an analogy with psychoanalytic maps of the personality, one could say that what falls under the definitional rubric of "mysticism" is as various as what falls under the rubric of "psycho-neuroses": one would not equate an obsessional neurosis with a borderline narcissistic disorder, nor should the latter be therapeutically engaged as the former is. This is not to discount the efficacy of positing that mysticism and its doctrines may contain elements of developmental determinants. Rather, it is to allow for the possibility that yet other forms may require not only adaptive but transformational models, and that even transformational models, which offer a generic mystical dimension to consciousness, are best served when reflexively "in dialogue" with representatives of the tradition in question, if only to ensure a correct framing of "the case" in question.

Dialogical Responses: Rolland, Bose, and Kosawa

Responses to Freud in the initial period of the psychology and religion movement came from three of his major correspondents: the disillusioned Catholic Romain Rolland, the Indian psychoanalyst Girindrasakar Bose, and the Japanese analyst Heisaku Kosawa. Like their counterparts in the psychology–theology dialogue, all three shared the general complaint concerning Freud's definitional strategy. It would be fair to say that the

---

[27] Parsons, *Enigma of the Oceanic Feeling*, 117.
[28] The paradigmatic statement of this school can be found in S. Katz., ed., *Mysticism and Philosophical Analysis* (New York: Oxford University Press, 1980).

three men thought that Freud's contribution was limited to what we can call the "common man's" Hinduism and Buddhism and that the wisdom of Eastern religions contained a depth dimension that transcended such developmental determinants. Again, like their aforementioned counterparts, they linked new definitional strategies to alternate conceptions of the person (i.e., theological anthropology) and the divine. Further, they offered a few new strategies that will add to our revised psychoanalytic tool kit.

Rolland's Counter

Rolland's request to Freud was that he investigate the oceanic feeling in the hopes that a "mystical psychoanalysis" might result. He affirmed the latter in his biographies of the Hindu saints by stating that he was convinced that the theories of the "modern psycho-physiologist" would be eventually able to harness the wisdom of mysticism. We have seen what Freud made of his request. Rolland's counter, which Freud rejected, implicated not only a new definitional strategy and conception of the unconscious but also an alternate framing of mystical practices and a revised instinct theory.

We have seen that Rolland defined the essence of religion as consisting in the mystical oceanic and that the latter necessitated a corresponding (transformational) change in the nature of the unconscious. Going further, he agreed with Freud's view of mystical practices up to a point. As he colloquially put it, the "ancient Yogis did not wait for Dr. Freud to teach them that the best cure for the mind is to make it look its deeply hidden monsters straight in the face."[29] He framed yoga as a "science of the soul" that helped one gain access to unconscious contents. On the other hand, Rolland found psychoanalytic evaluations of mystical practices to be limited. So it is, in differing from Freud, Rolland posited that the ultimate aim of Yoga was to help one access the deepest layers of the unconscious. In so doing, he explicitly engaged one of the Jamesian "marks" of mystical experience – "noesis" (i.e., mystical claims to knowledge) – framing it as the central problem of mysticism. Rolland understood that in dealing with complex matters of mystical epistemology, one had to engage the ruling philosophical figure of Immanuel Kant, who had argued the impossibility of truly knowing the divine (the "noumenon")

---

[29] Parsons, *Enigma of the Oceanic Feeling*, 66–67.

given the conditions and limits of human cognition. Without providing any compelling philosophical arguments, Rolland nevertheless claimed that "centuries before Kant" various Indian philosophers "had already predicated and even surpassed" his limited view. The secret, thought Rolland, lay in a cognitive faculty he termed mystical "intuition" that, accessed and developed through yoga, enabled one to transcend individual consciousness and merge with the Absolute.[30] Therein lay an impasse between him and Freud that never went beyond this initial stage. Nevertheless, the two men's correspondence can be credited with setting the problem.

Rolland linked to this a subsequent critique of Freud's structural model that amounted to questioning the adequacy of his instinct theory (which, in the nomenclature of religious studies, can be referred to as how to conceptualize "the body"). Rolland knew of and thought to be valid the Hindu tantric view of the body. The latter posits an esoteric physiology: a spiritual energy (kundalini) that circulates from the perineum to the crown of the head, moving through the chakras (i.e., psycho-spiritual centers) found at various points in the body. Tantra admits to there being sexual and aggressive energies, but holds that such energies characterize the lower chakras and are not to be simply sublimated but alchemically transformed into a higher spiritual energy. When such energies pierce all the chakras and ascends to the crown of the head, it culminates in divine realization. Yogic practices are designed, then, to awaken and develop one's kundalini. Some advanced practitioners, such as Ramakrishna, were capable of transmitting this divine energy to heal and raise the level of consciousness in believers (as he had done, notes Rolland, with his disciple Vivekananda).[31] From this new conception of the body it is not so much that Freud was wrong but limited. From the tantric view of the body and its energies, Freud got to only the "third chakra."[32] The latter suggests that one outcome of a bona fide dialogue between psychoanalytic

---

[30] Ibid., chapter 3.
[31] R. Rolland, *The Life of Ramakrishna* (Calcutta: Advaita Ashrama, 1965), 216, 240.
[32] The saying is attributed to Bhagwan Rajneesh. As Kripal comments: "When the Tantric guru Bhagwan Rajneesh observed that 'Freud only got to the third *chakra*,' he was saying at least two things, namely, that Freud's drive theory and tantra's *kundalini* yoga are comparable models of occult energy and sublimation, and that Freud missed the 'deeper' or 'higher' bliss of the id beyond the first three centers of the anal, the genital, and digestive systems (that is, the first three *chakras*). Freud, in other words, was not wrong; he simply did not go far enough." See J. Kripal, *Esalen: America and the Religion of No Religion* (Chicago: University of Chicago Press, 2011), 144.

and tantric conceptions of the body could end by relativizing psychoanalysis within the broader tantric physiology as but one stage in the ascent of the kundalini.

Bose's Complaint

Rolland was not the only proponent of Eastern religions with whom Freud corresponded. Commensurate with his desire to internationalize psychoanalysis, he was always on the lookout for those "brainworkers" and "cultural elite" who might aid his cause. He found another such prominent conduit in Girindrasekhar Bose (1887–1953), who became the primary advocate of psychoanalysis in India.

Freud's correspondence with Bose ran from 1921 to 1937, comprised close to two dozen letters, and was virtually concurrent with his correspondence with Rolland (1923–1939).[33] Bose received his medical degree from Calcutta Medical College (1910) and received the first doctor of science degree awarded in India (1921) for his doctoral thesis titled "The Concept of Repression." It was the publication of the latter, which contained some of the pivotal metapsychological insights and concepts he had come to formulate through practicing his own brand of psychotherapy, that was his initial intellectual salvo in his correspondence with Freud. When Bose gifted Freud on the occasion of his seventy-fifth birthday an ivory statue of the Indian god Vishnu (see Figure 6.1), Freud gave it a place of honor on his desk in London, noting how it symbolized the "proud conquest it [psychoanalysis] has made in foreign countries."[34] By 1922 Bose had helped found the first Indian psychoanalytic society in Calcutta, beginning a fruitful history of Indian psychoanalysts, not the least of which include S. C. Mitra and Tarun Sinha, successive presidents of the Indian Psychoanalytic Society after Bose's death, and Sudhir Kakar, a prominent student of Erik Erikson and the leading contemporary Indian psychoanalyst.

What is of importance for our purposes is how Bose, reflecting strategies we have seen before, countered Freud by offering revisions to psychoanalytic theory. Like Rolland, Bose proclaimed that Hinduism contained an introspective wisdom that pointed to the existence of a

---

[33] For a comprehensive overview and analysis of the Freud–Bose correspondence, see A. Hiltebeitel, *Freud's India: Sigmund Freud and India's First Psychoanalyst Girindrasekhar Bose* (New York: Oxford University Press, 2018).

[34] See Vaidyanathan and Kripal, eds., *Vishnu on Freud's Desk*, 81.

FIGURE 6.1 An ivory statue of the Hindu God Vishnu, gifted to Freud by the Indian psychoanalyst Girindrasekhar Bose on the occasion of his seventy-fifth birthday.

transformational dimension to consciousness. In so doing, he argued for an addition to Freud's structural model: a grand metapsychological concept he dubbed the "theoretical ego." The latter targets "the average man's 'I' that feels the continuity of experience" and, as such, can be said to be the "hypothetical entity which maintains the continuity of mental experience both conscious and unconscious . . . the thread which keeps the individual beads together in a necklace."³⁵ As such, the theoretical ego is "the great reservoir of all wishes both conscious and unconscious. It includes within itself the Freudian ego, the id, and the super-ego, in fact, all manifestations of mental life."³⁶ Bose, who had an allegiance to the Upanishads and Advaita Vedanta, seems to have imported Hindu philosophy into the notion of a theoretical ego. As Hiltebeitel notes, the latter embodies the characteristics of a *jivatman* (a "living Self") and employs Hindu images in its description: "[Bose's] Vedanta-oriented readers and patients could recognize it as synonymous with the *jivatman*: the self caught up in *samsaric* life that would nonetheless be theoretically (ontologically and "ultimately") free not only from reincarnation caused by karmic suffering, but from biological drives."³⁷

Bose formally articulated this transformational position in a small paper titled "The Psychological Outlook of Hindu Philosophy," delivered at the Indian Philosophical Congress in 1930. This paper can be framed as Bose's Hindu counterpart to Pfister's Protestant response to Freud as contained in his "The Illusion of the Future." Entering the definitional debate, Bose was willing to admit, as had Pfister, to a form of religion where God is a projection and designed to cater to infantile needs. He sees this "social type" encoded in the *Bhagavad Gita*, where one finds those who "believe" due to personal needs or external dangers and, as a result, creates "God out of his own mental image."³⁸ That said, he also argued that psychoanalysis needed to recognize the potentially adaptive value of religion: "religion served as a palliative for human suffering and was deemed therefore 'practical' for Bose rather than as the obsessive, collective neurosis that it was for Freud."³⁹ But then, going even further, he offered the example of the Upanishads, framed as a higher, introspective, and psychological form of religion. Here the religious seeker is redefined as bound not by feelings of need and danger but by the need for wisdom. This kind of person asks pertinent and sophisticated psychological questions, such as, "How do dreams arise" and "which is the agent in the body that feels pleasure?"⁴⁰ In asking such questions, and employing different introspective techniques such as yoga to find their answers, the early Upanishadic *rishis* accessed a deeper level of consciousness, termed

---

³⁵ See Hiltebeitel, *Freud's India*, 114. ³⁶ Ibid. ³⁷ Ibid., 119.
³⁸ G. Bose, "The Psychological Outlook of Hindu Philosophy," *Indian Journal of Psychology* 5 (1930): 119–146.
³⁹ Hiltebeitel, *Freud's India*, 126.
⁴⁰ Bose, "The Psychological Outlook of Hindu Philosophy," 125–126.

by Bose "pure consciousness" (consciousness without an object), which had the therapeutic effect of leading to a condition in which "all pains cease to exist, and there is a peculiar feeling of blissfulness."[41] In a psychoanalytic reframing of the Upanishadic claim that the meditative insight into Brahman results in "Sat, Chit, Ananda" (Truth, [pure] Consciousness, Bliss), Bose was offering a variant of Rolland's desire to see the establishment of a "mystical psychoanalysis."

Kosawa's Missive

The third important figure in the emergence of the psychology–comparativist dialogue was the Buddhist Heisaku Kosawa (1897–1968), the first president of the Japan Psychoanalytic Society and often referred to as the father of Japanese psychoanalysis. Kosawa was intrigued enough with Freud's ideas that, from 1931 to 1933, he took it upon himself to travel to Vienna, there to receive a personal analysis with Richard Sterba, one of Freud's colleagues, further being trained by Paul Federn, another one of Freud's colleagues, for the purpose of legitimating his status as a full-fledged analyst. He met with Freud (he said he loved the "sitting Buddha" in front of the bookshelf in Freud's study), engaged in a correspondence with him, even sent him as a gift a portrait of Mount Fuji (see Figure 6.2). Kosawa returned to Japan to set up his own practice, claiming that Japanese patients were best served by Japanese analysts.

In order to understand how Kosawa countered Freud's views on religion, one must first provide a brief summary of the nature of his Buddhist leanings. Brought up in a household harboring only a trace of Buddhism, things changed for Kosawa in his early twenties when he encountered Chikazumi Jokan (1870–1941), a monk in the tradition of Pure Land (Jodo Shinshu) Buddhism, and the writings of Shinran, its thirteenth-century Japanese founder. Pure Land traces its history to China and originating in India, and valorizes the Mahayana values of compassion for others and devotion to the saving power of the Amitabha Buddha (a "transcendent" divinity who had created a heavenly Pure Land to which adherents would travel after death). Mediated through Shinran and Jokan, Kosawa became enamored of the Pure Land distinction between *jiriki* (the power of the individual to save oneself) and *tariki* (the saving power of the Other, in this case, Amitabha). For Kosawa it

---

[41] Ibid., 133.

FIGURE 6.2 *Mount Fuji* by Yoshida Hiroshi (1929), woodblock in the Freud Museum, London. The accompanying plaque notes that it "was given to Sigmund Freud as a gift in 1932 by Japanese psychoanalyst Heisaku Kosawa. Dr. Kosawa came from Japan to Europe to study psychoanalysis and gave this print to Freud before beginning analysis with him. Freud wrote to thank Dr. Kosawa for 'the beautiful picture which presents to my eyes what I have read so much about and a sight which I myself have not been granted.'"

was *tariki* that finally held sway to the point that a signature insight of life was to realize the fact of one's weakness, frailty, defilements, and complete inability to manufacture enlightenment. So it is that Kosawa emphasized *shinjin*, or "true entrusting," that moment in which one realized that because one is incapable of procuring salvation by oneself one must turn to the Other (again, the compassion and grace of Amitabha). Even here one comes to understand that such faith is not part of the human equipment but due to Amitabha reaching out in love ("The voice with which I call Amida Buddha / Is the voice with which Amida Buddha calls to me").[42] The realization of Amitabha's unconditional love, grace, and saving power despite one's defilements led to a specific character change: the "melting" of resistance and anger, the turn to repentance, and, as a

---

[42] C. Harding et al., eds., *Religion and Psychotherapy in Modern Japan* (New York: Routledge, 2015), chapters 1 and 5.

result, the overwhelming gratitude for being unconditionally accepted and loved. While the comparison is oversimplified, one can at least see how some scholars have drawn affinities between this characterization of Pure Land Buddhism and Protestant Christianity.

Kosawa parlayed his differences with Freud into a critique of the latter's views on religion. For example, entering as those before him into definitional debates about religion, he claimed that *Totem and Taboo* was not aimed at a "unified" state of the religious mind, and hence not "really" about an analysis of religion at all. *Future of an Illusion*, based on Oedipus and its attendant emotions of fear and guilt, was also not a "true" form of religion. Rather, "true religion with a unified state of mind" was best exemplified in Shinran, Jokan, and Pure Land Buddhism. Moreover, the realized aim of Buddhism and its greatest figures, constituted by the melting of hatred and guilt into heartfelt repentance, gratitude, and compassion, was precisely that which psychoanalysis could help to facilitate. Again, fiddling with definitions of what "being religious" means, Kosawa held that it is this framing of a successful therapeutic intervention that was held up as a "religious state of mind." Buddhism and psychoanalysis, then, were wholly compatible. As he put it: "I cannot help but compare Dr. Freud's mindset with that of St. Shinran."[43] It is perhaps redundant to note that the general strategies employed by Kosawa echo those utilized by Pfister. That said, the exact details differ, one being a champion of Protestantism and the other of Pure Land Buddhism.

Reflexive Critiques

Freud's respondents shared the view that while psychoanalysis did indeed offer a tool kit that illumined the "common man's" element and developmental infrastructure of Eastern religions, his narrow definitional strategy in conjunction with the limited scope of his structural theory interfered with a fuller understanding and interpretation of other, more developed religious "cases." At the same time, there was another element that they felt interfered with a judicious treatment, namely, what we have called the lack of reflexivity.

Rolland, for example, leveled an ethno-psychological critique by arguing that Western psychologies contained value-laden cultural

---

[43] Ibid., 123.

assumptions. He chastised psychoanalysis for harboring "a Proud and Puritanical faith, whose prejudices they no longer see because those prejudices have become their second nature."[44] The real-life consequences, thought Rolland, could be disastrous: a mystic like Ramakrishna would undoubtedly be "placed in a lunatic asylum under a daily douche of psycho-therapy."[45] In other words, culturally conditioned models of the mind in conjunction with the lack of a transformational dimension could result in a misconstrual of the case and, invariably, therapeutic violence to the person.

Bose, on the other hand, targeted the universalism of Oedipus as the core nuclear conflict in the developmental cycle. Mirroring anthropological critiques of psychoanalysis and prefiguring the development of pre-oedipal (object-relations) theory, Bose argued that psychoanalysis had to be culturally reframed to fit the kinds of developmental vicissitudes found in Indian culture. Indian culture highlighted certain wishes (e.g., "the desire to be female"), born of identification and early narcissistic formation, that were more primal than the fear of castration. According to Bose's case histories, such wishes were "more easily unearthed in Indian male patients than in European."[46] In some cases, this new data would call for an "adjustment" of the oedipal wish. These revisions, in turn, impacted how Bose used them to analyze Hinduism. Developmentally speaking, he noted that in India, the "Oedipus mother is very often a combined parental image and this is a fact of great importance. I have reasons to believe that much of the motivation of the 'maternal deity' is traceable to this source."[47]

Similarly, Kosawa disputed the primacy of Oedipus. During the course of his correspondence with Freud he sent him a paper, "Zaiakuishikino nishu" ("Two Types of Guilt Consciousness: Oedipus and Ajase"), originally published in 1935 in the *Tokyo Journal of Psychoanalysis*. Freud found the Greek myth of *Oedipus Rex* and Western forms of literature such as Shakespeare's *Hamlet* fruitful as windows into the core psychological dynamic that determined human existence. In turn, Kosawa argued that Japanese culture had a culturally distinct form of a nuclear complex (i.e., the characteristic core of neuroses, which for Freud was the Oedipus complex), which found expression in the Pure Land myth of

---

[44] Parsons, *Enigma of the Oceanic Feeling*, 70.   [45] Ibid.
[46] See Vaidyanathan and Kripal, eds., *Vishnu on Freud's Desk*, 3.
[47] T. C. Sinha, "Development of Psycho-analysis in India," *International Journal of Psychoanalysis* 47 (1966): 430.

King Ajase. The latter, found in some notable Pure Land Buddhist texts (e.g., the Nirvana Sutra and Shinran's Kyogyoshinsho), describes the psychological dynamics between an Indian prince and his mother. While variations of the myth can be found, what is important is that Kosawa thought it represented a culturally distinct pre-oedipal complex he dubbed the "Ajase complex." In Kosawa's hands, the psychological core of the latter was constituted by the recognition that offspring invariably harbor feelings of hatred, ambivalence, and guilt toward their mothers and that the process of overcoming such feelings is facilitated through gaining insight into maternal acts of self-sacrifice and altruism. In other words, Kosawa's focus was more on the mother than the father, and hence on pre-oedipal dynamics rather than oedipal ones. Kosawa then used such insights to develop a new kind of relation with his patients: the *torokashi* (or "melting") technique. The analyst, evincing a form of unconditional maternal love and acceptance, could help "melt" hatred and resistance while engendering in the patient a form of heartfelt repentance. His therapeutic motto, again reflecting Buddhist influence, was "Shiran no kokoro wo motte, seishin bunseki wo suru" ("Doing psychoanalysis in the spirit of [or possessing the heart of] Shinran").[48] While Buddhism in and of itself may have been left outside the consulting clinic, it is clear that his therapy reflected a form of Buddhist-inspired transcendence.

These early reflexive critiques were followed by those of later members of the psychology–comparativist dialogue. For example, the contemporary Indian psychoanalyst Sudhir Kakar wonders if those classic-reductive psychoanalytic models that frame the Hindu striving for moksha as escapist and an abdication of the reality principle reflect cultural assumptions. He asks the extent to which normative ideas about maturity, the nature of reality, and positive/negative resolutions of conflicts and complexes end up being cast in the "scientific" language of "psychoanalytic universals." The latter, if applied without reflexivity, "lend credence to the position of an increasing number of third-world intellectuals who maintain that the western sciences of man, including psychoanalysis, are in fact culture-bound ethnosciences."[49] The Buddhist psychologist Lama Namgyal Dorje (Harvey Aronson) offers a portable lesson when, asking how one can engage the cultural other in a sensitive, respectful manner, he seizes on the observations of the social theorist Richard Schweder, who

---

[48] C. Harding et al., eds., *Religion and Psychotherapy in Modern Japan*, 128ff.
[49] S. Kakar, "Reflections on Psychoanalysis, Indian Culture, and Mysticism," *Journal of Indian Philosophy* 20 (1982): 289–297.

thinks any encounter with "the other" involves four distinct stages: (1) *thinking by means of the other*, which obliges us to respect the other to the extent that we recognize that they have harnessed truths unavailable or deeply buried in our own culture; (2) *getting the other straight*, which necessitates an understanding of the internal logic, worldview, and values of another culture as well as the admission that they are relatively true; (3) *seeing areas where others may have limitations*, which realizes that other cultures, like our own, are incomplete; and (4) *being aware of oneself in the context of engagement with the other*, which heightens the reflexive self-awareness of how one's own culture operates unconsciously, and sometimes in a prejudicial manner, in the encounter with the Other.[50]

Dialogical Critiques: Second Period

From the perspective of those participating in the psychology–comparativist dialogue in the second and third periods, Freud's first-period psychoanalytic studies are cast as suffering from the general inadequacies of comparative studies of that era: limited and inadequate translations; misleading and incomplete secondary scholarship; little if any patient data or input from practitioners, lamas, and gurus; superficial comprehension of the complexity of Eastern traditions; and absence of personal familiarity with meditational techniques. Such factors are exacerbated by the lack of reflexivity: an "ethno" dimension that increased the possibility of reductive, colonialist, and Orientalist interpretations.[51]

Dramatic social, political, and religious shifts in the 1950s and 1960s led to discernible changes in the sophistication of the psychology–comparativist dialogue. This new cultural soil gave rise to the beatniks and the hippies, the civil rights movement and anti-war sentiments, the San Francisco Zen Center, the Esalen Institute, and, later, Chogyam Trungpa Rinpoche's Tibetan Buddhist Naropa University. There was general disillusionment with reigning forms of Christian morality and doctrine, seen as mendacious and politically linked to racism (Southern segregation) and colonialism (the Vietnam War). Multiple forms of therapy were widely disseminated and the taking of entheogens and sexual experimentation authorized. Many looked to the East for cultural

---

[50] H. Aronson, *Buddhist Practice on Western Ground* (Boston: Shambala, 2004).
[51] See Parsons, "Themes and Debates in the Psychology–Comparativist Dialogue" and "Psychoanalysis Meets Buddhism."

resources, touted such figures as Gandhi and the Dalai Lama, and, most important for our purposes, developed a singular fascination with Eastern religions. Linked to this was the slow translation of Asian religious ideation and practices into Western psychological terms. The most impactful of the Hindu and Buddhist "missionaries" were familiar with Western psychological models, framed their traditions in tandem with that nomenclature, sought out noted Western psychologists for dialogue, and enjoined an emerging cadre of Asian psychologists to join in.

The psychoanalytic studies stemming from the second period (1945–1969) resulted in two significant advances: (1) the incorporation of meditational practices as part of the therapeutic process and (2) the adjustment of psychoanalytic aims of health. These advances evince an adaptive view of religion as well as what we have called reflexivity. The earliest of these advances are apparent in the well-known series of encounters between Buddhist practitioners, intellectuals, and psychologists (e.g., D. T. Suzuki, Shin'ichi Hisamatsu, Akihisa Kondo, Koji Sato) and Western intellectuals and practitioners within the psychoanalytic tradition (e.g., Karen Horney, Erich Fromm, Herbert Fingarette, Ed Maupin) – encounters that led to the creation of journals (e.g., *Psychologia, American Journal of Psychoanalysis*) and publication of significant books (e.g., *Zen Buddhism and Psychoanalysis*) devoted to the furthering of dialogue.[52]

To illustrate these important shifts, we may turn to a few notable figures. For example, Karen Horney is an illuminating example of dialogue and reflexivity at work. She met D. T. Suzuki in the winter of 1950 through the auspices of the Japanese psychologist Akihisa Kondo and two of her patients, Cathy and Cornelius Crane. Horney also began meditating under the tutelage of Suzuki at that time, followed by a summer tour through Japan and its Zen monasteries in 1952. It is clear that her mediational practice and dialogue with Suzuki and Japanese psychologists led her to reconfigure two central aspects of her "neo-Freudian" psychology: the "Real Self" and wholeheartedness. The Real Self was conceptualized as that inner core which drives self-realization, self-regulation, growth, joy, and wholeness. If the expression of the Real Self is blocked, then the person develops an inauthentic false-self orientation, catering to the whims of others and society at large. On the other hand, among the aims of a person exhibiting the expression of the Real

---

[52] See Parsons, "Psychoanalysis Meets Buddhism," 190ff.

Self was that of "wholeheartedness." Wholeheartedness points toward someone who is entirely absorbed in their actions, operating with all faculties while remaining at the same time quite oblivious to themself. One is emotionally sincere, authentic, and capable of putting all of one's energy and attention into the task at hand. As an example, Horney offered her observation of a professional waiter at an upscale New York restaurant who displayed impeccability, attentiveness, and absorption "in the moment" that could be applied to any endeavor undertaken during one's everyday existence.

This "reflexive" reframing of psychoanalytic therapy and normative conceptions of health was clearly influenced by Horney's dialogue with Suzuki and Japanese Buddhist psychologists. Horney thought that the mental skills and attributes developed through practicing "mindfulness" (e.g., focused attention and observation, mindful detachment, self-forgetfulness, and a general nonjudgmental attitude) were advances on Freud's techniques and could be integrated with great results into the clinical session. While therapy inevitably focused on engaging the content of experience, Horney began to shift her focus to not simply content but changing one's relationship to one's experience. Change became conceived of less in terms of striving to be something else and more in terms of simply accepting what one is in the present moment. It is in the acceptance itself that "change" occurs. Indeed, part of expressing the Real Self was dependent on the ability to be mindful, while wholeheartedness was facilitated by training the mind to be in the "now" moment.[53]

Erich Fromm followed suit by noting, in his *Zen Buddhism and Psychoanalysis*, how his conversations with Buddhists had altered his conclusions about the nature and aims of psychoanalytic therapy. Commenting on Freud's definition of health as found in his "psychoanalytic motto" ("Where Id was, there Ego shall be"), he observes that Freud's ideal was essentially negative, dealing with localized features of the unconscious such as symptom formation, conflict, and trauma. A more positive aim of health would enlarge Freud's purview by addressing what he called the "full recovery" of the unconscious and the "total experience of the total man." For Fromm, this meant overcoming the split between the socialized personal identity and the universal, empathic recognition of all potentialities and identities within oneself, thus "giving up the illusion of the separate ego."[54] Helpful in attaining this ideal was

---

[53] Ibid. [54] Ibid., 195.

the practice of Buddhism. He agreed with Suzuki that the experience of satori (as an instance of the general rubric of "mystical experience") was not a regression to primary narcissism, as many psychoanalysts continued to posit. Rather, for Fromm, satori was "the reception of the pre-intellectual immediate grasp of the child but on a new level, that of the full development of man's reason, objectivity, individuality. While the child's experience, that of immediacy and oneness, lies before the experience of alienation and the subject–object split, the enlightenment experience lies after it."[55] Fromm also agreed that the therapeutic integration of such experiences led to what Suzuki had called being an "artist of life," which included being freed from the regressive pull of the mother and authoritarian rule of the father, having arrived at the full development of reason, overcoming narcissism and greed, and being creative.

Two other reflexive, adaptive reformulations of psychoanalytic theory are important: that of Herbert Fingarette and Ed Maupin. Fingarette used the advances of ego psychology to promote a simple thesis: Zen is but a culturally relative form of psychoanalysis. But the sophistication and skillfulness of Fingarette's presentation, which utilized a case history (the first used within psychoanalysis in its dialogue with Buddhism) and a spectrum of ego-psychological terminology, went well beyond previous efforts. Fingarette argued that the paradoxical language of Zen (terms such as anatta) was not indicative of pathology but rather a culturally specific use of therapeutic terms that, when properly translated and contextualized in the therapeutic context, had exact analogs in the psychoanalytic clinical setting. For example, Fingarette argued that what was "lost" in Zen was not the self per se but the "transference self" with its attendant forms of anxiety and intrapsychic conflict. Harkening back to Freud and Rolland, Fingarette gave adaptive value to pre-oedipal states by arguing that "Zen therapy" enriched the autonomous ego with the residues of the "oceanic feeling" tempered by a lack of self-consciousness.

Ed Maupin, on the other hand, argued that Zen was indeed a "therapy" that worked via a series of regressed states. In its initial phase, it uncovered and "worked-through" the phase of primary process residue linked to the Oedipus complex. One then had access to the deeper, pre-oedipal fantasies of grandiosity and omnipotence. Once this phase had been managed (with the help of the Zen therapist/master), one then had the internal fortitude necessary to access the intuitive insight contained in

---

[55] Ibid.

the momentary insight into anatta, which afforded one the experience of wholeness and oneness. Additionally, Maupin introduced the idea of the "trained unconscious." What Zen-inspired regression tapped for Maupin were not only developmental vicissitudes but also perceptual and motor abilities registered in the unconscious – abilities waiting to be accessed, developed, and utilized. Zen training in archery and the martial arts was a case in point. The latter could lead to altered states of "flow" and even "supernormal" performances.[56]

Dialogical Critiques: Third Period

The inevitable effects of the culture-wide dissemination of Eastern religions, figures, and practices in the second period was the creation of a new cadre of young adults who took seriously such practices and engaged them on both existential and intellectual grounds. In the third period (1970 to present), many of them invested in careers (psychoanalysts, university professors, researchers), adding a new level of erudition to the dialogical relation between psychoanalysis and Eastern religions. Many of these practitioners and scholars continue to wear more than one professional hat: practicing psychoanalysts (who have been analysands) as well as teachers of meditation (who have been students of an assortment of masters/gurus). Their ongoing researches have been driven by a growing social base that is psychologically informed yet also hungry for spiritual nourishment – a trend evinced by the widespread growth of retreat centers, weekend workshops, local centers touting personal growth, and individual integrations of Eastern practices alongside psychoanalytic ones. It is not surprising, then, that the power of this social base has crept into multiple aspects of the practice of analysts and of the therapeutic expectations of analysands. The analyst Paul Cooper, for example, thinks that there is an undeniable cultural drift in this direction. He draws attention to the empirical fact that many of his analysands understand psychoanalytic therapy as part of their spiritual growth. He also notes that spiritual practices have influenced multiple dimensions of psychoanalytic therapy (e.g., theory, technique, training, supervision).[57]

---

[56] Ibid., 195ff.
[57] P. Cooper, "The Disavowal of the Spirit: Integration and Wholeness in Buddhism and Psychoanalysis," in *The Couch and the Tree*, ed. A. Molino (New York: North Point Press, 1998), 231–246.

While a comprehensive summary of such advances is beyond the limits of this chapter, two central trends can be noted. First, there is general agreement that psychoanalysis has a better grasp of the origins, subtleties, and vicissitudes of developmentally based behavioral patterns. Particularly with respect to deep neurotic deficiencies, it is psychoanalytic therapy, and not Eastern teaching and practice, which is the superior healing enterprise. This is in part due to the fact that Eastern religions have not amassed the detailed clinical evidence needed to theorize that dimension of the human personality. Importantly, and to this end, clinical evidence supports certain classic-reductive analyses: how the doctrine of "no-self" can ward off the burden of creating an adaptive identity and rationalize the lack of self-esteem, and how feelings of emptiness and the notion of "enlightenment" can be cathected narcissistically to cater to the needs of archaic forms of grandiosity ("I am enlightened, you are not"). Further, meditation can be problematic if unearthed unconscious content is simply observed (as meditation advises) and not engaged and worked through (as psychoanalysis advises). Finally, evidence from the use of Rorschach tests, case histories, and detailed observations from meditation-based communities also suggests that some "masters" exhibit forms of defensiveness, grandiosity, and pathology.[58] To be sure, such studies do not render all Buddhist thought, teaching, and teachers as indicative of pathology. Rather, assuming Buddhism is, like psychoanalysis, a healing enterprise, such studies offer conceptual frameworks for spying pathology when it occurs. To give further examples, such studies have noted the problematic dimensions operative within the transference that invariably marks the master–disciple relationship. Well catalogued in what can be called the "scandal literature," the list of problematic behaviors ranges from sexual and power abuse to outright criminality. Following in the footsteps of Freud, this literature has also been extended to the sociopolitical realm, as is illustrated in the studies on "Zen nationalism." The focus of the latter is on the racist, xenophobic, and misogynistic advice given by Zen masters to their students in the service of promoting Japanese fascism during World War II.[59]

A second trend, facilitated by theoretical developments into the developmental line of narcissism, object-relations, and transformational theory, is marked by the attempt to theorize how Buddhist practice is

---

[58] See Parsons, "Psychoanalysis Meets Buddhism."
[59] See B. D. Victoria, *Zen at War* (Lanham, MD: Rowman & Littlefield, 2006); B. D. Victoria, *Zen War Stories* (New York: Routledge, 2003).

not simply therapeutic and adaptive (as the second period studies argued) but soteriological; that Eastern religions catalog experiences and states that are outside the borders of existing psychoanalytic theory (in our terminology, the need to acknowledge a transformational dimension). The psychoanalyst Mark Epstein speaks to this when he says that something in Buddhism "reaches beyond therapy, toward a farther horizon of self-understanding that is not ordinarily accessible through psychotherapy alone."[60] Buddhism goes farther than psychoanalysis asking who the "I" is behind, for example, feelings of narcissistic emptiness and rage. In asking us to acknowledge the relativity of the narcissistic emotions, it lessens the import and centrality of such feelings. The shift from identifying with reactive emotions to looking at the foundational "I" and self that lie behind those feelings and is often identified with it is, according to Epstein, "the most important contribution Buddhism has to offer to the world of psychotherapy."[61] The key for Epstein and others lies in the correct practice of meditation. Properly practiced, meditation permeates the inner world so thoroughly that "no aspect remains available for narcissistic recruitment."[62] How the latter is to be understood and synthesized into a more inclusive healing enterprise that is clearly an expansion of psychoanalytic theory then becomes the task at hand.

A general frame for this attempt at synthesis lies in the work of the practicing psychoanalyst and Buddhist meditation teacher Jack Engler. Initially, Engler, like some of his counterparts in the psychology–theology dialogue, proposed a stage approach in which psychoanalysis and Buddhism map discrete states of a single developmental sequence, the former describing the lower stages of what he calls "conventional" development, the latter the more subtle, spiritual stages of what he calls "contemplative" development. In speaking to how these stages relate, Engler is not without recourse to the more pathological treatment of Buddhism, noting that mystical therapies like Buddhism can attract and even exacerbate the condition of those with narcissistic self-disorders. Such persons are not yet ready for the rigors of meditative life and better off with psychoanalytic therapies, which seek to help them "grow" a self. Once a cohesive enough self has developed, one can then engage in meditational exercises designed to gain insight into the reality that there is no enduring self, hence the phrase: "You have to be somebody before you are nobody." The two healing systems, then, are seen to have

---

[60] M. Epstein, *Thoughts without a Thinker* (New York: Basic Books, 1995), 130.
[61] Ibid., 220.   [62] Ibid., 134.

different aims: psychoanalysis aims to grow a cohesive self, Buddhism to realize there is "no self." Drawing on studies of meditation that explain how the heightened state of attention and concentration available to meditators allows them to retrace the representational process whereby a sense of self and other comes to exist, Engler claims that the insight into no-self literally breaks apart the underlying continuity of self. This insight is so profound that it entails an end to suffering altogether – a state, Engler observes, that Freud and psychoanalysis in general views as an "ideal fiction." Engler is quick to point out that the insight into anatta is not necessarily a discovery. Speaking reflexively, from the Buddhist perspective the common-sense understanding that an enduring self exists is an illusion. Indeed, Engler proposes the radical claim that the construction of a separate, enduring continuous self is a compromise formation with defensive aims. In other words, there is a deeper form of repression: we repress the fact of an unconstructed non-core to existence.[63] One could say that Engler, much like the tantric view of psychoanalysis as belonging to the lower chakras, is enabling a psychology–comparativist dialogue that ends up relativizing psychoanalytic theory and practice.

The psychoanalyst Jeff Rubin has modified Engler's sequence, arguing that his efforts amount to a "pseudo-complimentary" approach in which "the complexity and multidimensionality of human experience and development is obscured by linear, hierarchical, developmental models."[64] Rather, Rubin argues that the relation between psychoanalysis and Eastern religions "is more complex than the existing accounts suggest, forming not a singular pattern of influence but rather resembling a heterogeneous mosaic composed of elements that are – depending on the specific topic – antithetical, complementary and synergistic."[65] By "synergy" Rubin means that psychoanalysis investigates unconscious determinants, idealizing transferences, life-cycle difficulties, and the like, while Eastern techniques can help psychoanalysis with non-self-centered subjective states. These states are neither pathological or developmentally archaic states of nondifferentiation. Evinced by being in love, right-brain artistic activities, flow states, and meditative absorption, they are defined by Rubin as being "open to the moment without a sense of time,

---

[63] See J. Engler, "Therapeutic Aims in Psychotherapy and Buddhism," in *Transformations in Consciousness*, ed. K. Wilber, J. Engler, and D. Brown (Boston: Shambala, 1986), 17–52.
[64] J. Rubin, *Psychotherapy and Buddhism* (New York: Plenum Press, 1996), 49.
[65] Ibid., 51.

unselfconsciousness but acutely aware, highly focused and engaged yet related without fear," being further characterized "by heightened attentiveness, focus and clarity, attunement to the other as well as the self, non-self preoccupied exercise of agency, a sense of unity."[66] Thus framed, the respective views of personhood found in psychoanalysis and Eastern religious traditions are not better than one another. They are different and yet can be mutually enriching; they are "alternating positions of being rather than hierarchically ordered stages."[67] The melding together of psychoanalysis and Eastern modes of subjectivity can lead to "a bifocal conception of subjectivity." Rubin sees a new self emerging – a "species-self ... for whom both individuation and non-self centricity are seen as two interpenetrating facets of what it means to be a human being."[68]

[66] Ibid., 69. [67] Ibid., 75. [68] Ibid., 197.

7

Psychoanalysis and Religion beyond Freud

It was primarily after World War II, in the second (1945–1969) and third (1970 to present) periods of the psychology and religion movement, that classic Freudian psychoanalysis, having achieved the founder's wish of international dissemination, being informed by a new clinical base from diverse cultures, alternate complexes not named Oedipus, and a generational turnover of theorists, began to evince the creation of new clinical techniques and formulations. During this time, there emerged dozens of diverse figures who not only have come to dominate the contemporary "what" of psychoanalysis but have done so in ways that creatively assimilate the best of Freud while repudiating some of his less-compelling formulations. It is safe to say that Freud himself would have been uncomfortable with at least some of these innovations, particularly those that valorize an appreciative view of religion. At the same time, Freud was willing to admit that his efforts at applied psychoanalysis reflected his own proclivities; that his various analyses of religion were his "personal views, which coincide with those of many non-analysts and pre-analysts, but there are certainly many excellent analysts who do not share them"; and that his preferences "need deter no-one from using the non-partisan method of analysis for arguing the opposite view."[1] Indeed, many of his heirs took him up on that offer.

The sheer number and variety of individual theorists and new formulations that have been subsequently housed under the banner of "psychoanalysis" necessitate that choices have to be made, and our selection is

---

[1] See Freud and Pfister, *Psychoanalysis and Faith*, 117.

based on how certain theorists and concepts best illustrate the development of adaptive and transformational psychoanalytic models. In so doing, we are not saying that Freud should be wholly left behind. Indeed, properly qualified and judiciously applied, his formulations still have merit as part of our *inclusive* formula. It is, however, to point out that his various analyses are dependent on a specific model of the mind, a narrow definition of religion, and can benefit by more developed psychoanalytic formulations that are capable of nonreductive treatments of phenomena related to a more expansive rendering of religion.

EGO-PSYCHOLOGICAL ADVANCES

In theorizing about the ego, Freud established two intersecting models: (1) the ego as a "mechanism" (e.g., repression, sublimation, regression, projection), which functioned to defend against unwanted unconscious drives while helping one adapt to external reality, and (2) the ego as the repository of what Freud referred to as "abandoned object-cathexis," which in experience-near language amounts to the felt sense of I or Self. The latter was conceived by Freud as being built up in part of idealizations and identifications with loved "objects" such as one's parents and significant others. Over the course of development, previously loved and idealized objects (persons) are partially left behind (which is to say, "de-idealized"), as is the norm during the process of maturation. At the same time, such identifications are internalized and memorialized as part of one's own psychological structure (i.e., one's ideals, values, aims, and pursuits). These two lines of ego theorizing became the theoretical basis for the development of ego psychology and object-relations theory, the former building more on the mechanistic ego and the latter the "relational" self. That said, the difference between the two is not as binary or absolute in theory or in practice. For example, we will see that Erik Erikson's ego psychology contains a good bit of theorizing about the pre-oedipal or narcissistic line of development, even if not named as such. We will attend to ego psychology in this section, and object-relations in the next.

A Brief History

The emergence of ego psychology is initially apparent in the work of Anna Freud (Sigmund's daughter), who tellingly wrote a book published just before Freud died called *The Ego and the Mechanisms of Defence* (1936). This book, often thought of as the founding text of ego psychology, opened the gates for a host of theorists in the second period (e.g., Heinz Hartmann, Ernst Kris, David Rappaport, Erik Erikson) who offered theoretical advances in the psychoanalytic concept of the ego.[2] While their individual formulations varied, the net effect of their theorizing as a group was the resurrection of the ego as a center of initiative and energy whose motivations and actions, in contrast to Freud's view, are far less determined by the dynamic upsurge of the id. This is well captured in the ego-psychological notion of a "conflict-free ego sphere." In the latter the ego is not simply a mediator between the desires of the id and reality, between the pleasure and reality principles, nor is it hopelessly mired between a rock (the id) and a hard place (the super-ego). Rather, the ego is conceived to have its own "battery," so to speak, its psychic inventory including the transformative possibilities actualized through play and mastery, the use of reason and reflection, the intrinsic pleasure of exercising curiosity, and the capacity for synthesis and integration. In sum, the ego psychologists went a good deal further in conceptualizing the structural capacities and independence of the ego than did Freud. In applying a "sociology of knowledge" approach (i.e., What is the relation between social soil and the emergence of new theoretical models?), sociologists are fond of noting that postwar capitalistic, technological American culture, quite unlike Freud's European social soil, occasioned (if not demanded) the theorization of an "executive ego." Insofar as it was the American-based Erik Erikson that is usually thought to be the reigning figure of ego psychology, there seems to be some credence to that view.[3]

Key Formulations

The application of ego psychological advances has had a profound effect on the psychoanalytic theory of religion. This can be illustrated with respect to a few of their key formulations. Best represented in Erik Erikson's *life-cycle theory*, ego psychology posited that the ego itself undergoes a process of development. In contrast to Freud, whose libido

---

[2] See A. Freud, *The Ego and the Mechanisms of Defence* (New York: Routledge 1992 [1936]); E. Kris, *Psychoanalytic Explorations in Art* (New York: International Universities Press, 1952); H. Hartmann, *Ego Psychology and the Problem of Adaptation* (New York: International Universities Press, 1958); D. Rappaport, *The Structure of Psychoanalytic Theory* (New York: International Universities Press, 1960); and E. Erikson, *Identity and the Life Cycle* (New York: W. W. Norton, 1994 [1959]).

[3] See H. Stuart Hughes, *The Sea Change: The Migration of Social Thought, 1930–1965* (New York: Harper and Row, 1975).

theory was confined to the development of the sexual instinct from infancy through puberty, Erikson posited eight stages of the development of the ego that ran from the pre-oedipal period of nursing with the mother through the challenges of old age. Each stage had both an "existential" and "ethical" dimension. For example, in the earliest, pre-oedipal phase of development (the stage of *infancy*) the *existential* challenge faced by the infant is whether the world is more or less a trustworthy place ("trust versus mistrust"). The latter is decided in the main by "good-enough" mothering and the absence of serious trauma. If successfully navigated, nascent capacities for the development of the *virtue* of hope (the *capacity* to be hopeful) is facilitated. Erikson posited seven more stages of development, each with its own existential crisis and hoped-for ethical capacities: *early childhood* (autonomy versus shame/doubt; will), *play age* (initiative versus guilt; purpose), *school age* (industry versus inferiority; competence), *adolescence* (identity versus identity diffusion; fidelity), *young adulthood* (intimacy versus isolation; love); *adulthood* (generativity versus stagnation; care); and *old age* (integrity versus despair; wisdom). While religious ideation and practice can help one navigate the challenges of the life cycle at any stage, Erikson is particularly interested in how religion helps those with issues surrounding trust, forging an identity, exercising generativity, and managing the despair of old age.

Importantly, Erikson's developmental sequence was ruled by *epigenesis*, a term taken from embryology that denotes that later developmental stages unfold from previous ones (as apparent in the development of an embryo). In this hierarchical system of increasing differentiation, inadequacies of early stage resolution (e.g., "being mistrustful") can be reworked and resolved in subsequent ones. For example, if one, due to a lack of pre-oedipal love and support, came to hold an essentially pessimistic and mistrustful view of the world, then a way to repair that deficit might be through religion. Female divinities like Mother Mary, the daily remembrance of which can be affirmed in necklaces, pins, and car dashboards, and scriptural referents denoting a "psychology of the face" (e.g., "The Lord make His Face to shine upon you and be gracious unto you. The Lord lift up His countenance upon you and give you peace") can repair by igniting adaptive memories of pre-oedipal trust and benevolence. To take another example, Erikson points to his work with adolescents, with whom he had occasion to engage extensively in his clinical home at the Austen Riggs Center in Massachusetts. For adolescents, the existential challenge was establishing a solid sense of identity (versus self-fragmentation and identity diffusion) with the corresponding capacity and virtue being that of fidelity (of "being able" to commit). A religious worldview, properly communicated, could certainly help one solidify who and what one is as well as mediate a series of ethical values and aims conducive to formulating a life-cycle plan. In this sense, religion can help those adolescents who are identity challenged. Providing psychoanalytic sophistication to Pfister's valorization of pastoral psychology as adaptive, Erikson goes on to note the psychological efficacy of transference relationships with religious figures/pastoral psychotherapists. The latter, in conjunction with the ability of religious symbols and narratives to speak to unconscious functioning and rituals that integrate one into a community, could be resources to help one revisit and resolve previously mismanaged developmental challenges. For example, in such a scenario the capacity (and virtue) linked to the pre-oedipal stage, that of hope, once repaired, resurrected, and made existentially available, could eventually morph into a capacity more psychologically and religiously advanced, namely, "faith." While only hope, and not faith proper, is available to infants, the capacity to hope is the basis for and can transmute into faith when run through religious ideation in tandem with the more advanced cognitive and volitional capacities of adolescents. In this way, then, the resources of religion can help the adolescent to form the kind of trustful relationships and solid identity for use in adapting to the vicissitudes of life.

Life-cycle theory also entails a revision of Freud's instinct theory. Freud had emphasized a somatic base for the unconscious, concentrating on aggression and sexuality. Erikson countered by offering a more positive view of the animalistic urges found in humans. He did not deny that sex and aggression and their vicissitudes were deeply ingrained in who we are and what we do. But his researches into ethology and ecology led him to conclude that animals, evinced in care for their young and their awareness of and respect for environmental cycles, exhibited an instinct for "generativity." Translated for humans, this meant that there was a powerful biological need and wish to maintain and further one's family, society, and the human species that transcended even one's own egotistical desire for survival. This instinct, grounded in biology and present in archaic dimensions of the unconscious, was also linked to higher cultural products, including art and religion. A good example of how religion might aid in the development of generativity and care lies in its application to later stages of the life cycle. The wisdom accumulated through generations and housed in theology, doctrine, and scripture models behavior aimed at becoming more trustworthy to others while valorizing those existential tasks devoted to the betterment of subsequent generations. Moreover, for the aged, religion offers resources for meeting inevitable death with the existential challenge of integrity (as opposed to despair) by offering a form of "ultimate" identity above and beyond the more finite, transient one of earthly existence.

Life cycle theory added two further revisions to Freud's view of the ego: *autoplastic versus alloplastic adaptation* and *regression versus regression "in the service" of the ego*. The former, initially formulated in the works of Heinz Hartmann, counters Freud's conflict model between the individual and civilization. Recall that Freud held that the individual, because of the aggressive instinct, was always in opposition to society and its institutions. In this view, adaptation to the religious cultural super-ego and its regnant values required accommodation and renunciation, hence being framed by ego psychologists as an instance of "autoplastic" adaptation. Alloplastic adaptation, on the other hand, countered by signaling the capacity of individuals to change culture by utilizing the resources of religion. The Baptist minister and civil rights activist Martin Luther King Jr.'s reliance on his faith to demand racial equality is a paradigmatic case in point. But so too are Martin Luther's Protestant reformulation of the overly strict, medieval, "heteronomous" Catholic understanding of morality in favor of being "justified by faith" alone and Gandhi's proclamation of ahimsa (nonviolence) and satyagraha to effect social change. In sum, religion is now seen as not simply a reflection of society's values and a reigning super-ego but a (revolutionary) means to change it.

This new formulation also served to revise Freud's views on the cultural super-ego. The ego-psychological view would not dismiss Freud's model, emphasizing as it does how religious ideology and morality, as communicated by the parents and significant others, become part of one's individual super-ego through the developmental process. At the same time, utilizing the notion of alloplastic adaptation, they would add a more positive rendering of the potential psychological benefits of the religious cultural super-ego. This is well represented in Erikson's view of the *homo religiosus*, of which Gandhi, Martin Luther King Jr., and Luther were all examples. The latter term is defined as a person who, embodying the existential and cultural conflicts of an era, offers themselves up as a type of patient whose cure (their new formulation) effects changes for whole groups of peoples. In effect, by offering a solution of identity dilemmas to the waiting public, the *homo religiosus* inscribes new values as part of the ongoing reformation of the cultural super-ego. For Freud, the function of the cultural super-ego was to keep aggression at bay, mostly through fear and guilt. For the ego psychologist, the cultural super-ego additionally contains a storehouse of psychological wisdom, modified through the generations, which could be used for edification and personal growth.

Implicit in the above is another important consequence: religious institutions are not, as Freud would have it, always "unpsychological" in nature. Alloplastic adaptation countered Freud's view of the intrinsic animosity between the individual and society with the notion of the "average expectable environment." Alloplastic adaptation differed from Freud's conflict model by holding that each individual had the natural capacity to adapt to a range of different cultural environments. In this view, social institutions like religion were not so much antagonistic to the individual but correlated with, indeed, enabled the capacities to overcome, the stage-appropriate existential challenges every individual faces (e.g., creating a workable identity, navigating the anxiety of death, facilitating close relationships). In addition to the examples offered above, one can cite Erikson's notion of a *moratorium*. The latter references those institutions and social spaces that allow time for the exploration and experimentation of cultural options regarding work, sex, gender, relations with others, values, and ultimate questions concerning life's meaning. The richer a society is, the more institutions it will offer to help facilitate such a process. For example, for many it is the university, where one is enjoined to experiment with such core existential issues. Career trajectories are often formulated, reformulated, and changed again. Sexual mores and orientations can be rehearsed and settled. Values are developed and a sense of self won. The armed forces, Peace Corps, and even juvenile detention centers might also be illustrations of psychosocial moratoriums. In Erikson's view, religious institutions, notably, the monastery, also fit the bill, functioning akin to the psychological clinic in their valorization of introspective techniques (prayer, mediation), psychological wisdom, the love and support of a "religious form" of group therapy, and religious professionals (monks, nuns, abbots, priests, gurus, etc.) who function as transference figures. In other words, such religious institutions give one a culturally valorized and authorized social space and needed time to work out stage-appropriate existential challenges.

The second important ego revision listed above, that of regression versus regression "in the service of" the ego, was initially formulated by Ernst Kris, the psychoanalyst and art historian. He noted that even the analytic session, in its use of free association, depended on a regressive process. Kris went on to show how the fantasied formulations of artists also depended on a regression "in the service of" the ego. Erik Erikson, in applying this concept to religious introspective techniques (like prayer), similarly framed regression as a way of moving forward (what he called "teleological") rather than backward and fixated (which he linked with Freud and called "originological"). Freud emphasized that believers, faced with the existential challenges and exigencies of life, adapted by "regressing" to an earlier phase of development (childhood) in which seeking the aid of the parental unit (particularly the father) was a workable solution (regressive adaptation) to one's problems. Erikson, on the other hand, was able to theorize how in certain forms of religious introspection one can discern in the "inner cosmos" of believers what he called "dim nostalgias," which, evoked through religious ideation and practices, served not simply a regressive but teleological function. One of these nostalgias was pre-oedipal, being "the simple and fervent wish for a hallucinatory sense of unity with a maternal matrix ... symbolized by the affirmative face of charity, graciously inclined, reassuring the faithful of the unconditional acceptance of those who will return to the bosom."[4] The second of these nostalgias was oedipal, being "the paternal voice of guiding conscience, which puts an end to the simple paradise of childhood and provides a sanction for energetic action."[5] Adaptively put, such symbols at their best not only elicit developmental themes but also help repair psychological deficits. This, then, is what the notion of regression "in the service of" the ego means when utilized as part of an adaptive psychoanalytic theory of religion. The difference between Freud and the ego psychologists on this point becomes clear when Erikson, casting doubt on Freud's myopic emphasis on the negative consequences of regression, goes on to ask: "must we call it regression if man thus seeks again the earliest encounters of his trustful past in his efforts to reach a hoped-for and eternal future? Or do religions partake of man's ability, even as he regresses, to recover creatively? At their creative best, religions retrace our earliest inner experiences ... it is a regression which, in retracing firmly established pathways, returns to the present amplified and clarified."[6]

The above advances of ego psychology are evident in Erikson's most famous book, *Young Man Luther*. In embracing Freud's oedipal theory, it contained an "originological" Freudian analysis of Martin Luther, the conclusion being that he suffered from an obsessional neurosis. But then,

---

[4] E. Erikson, *Young Man Luther* (New York: W. W. Norton, 1958), 263–264.   [5] Ibid.
[6] Ibid.

weaving in theoretical developments within ego psychology (as listed above), he went on to show how such advances accounted for the ways in which Luther, through religion and the monastic setting, engaged and transcended such developmental determinants. Recall that Freud, in his letters to Pfister and in his analysis of the seventeenth-century painter Christoph Haizmann, was receptive to how religious ideation might heal in a suggestive-supportive manner. But Erikson, writing in the "second period," which saw the full flowering of the psychology–theology dialogue and pastoral psychology, was able to provide more nuanced psychoanalytic theorizing for how religious institutions, practices, and figures could be instrumental in facilitating healing and adaptation. In the next chapter we will have occasion to illustrate ego-psychological advances at work in our treatment of another Christian figure, St. Augustine.

To sum up, Freud's stress on libido theory (infantile sexual development) in tandem with his structural model, the focus on Oedipus, the inherent conflict between the individual and civilization, and a narrow definition of religion led to an interpretative bias: religion as childish, defensive, regressive, and possibly pathological. The advances of ego psychology (multiple reformulations of the ego, the developmental cycle, the id, and the super-ego) offered a new "flashlight" and model for exercising the psychology "of" religion project, which led to a functional view of religion as constructively adaptive and healing. In turn, these advances were conjoined to a shift in their "definitional strategy" that went well beyond that preferred by Freud. This is again best illustrated in Erikson, who was seeped in theological thought like that offered by his contemporary Paul Tillich, the nineteenth-century Danish philosopher and theologian Soren Kierkegaard, and mystical authors both east and west. His books on religious figures such as Luther and Gandhi indicate that Erikson's framing of the "what" of religion was hardly that of Freud, who, as we have seen, in railing against those "philosophers" that "stretched the meaning of religion," preferred limiting its purview to that of the "common man." This shift in the definitional strategy is one that was also valorized, as we saw in the preceding few chapters, by the dialogical projects, and will be evident again in our survey of object-relational and transformational theorists.

Finally, before we leave the ego psychologists, a cautionary tale is in order. While allowing that the advance of ego psychology gives impetus to those championing an adaptive view of religion, the application of such insights must be tempered with reflexivity. For example, recalling some of the anthropological critiques offered in Chapter 2, different cultures may prefer, even invent, ego defense mechanisms not valorized in Western, capitalistic cultures (as we will illustrate in the next chapter). Again, taking life-cycle theory as our focus, Erikson's stress on adolescence may have been relevant for postwar America in the 1950s and 1960s, but anthropologists have long noted that the name, length, and vicissitudes of a stage named "adolescence" (and indeed any stage) is at the very least culturally variable. In some cultures, the notion of a prolonged adolescent stage remains unnamed and unimportant. One can add to this Erikson's own student, the Indian psychoanalyst Sudhir Kakar, who, in emphasizing the need for ethnographic data, offers quite a different sequence of life-cycle stages based on the cultural valorization of Hindu thought. The concept of "identity" may be portable, but what that means (e.g., "Indian identity" versus "American Protestant identity") is culturally variable.[7] Indeed, noting that Erikson's Protestant heritage and belief are echoed in the seemingly Christian "virtues" of faith, love, and hope that adorn his professed ideal outcome of life-stage maturation, reflexivity must be extended to the norms and aims that animate his version of life-cycle development as a whole. In other words, one must be reflexively aware of the "ethno" elements in life-cycle theory lest one fall prey, in its application, to colonialism and Orientalism.

OBJECT-RELATIONAL ADVANCES

We have noted that sociologists have commented on the link between ego psychology, postwar capitalistic culture, and the theoretical elaboration of an executive ego. Similarly, they observe that another notable characteristic of postwar culture was the growing prevalence of fatherless families and, in those with both parents intact, how economic conditions and parental absence led to a growing inability to monitor children. The result was the emergence in the clinic of new types of neuroses. Generally speaking, what clinicians saw in their patients was the preponderance of a new set of symptoms: feelings of fragmentation, emptiness and

---

[7] See Kakar, *The Inner World*, chapter 2.

meaninglessness, low self-esteem, sensitivity to disappointments, slights and failure, hypochondria, exaggerated idealization of powerful figures, the need to merge with perceived sources of strength, eruptions of archaic grandiosity, narcissistic rage, and lack of empathy.[8] Freud had been invested mainly in the analysis of hysteria and obsessional neuroses, a fact culture theorists attribute to his sociocultural surround and its tendency to manufacture such forms of mental distress. Only rarely did he have occasion to theorize about the developmental phase before Oedipus (the "pre-oedipal" or "narcissistic" line of development) and, as we have seen, apply it to religion. It was the object-relations theorists who, in part due to the influx of new clinical data, undertook what became a robust round of new theorizing on the pre-oedipal, narcissistic line of development. The clinical issue centered on early relationships and how the vicissitudes of the processes of idealization, identification, and internalization gave rise to what all humans need: a "cohesive" self (or a firm sense of healthy "narcissism"). The development of a cohesive self is linked to the capacity for empathy. In other words, clinically speaking, a healthy sense of narcissism is the opposite of the common, pejorative use of that term (i.e., "narcissist"). One must have a good sense of self before one can be a self to others. This new line of theorizing tends to downplay Freud's insistence on the biological, instinctual, and triangular (i.e., oedipal) in favor of the relational and dyadic (mother–child). Indeed, according to object-relations theory, Freud's oedipal theory and need to contain instinctual upsurge becomes most relevant when the more important, developmentally based, "good-enough" relationships break down.

As with the ego psychologists, there is an abundance of figures who can be subsumed under a liberal rendering of the label "object-relational theorists." And again, as in the preceding section, we will limit our survey to but a few who have been utilized most extensively among those using object-relations to interpret religious phenomena: Heinz Kohut, D. W. Winnicott, Ana-Maria Rizzuto, and Sudhir Kakar.[9]

---

[8] For a good summary treatment of this, see C. Lasch, *The Culture of Narcissism* (New York: W. W. Norton, 1979).

[9] To be sure, the list of those classified as object-relations theory is a long one. For a good survey, see J. Greenberg and S. Mitchell, *Object Relations in Psychoanalytic Theory* (Cambridge, MA: Harvard University Press, 1983). For an overview of additional applications in the object-relational theory of religion, see J. Jones, *Contemporary Psychoanalysis and Religion: Transference and Transcendence* (New Haven, CT: Yale University Press, 1993).

Kohut's Self Psychology

Heinz Kohut (1913–1981), an Austrian-American psychoanalyst who was a major figure in the innovative Chicago Institute for Psychoanalysis, is known for formulating what he called self psychology, an object-relations theory about the narcissistic line of development. Starting from Freud's postulation of primary narcissism (that phase being the origin of Romain Rolland's oceanic feeling), Kohut goes on to stipulate how that original ego feeling slowly develops into the firm, continuous, stable sense of a mature "I" that he called having a "cohesive" self (i.e., the developmental line of narcissism). The infant is, of course, vulnerable, fragile, and dependent on the parental unit for sustenance and support. Such vulnerability becomes heightened as the original Edenic, oceanic feeling of omnipotence and connectivity fades relative to the growing awareness of external reality, the parents as separate "objects" not under the infant's control, and the demands of inner needs. In striving to counter such helplessness and vulnerability, and in the attempt to grow and achieve a measure of initiative, independence, and self-cohesion, the infant's narcissistic line of development morphs into two related "archaic" narcissistic structures: the grandiose self and the idealized parent imago. The two structures are inexorably related yet evince different strategies used by the child to maintain self-equilibrium and adapt to a social world populated by stronger Others. The recourse to grandiosity is illustrated by developmentally phase-appropriate behaviors where, for example, the child boasts about being a god or a superhero. In other words, it is normal ("phase-appropriate grandiosity") for children to inflate their feeble selves into powerful cultural figures like superheroes to create a sense of initiative and power. When faced with such behavior, the parent or adult usually smiles and feeds the fantasy (i.e., "mirroring" the grandiosity of the child). The parent also does this when the child achieves developmental milestones (riding a bicycle, tying shoes, getting good grades, etc.), spontaneously and naturally mirroring and encouraging the child ("good-enough" parenting). As the child matures, the need for eruptions of archaic grandiosity decline due to good enough parenting and mirroring. Archaic grandiosity is gradually transformed into more mature narcissistic structures evincing acceptance of self and realistic self-esteem. If, due to trauma or poor parenting, archaic forms of expressing grandiosity are not tempered and transformed, then low self-esteem, sensitivity to slights and disappointments, and outright displays of adult, archaic grandiosity may result.[10]

We can show the difference between the uses of this model and Freud's classic oedipal one by revisiting the latter's portrait of Spiderman. We previously saw how Spiderman could be read along Freudian lines as appealing to (in particular) boys and young men who are experiencing, even if unconsciously, oedipal distress. In the best-case scenario, identifying with Spiderman allows them to inwardly assuage (and occasionally "act out"), in a culturally appropriate and experience-distant way, their conflicts through fantasy and identification with Spiderman "on the screen" of the movie theater. Kohut's analysis, while validating Freud's oedipal reading, would complement it by adding a self-psychological analysis. Here the focus of the origin myth is not Peter Parker's feeling of guilt over letting a robber kill Uncle Ben, which led to his crime-fighting days as Spiderman and need to hide his identity (namely, the anxiety linked to the "secret identity" of oedipal conflict). Rather, it is the fact that he became Spiderman as a result of being "infected" by a poisonous, radioactive spider. In the classic psychoanalytic view, spiders are symbols of the venomous, dangerous, suffocating, castrating mother. To be bitten and infected by one is, according to Kohut, a metaphor for a developmental sequence in which one never received maternal mirroring and empathy. The result is feelings of inadequacy, low self-esteem, and exhibitionistic outbursts of grandiosity (namely, thinking one is a superhero). This fits with the framing of Peter Parker as a nerdish, unpopular, weak high school teenager beset by bullies. Of course, it is one thing to have cultural outlets like the Marvel universe to appease one's need (through identification) for grandiosity but an entirely different one to offer religious narratives that authorize individuals to proclaim that they are the second coming of the Messiah. For Kohut, the underlying psychology is the same, even if the institutions (art, religion) offer different solutions, some of them dangerous, for those who are narcissistically challenged.

The second way of adapting to reality (the "idealized parental imago") involves the parental unit and starts with the idealization of and need to merge with them (a process Kohut refers to as merging with

---

[10] For brief summary statements of Kohut's psychology, see H. Kohut, "Forms and Transformations of Narcissism," in H. Kohut, *The Search for the Self*, 2 vols., ed. P. Ornstein (New York: International Universities Press, 1978), 427–460; H. Kohut and E. Wolf, "The Disorders of the Self and Their Treatment: An Outline," *International Journal of Psychoanalysis* 59 (1978): 413–425.

"self-objects"). The parents are understood by the child as centers of support and power (hence "god-like"). As development proceeds, the idealized parents slowly lose their status as moral arbiters and models for adapting to reality, being "de-idealized," internalized, and psychologically transformed into values, aims, and blueprints for life (in short, what Kohut refers to as the building of mature "psychological structures"). If the parents are not available for idealization due to their absence or their nonempathic relation to their offspring, then the child may engage in trying to "regrow" that lost dimension of self by finding and merging with perceived "self-objects" of power. To a certain extent we all do this throughout the life cycle. But there is a difference between merging with an idealized Other that enables the morphing of archaic forms of narcissism into mature structures by mediating mature values and aims (e.g., President Kennedy's "Ask not ..."; King's "I have a dream") and those (e.g., totalitarian dictators) who, in demanding conformity, cater to untransformed, archaic needs to merge with a powerful, all-embracing, god-like persona.[11]

In sum, if development proceeds normally, then the transformation of archaic forms of narcissistic structures to mature ones leads to realistic self-esteem, a workable set of values, and the capacity to create and actualize a life plan in accordance with an accurate understanding and assessment of one's talents. If not, then a range of "narcissistic personality disorders" and their clinical signs (e.g., meaninglessness, fragmentation, hypochondria) may result.

Gurus and Megachurches

A good illustration of the application of Kohut's theory to religion in the United States can be found in the cultural popularity of Eastern gurus (starting in the 1960s) and in the current appeal of megachurches. An object-relations approach as to the "why" of such popularity would, in dialoguing with sociologists, note that for many in the postwar era, the Judeo-Christian tradition, due to its perceived complicity in problematic sociopolitical adventures (racial segregation, the Vietnam War, overly rigid sexual mores), began to lose its appeal.[12] In effect, many younger

---

[11] See note 10.
[12] To be sure, there were many within Christianity (e.g., the Quakers, African American Baptist churches, liberal Christian denominations in general) who were active in the pursuit of social justice, demonstrated against the Vietnam War, and sought to reform

Americans "de-idealized" such religious forms. As a result, the narratives and symbols of traditional Western religions were no longer compelling or believable. In this view, then, the psychological ability to idealize is the "developmental infrastructure" of the later capacity to believe ("faith" entails "idealization"). Commensurate with this are psycho-historical, sociological analyses (notably Christopher Lasch's work *The Culture of Narcissism*) that point to how the disruption of the nuclear family in tandem with shifts in economic conditions and the sociopolitical sphere exacerbated the prevalence of narcissistic disorders. In modeling civilization as a kind of "organism," the cultural imagination responded by creating new religious forms in which self-disorders could be addressed in an experience-distant, adaptive fashion.

In the case of the guru, Western culture enabled idealization in that the guru, as a cultural "self-object," was framed as "perfect" (enlightened) and god-like. For those with self-deficits, such a figure was attractive in that it afforded the opportunity for what the Indian psychoanalyst Sudhir Kakar calls a "developmental second chance."[13] The developmental sequence of transforming the archaic narcissistic structures of the grandiose self and idealized parent imago did not go well or were in the process of failing. It is these deficits that the seeker attempts to rectify by "regrowing" and thus transforming archaic structures into more mature ones. Given the variety of guru figures available, object-relations would hold that one's choice would be directed by "parental style," meaning the extent to which the guru exhibits characteristics reminiscent of one's actual parents. The relation to the guru, marked by submission, devotion, and idealization, facilitates regression. Once in this relationship, the power of the guru to heal is, like that of the patient–analyst relationship,

---

the church's stance toward women, gays, and lesbians. But many also saw conservative figures and denominations within Christianity as promoting the Vietnam War, patriarchy, racial segregation, and rigid sexual mores. Feminist theology (e.g., Mary Daly and, later, Rosemary Radford Ruether and Elizabeth Schüssler-Fiorenza), the quest for racial justice, and the LGBTQ movement (e.g., the 1969 Stonewall Inn incident in Greenwich Village) found their origins in the decade of the 1960s. While some fought to reform Chrsitianity, others were disillusioned enough to abandon it altogether. See, for example, M. Daly, *The Church and the Second Sex* (Boston: Beacon Press, 1986 [1968]); G. Wacker, *America's Pastor: Billy Graham and the Shaping of a Nation* (Cambridge, MA: Harvard University Press, 2014); A. Cross, *When Heaven and Earth Collide: Racism, Southern Evangelicals, and the Better Way of Jesus* (Montgomery: New South Books, 2014).

[13] See S. Kakar, "The Guru as Healer," in S. Kakar, *The Analyst and the Mystic* (Chicago: University of Chicago Press, 1991), 35–54.

exponentially enhanced. An "idealizing transference" is ignited in which every move, glance, touch, or word of the guru becomes an opportunity for the seeker to feel valued, mirrored, and loved. The regression may be so deep as to engage the earliest memories (e.g., soiled diapers) wherein some external "object" came and rescued one from the feeling of helplessness and fragmentation (what can be called the "Humpty Dumpty syndrome"). An adaptive rendering of this relationship would hold that reconstituting the idealization/internalization process through the guru can help one transform archaic narcissistic structures into mature ones. That said, as one can imagine, things can also go horribly wrong. If the guru is suffering from unresolved narcissistic issues of their own (e.g., the archaic grandiose need to be admired as a god) while the seeker suffers from low esteem, then the possibility for abuse is magnified (as is evident in what we in the preceding chapter called the "scandal literature").

The psychology underlying the rise and popularity of the guru is applicable to similar religious phenomena. For example, take the immense popularity of the "megachurch." In the analysis of the latter offered by Christine Miller and Nathan Carlin, they too begin by affirming how the disruption of the nuclear family in tandem with shifts in economic conditions and the sociopolitical sphere exacerbated the prevalence of narcissistic disorders. The megachurch, like the guru phenomenon, stepped in to fill the void. Narrowing their analysis to Joel Osteen's Lakewood megachurch in Houston (the largest in the country), they list the multiple ways it serves to elicit idealizing transferences and opportunities for healing self-deficits. The latter include (1) a "light" theology that emphasizes a nonjudgmental attitude and the value of collective solidarity; (2) the presence of and multiple opportunities for exercising parental style (insofar as Lakewood offers a variety of pastors, only one of which is Joel Osteen, who are framed as being "from God" and available for idealizing transferences); (3) sermons that mediate total acceptance, mirroring, and affirmation ("You are God's masterpiece ... God accepts you ... God approves you"); and (4) the presence of therapeutic handlers during the service who are available to listen to the suffering and complaints of parishioners.[14]

---

[14] C. Miller and N. Carlin, "Joel Osteen as Cultural Self-Object: Meeting the Needs of the Group Self and Its Individual Members in and from the Largest Church in America," *Pastoral Psychology* 59 (2010): 27–51.

Winnicott and Transitional Objects

Alongside Kohut, another framing of the developmental line of narcissism that has been widely used is that offered by the British pediatrician and psychoanalyst D. W. Winnicott (1896–1971). This is particularly true of his terms "transitional objects" and "transitional phenomena."[15] Based on clinical observations of infants and children, Winnicott used such terms to explain what happens in their inner world during the developmental process of separation (from parents) and individuation (becoming a self). The crucial observation for Winnicott lay in the emergence in the child's life of an object, such as a blanket or stuffed animal, to which the child develops an intense bond and from which it receives nurturance. Such objects aid in the process of individuation and the mastery of the world "out there." Winnicott suggested that transitional objects symbolized the absent mother, the latter being inevitable during the course of a normal developmental cycle. Further, for Winnicott the initial capacity to form transitional objects is also the first attempt at symbolizing: it denotes the child's capacity to symbolize the absent parental unit. Transitional objects, in offering a remembered nurturing maternal presence, provide the self-confidence and inner calmness necessary to creatively explore, master, and integrate the challenges posed by external reality.

Such objects punctuate the landscape of culture, art, and religion. Take, for example, the little boy's relationship with the alien in the film *E.T. the Extra-Terrestrial* (who, not so coincidentally, ends up hiding as part of the boy's stuffed animal collection), the tiger in the comic strip Calvin and Hobbes (a simple stuffed tiger when the parents are around but a living co-creator of a world of fantasy when alone with Calvin), and Linus's blanket in *Peanuts*. As may be evident in such examples, the transitional object points to an area of experience to which both inner psychological and outer cultural reality contribute. Hobbes, insofar as he is an object of play given to and not created by Calvin, is constituted by culture. Yet Calvin also creates Hobbes, breathing life into him and investing him with meaning in their joint efforts to playfully engage and master external reality. For Winnicott this fact points to an unchallenged "third" area of experiencing, both real and unreal, which undercuts Freud's simple opposition between inner and outer reality and their correlates, the pleasure and reality principles. This third area is what he

---

[15] See D. W. Winnicott, *Playing and Reality* (New York: Penguin, 1971).

refers to as the "substance of illusion" – an inner/outer space illumined by transitional objects. "Illusion," in this Winnicottian sense, is not so much "delusion" (as Freud would see in religious worldviews) but the more accurate and necessary psychological rendering of how human beings live their lives. In moving away from Freud's firm adherence to a strict empiricism, Winnicott offers us a new psychoanalytic epistemology for how we come to know and interact with the world.

This epistemology extends beyond the reference to transitional objects. For Winnicott, the ability to find a transitional object for use in creatively adapting to external reality designates a human capacity that expands and deepens throughout the life cycle. Examples of the latter are the investigations of science, the creative renderings of the arts, and even religion. In contrast to Freud, Winnicott does not always distinguish between the three in stark terms. This lies in part due to the fact that for Winnicott, the very definition of what constitutes a healthy person is the ability to creatively engage and master an external reality that, as an "X out there," is never fully understood or mastered. For Freud, any religious worldview, because it could not be empirically confirmed, was at least an illusion, if not a form of delusion and pathology. Winnicott, on the other hand, would say that because we never get to the "X" that defines the "real" of external reality, the task of "reality acceptance" is lifelong.[16] Religion, along with science and art, offers us creative resources for engaging and adapting to the ultimately unknowable "X" that lies "out there."

God Representations West and East

Winnicott's theory has been applied to multiple religious phenomena. For example, take certain forms of religious practices and rituals such as prayer and communion. Both cases are effective in that they symbolize "something more" than the fact of objective, material existence. As such, they can be framed as serving an adaptive function when conceived of as essentially transitional, rather than delusional, in nature. This function can be extended to apply to one's belief system and religious worldview as a whole. With regard to the latter, no single theorist has detailed this more than the Catholic psychoanalyst Ana-Maria Rizzuto.[17] Contra Freud, Rizzuto thinks that belief "is an integral part of being human, truly

---

[16] Ibid.
[17] A. Rizzuto, *The Birth of the Living God* (Chicago: University of Chicago Press, 1979).

human in our capacity to create nonvisible but meaningful realities capable of containing our potential for imaginative expansion beyond the boundaries of the senses."[18] Belief is always linked to a religious worldview, the latter being referred to by Rizzuto as a "God representation." It is here that Rizzuto invokes Winnicott: "God, psychologically speaking, is an illusory transitional object."[19] Indeed, it is a "special" transitional object – one formed not from "plushy fabrics" like teddy bears and blankets but from "representational materials" that initially, as Freud would have it, find their source in the primary objects of infancy and childhood. However, going further than Freud, Rizzuto argues that the God representation is an overdetermined "quilt" and "work of art" influenced by culture at large, incorporating sexual and nonsexual elements, pre-oedipal and oedipal elements, representational and ideational components, and, in explicitly evoking Erikson's life-cycle theory, capable of evolving during subsequent life stages to the extent that it can supersede developmental determinants (like oedipal dynamics and the "Father").

We can unpack the aforementioned factors that contribute to the formation of a God representation in more detail. First, culture at large is complicit. Due to the child's natural inquisitive nature and the inescapable fact of culturally available religious narratives, Rizzuto posits that a rudimentary God representation is mediated to the child through the parents and, behind them, culture at large. Second, developmental factors are adduced, for a God representation becomes unavoidably imbued with relational and developmental depth. Here Rizzuto goes beyond Freud in arguing how clinical studies show that the God representation can be composed of paternal and maternal elements as well as reflect pre-oedipal and oedipal developmental configurations. Third, what Freud refers to as "secondary process thought" also contributes to the formation of the God representation. In making clear how this happens, Rizzuto distinguishes between the "concept of God" and the "image of God." The former is the God of the theologians and philosophers fabricated at the level of secondary-process thought, which follows the rules of philosophical inference, argumentation, and theorizing. The "images" of God find their source in the developmental vicissitudes of the representational process marked by idealization, identification, and internalization. These two aspects can and do coexist in any God representation. "Image"-based

---

[18] Ibid., 47.   [19] Ibid., 177.

religious symbols and narratives point to developmental contributions, while "conceptual" aspects are due to secondary-process cognitive reflection. Finally, in adopting Erikson's notion of epigenesis, Rizzuto holds that the God representation is available for evolution, transformation, and use throughout the life cycle. Epigenesis means that the God representation need not be subject to the determinism of the archaic infantile past but can be reworked, refined, and transformed. Crucial to the latter process is the ongoing integration of the conceptual aspects of the God representation with the deeper, developmentally and interpersonally based images of God. A dialectical process between the two is posited as taking place through significant experiences, idealized mentor figures of all kinds (from a psychoanalyst to a pastor) who elicit transference, and the individual psychical work of self-scrutiny and self-reflection. Through such auspices a process akin to the analytic session takes place, resulting in the integration and transformation of conceptual and image-based aspects of the God representation. In this schema, "conversion" is defined as "the ego-syntonic release from repression in a given individual of an earlier (or even present) parental representation linked to a God representation."[20] Importantly, Rizzuto thinks that a God representation, being a quilt and work of art to which multiple sources contribute, can contain transformational mystical insights as well: "The developmental process of forming a God representation is exceedingly complex and is influenced by a multitude of cultural, social, familiar, individual phenomena ranging from the deepest biological levels of human experience to the subtlest of spiritual realizations."[21]

Rizzuto admits to confining her analysis to Western religious traditions, especially Christianity, indicating that answers to problems concerning the universality of a God representation need clinical contributions from other cultures. At the very least, as indicated by the cautionary tale of reflexivity, the terminology employed ("God" representation) would have to be modified. For example, Theravada Buddhism does not admit the existence of God while proclaiming the self to be empty and non-enduring (anatta). The notion of a God representation here is awkward and carries with it charges of colonialism and Orientalism. Taking this to heart, the Indian psychoanalyst Sudhir Kakar provides an important "reflexive" expansion on Rizzuto's views by offering a culturally sensitive, postmodern view of how a God

---

[20] Ibid., 51. [21] Ibid., 182.

representation might function in a non-Western religious tradition. Speaking to the psychological terrain of the Hindu inner world, he refers to a "cluster of ideas," the "heart" of which consists of the Hindu notions of moksha, dharma, and karma. The latter, thinks Kakar, provides "a coherent, consistent world image in which the goal of human existence, the way to reach this goal, the errors to be avoided, and the obstacles to be expected along the way" are offered to the individual.[22] It is in speaking to how this "image" is internalized and functions that Kakar becomes Winnicottian, claiming that it is initially mediated through the mother and that "such world images (in any culture) constitute a third distinct category, both 'real' and 'unreal,' a meta-reality which is neither deterministically universal nor utterly idiosyncratic but which fills the space between the two ... exercis[ing] an influence on individual thought and behavior that is somewhat comparable to the working of the reality and pleasure principles."[23]

Becoming even more reflexive, Kakar, in noting that the "goal" of Hindu thought is best expressed in the Upanishadic notion of moksha, laments the strong tradition within psychoanalysis that tends to render it in pathological terms. The latter, for Kakar, reveals the implicit ethnopsychology value system and unfortunate colonialist tendencies of Western psychoanalysis. Indeed, recalling a cautionary tale unpacked in Chapter 5 (i.e., Freud's valorization of the Empedoclean mythology of Eros and Thanatos), Kakar thinks that the Hindu worldview, with its introspective discipline of yoga and aim of moksha, offers a vision of reality that is simply different, if not in some sense more profound, than that offered by Freud:

> The psycho-analytic vision of reality ... is primarily influenced by a mixture of the tragic and the ironic.... Fittingly enough, Oedipus, Hamlet and Lear are its heroes.... The tragic vision and its ironic amelioration are aptly condensed in Freud's offer to the sufferer to exchange his unbearable neurotic misery for ordinary human unhappiness. On the other hand, the yogic (or more broadly, the Hindu) vision of reality is a combination of the tragic and the romantic.... The new journey is a search and the seeker, if he withstands all the perils of the road, will be rewarded by an exaltation beyond normal human experience. The heroes of this vision are not the Oedipuses and the Hamlets but the Nachiketas and the Meeras.... These different visions of reality ... may converge in some respects yet diverge in others. To call such a deviations "pathological" or "ignorant" is to confuse a vision of reality with *the* reality and thus to remain unaware of its relativity.[24]

---

[22] Kakar, *The Inner World*, 15.   [23] Ibid., 50–51.   [24] Ibid., 28–29.

Through the auspices of Winnicott, Rizzuto, and Kakar, then, and linking it with our elaboration of its less sophisticated version (the "summary formula" introduced at the end of Chapter 4), what we have is a revised psychoanalytic theory of religious worldviews that can incorporate Freud's myopic oedipal and reductive analysis yet goes well beyond him by expanding his definition of religion, bringing in a reflexive mentality, and allowing a place for adaptive and transformational perspectives. We will have occasion to illustrate its workings in the case histories we will analyze in the next chapter. Before we do, let us first turn to developments in the psychoanalytic transformational school.

TRANSFORMATIONAL ADVANCES

In the above, as well as in previous chapters, we have seen that some of Freud's heirs and respondents championed an expansion of psychoanalytic models to accommodate the more rare types of insights and states as experienced by mystics and saints. While Freud demurred, transformational theory has taken up the challenge by attempting to theorize that lacuna in psychoanalytic theory.

Reformulating the Unconscious

An initial case in point is that of Erik Erikson. We earlier presented him as a good example of the adaptive psychoanalytic approach to religion. We can now add that he also saw fit to articulate a transformational dimension. In addition to the two "nostalgias" (pre-oedipal and oedipal) cited earlier, Erikson noted that monastic techniques enabled access to an even deeper "third nostalgia," which references "the pure self itself, the unborn core of creation, the – as it were, preparental – center where God is pure nothing: *ein lauter Nichts*, in the words of Angelus Silesius." Erikson goes on to cite other examples:

> God is so designated in many ways in Eastern mysticism. This pure self is the self no longer sick with a conflict between right and wrong, not dependent on providers, and not dependent on guides to reason and reality.... One basic form of heroic asceticism, therefore, one way of liberating man from his existential delimitations, is to retrace the steps of the development of the I, to forego even object relations in the most primitive sense, to step down and back to the borderline where the I emerged from its matrix ... the Eastern form

cultivates the art of deliberate self-loss: Zen-Buddhism is probably its most systematic form.[25]

Erikson's references to the Christian mystic Angelus Silesius and Zen (the inclusion of the latter reflecting its emerging popularity in the 1950s and 1960s), signify both an advance on theory and a new definitional strategy with regard to religion. In accounting for this deeper level of awareness, Erikson argued, in addition to his reformulations of the ego, the id, and the life cycle, and along the general lines advocated by Tillich, Rolland, and Bose before him, for another existential and "transformational" level of the human personality. This level engages, over and above the psychosocial developmental contribution to one's life, those concerns and anxieties about foundational issues of existence: the "ultimate questions" of death, nothingness, and meaning. The import of Erikson's extension of psychoanalytic theory is clear: the deepest level of selfhood is that in which we become aware of our contact with divinity.

A commensurate if alternate formulation can be found in another transformational theorist, the British psychoanalyst Wilfred Bion (1897–1979). While Bion was heavily influenced by Freud and object-relational theorists, his formulations were so unique and complex that he deserves his own place in the history of psychoanalytic thought. What is of particular interest to us is a specific concept that reflects a transformational dimension, that of "O," which he defined as "ultimate reality, absolute truth, the godhead, the infinite, the thing-in-itself. O does not fall in the domain of knowledge or learning save incidentally; it can be 'become,' but it cannot be known."[26] Bion insisted that O is unknowable, ineffable (beyond language), a "groundless ground," and, as a result, cannot be fully apprehended by human cognition. Since he was influenced by Kant, one could say that the closest philosophical correlate would be Kant's concept of the "noumenon" (or "thing-in-itself"). With respect to Western religious thought he is closest to "apophatic" (unsaying) theology, a strong line of mystical thought that can be found in numerous figures from Dionysius through St. John of the Cross (who Bion cited numerous times in this regard). At the same time, O is seen by Bion as the foundational ground of psychoanalysis and of psychoanalytic therapy. In the contemporary scene, the integration of a groundless ground with psychoanalytic therapy has made his formulations particularly attractive

---

[25] Erikson, *Young Man Luther*, 264, 119.
[26] P. Cooper, *Zen Insight, Psychoanalytic Action* (New York: Routledge, 2019), 98–99.

to psychoanalysts who are also Buddhist meditation teachers. They find in Bion a theoretical bridge allowing a connection between the "nondual" ground accessed through meditation and psychoanalytic theorizing about developmental contributions.[27]

While Bion, Erikson, and multiple figures in psychoanalysis (as detailed in the following sections) and in the dialogical projects share the common thread of arguing for a transformational dimension to the human personality, we have advocated the cautionary tale that warns against a simple-minded perennialism, as if the deepest root and mystical core of all religions is "the same." Rolland was guilty of this, and Erikson's virtual equation between the thought of Zen Buddhism and Angelus Silesius represents a cavalier treatment of mysticism(s) that would be deemed problematic by contemporary academics. Differences remain concerning the nature of that transformational "core" not only between religious traditions but often within the multiple figures that dot the landscape of each individual tradition. In other words, even transformational theory, lest it fall into the trap of advocating a universal, generic, psychologized religious ground, must continue to engage in dialogue, taking into account the particularities of each case as it is encountered. That said, the advance of transformational models "in dialogue" is that they extend psychoanalytic metapsychology by legitimating religious dimensions of the human personality in a nonreductive way.

Religious Practices

If there exists a transformational dimension to the unconscious, then what resources can be utilized to theorize about its access and development? In providing continuity between transformational reflections on this matter with Freud, recall that one line of argument he offered was evident in the psychoanalytic motto, where he remarks that "certain mystical practices" could pierce the usual barriers between the id and ego so that one could gain insight into "the depths of the ego and in the id which were otherwise inaccessible." While he cast doubt that "ultimate truths" and "salvation" could be had by such a route, he nevertheless went on to say: "it may be admitted that the therapeutic efforts of psychoanalysis have chosen a similar line of approach." While Freud preferred a technique such as free

---

[27] Ibid.

association as the road to unearthing the content of the unconscious, he was admitting that there were other ways, if in his view less satisfactory, of doing the same. Rolland and multiple figures in the psychology–comparativist dialogue disagreed, arguing that mystical practices went beyond a simple regression to developmental stages to engage a level of consciousness where the individual ego found its origin in a deeper, more expansive "Absolute." It is here that various transformational formulations step in to fill the seeming impasse between Freud and his respondents.

In framing this problem, it is useful to recall that Freud's invention of free association was in part due to his failure at hypnosis. Meanwhile, his British colleague Frederic Myers and his Society for Psychical Research (briefly mentioned in our introductory chapter) continued to champion hypnosis as a central way to get into trance states, seen as the springboard for diving into the deepest states of the (transformational) unconscious. Importantly, in the contemporary academic study of comparative religion, such trance states continue to be heralded as the eventual result and aim of religious introspective practices.[28] Like Myers, the argument from such academics is that trance states, once attained, become the inner springboard for accessing intuitive knowledge about the nature of the divine (what James referred to as the "noetic" dimension of religious practices).

Within psychoanalysis, it was only the later ego psychologists who came to center their analysis on how hypnosis works. Heinz Hartmann and, later, Gill and Brenman seized on what they called the contrasting notions of "automatization" and "deautomatization" to describe the process of hypnosis. Arthur Deikman then carried this project forward by using their formulations to analyze empirical data concerning subjects in contemplative meditation.[29] In defining automatization and deautomatization, he noted that as human development proceeds, our perceptual, motor, and behavioral systems undergo a slow process of automatization until they operate on a "second-nature" or "automatic" level. For example, seemingly unconscious or preconscious phenomena like perceptual focusing or audio processing, infant and childhood tasks like walking

---

[28] See R. Forman, ed., *The Problem of Pure Consciousness* (New York: Oxford University Press, 1990), and J. Garb, *Shamanic Trance in Modern Kabbalah* (Chicago: University of Chicago Press, 2011).

[29] A. Deikman, "Deautomatization and the Mystic Experience," in *Understanding Mysticism*, ed. R. Woods (Garden City, NY: Image Books), 240–260.

and talking, or learned routines like tying one's shoes and driving are all functions that, while once requiring attentional energy and concentration, are considered at the adult level to be routine. As one matures, one invests less intentional energy on such functions, allowing for the allocation of energy saved to new and more complex tasks like abstract reasoning. So, for example, in first learning to drive an automobile one's attention is entirely devoted to steering; later, one can engage in abstract problem solving, fantasizing, or conversing to the extent that miles on the highway have passed without notice. A potential drawback of the process of automatization, thinks Deikman, is that certain "archaic" modes of perceiving and relating may be left in a nascent state or entirely abandoned. To a certain extent, which modes get left behind may be due to culture. The capitalistic cultures of the West, for example, with their valorization of intense work, invariably favor a socialization process that demands the cultivation of cognitive modes of operation directed toward attachment to materiality and the sense world. In contrast, Deikman thinks that there exist less valued, archaic modes of cognition that are targeted by those practices (prayer, contemplation, meditation) that encourage detachment from and renunciation of the sense-world.

Deikman's introspective, meditational move, then, proceeds as follows: detachment and removal of ties to the sense world, a return inward and contemplation (which leads to deautomatization, a prominent feature of which is the silencing of thoughts), and the opening and cultivation of new modes of knowledge. While such formulations may leave much to be further reflected on, what is important is to note that while psychoanalytic techniques like free association have their place, there exist other introspective techniques housed in religious traditions, authorized and theorized by later psychoanalytic thought, which may enable one to gain access to transformational kinds of knowledge.

There is a second line of transformational reflections, following from texts in the Freudian corpus, on the possibility of accessing deeper dimension of the unconscious. The texts in question address a dimension of religion that Freud took seriously: the paranormal. During his era many psychologists earnestly investigated such phenomena, not the least of which were Freud's colleagues William James, Frederic Myers, and Carl Jung, all of whom were convinced of their importance and reality. Indeed, Freud actually penned not one or two but *six* essays on what he called the one and only "kernel of truth" that he found in the data of paranormal studies, namely, the fact of telepathy (what he preferred to call "thought transference"). In theorizing about the manifestation of telepathy, Freud insisted that two general conditions were needed. First, telepathy was facilitated when two people were emotionally tied (the paradigmatic example being parent and child). In other words, a certain empathy was cast as conducive for the transmission of telepathic knowledge. Next, he recognized that receptivity to telepathic messages was enabled by having one's attention diverted from the objects of ordinary everyday rational consciousness or by being in certain altered states (and here sleep and the dream life were paradigmatic examples). Finally, in asking his readers to "have kindlier thoughts on the objective possibility of thought-transference and at the same time of telepathy," Freud offered a working theory to explain such phenomena:

> The telepathic process is supposed to consist in a mental act in one person instigating the same mental act in another person.... The analogy with other transformations, such as occur in speaking and hearing by telephone, would then be unmistakable.... It would seem to me that psycho-analysis, by inserting the unconscious between what is physical and what was previously called "psychical," has paved the way for the assumption of such processes as telepathy.... One is led to a suspicion that this is the original, archaic method of communication between individuals ... the older method might have persisted in the background and still be able to put itself into effect under certain conditions.... It is a kind of psychical counterpart to wireless telegraphy.[30]

Freud's reference to an "original, archaic method of communication," which can become operative under specific conditions (i.e., altered and deautomatized states), recalls our earlier analysis of his characterization of mystical practices as unearthing the "primordial depths" of the unconscious. While Freud's commentary was limited to the above, it should be noted that those in the transformational school have been more open to advancing psychoanalytic theorizing about such matters and have done so by pointing to Freud's earlier attempts as authorizing their efforts. For example, Heinz Kohut, citing Freud's views on telepathy, claims that among the altered states found in the analytic session was a deep form of empathy that resulted in "thought transference." For Kohut, empathy is innate but increasingly overlaid by other, nonempathic modes of knowing during the course of development. He claimed that psychoanalytic practices, physiologically speaking, required both a certain level of somatic relaxation (as is true of many religious practices) and the "intentional curbing of the usual cognitive processes."[31] These conditions allow for

---

[30] S. Freud, "Dreams and Occultism," in *New Introductory Lectures*, S.E. 22: 49–50.
[31] Kohut, "Forms and Transformations of Narcissism," 453.

the emergence of empathic modes of communication that could, in their extreme form, be considered to be telepathic. Sudhir Kakar, in following Freud and Kohut, goes further in his concept of an "amplified empathy." Contrasting Freud's structural model with the concept of personhood found in the Upanishads, Kakar recasts the Hindu aim of moksha as "not limited to gaining this awareness of 'I' in a composite self. Rather, it is held that this ultimate 'man's meaning' is not realized until a person also has a similar feeling of 'I' in the selves of others, an empathy amplified to the point of complete identification."[32] Importantly, in valorizing buried, archaic modes of knowing, Kakar goes on to affirm a modified theory about the nature of the unconscious that might account for unusual psychic phenomena:

In the Hindu ideal, reality is not primarily mediated through the conscious and pre-conscious perceptions, unconscious defences and rational thought processes that make up the ego; it emanates from the deeper and phylogenetically much older structural layer of personality – the id, the mental representative of the organism's instinctual drives. Reality, according to Hindu belief, can be apprehended or known only through those archaic, unconscious, pre-verbal processes of sensing and feeling (like intuition, or what is known as extra-sensory perception).[33]

Indeed, as Kakar notes, it is the aim of Hindu mystical practices to empower one to access such modes of knowing.

---

[32] Kakar, *The Inner World*, 19.
[33] Ibid., 20. Such transformational openings offer the basis for a number of new psychoanalytic hermeneutical applications: (1) the possibility, in addition to Freud's view of the *reductive* (tribal unity with its attendant racism) and *adaptive* (aim-inhibited forms of Eros) interpretations of the love command, of a (transformational) metapsychological basis for the essential interdependence of all humans (also found in a related metaphor, that of the Buddhist Indra's Net) – one that recognizes and promotes a form of Eros based on a what can be called a "species unity" that transcends all national, racial, gendered, and religious differences; (2) a metapsychological and clinical justification for what the pastoral psychologist rebrands as altruistic, vicarious suffering (i.e., the amplified empathy established in the therapeutic session occasions healing and the "taking on" of the analysand's suffering); and (3) the metapsychological basis for a "divine" form of telepathy (i.e., the mystical notion of intellectual locutions as found in St. Teresa's *Interior Castle*, mansion 6, chapter 3, especially the last paragraph). To be sure, our *inclusive* approach allows that, for example, the use of the love command is "nothing but" in the service of racism and tribalism. But, depending on the case, it might also point to an attained religious maturity that illustrates the recognition of the Other and the presence of genuine Levinasian altruism.

Religious Intent and the Ascent of Eros

Alongside an attempt to theorize transformational dimensions of the unconscious and religious introspective practices, there exists a third area of investigation: that of justifying the religious *intent* to access such dimensions in a nonreductive way. In *Future of an Illusion* Freud advocated the view that religious intent should be rendered as a form of regressive adaptation to the exigencies of external reality. However, one can find in Freud's corpus theoretical openings that provide a textual basis for alternate theorizing found in transformational models. In particular, the latter is evident in what we can call the "psychoanalytic ascent motif," the latter found in Freud's *Group Psychology and the Analysis of the Ego* (1921). There Freud, drawing yet again on great thinkers and "intuitive psychologists" of the Western past, and by way rebutting those who sought to dismiss his views of sexuality as narrow and reductive, articulated what he referred to as "the wider sense" of his use of the term "Eros":

> Libido is an expression taken from the theory of the emotions.... We call by that name the energy ... of those instincts which have to do with all that may be comprised under the word "love." The nucleus of what we mean by love naturally consists ... in sexual love.... But we do not separate from this ... on the one hand, self-love, and on the other, love for parents and children, friendship and love for humanity in general, and also devotion to concrete objects and to abstract ideas.... By coming to this decision, psycho-analysis has let loose a storm of indignation.... Yet it has done nothing original in taking love in this "wider" sense. In its origin, function and relation to sexual love, the "Eros" of the philosopher Plato coincides exactly with the love-force, the libido of psychoanalysis ... and when the apostle Paul, in his famous epistle to the Corinthians, praises love above all else, he certainly understands it in the same "wider sense."[34]

In his book *The Ego and the Id* (1923), Freud used Plato's chariot metaphor (elaborated in Plato's *Phaedrus*) to speak of his structural model: the "rider" (*das Ich*) was always at pains to control what Plato called the noble (for Freud *das Über-ich*) and ignoble (for Freud *das Es*) horses. One could further point out that the psychoanalytic ascent motif is dependent on sublimation. The latter becomes the lever for redirecting sexual love to "higher aims" like the love of abstract ideas. What limits Freud's ascent upward is the chain that tied sublimation to the downward

---

[34] S. Freud, *Group Psychology and the Analysis of the Ego*, in S.E. 18: 90–91.

pull of the instincts and the unconscious. Unlike Plato's account, then, Freud's steeds were neither winged nor capable of flight to the Platonic mystical goal of ascent, evident in his work *The Symposium*, which he called the "Sea of Beauty." It is the vision of that Sea that makes one a "friend" of God. With regard to the reach of love upward, then, Freud's theory is limited relative to that offered by Plato.

Transformational models, on the other hand, endeavor to move beyond Freud's chaining of Eros to create a metapsychological space for Plato's "winged" Eros. No single psychoanalyst has spoken more directly to this point than the French psychoanalyst Jacques Lacan (1901–1981) and his concept of "The Real." From a religious perspective, the latter is akin to a "thing-in-itself," an Absolute that is ineffable, undifferentiated, and primordial. Importantly, Lacan, in referencing a philosophical version of this primordial reality, pointed to the neo-Platonic sage Plotinus (204–270) and his rendering, in his famous book *The Enneads*, of what he called the "One." Lacan stated that mystical utterances were the "best thing you can read," adding that his own work should be regarded as essentially "of the same order" as mysticism.[35] As some have observed, Lacan has shifted psychoanalytic conceptions of language, the unconscious, truth, and healing toward a perspective commensurate with philosophical and religious mysticism.[36]

What is of specific interest to us is how Lacan's formulations have been used to frame a form of desire (Eros) that goes beyond sexuality while authorizing a nonreductive perspective on the religious desire or intent to seek the divine. Speaking of the Plotinian "One," Lacan states that it is linked to a form of desire or Eros that Lacan called *jouissance*. The latter is a special form of desire that "goes beyond" sexual objects. Lacan found such a *jouissance* in Christian mystics such as St. Teresa and her bridal mysticism. The latter is charged with sexual metaphors, yet, in Lacan's view, is also charged with an energy, both pleasurable and painful, that "goes beyond" sexuality. A portrait of *jouissance* in the religious register is seen in Bernini's statue titled "The Ecstasy of Saint Teresa," which depicts Teresa in a state of helplessness with an angel above her holding a spear. Commenting on the Freudian take on this

---

[35] J. Lacan, "God and the Jouissance of Women," in *Feminine Sexuality: Jacques Lacan and the école freudienne*, ed. J. Mitchell and J. Rose (New York: W. W. Norton, 1982), 137–149.

[36] See R. Webb and M. Sells, "Lacan and Bion: Psychoanalysis and the Mystical Language of Unsaying," *Theory and Psychology* 5 (1995): 195–215.

statue, Lacan says: "she's coming, there is no doubt about it." But then adds: "And what is her *jouissance*, her coming from?"[37] His answer is that Teresa's mystical-erotic utterances "go beyond" developmental considerations, are directed to a deeper form of Eros, and, as a result, ask us to open up psychoanalytic metapsychology to a conception of mystical desire that, as with Plato, indicates the need for winged steeds. We will further illustrate this concept at work in the next chapter.

Revisiting Religious Therapies

The above narrative suggests that we should think anew about how to frame certain (mystical) kinds of religious forms of introspection and healing. We have seen that Erikson, by positing a third nostalgia (that of the "pure self"), intimated that mystical forms of therapy in the monastic setting go beyond classic-reductive and adaptive analyses, requiring transformational theory to fully account for its nature and results. A related example lies in the contested interpretation of Rolland's oceanic feeling (as mentioned in the previous chapter). For Freud, the oceanic feeling was akin to a "developmental appendix," a residue from an early stage that for some people maintained its presence in the background of the more developed, individuated ego of adulthood. But recall that subsequent surveys of Rolland's written works on the oceanic feeling revealed how he framed its state-like status to be an advanced stage appropriate to spiritual achievement akin to, but not necessarily identical with, similar claims found in Sri Ramana Maharshi and St. Teresa of Avila (i.e., *sahaja samadhi* and the *spiritual marriage*, respectively). The latter, framed by Maharshi and Teresa as advanced forms of the mystical life, necessitated the gradual disillusionment of and detachment from worldly matters, carrying with it existential and ethical dimensions. Freud's analysis, then, failed to account for the developmental or "process" dimension of Rolland's mysticism.

It is here that a transformational approach can be of value. We earlier saw how Kohut's psychology could be utilized in the service of both classic-reductive and adaptive applications. We can now add that, in addressing anew the nature of Rolland's oceanic feeling, Kohut felt the need to expand his theory to include a transformational dimension. Of relevance here is his concept of "cosmic narcissism," which clearly

---

[37] Lacan, "God and the Jouissance of Women," 147.

captures the transformational religio-ethical goal of his psychology and, when applied to Rolland, accounts for the existential and ethical dimensions of the oceanic feeling. Cosmic narcissism is a developmentally mature attainment indicative of ethical and existential achievement above and beyond the results of even a successful analysis. Explicitly referencing Rolland's "oceanic feeling," Kohut insists that cosmic narcissism is state-like, consisting in "a shift of the narcissistic cathexis from the self to a concept of participation in a supraindividual and timeless existence."[38] Cosmic narcissism "transcends the bounds of the individual," and one lives "sub specie aeternitas" without elation or anxiety, bathed in a continual communion with a contentless, supraordinate Self, participating in "supraindividual ideals and the world with which one identifies."[39] We can refer to Kohut's rendering, then, as the "developmental" or process dimension of the transformational.

Importantly, Kohut goes on to conjoin to his religio-ethical ideal a cultural agenda. Freud had suggested that religion be replaced by a humanistic "secular cure of souls," while Rolland was asking him, through analyzing mystical phenomena like the oceanic feeling, to move closer to a "mystical psychoanalysis." In his essay "On Leadership," Kohut moves closer to Rolland by suggesting the need for a new, unchurched rational religion, "an as yet uncreated system of mystical rationality which could take the place of the religions of the past."[40] He then points to "instances of heroic men of constructive political action who have achieved a transformation of their narcissism into a contentless, inspiring personal religion," further opining that humanity will have to produce such types in greater numbers in order to survive.[41] As to who might embody such an achievement, Kohut points to Dag Hammarskjöld, the former secretary-general of the United Nations: "Dag Hammarskjöld ... an example of this type, describes his contentless mysticism in the following words: 'Faith is a state of mind and of the soul ... the language of religion is (only) a set of formulas which register a basic religious experience.'"[42] It is not surprising that Rolland, well before Hammarskjöld, argued in favor of not only a mystical psychoanalysis but also the League of Nations (the historical prelude to the

---

[38] Kohut, "Forms and Transformations of Narcissism," 455–456.
[39] Ibid. See also the argument in Parsons, *Enigma of the Oceanic Feeling*, chapters 5–7.
[40] H. Kohut, "On Leadership," in *Self Psychology and the Humanities*, ed. C. Strozier (New York: W. W. Norton, 1985), 70.
[41] Ibid.   [42] Ibid.

United Nations). In Kohut and Hammarskjöld, then, we have come full circle.

The above considerations reaffirm that we look at the process dimension of mysticism as akin to religious therapy. It may well be that, in certain cases, classic-reductive and adaptive models, if taken in the spirit of our "star metaphor," can illumine those aspects of mystical therapies that remain poorly articulated and understood in the traditions proper, providing an antidote to the many ways in which human developmental baggage and social institutions are complicit in obfuscating the religious journey. At the same time, transformational models "in dialogue" allow for the diversity of religious therapies and hence the continued expansion and falsification of psychoanalytic theory with respect to new data sets that go beyond Freud's limited models.

8

Revisions and Applications

Our presentation of the important theoretical advances that have marked the psychoanalytic theory of religion after Freud has given us an appreciation of the differences between the classic-reductive, adaptive, and transformational approaches. Combined with our earlier emphasis on the need to include reflexive and dialogical dimensions, we can now proceed to illustrate the application of that formulaic shift. To that end, we will present two case histories, one Western (St. Augustine) and the other Eastern (Sri Ramakrishna). Our respective analyses will differ in that they are designed to illustrate different aspects of the workings of a reflexive, dialogical, inclusive psychoanalytic approach. That said, our analyses and conclusions with regard to the two cases will not be mutually exclusive and the lessons learned can be carried forward.

The first section (on St. Augustine) highlights how the Winnicottian notion of a transitional "God representation" works through the course of a life. We have seen that Freud thought the faith journey to be characterized by regressive adaptation and conversion by oedipal dynamics. However, since a God representation is formed through numerous factors and evolves through time, thus framing belief systems as a work of art, quilt, or tapestry, it is susceptible to being illumined by the varying analyses as offered by classic-reductive, adaptive, and transformational approaches. The second case (on Sri Ramakrishna) highlights the challenging dynamics of gender identity and sexuality (Eros) relative to the Divine. We know what Freud thought about sexuality and gender, but our analysis of the case of Ramakrishna will feature the need for not only inclusivity and dialogue but especially reflexivity as concerns the dynamics, transformations, and ultimate aim of Eros during the course of a religious life.

Again, our examples by no means exhaust the uses of our formula. The revised psychoanalytic tool kit unfurled in these pages has multiple tools and options. Which ones are best suited for application is dictated by the case in question. In picking but *some* of these tools and options in the below cases, then, it is to be emphasized that they are but two instances of a revised psychoanalytic theory of religion at work. They provide instances of how a revised psychoanalytic theory can be used while telescoping how it might be employed going forward.

THE EVOLUTION OF ST. AUGUSTINE'S GOD REPRESENTATION

The written corpus of St. Augustine (354–430) is influential enough with regard to the subsequent course of Christian theology to mark him as one of its seminal figures. Of all his writings, it is arguable that the most widely known is his spiritual autobiography, the *Confessions* (397–400). While the genre of autobiography (indeed, the word "autobiography" itself) is not older than the eighteenth century, the *Confessions* has been retrospectively framed as the very first Western autobiography, containing the central elements of introspection, self-discovery, and the awareness of how past events influence present consciousness. Dovetailing with this is the fact that in one of his earliest books (the *Soliloquies*) Augustine remarks that what he seeks to know are two things: God and the soul. Augustine's apprehension of both in his *Confessions* evolved relative to life stages, significant events, experiences, education, and relationships. This is admitted by Augustine himself, who, in his *Confessions*, tells us in detail about the circumstances surrounding each life stage and how they were related to the state of his soul and his knowledge of God. It is the latter in conjunction with Augustine's autobiographical, "case-history" style of narration that has occasioned multiple and varied psychological analyses of the nature and determinants of his religious journey. Of these the most important have been from the camp of psychoanalysis, giving rise to what can be called a psychoanalytic "reception history" of Augustine's *Confessions*. Even more germane to our interests is the fact that these studies display a kind of evolution that marks our three perspectives (classic, adaptive, transformational). Additionally, Augustine's "case history" speaks to many of the core issues (e.g., theological anthropology, conceptions of the Divine, definitional strategies regarding religion) we have explored surrounding Freud and his respondents in the psychology–theology dialogue.

Taking this into consideration, and for the sake of clarifying the application of our three psychoanalytic models set within the notion of an evolving God representation, one can divide Augustine's narrative (spun over thirteen "books," each of which is divided into smaller sections or "chapters" of a few pages each), into four phases: his boyhood (books 1 and 2), adolescence (books 3–6), young adulthood (books 7–9), and mature adulthood (books 10–13).

Boyhood: Classic-Reductive Models and the Father God

Augustine's autobiographical reflections start with his infancy and boyhood. As one would expect, classic-reductive studies spy a pattern of Oedipal conflict linked to his emerging belief system.[1] There is some justification for this given that Augustine describes his initial and relatively unsophisticated understanding of God as follows:

> When I was still a boy, then, I had heard of an eternal life promised us through the humility of our Lord God stooping to our pride. My mother had great hope in you, O God, and as soon as I came out of her womb I was marked with the sign of the Lord's cross and was salted with His salt.... We saw, God, how men prayed to you and, with our limited capacities, we formed an impression of you as of someone great, who was able, even when not present to our senses, to hear us and to help us. For when still a boy I began to call upon you.[2]

Here Augustine confirms the centrality of his surrounding culture (his mother and the community behind her) in mediating to him his initial conception of God. In describing that initial conception, he emphasizes the paternal, fatherly nature of an object-God ("someone great") and, relationally, his need through prayer for protection. We can see how a Freudian model fits here: the Father God existing as an object to answer wish-fulfilling prayers. Indeed, Augustine later goes on to say how his own prayers were directed at the alleviation of his immediate boyhood concerns, notably, the fact that he was beaten at school.

---

[1] The edited volume by D. Capps and J. Dittes titled *The Hunger of the Heart: Reflections on the Confessions of Augustine* (West Lafayette, IN: Society for the Scientific Study of Religion, 1990) has culled together the leading oedipal analyses of Augustine over the past half-century.

[2] Augustine's *Confessions* book 1, chapter 9 (henceforth designated by book and chapter, in this case 1.9). All citations are from *The Confessions of St. Augustine*, trans. Rex Warner (New York: Mentor, 1963).

Classic-reductive studies have further argued the link between this concept of God and what they think to be evidence of a determining developmental (oedipal) infrastructure. For example, throughout the *Confessions* Augustine had almost nothing to say about his father Patricius. What little he did say reveals that he saw him as unempathic, willful, lustful, and, despite his later conversion to Christianity, essentially a pagan. Notably, in *Confessions* 3.4, Augustine passes coldly over his father's death, devoting to his demise but one dismissive sentence (and that in parentheses). Augustine claimed (in *Confessions* 2.3) that Patricius "saw in me only a hollow thing," despite the fact that he tried to facilitate Augustine's education through his contacts with bureaucratic powers (which bore fruit, as Augustine not only received a fine education but was a teacher of the rhetorical arts before his later status as Bishop of Hippo).

Mother Monica is a different story. Augustine references her in the pages of the *Confessions* more than anyone but God. Classic-reductive studies depict her as fostering an erotic attachment with her son: as hypermoral and hostile toward sex; as domineering, controlling, and ultimately winning the battle with her rebellious son. The evidence amassed to buttress these claims is compelling. In *Confessions* 9.13 Augustine himself tells us Monica was possessed of an "overly carnal" attachment to him: "she loved having me with her, as all mothers do, only she much more than most."[3] She played a role in getting him to release not one but two concubines as unfit for his move up the professional ladder. She also maintained a certain power relation over him by strategically telling him of "prophetic" dreams and visions. When puberty hit and Augustine and his father returned from the public baths one day, Patricius told Monica of Augustine's growing physical maturity, whereupon Monica took him aside "with a holy fear and trembling ... For it was her wish, and I remember how privately and with what great anxiety she warned me not to commit fornication and especially not to commit adultery."[4] It seems Monica undermined the role of Patricius as Augustine's father ("She tried earnestly, My God, that you should be my father, not him"[5]). If the super-ego is an internalization of the moral attitudes and values of the parents (Monica and the "Father" behind her) then we have here a good indication of at least part of the attitude toward sexuality internalized by Augustine during his developmental years.

---

[3] *Confessions* 5.8.   [4] Ibid., 2.3.   [5] Ibid., 1.11.

Classic-reductive models go on to see this oedipally based "developmental infrastructure" as determinative for the various episodes that punctuate the subsequent course of Augustine's religious journey. Most important is his later, full conversion to Christianity as detailed in book 8. In his adolescence, Augustine had drawn away from Christianity, becoming a teacher of the rhetorical arts in Carthage and then later in Italy. At that point in his life his father had passed away, and Monica, having followed him to Italy, was now his live-in housemate. Becoming once again interested in Christianity, Augustine relates how he came back to the fold through a famous conversion scene. Crucially, his conversion was not simply to Christianity but to celibacy, for the cultural narrative at that time valorized celibacy as a path to Christian perfection. Augustine's confessional testimony reveals that a clear psychological struggle was taking place. Classic-reductive analyses observe that one finds the language of shame, fear, self-reproach, and even an auditory hallucination in which Augustine heard the words "take up and read" (*tolle lege*, a reference to scripture). Classic-reductive views see this struggle as the war between the unconscious and the super-ego. The conversion was "really" a kind of psychic compromise in which Augustine, now possessed of Monica as house-mother and having "killed" his father, had truly won the oedipal battle in every way except that of the overtly sexual. If unconscious desire was in part satisfied, there would be a price to pay. That price was celibacy. In return, he could have not only Monica but the love of God "the Father": his continued protection, favor, and guidance.

These studies again follow Freud in seeing a link between Augustine's developmental infrastructure and his later theology. In effect, they suggest "continuities" between Augustine's life and thought, what we earlier framed as a "basement theology."[6] Indeed, more than a few prominent theologians have found value in this interpretative lens. They point out that one cannot ignore how a Freudian take on Augustine illumines developmental factors involved not only in

---

[6] D. Capps and J. Dittes reveal that the term "basement theology" was coined as a result of a 1964 Yale University Divinity school seminar, centered on continuities between the life and thought of various religious figures, which met in the basement, the idea being that classes in theology, which met "upstairs," neglected such continuities. As Capps and Dittes put it, "the seminar ... invited students to a kind of theological work that some, accustomed to the theology "upstairs," felt risky and alien ... it was clear that they were engaging in a risky underground, even subversive activity." In *The Hunger of the Heart*, ix.

"his doctrines of predestination, the damnation of unbaptized infants, and the use of religious coercion but also in his understanding of grace, original sin, creation, church, sacraments, and the image of God as father that underpins them."[7] David Bakan exemplifies the most reductive and pejorative pole of these studies when he concludes that Augustine's *Confessions* played a role in the "spiritual retardation of mankind," his historical influence reflecting the "immaturity of mankind."[8]

Some object-relational studies have also fed this more reductive line of interpretation.[9] Here the deficiencies are seen to have impacted the narcissistic line of development. For example, Augustine's continued depreciation of Patricius and virtual omission of him in the text is now read not simply or primarily as indicative of oedipal hostility but as the failure of Patricius to provide an idealized parental figure for Augustine's budding sense of his male self (read clinically, and hence non-pejoratively, as "male narcissism"). The "overly carnal" attachment of Monica to her son, seen in her weeping fits and what she communicated to Augustine as her divinely inspired dreams, reveals not only her need to control Augustine and unconscious incestuous gratification but also evidence of her depressive narcissistic personality and need to use Augustine as a self-object to regulate her fluctuating self-esteem. The "disorder" Augustine recounts of his youth (e.g., his stories about lying and stealing, his problems with commitment, fidelity, and sexual promiscuity) becomes a consequence of narcissistic injury and rage, located in the emotional and physical abuses suffered in school beatings, the consequent mocking of his parents, a controlling Mother, and in a troubled separation-individuation process. Such developmental snafus account for Augustine's need, after his father's death, for what we will see below as the idealization of a parade of religious male figures (e.g., Faustus, Ambrose).

---

[7] See William B. Parsons, *Freud and Augustine in Dialogue* (Charlottesville: University of Virginia Press, 2013), 22.

[8] See D. Bakan, "Augustine's *Confessions*: The Unentailed Self," in Capps and Dittes, eds., *The Hunger of the Heart*, 111.

[9] Again, one can find many of the most influential object-relational studies culled together in Capps and Dittes, eds., *The Hunger of the Heart*. For a further sampling of object-relational analyses of Augustine, see W. Beers, "The Confessions of St. Augustine: Narcissistic Elements," *American Imago* 45 (1988): 107–125, and Sandra Dixon, *Augustine: The Scattered and Gathered Self* (St. Louis: Chalice Press, 1999).

Dialogical Responses to the Classic-Reductive Approach

There are interlocked responses from dialogical respondents (historical, literary, and theological) that, in supporting each other (hence not mutually exclusive), offer convincing counters that make one pause to consider the finality of the conclusions of the classic-reductive school.[10] Historians have in common with anthropologists the notion that going back centuries into the past, even if the Western past, is tantamount to going to a different culture. They question whether classic-reductive studies are reflexive, and whether they have accurately placed Augustine's narrative within his sociocultural milieu. So it is that historians such as Paula Fredriksen, in noting that Augustine's references to "carnal desire" and "fornication" are seen in psychoanalytic studies as revealing important and unconscious sexual meanings, rightly point out that the Latin term Augustine actually uses (*Et illius carnale desiderium*) is meant, in his sociocultural and religious context, to be construed more widely as "earthly (or worldly) affection" and attachment.[11] Similarly, Augustine's use of the term "fornication" occurs in nonsexual contexts and is to be understood as pertaining to his important religious notion of how desire, because of original sin, is essentially disordered (where "rightly ordered" is defined relative to how Eros has as its aim the ascent to the Divine). In other words, Augustine's notions of disorder and attachment to worldly matters intends to convey an existentially deeper religious subjectivity than that captured by recourse to an oedipal model aimed at spying only his conflicted sexuality.

Literary critical methods offer a related set of cautionary tales. They note that Augustine's narrative is composed of not only actual life experiences but also elements taken from scripture, philosophy, and literature. Augustine was educated, as he himself says, to realize the cultural idea of the "orator," to "become master of the spoken word ... to learn the art of words, to acquire that eloquence that is essential to persuade men of your case, to unroll your opinions before them."[12] What this means is that Augustine's narrative in the *Confessions* must be taken for what it is: an intentional, constructed work of art that borrows heavily from literary

---

[10] For a summary treatment of historical, literary-critical and theological perspectives, see Parsons, *Freud and Augustine in Dialogue*, especially 18ff.
[11] P. Fredriksen, "Augustine and His Analysts: The Possibility of a Psychohistory," *Soundings* 61 (1978): 206–227.
[12] *Confessions* 1.16.

sources.¹³ In portraying his own self, Augustine undoubtedly utilized some of his own personal experiences. But in the last analysis the *Confessions* portrays a "fictionalized self, an allegorically and rhetorically constructed self, rather than a literal self."¹⁴ Augustine used his own life experiences in conjunction with literary sources to construct an archetypal Self that transcends his own biography, speaks to the universal human condition, and functions as a religious, edifying discourse concerning the nature, limits, and possibilities of human transformation. As a result, it asks for caution with regard to the attempt to isolate the "real," "historical" Augustine behind the text. The issue thus becomes how to engage the problems of the constructed subject and what is clearly the use of borrowed literary units in narrating a life history. We will see the value of this cautionary tale below, especially in deciphering the meaning of his famous vision at Ostia.

Finally, theological perspectives supplement both the historical and literary critiques by asking us to consider whether classic reductive models possess enough explanatory power to illumine the deepest recesses of Augustine's religious nature. Augustine himself supports this when, on reflecting on his boyhood conception of the Divine, offers his opinion, not unlike that of Pfister and Tillich, that the concept of an object-based, heteronomous God is necessarily mistaken. He notes how many people, "when they read or hear the words which we are discussing think of God as though He were a kind of man or else like some great force associated with an enormous mass, and they imagine that by some new and sudden decisions He made heaven and earth outside Himself."¹⁵ The crux of the problem, thinks Augustine, is "due to the fact that some people are used to thinking in material terms," adding that "such people are still feeble little creatures."¹⁶

The key word here is "material." In multiple books of the *Confessions* Augustine remarks on how material conceptions of God are but figments of the imagination; how God, "corporeally conceived," renders belief "empty" and incapable of transformation (*Confessions* 4.2, 4.7, 4.15–16). Psychoanalytically conceived, the notion of "materiality" is that of projection: we are merely making an "object-God" in our own

---

¹³ See P. Courcelle, *Recherches sur les "Confessions" de S. Augustin* (Paris: Boccard, 1968), and R. McMahon, *Augustine's Prayerful Ascent: An Essay on the Literary Form of the Confessions* (Athens: University of Georgia Press, 1990).
¹⁴ See D. Jonte-Pace, "Augustine on the Couch: Psychohistorical (Mis)readings of the Confessions," *Religion* 23 (1993): 72.
¹⁵ *Confessions* 12.27.   ¹⁶ Ibid.

image. And, as with Freud, this means that such a rudimentary paternal concept of God carries with it developmental baggage: we are projecting unresolved and conflicted psychic content onto a culturally valorized sacred canopy. Certainly, Augustine, like Freud, understood that such rudimentary conceptualizations of the Divine, if left there, carried with it a certain ethical and existential risk. Such "corporeal" conceptualizations of the Divine were synonymous with a lack of spiritual depth and incapable of offering personal transformation. In other words, linked to his critique of this rudimentary "conceptual" dimension of a God representation was a moral one. So it is that Augustine, recalling how as a boy his prayers to God were more in the form of wish-fulfillment, opines that such a belief system did not entail self-transformation and, as such, merited the designation of "foolishness" (*Confessions* 1.9). One can then surmise that Augustine's later evaluation of his boyhood faith was that it, like the state of his soul at that time, was disordered, even if it had the potential of becoming less so through the vicissitudes of life and reflection.

Even given such critiques, one cannot simply dismiss classic-reductive studies out of hand. The dialogical use of the star metaphor and our stress on inclusivity allows that "faith seeking understanding" (as Augustine would have it) may well be encumbered, to some extent, by developmental baggage. Inclusivity holds that there may well have been oedipal and pre-oedipal elements operative in the "quilt" of Augustine's God representation and the value of applying a "basement theology" approach to some of his more dubious theological formulations. At the same time, the dialogical responses and the later changes evident in Augustine's God representations suggest the additional need for adaptive and transformational approaches to understand the full range of his faith journey.

Adolescence: Manicheanism and Adaptive Views

Such considerations become immediately relevant when one turns to Augustine's narrative (books 3–6) summarizing a nine-year period of his life (19–28) – one that psychologists would refer to as late adolescence to early adulthood. While anthropologists warn us that the life stage we call "adolescence" is not universal and, where present, culturally variable, being next to nonexistent in some societies and certainly not as significant or long as it is in our own, we would be justified to say that certain hallmarks of adolescence as we know them are present in Augustine: the struggle with sexuality, the need to form an identity, the search for answers to the big questions of life, and a *moratorium* that granted him the space and time to resolve such pressing issues.

Augustine tells us of several life changes that, while not unusual for the turmoil of adolescence, are surely of import. Most significantly, with respect to the Oedipal triangle, he informs us that his father had died when he was seventeen – a fact that cannot help but be a psychic earthquake for any teenager in any culture or historical era. Psychoanalysts would say that this cemented, at least unconsciously, Augustine's victory in the oedipal competition, which, in turn, could only have led to increased guilt. Interestingly enough, having left behind his childhood Christianity, it was this event that led him to a new and heightened interest in religious matters. As he put it, it was "in my nineteenth year (my father having died two years previously)" that the change came: "I was on fire, then, My God, I was on fire to leave earthly things behind and fly back to you."[17]

It is impossible for the psychoanalyst to "read" this as anything other than a belated mourning for Patricius, who, now departed, was, according to the Christianity Monica had socialized him into, with God in heaven. One could only "fly back" to him if one left "earthly things." In short, like many adolescents without fathers, he needed an idealized paternal figure. Augustine may have felt guilt but also mourned the loss of his protector and guide. He undoubtedly experienced heightened anxiety, fear, and confusion with respect to his masculine identity (male narcissism). Added to this was a strained relationship with Monica, who, now bereft of a husband, sought emotional sustenance from her son. As mentioned before, Augustine said that Monica "loved having me with her, as all mothers do, only she much more than most," a "disorder" he attributed to the heritage of Eve. Finally, typical of adolescence and many young men of his era, Augustine engaged in a significant romantic relationship. Augustine's rhetorically elegant description of the physical and emotional upheaval of puberty and adolescence in *Confessions* 3.1 has proved to be timeless: "I was in love with love.... Being in love with love I looked for something to love; I hated security and a path without snares.... I was fettered happily in bonds of misery so that I might be beaten with ... the rods of jealousy and suspicions, and fears and angers and quarrels."

---

[17] Ibid., 3.4.

It is this life situation that informs a significant change in his God representation. Having drawn away from his boyhood Christianity, Augustine became intrigued by the Manicheans (later deemed a heresy), who, in offering a more sophisticated intellectual approach, were championed by many of those in Augustine's circle (Augustine now being a teacher of the rhetorical arts in nearby Carthage). Indeed, Augustine tells us that what attracted him was their erudition, embodied in the figure of what he thought at the time was their wise bishop Faustus and the intellectual power of their belief system. Most determinative in his gravitation toward the Manicheans was, he tells us, his almost singular obsession with the problem of evil (simply put: Why do people sin, and why do bad things happen to good people?). As the historian Peter Brown notes, the "Manichean answer to the problem of evil is the core of the Manichaeism of the young Augustine."[18]

What, then, was the Manichean "answer" to why people sin? In essence, it boils down to a dualistic conception of the universe in which co-eternal good and evil "substances" were at war. Augustine labeled the evil entity a "Dyad" (which consisted of "anger as in deeds of violence and lust") and the good substance a "Monad," which, accessed through the judicious use of one's reason, was untainted and lacked the harsher paternal qualities of punishment and vengeance.[19] Crucial to this dualism was the notion that one's "sin" was due to the intrusion of the Dyad. As Augustine later put it in a kind of retrospective self-critique:

> I was still of the opinion that it is not we ourselves who sin, but some other nature which is in us; it gratified my pride to think that I was blameless and, if I did something wrong, not to confess that I had done it, so that you might heal my soul, because my soul had sinned against you. Instead, I liked to excuse myself and accuse something else – something that was in me, but was not really I.[20]

The importance of a dualism to offset his adolescent crises cannot be overstated. As Brown once again notes, in pointing to the above quote: "the need to save an untarnished oasis of perfection within himself formed, perhaps, the deepest strain of his adherence to the Manichees."[21]

We have here, then, the inauguration of a new episode in Augustine's life: a change in the state of his soul (due to adolescence) and, in Rizzuto's terms, a corresponding change in both the image-based and conceptual components of his God representation. What can we say about it that

---

[18] P. Brown, *Augustine of Hippo* (Berkeley: University of California Press, 1969), 46.
[19] *Confessions*, 4.15. [20] Ibid., 5.10. [21] Brown, *Augustine of Hippo*, 51.

might go beyond Freud? One of the pivotal observations is that alongside the changes in family and sexuality was the establishment of a career trajectory. As noted, during these years, Augustine toiled, first as student and then as teacher, in what in that day was referred to as the "rhetorical arts." Here Erikson is of value, for one could refer to this academic pursuit in terms of a *moratorium* – a liminal social space akin to a modern university, which gave the young Aurelius the time, leeway, and exposure to diverse enough ideas to experiment and mold a sense of identity and purpose. In the case of Augustine, his reading in humanistic and philosophical literature led to what can aptly be referred to as a "deidealization" of his previous boyhood indoctrination into Monica's Christianity. As he put it: "I therefore decided to give my attention to the study of the Holy Scriptures and to see what they were like.... They seemed unworthy of comparison with the grand style of Cicero."[22] While Augustine eventually rejected Cicero, this quote is indicative of the effect new ideas (the "conceptual" dimension of his God representation) were having on his native Christian belief system. He needed an "ideology" and worldview that made sense and would enable the stage-appropriate task of forming a workable "identity." His childhood Christianity was not capable of providing that needed function.

But why move to the Manichean worldview? Erikson's "adaptive" theory and focus on identity would supplement Augustine's given intellectual and "conscious" reason (i.e., the need to fashion a theodicy or the defense of evil) as his motive by noting the role of unconscious forces. The death of his father, the loss felt as a result, and the need to contain unruly instinctual forces were the deeper reasons for his sudden interest in theodicy. Augustine's retrospective insight into how the Manichean worldview enabled him to evade responsibility for sin is psychoanalytically understood as the need to repress the stage-appropriate emergence of strong, conflicted unconscious desires and tendencies – feelings undoubtedly exacerbated by the continued presence of a domineering mother and loss of a father who both constrained and guided. Indeed, it is noteworthy that Augustine's description of the "evil" substance is an exact equivalent of the instinctual core of the Freudian unconscious: "I called the other a Dyad – anger as in deeds of violence, and lust as in sins of impurity."[23] For Freud the devil (in this case the Dyad), culturally constituted through psychic splitting, is but the projected personification of repressed,

---

[22] *Confessions* 3.5.   [23] Ibid., 4.5.

unwanted unconscious instincts.[24] Augustine, in the throes of adolescence and newfound feelings of sexuality, aggression, and guilt, had found the perfect worldview for dealing with his unconscious and his need for cohesion. Added to the mix was the idealized paternal figure he needed: the bishop Faustus. Interesting in this regard is that Augustine waited almost a decade for Faustus to actually show up at his school. The idealization of and long wait for Faustus indicates the strong need for a paternal, idealized, cultural self-object capable of providing the function of protection, nourishment, and guidance. Here again we see the value of an "adaptive" approach with regard to the advances of ego psychology and object-relations theory.

To sum up, what can be said about books 3–6 is that they show a dramatic change (from Christianity to a Manichean dualism) in Augustine's God representation. This shift can be described as due to several related factors: a change in life stage, the deidealization of Augustine's boyhood Christianity, a growing intellectual sophistication, an enabling social space and *moratorium*, the accessibility of idealized cultural self-objects (such as Faustus), an obsession with the need to defend against strong instinctual forces, and the need to fashion a working identity. Such changes seemed to be adaptive and enabling: they allowed him to navigate the vicissitudes and exigencies of a significant period of his youth until he was ready, as Augustine himself would come to note, for more profound changes. Meanwhile, Augustine had found a suitable worldview to buttress his flagging sense of masculinity, stonewall strong feelings of guilt and conflict, and counteract the pressure from a domineering mother.

Adulthood: Vision and Transformational Approaches

We earlier summarized Augustine's retrospective critiques of his boyhood God representation. Augustine had a similar retrospective critique of his Manichean phase, claiming that the dualism offered by the Manicheans led him to make the continued mistake of "materiality." The notions of the Monad and the Dyad amounted to "substances" that were objects "out there" and, as a result, nothing more than projected figments of his imagination. As he puts it, he tried to "imagine" God using concepts like "size," "weight," "bulk": "my eyesight could reach no further than

---

[24] See A. Rizzuto, *The Birth of the Living God* (Chicago: University of Chicago Press, 1979), 20ff.

bodies and the sight of my mind no further than a fantasy."[25] Further, as we have seen, Augustine thought this imagined notion of a Monad and Dyad forestalled the required task of introspection and its correlate, inner transformation. This was because they fed the notion that his feelings of lust and anger were not really his, but the result of the Dyad working within him.

But things were about to change. In his adulthood, Augustine's God representation undergoes a definitive evolution, which marks his entry into a mature Christian faith. After leaving Africa for Italy, Augustine came to distance himself from the Manicheans, gravitating back to Christianity. Central to his return was the fact that Italian Christianity was being heavily influenced by philosophy, particularly that of Plato and his followers. Many prominent Christian leaders, particularly Bishop Ambrose, whose sermons Augustine attended, were using Platonic ideas to fortify and add sophistication to the teachings of the New Testament. Disillusioned with Manicheanism, Augustine related to a friend that he was open to being "taught" again. In other words, a new evolution of his God representation was in the offing.

Central to this change were two visions, one at Milan and the other at Ostia. Through his association with Ambrose and wider Christian friends, a conceptual change in his God representation was about to occur. To this point, he says he started reading "some books written by the Platonists," specifically those of Plotinus, one of Plato's later followers. As noted in the previous chapter Plotinus's major work, *The Enneads*, proclaimed an introspective, ineffable "something" at the heart of all reality, which he called the One. That said, Plotinus made it clear that no description of the One could possibly do it justice, unless one used negative terms, for it was totally transcendent, prior to any existing thing, without any distinctions, beyond duality, and beyond even "Being" and "non-Being." In that sense it was "apophatic" and recalls what Erikson said about Angelus Silesius's notion of God: *"ein lauter Nichts"* (a "pure Nothing"). In fact, Plotinus and "apophatic theology" are linked, having had a long history in Christian mysticism. To be sure, this history is theologically complicated, and by no means can we say that its multiple and various formulations are identical with that of Plotinus. It is, however, to say this movement was authorized by Augustine, who, while "Christianizing" Plotinus (Augustine has been referred to as a

---

[25] *Confessions* 3.7.

"Christian neo-Platonist"), was, like him, advocating for the actual vision of God over merely "talking" about it – what we in the modern world are apt to call a mystical experience (Augustine's own nomenclature is the vision of God [*visio Dei*] or "intellectual vision"). And so it is in book 7 he describes an introspective movement to a place "deeper than the deepest recesses of my heart" and above the summit of his soul, "higher than the highest I could reach."[26] Having arrived at this inward place, he glimpsed an ineffable light:

> I entered and I saw with my soul's eye (such as it was) an unchangeable light shining above this eye of my soul and above my mind. It was not the ordinary light which is visible to all flesh, nor something of the same sort, only bigger, as though it might be our ordinary light shining much more brightly and filling everything with its greatness. No, it was not like that; it was different, entirely different, from anything of the kind. Nor was it above my mind as oil floats on water or as the heaven is above the earth. It was higher than I, because it made me, and I was lower because I was made by it. He who knows truth knows that light, and he who knows that light knows eternity. Love knows it. O eternal truth and true love and beloved eternity! You are my God; to you I sigh by day and by night.[27]

The importance of vision for Augustine cannot be overstated. As a noted theologian put it, Augustine's "mysticism" runs like a central thread throughout his works: "If there is one constant running through all of Augustine's thinking, it is his preoccupation with the question of happiness.... But the answer is equally uniform: what makes man happy is the possession of God, a possession achieved by way of vision."[28]

The conceptual component of his God representation had shifted in a dramatic way. God was now conceived of as incorporeal, as immutable, and as transcending the ability of the material senses and imagination to conceptualize. This God Augustine would frame paradoxically: "everywhere you are present in your entirety, and no single thing can contain you in your entirety."[29] The location of God was, as we intimated above, now "deeper than the deepest recesses of the heart" and above the summit of the soul.[30] It was this inward and upward God he contrasted with the "empty" "phantasm" God of the "senses" endemic to his earlier Manichean period as well as the rudimentary concept of the heteronomous God he held with the "limited capacities" of boyhood. Framing it with respect to more contemporary terms, Augustine came to the

---

[26] Ibid., 3.6.   [27] Ibid., 7.10.
[28] See B. McGinn, *The Foundations of Mysticism* (New York: Crossroad, 1991), 232.
[29] *Confessions* 1.3.   [30] Ibid., 3.6.

conclusion that in rare cases of states of altered consciousness one might glimpse the Light itself. Indeed, he intimates that such a vision requires one be in something akin to a state of "virtual death" (what we today would call a near-death experience).[31]

This "vision at Milan" signals a crucial juncture in Augustine's spiritual journey. Now, for the first time, Augustine claimed that he understood the changeless, incorporeal nature of God, that "he loved [God] and not a phantom instead of you."[32] As for "evil," as a result of his vision he knew that evil was not a "substance," as he had been taught by the doctrines of Manichaeism, but located in his own will: "a perversity of the will turning away from you, God, the supreme substance, toward lower things."[33]

Augustine goes on to speak in *Confessions* 9.10 of a linked mystical event, the famous vision at Ostia, in which he and his mother were immersed in conversation "standing alone, leaning in a window that looked onto the garden inside the house where we were staying, at Ostia on the Tiber." As they talked they reached a point where they considered how much greater the pleasures and joys of eternal life were than anything that could be granted by the senses and by transient, earthly, corporeal delights. He then goes on to relate a mystical ascent, a dominant feature of which is the stress on silence ("So we said: if to any man the tumult of the flesh grew silent [*sileat*], silent the images of the earth and sea and air ... the very soul") in which both mother and son participated, culminating in a "contact with that eternal wisdom which abides above all things." He then goes on to indicate that such a vision was a foretaste of the beatific vision, the ultimate aim of Christians:

[S]upposing that this state were to continue, that all other visions, visions of so different a kind, were to be withdrawn, leaving only this one to ravish and absorb and wrap the beholder in inward joys, so that his life might forever be like that moment of understanding which we had had and for which we now sighed – would this not be: *Enter into thy Master's joy*? and when shall that be? Shall it be when *we shall all rise again*, though we *shall not all be changed*?[34]

This description is important for two reasons. The first is that it seems unusual that Augustine would ascend to God together with another person and even more so that it was his mother. It is the presence of Monica that has led Freudian classic-reductive theorists to interpret the Ostia vision as evidence of Augustine's continued oedipal problems. They

---

[31] See the discussion in Parsons, *Freud and Augustine in Dialogue*, chapters 2 and 3.
[32] *Confessions* 7.17.   [33] Ibid., 7.16.   [34] Ibid., 9.10.

point out that the vision could be seen as a metaphor for incest, as culminating in a kind of orgiastic, mystical climax. Object-relational theorists, on the other hand, recalling Rolland's oceanic experience, have been more apt to champion an adaptive reading in which the presence of Monica signifies a regression to pre-oedipal nurturance, the rekindling of feelings of love and trust, and the subsequent therapeutic effect of a restored sense of goodness and wholeness.[35]

The adaptive application of Rizzuto's formulation would integrate the above by recasting them in terms of changes in both the developmentally based "images" and more philosophical "conceptual" components of Augustine's God representation. This change would be theorized as due to the interaction of a few pivotal factors: the availability of idealized transference figures such as Bishop Ambrose, the integration of significant writings/texts (e.g., the books of the Platonists), pivotal conversion and mystical experiences, and a long period of intense inner reflection and "soul-searching." To unpack these factors further, Augustine portrays Ambrose in idealized terms as "exceptionally learned," "honored by people of importance," and, most significantly, commanding the respect and devotion of Monica.[36] Intimating that a form of transference occurred, Augustine goes on to say: "That man of God welcomed me as a father.... I began to love him at first not as a teacher of the truth but simply as a man who was kind and generous to me."[37] Ambrose, then, served as a kind of fatherly sponsor for rekindling Augustine's interest in Christianity, because *this* kind of Christianity, as opposed to his previous take on Christianity, was imbued with philosophical sophistication. It is significant that Ambrose, among others, used neo-Platonic ideas in his sermons. As Peter Brown notes: "it is possible to trace literal borrowings from Plotinus in the bishop's sermons."[38] This suggests that the impact of texts ("the books of the Platonists") was heightened precisely because they were mediated by idealized significant others. Augustine's enormous capacity for inner reflection added to this mix. As Brown again notes: "as with many immensely fertile thinkers, it is difficult to imagine Augustine as a reader. Yet, what happened at this crucial time and in the years that follow was a spell of long and patient reading, apparently aided by some

---

[35] See the essays by C. Kligerman, J. Dittes, and V. Gay in Capps and Dittes, eds., *The Hunger of the Heart*.
[36] *Confessions* 6.1–3.   [37] Ibid., 5.13.
[38] Brown, *Augustine of Hippo*, 94–95, 80–105.

discussions."³⁹ Such ideas were, as is evident, "thoroughly absorbed, 'digested,' and transformed by Augustine."⁴⁰

The therapeutic leverage mediated through the figure of Ambrose and others, alongside the transformative effect of ideas, pivotal visions, and "soul-searching," engaged not only the conceptual dimension of Augustine's God's representation but the developmentally based image aspects as well. His mystical experiences as well as his conversion experience to Christianity are seen in Rizzuto's terms as the "ego-syntonic" release of the developmentally based "images" (both paternal [oedipal] and maternal [pre-oedipal]) of God, now unearthed and released to be consciously acknowledged and therapeutically "worked through."

What, then, of the transformational? The way to justify a transformational reading comes through dialogue with theological and literary perspectives. Theological analyses of the Ostia vision, dependent in part on literary criticism, remind us that Augustine was a professor of rhetoric as well as a bishop. Strictly speaking, the vision at Ostia is not an autobiographical text revealing unconscious content but rhetorically constructed and hence fictional. Augustine never "really" ascended with his mother to the One. What, then, was Augustine trying to convey in this text? We have already said that Augustine was influenced by Plotinus, but that he also "Christianized" him in significant ways in order to distinguish Christian mysticism from that of Plotinus. This text shows that effort at work. The first issue regards gender. Throughout the *Confessions* Monica is portrayed as the paradigmatic person of faith. The fact she was a woman is crucial in that the notion that an "unlearned" woman like Monica could take an active role in the upward ascent to vision would be foreign to Plotinus. The second and linked issue regards the framing of Monica as a symbol for community. For Plotinus the ascent upward was solitary: "the flight of the alone to the Alone" (i.e., the One). But Augustine situates the ascent to vision with Monica in a "walled garden" (he and Monica "were standing alone, leaning in a window which looked onto the garden inside the house we were staying"). For Augustine this walled garden was a metaphor for the church. The rhetorically embellished message, then, was that was the ascent to God is communal. There is a heavenly tabernacle and an earthly one, and it is by dint of membership in the latter that vision is eventually attained.⁴¹ In sum, the earlier

---
³⁹ Ibid., 95.   ⁴⁰ Ibid.
⁴¹ See the discussion in Parsons, *Freud and Augustine in Dialogue*, chapter 1.

psychoanalytic studies we adduced misread Augustine. Their lack of dialogue amounts to a singular fact: they did not get "the case" right. This does not negate other evidence that may point to oedipal and pre-oedipal determinants in the quilt of Augustine's God representation. Rather, it questions the extent to which such determinants account for his visions.

If this is accepted, then we are still left trying to understand the interpretation of mystical vision. Is it merely a reflection of developmental issues or, as transformational theory has it, the "third" dim nostalgia beyond the paternal and maternal, the "unborn core of creation" Erikson references and of which the mystics speak? A transformational approach, unlike the classic reductive or adaptive one, would grant the legitimacy of vision. Recall that Erikson's valorization of a transformational dimension references Silesius and Plotinus, insofar as the former was influenced by Christian apophatic theology. Moreover, as noted earlier, Augustine emphasizes that vision is enabled by being in an altered state ("virtual death"). Indeed, Augustine's "ascent" motif (to the Light) emphasizes the refrain of "silence": that of images and thoughts. As one ascends upward, one becomes more silent, which is grist for Deikman's ego-psychological de-automatization theory of what happens during contemplation and the possible activation of mystical intuition. It is there that Augustine, with his "soul's eye," saw the ineffable Light. To be clear, this does not mean that transformational theory necessarily morphs into an adjunct of Christian mystical theology. On the contrary, by positing a generic metapsychological space for the More, it allows for a nonreductive dialogue with any of the variety of mystical encounters understood as being (depending on individual cases) potentially different in degree and perhaps in kind. In other words, using transformational theory does not necessitate subscribing to a perennial core of vision or mysticism. As unpacked in the last chapter with respect to Rolland's oceanic feeling, a psychoanalytically informed constructivist approach does not, epistemologically speaking, adjudicate between alternate and sometimes opposed religious framings of the mystical More, nor does it reduce all differences to a common core. Rather, in the spirit of dialogue, a Winnicottian God representation frames such differences as legitimate dimensions of any belief system: it is a "third" area between "reality" and "unreality" that is tolerated, unchallenged, and nonpathological. Referring back to our earlier discussion concerning the debate over the school of perennialism and that of constructivism, one could say that a God representation, conceived in Winnicottian terms as "transitional," functions as the developmental infrastructure of constructivism.[42]

This analysis has additional explanatory value. Augustine's newfound God representation was also correlated with a new state of his soul: a soteriological regimen, what to the contemporary psychological mind may appear as a form of religious therapy, with the caveat that its aims and normative ideals of health are different, but no less valid, than that of classic psychoanalysis. Recall from the preceding chapter that Kakar, in speaking of Hindu God representations harboring Upanishadic mystical orientations, noted that their aims and goals were different from classic Freudian ones. Their "vision of reality" and aims of "therapy" are optimistic and romantic, culminating in an "exaltation beyond normal human experience." While Augustine was clearly not a Hindu, Kakar's general observations are portable and apply to Augustine's Christian formulations. The goal for him was revealed through vision in that the latter was episodic, a foretaste of the life to come (the "beatific vision"). What was demanded in this life, then, was a reformation of the soul, a "reordering" of one's "disorder" in accord with vision. It is to that end that his soteriological regimen ("religious therapy") was devoted. In this soteriological context, even his celibacy, which may have been determined to a certain extent by developmental factors, is now framed "in the service of" the higher mystical injunction of detachment from worldly matters.

Significantly, it was only after vision that Augustine gains access to the interior life. The many innovative psychological insights he subsequently came to (especially evident in books 10–13) have intrigued both psychologists and theologians. They see in his formulations recognition of the

---

[42] See the discussion in Parsons, *Freud and Augustine in Dialogue*, 100–101. The value of this approach is portable and can be seen in recent developments in the psychology-comparativist dialogue, specifically those concerning alternate ways of framing the Buddhist "More" as found in the works of the psychologists Jack Engler and Mark Epstein (both addressing vipassana [insight] form of meditation) and that of Judith Blackstone (a psychologist in a tantric Tibetan Buddhist lineage). Utilizing the Tibetan distinction between Rangtong and Shentong forms of meditational insight, Blackstone claims that Engler and Epstein are in the former camp, while Shentong (which she valorizes) leads to a deeper, alternate conception of the More. In other words, not all Buddhism holds to a core version of the Divine (see J. Blackstone, *The Empathic Ground* [Albany: State University of New York Press, 2007], chapter 1 and 48ff.). A related point could be said for the doctrine of reincarnation. Psychoanalysis cannot hold to a "lives-cycles" theory, lest it become an adjunct to those religious traditions that believe in reincarnation. But the latter can be admitted and clinically justified if viewed transitionally.

power of sexuality, the hidden quality and opaqueness of the unconscious, the conflicted nature of our various desires and "wills," and the attempt to fashion a therapeutic soteriology that included confession, catharsis, renunciation, and active recognition of how past events determine present habits. So it is that A. C. Outler suggested that Augustine "was far and away the very best – if not the first – psychologist in the ancient world. His observations and descriptions of human motives and emotions, his depth analyses of will and thought in their interaction, and his exploration of the inner nature of the human self – these have established one of the main traditions in European conceptions of human nature, even down to our own time. Augustine is an essential source for both contemporary depth psychology and existentialist philosophy."[43] The pastoral psychologist Donald Capps adds that the *Confessions* is a text in which catharsis, the recall of past events, and an attempt at self-transformation are apparent.[44] Even the noted Augustine scholar Eugene TeSelle has been moved to echo these sentiments, adding that "Augustine is the one who taught the West about selfhood, its freedom, its affections and their disordered orientations, its object-relations, especially in the model of love. Perhaps these insights are the result of Oedipal or narcissistic conflicts, resolved or unresolved. But even if they are unresolved, he did conceptualize the dynamics of the self."[45]

Again, as noted above, this is not to claim that there is an exact equivalence between psychoanalysis and Augustine's mystical therapy. Rather, it is to point out that this evolution in Augustine's God representation represented a step forward, which brought him into line with proponents of the psychology–theology dialogue from Pfister and Tillich onward. In learning from those efforts, a psychoanalytic theory of religion that is reflexive, dialogical, *and* inclusive, with its multiple models offering their respective judicious and qualified contributions, is best positioned to fairly treat the evolution of Augustine's God representation.

---

[43] J. Dittes, "Continuities between the Life and Thought of Augustine," in Capps and Dittes, eds., *The Hunger of the Heart*, 120.
[44] See D. Capps, "Augustine as Narcissist: Of Grandiosity and Shame," in Capps and Dittes, eds., *The Hunger of the Heart*, 169–185. For an in-depth textual treatment of the multiple ways in which Augustine prefigured the insights of psychoanalysis, see Parsons, *Freud and Augustine in Dialogue*.
[45] E. TeSelle, "Augustine as Client and as Theorist," in Capps and Dittes, eds., *The Hunger of the Heart*, 215.

THE EROS OF RAMAKRISHNA'S TANTRIC JOURNEY

For many Hindus the importance of Sri Ramakrishna rivals that of Augustine for Christians. Indeed, the name of Ramakrishna was known even to Freud. Recall in his letter to Freud of December 5, 1927, Rolland remarked not only about his "oceanic feeling" but also about his current work on mysticism east and west, eventually published as his biographies of Ramakrishna and Vivekananda (which he later sent to Freud). Fortunately, as with the case of St. Augustine, there now exist more than a few psychoanalytic studies of Ramakrishna. As a group, the latter not only illustrate the evolving nature of psychoanalytic theory but engage many of the core issues surrounding Freud's analysis of Eastern religions and the counters offered by his respondents in the psychology-comparativist dialogue. Drawing on these studies, then, we will highlight how a revised psychoanalytic theory of religion can best illumine a pivotal aspect of Ramakrishna's religious journey: the nature and vicissitudes of Eros as related to his intent and desire to achieve divine realization.

The Case of Ramakrishna

Ramakrishna (1836–1886) was semi-literate and left no written corpus. Rolland and others were relying on the biographies written by his disciples, of which the one manufactured by "M" (his disciple Mahendranath Gupta) is considered to be the most reliable. These biographies detail his upbringing, pivotal relationships, events of his adult years, emergence as a religious figure, religious visions, and mystical practices (or "sadhanas"). Ramakrishna's family had been brought up in a theistic Hindu tradition (the Vaishnava tradition), which centered on the male god Vishnu and his divine reincarnations (or "avatars") Rama and Krishna (hence his religious title "Ramakrishna"). At the same time, he was also devoted to the goddess Kali, the female half or consort to another high god, Siva, spending time as a curator of a Kali temple near his house.[46]

His spirituality can be linked to the ideas contained in a few seminal Hindu texts. The first is *The Upanishads*, which are the revealed texts at the end of those multiple scriptures referred to as the "Vedas." Since they

---

[46] For an overview of the biographers and life of Ramakrishna, see J. Kripal, *Kali's Child: The Mystical and the Erotic in the Life and Teachings of Ramakrishna* (Chicago: University of Chicago Press, 1995).

are the last installment of those scriptures, they are referred to as "Vedanta" (i.e., the "end" of the Vedas), much like the New Testament (for Christians) is the last installment of the Bible. The Upanishads introduced yoga as a technique for accessing the Divine and valorized the absorption of the soul, or atman, into the "divine ocean," or Brahman, the latter understood to be nondual, inexpressible, without "discerning characteristics" (the term being *nirguna*) and existing alone "without a second" (the term being *advaita*). The second text is the *Bhagavad Gita*, a long poem consisting of a dialogue between Krishna and the warrior Arjuna, thus valorizing a theistic relationship to the Divine. That relationship was characterized as consisting of faith, devotion (bhakti), and the command to do one's allotted caste duty in society with detachment and an attitude of service. The third text is *The Puranas*, a series of scriptures containing tales of the gods, which, among other things, promoted the existential practice of certain modes of devotion (called *bhavas*), each patterned after particular kinds of relationships (wife–husband, servant–master, mother–child, friend). The fourth and final text is the *Tantras*, a series of texts centered on a physiological and mystical current in the body (kundalini and its physiological correlate, the chakra system). The practices and rituals advocated by tantric literature were often seen as subversive in their promotion of transgressive sexual and dietary practices, the latter designed to promote detachment and the cultivation of kundalini.

The English translations of the biographies (which were written in Bengali) omitted what Ramakrishna, in his oral teachings to his disciples, called "secret talk," the content of which was highly erotic. This was intentional, as it was bound to be seen as scandalous by a Western audience and enabled his disciples to portray Ramakrishna as an exponent of Vedanta, that Upanishadic tradition aimed at a "nondual" type of mystical union. The latter bore enough of a resemblance to the Western neo-Platonic mystical tradition that Ramakrishna's heirs and "missionaries" had a better chance of finding success in their endeavors. That strategy, in fact, worked, evinced in the Western institutionalization of the Vedanta Society, the buildings of which can be found in many Western cities. Through time, however, scholarship has reinstated Ramakrishna as a tantric practitioner. It is the latter that best illustrates the nature and dynamics of Ramakrishna's religious intent or desire (Eros) and, as one might imagine given its sexual dimension, psychoanalytic intrigue. As such, it will be the focus of our investigation here.

A general frame for our discussion can be had by recalling the previous chapter where we cited Freud's "psychoanalytic ascent motif," how it was indebted to Plato's ascent of Eros in his book *The Symposium* but stopped short of Plato's winged horses in their flight upward to the Sea of Beauty. Ramakrishna, on the other hand, promoted an ascent of Eros that is a cultural variant of that offered by Plato and recalls Rolland's counter to Freud concerning tantra, its view of the "body," and the need to revise psychoanalytic instinct theory. Indeed, Ramakrishna's ascent assumed a tantric mystical physiology of the body in which the kundalini rises through the chakra system, integrating the wisdom released in each chakra until the ascent of kundalini reaches the final (crown) chakra at the top of the head. This ascent required celibacy and mystical practices in that seminal fluid is the raw material ("rocket fuel," so to speak) that, properly cultivated through yogic practices, is alchemically transformed into the spiritual energy of kundalini. Importantly, the ascent involves potentially transgressive sexual themes. Ramakrishna describes the ascent as follows:

This is very secret talk! I saw a boy of twenty-three exactly like me, going up the subtle channel, erotically playing with the vagina-shaped lotuses with his tongue! First the Anus [*guhya*], then the Phallus, then the Navel, the four-petaled, the six-petaled, the ten-petaled – they were all dropping – now they became aroused! When he got to the heart – I remember it well – after he made love to it with his tongue, the drooping twelve-petaled lotus became aroused – and blossomed forth! After that, the sixteen-petaled lotus in the throat and the two-petaled lotus in the forehead [became aroused]. Finally, the thousand-petaled lotus blossomed forth! *Ever since then I have been in this state.*[47]

The reference to the "subtle channel" is to kundalini, while "this state" refers to divine realization (the opening of the crown chakra). The above quote, then, affirms our claim that what we have here is Ramakrishna's culturally variant ascent motif – one that references an erotically tinged tantric psycho-mystical physiology. It is in the context of this ascent motif that Ramakrishna's various visions and practices make religious sense. Most pivotally, it casts light on a central vision that Ramakrishna's biographers agree was the religious event that ignited the trajectory and aim of his spiritual path (thus being analogous to Augustine's vision at Milan and Ostia). The vision in question is that of the goddess Kali, which occurred when Ramakrishna was in

---

[47] Ibid., 127.

late adolescence and the curator of a Kali temple. Frustrated by his inability to realize the vision of the Mother, Ramakrishna resorted to drastic steps:

> There was then an intolerable anguish in my heart because I could not have Her vision. Just as a man wrings a towel forcibly to squeeze out all the water from it, I felt as if somebody caught hold of my heart and mind and was wringing them likewise. Greatly afflicted by the thought that I might not have Mother's vision, I was in great agony. I thought that there was no use in living such a life. My eyes suddenly fell upon the sword that was in the Mother's temple. I made up my mind to put an end to my life with it that very moment. Like one mad, I ran and caught hold of it, when suddenly I had the wonderful vision of the Mother, and fell down unconscious.... And what I saw was a boundless infinite conscious sea of light! However far and in whatever direction I looked, I found a continuous succession of effulgent waves coming forward, raging and streaming from all sides with great speed. Very soon they fell on me and made me sink to the abysmal depths of infinity.[48]

It should be reiterated that while Kali is framed differently throughout the history of Hinduism, for our purposes what is relevant is how she is understood as the female half or consort of the male god Shiva, at certain historical junctures usurping him and becoming the reigning deity of a local temple (as was the case with Ramakrishna). Her iconic representation is that of a virtually nude woman, dressed only with a garland of severed heads, with four arms (two on either side), her legs standing on her quiescent male half (the god Siva, portrayed as lying on his back and sometimes attached to a rising snake). Her two right arms symbolize aid and boons, while the two left arms, one with a sword and the other a severed head, symbolize the way to mystical union with her (i.e., the metaphorical directive of the need to "cut off one's ego" to achieve union with the divine ocean). In reaching for Kali's sword, then, Ramakrishna was following a scriptural directive. The garland of heads around her virtually nude body mirrors this theme (i.e., the severed heads of those who have succeeded in union), while her foot on top of the quiescent Siva and the resultant rising snake can be taken to signify, among other things, the "pumping out" of both cosmic divine energy (or "Shakti") and its physical manifestation in the body (i.e., kundalini).

---

[48] As cited in Kakar, *The Analyst and the Mystic*, 11–12.

The Analysis

Armed now with the two basic elements of our "case" (the erotically tinged ascent motif and the vision and symbolism of the Mother), the question is how subsequent psychoanalytic studies have seen fit to interpret Ramakrishna's Eros and how, taken together, they argue for the valorization of a reflexive, dialogical, inclusive psychoanalytic theory of religion.

Classic-Reductive Studies

The classic-reductive analyses of Ramakrishna's Eros ensure that his religious intent and visions are reduced to developmental processes, usually followed by a pejorative evaluation regarding its value for healing and adaptation to reality. The psychoanalyst Jeffrey Masson speaks for this perspective when, citing Freud's case history of the schizophrenic (then called "dementia praecox") Daniel Schreber, concludes that Ramakrishna "had delusions and hallucinations at least equal to if not greater than that of Schreber."[49] This, as we saw in Chapter 6, is the type of "unreflexive" interpretation Rolland had in mind when, in response to Freud, he warned that psychoanalysts were apt to put Ramakrishna in an insane asylum. Again, following Freud's views on Hindu worldviews as set forth in his essay on the Acropolis, Masson confidently states that Vedanta philosophy, with its emphasis on the Ocean of Being as the "truly" Real entity and, as a result, the world as we see it an illusion (i.e., maya), signifies the pathological processes of "derealization" (the world is not real) and "depersonalization" (the self is not real).[50] Narasingha Sil, a psychoanalytically inclined historian, in specifically addressing the vision of Kali and endorsing the lead of Masson and Freud, warns that "it is necessary to understand the origins and nature of Ramakrishna's psychosis ... in order to make any sense of his theosis."[51] In typical classic-reductive parlance, this signifies that it is developmental trauma that is the true cause of any and all of Ramakrishna's visions. As to the latter, Sil suggests that Ramakrishna was most likely

---

[49] J. Masson and T. C. Masson, "The Study of Mysticism: A Criticism of W. T. Stace," *Journal of Indian Philosophy* 4 (1976): 109–125.
[50] Ibid. And see J. Masson, *The Oceanic Feeling* (Dordrecht: D. Riedel, 1980); "Indian Psychotherapy?," *Journal of Indian Philosophy* 7 (1979): 327–332; and "The Psychology of the Ascetic," *Journal of Asian Studies* 35 (1976): 611–625.
[51] N. Sil, *Ramakrishna Paramahamsa: A Psychological Profile* (Leiden: Brill, 1991), 5.

seduced in childhood, which, along with the death of his father and brother, led to a greater identification with women. The vision of the divine Mother, then, becomes not so much a "father" religion as it does a "mother" religion. Ramakrishna's meditative trances were regressive and led to the hallucination of "union" with her, being most likely the "outcome of his depression and aggression towards the most important object (the Mother goddess) in his life ... and thus, in Freudian terms ... a classic case of the shadow of the object falling upon the ego."[52]

Of course, for Freud, religion is linked to not simply one but any number of manifestations of the libido, and gender identity is not fluid but essentialized. Classic-reductive studies of Ramakrishna follow suit. For example, Sil thinks his willing participation in the *bhava* of wifely devotion (found in the *Puranas* as a prescribed religious practice) in which Ramakrishna, identifying with Krishna's lover Radha through cross-dressing, should be interpreted as the religious excuse for the expression of his feminine identification and urges.[53] Seizing on his virginity and simplicity, Sil further frames him as a *"puer aeternus"* (eternal boy).[54] Masson proclaims that Ramakrishna was a "happy pervert" precisely because the pathology inherent in his religio-cultural surround countenanced, if not encouraged, bizarre behaviors like cross-dressing. Indeed, noting that Plato's ascent to the Sea of Beauty starts with the beauty of boys, Masson goes so far to suggest that the ascent of Eros to the Divine in both Plato and Ramakrishna was but "an intellectually sublimated reversal of the homosexual relationship."[55] Jeffrey Kripal, a psychoanalytically informed Indologist, joins this line of interpretation by spying in Ramakrishna unconscious, unresolved homoerotic elements. In so doing he points to two significant facts of the vision of Kali: (1) the culturally shared, tradition-based drama where Kali's sword demands one's severed head in return for mystic vision and (2) Ramakrishna's personal, idiosyncratic, homoerotic "vocabulary of desire" ("anxious longing," "enkindling," "attraction," "strange sensation," and "wrung like a wet towel"). Performing exegesis on the former with respect to Hindu iconography (where being "beheaded" by Kali's sword, psychoanalytically speaking, signifies male castration fears) and rooting the latter in Ramakrishna's later linguistic conjunction between his desire for the Mother and homoerotic longing for his boy disciples, Kripal concludes it was the shame

---

[52] Ibid., 118.   [53] Ibid., 34.   [54] Ibid., 32.
[55] J. Masson and C. Hanly, "A Critical Examination of the New Narcissism," *International Journal of Psychoanalysis* 57 (1976): 59–60.

Ramakrishna felt over illicit homoerotic desires that was complicit in his first vision of Kali.[56]

Despite evident differences of interpretation, all the above fits in well with the general classic-reductive approach that sees Ramakrishna's Eros as reflective of developmental determinants. In emphasizing the reflexive dimension of our formula, we may ask the extent to which such analyses allow room for ethnographic reflection. That can be answered in the negative as, on the whole, they follow in the footsteps of Freud's psychoanalytic universalism, as we saw in *Totem and Taboo*, which eschews the kind of meaningful dialogue with other social sciences that would allow space for culture to play a definitive role in the interpretative enterprise. They do not see psychoanalytic theory as an ethnoscience that, applied cross-culturally in an unreflective manner, can harbor a form of orientalism and colonialism that reflects the norms and values of Western society, thus interfering with a true appreciation of the nuances and subtleties of the phenomenon in question. As a result, Ramakrishna's gender identity and sexual orientation is easily labeled and pathologized, with nary a reflexive thought about how psychoanalytic views on gender and sexuality may reflect Western cultural constructions and norms.

Again, one may ask: Do these models evince any meaningful dialogue with comparativist perspectives? The reductive universalism championed in these studies holds that no religion harbors "ontological" truths. The mystical assumptions (the "More") of Eastern religions are a priori negated, being traceable to the vicissitudes of development and conflict between the structural elements of the psyche, there to be diagnosed as pathological. But it is questionable whether they have done the textual and theological work that allows them to so easily obviate the need for a richer dialogue. It is pertinent in this regard to look to two Indologists, Wilhelm Halbfass and Richard Gombrich, who have offered definitive critiques of the selective, misleading appropriation of the texts and theology of the Hindu tradition exhibited in these classic psychoanalytic studies.[57] It would not be an overstatement to say that the word "dialogue" ceases to have any meaning when the tools employed in the cross-cultural study of religion are so cavalierly ignored. Without entirely negating the worth of classic-reductive models (their qualified value being

---

[56] See Kripal, *Kali's Child*.
[57] R. Gombrich, "Review of *The Oceanic Feeling*, by Jeffrey Masson," *Journal of the Royal Asiatic Society* 1 (1983): 75–78; W. Halbfass, "Review of *The Oceanic Feeling*, by Jeffrey Masson," *Journal of Asian Studies* 41 (1982): 387–388.

detailed below), such cautionary tales suggest the need to look to psychoanalytic studies that employ reflexive and dialogical adaptive/transformational models.

Reflectivity and Dialogue: Adaptive Studies

To this end, the Indian psychoanalyst Sudhir Kakar offers us a very different portrait of Ramakrishna. Kakar is particularly fond of ego-psychology and object-relations theory as found in Erikson, Kohut, and Winnicott, all of whom, as we have seen, rejected Freud's myopic, pejorative evaluation of religion. So too is he adamant about his call for a "radical revision" of psychoanalytic theory and the need to include what anthropologists refer to as the "native's point of view."[58] The pervading theme of his written corpus lies in denying the (culturally mandated) discovery of an absolute truth, walking the fine line between psychological universalism and cultural relativism, and respecting different (and equal) visions of reality, mental health, gender identity, and selfhood. Kakar, then, is unrelentingly critical of those psychoanalysts like Masson and Sil who pathologize religious mystics like Ramakrishna. As one might expect, he sees in the latter the Orientalist and colonialist tendencies of psychoanalysis. Their efforts, he says, are "neither careful enough nor sensitive enough to its subject matter," resulting in the "banal oversimplification of human motives and debunking of human endeavors."[59] Such work, continues Kakar, is of "special interest to an Indian psychoanalyst" for it is the "refusal of psychoanalysts to engage themselves with the mystical model of man and their predilection to dismiss it perfunctorily" that is but "another example of Western parochialism in the human sciences."[60] Kakar insists that all attempts at cross-cultural applied psychoanalysis must be qualified by taking into account new information gleaned through specifically Indian case history material and relevant ethnographic observations. Kakar, then, not only champions the use of "adaptive" psychoanalytic theories of religion; he literally extends their cross-cultural applicability by creating, through his case histories and inclusion of relevant ethnographic detail, a new form of

---

[58] Kakar, *The Analyst and the Mystic*, 3, 14.
[59] S. Kakar, "Reflections on Psychoanalysis, Indian Culture, and Mysticism," *Journal of Indian Philosophy* 10 (1982): 296.
[60] Ibid., 289, 292.

culturally sensitive metapsychology. This is another instance of what we mean when we speak of the need for psychoanalysis to be "reflective."

On the one hand, Kakar is not beyond spying the continued presence and of developmental elements in Ramakrishna's life. On the other, unlike the classic reductive models, he is also willing to look for adaptive and transformational elements. This means a total engagement with the religio-cultural context that guided Ramakrishna's sense of self, sexuality, and gender identity. For example, in the case of Ramakrishna's desire to achieve liberation, Kakar thinks that the tantric striving for deeper insight into the foundational nature of the self cannot be reduced to mere pathology and regressive states. To be sure, he allows for the latter, as he understands that what he calls the "motivational skein" of the religious intent to seek the Real is complex and, as per our "star" and "baggage" metaphors, may be overdetermined in a way that includes developmental contributions. However, he departs from classic-reductive and adaptive approaches when he includes one of our "transformational" theorists, Jacques Lacan (whom he refers to as one of the "mystics of psychoanalysis"), to legitimate the psycho-mystical quest for the Divine:

> Lacan ... has postulated that man's psychic life constantly seeks to deal with a primordial state of affairs which he calls the Real. The Real itself is unknowable, though we constantly create myths as its markers. Perhaps the principal myth involves the rupture of a basic union, the separation from the mother's body, leaving us with a fundamental feeling of incompletion. The fantasies around this insufficiency are universal, governing the psyche of both patients and analysts alike. In the psyche, this lack is translated as desire, and the human venture is a history of desire as it ceaselessly loses and discovers itself in (what Lacan calls) The Imaginary and, with the advent of language, The Symbolic order. Born of rupture, desire's fate is an endless quest for the lost object; all real objects merely interrupt the search.... The mystical quest seeks to rescue from primal repression the constantly lived contrast between an original interlocking and a radical rupture. The mystic, unlike most others, does not mistake his hunger for its fulfillment. If we are all fundamentally perverse in the play of our desire, then the mystic is the only one who seeks to go beyond the illusion of The Imaginary and, yes, also the *maya* of The Symbolic register.[61]

Kakar goes on to add more sophistication to the nature of this striving. As we have seen, the term given to this devotion – bhakti – marked much of Ramakrishna's life. Here is where Kakar calls for a culturally sensitive, reflective form of psychoanalytic theorizing. Recalling anthropological critiques (in Chapter 2) that countered Freud by calling attention to the

---

[61] Kakar, *The Analyst and the Mystic*, 27.

need to allow for culturally specific defense mechanisms, Kakar obliges by reflexively framing *bhavas* as a culturally distinct Indian ego defense mechanism akin to Freud's understanding of the nature and function of "sublimation" in Western culture. *Bhava* is defined by Kakar as a passionate form of devotion done "with all one's heart ... soul ... might."[62] So framed, it engenders an intense form of experiencing similar to extreme forms of love, grief, and fear. While such passion may well unearth developmental issues, it can also transform them into the altered, ecstatic state that bequeaths visionary products.

Again, Kakar insists that the relative notion of gender identity, when run through the aims and practices of tantra, is best understood in terms of actualizing a culturally alternate gender ideal: that of divine androgyny. Such an ideal is not seen as "abnormal" or "perverted" or anything other than one of many equal, if different, cultural and religious solutions to the existential challenges surrounding universal conflicts about gender identity and sexual orientation. To this end, he notes that object-relations theory does not posit, as did Freud, that both boys and girls are initially born as "little men" but, because the mother is the first "object" with which we identify, posits them as "little women." For males, this means that the de-repression and "ego-syntonic" (i.e., accepted by the ego) integration of one's primary femininity is a developmental task – one recognized in Hinduism and targeted by many of its tantric practices.[63] Armed with this new model, Kakar interprets Ramakrishna's various practices as activating what Winnicott called the "pure female element."[64] The de-repression and integration of the latter may well be heralded, in certain cultures and religions (as with tantra), as a gender ideal (i.e., divine androgyny) to be realized.

Kakar goes further by linking the achievement of divine androgyny to a specific form of the multiple, available, and relatively equal modes of adaptation to reality. For example, one such Western ideal mode is expressed in the oft-used notion of the "Protestant ethic," which valorizes the need for continual "doing," "mastery," and even "active opposition." Tantra, however, valorizes a more "feminine" mode, reflected in the Hindu notions of *ananda* (the bliss of divine grace) and "focused receptivity." The latter terms are defined with respect to a permanent form of psychological transformation centered around a receptive, empathic

---

[62] Ibid., 18.
[63] See Kakar, *Shamans, Mystics, and Doctors*, chapter 6 ("Tantra and Tantric Healing").
[64] Kakar, *The Analyst and the Mystic*, 30-34.

attunement with the flow of everyday events, championing a subjectivity imbued with the delight of creative apperception and the virtues of simply "being" and the more relaxed attitude of "reception absorption."[65] By offering a reflexive portrait of gender and sexuality, then, Kakar shows a way out of the hegemony of an unreflexive, culturally assumed essentialist view, which can prejudice psychoanalytic interpretations of religious phenomena.

Reflexivity and Dialogue: Transformational Perspectives

Kakar's use of Lacan to legitimate the mystical intent of Ramakrishna is carried forward by Kripal. We have seen that Kripal employed classic-reductive models in arguing that Ramakrishna was a tantric practitioner whose visions were fueled by unconscious homoerotic desire. However, he then turns around and, by way of critiquing Masson, offers a reflexive, transformational way to go beyond the classic-reductive approach. In explicitly rejecting Masson's "dogmatic, universalizing rhetoric" and the "ontological reductionism it implies," Kripal insists that Ramakrishna's mystical visions were at times revelatory.[66] The central problem of his analysis is how to illumine the developmental dimension of Ramakrishna's religiosity while simultaneously legitimating the ontological ground revealed in his mystical visions. In so doing, Kripal promotes a reading of Ramakrishna's mysticism (and here he explicitly draws analogies with Plato's ascent motif) that would account for "a homoerotic infatuation harnessed and 'winged' for ecstatic flight."[67] His aim is to relate mystical experience to both "the physical and emotional experience of sexuality and ... the deepest ontological levels of religious experience."[68] Kripal does this by building a dialogue that includes a new cross-cultural category he calls "the erotic," which utilizes Lacan and the "mystics" of psychoanalysis and (in taking a portable lesson we found best articulated in the psychology–theology dialogue) the philosophical, dialectical take on Freud advocated by Paul Ricoeur.

Unpacking this dialogical project piece by piece, Kripal defines his cross-cultural category of "the erotic" as "a dimension of human experience that is simultaneously related both to the physical and emotional experience of sexuality and to the deepest ontological levels of religious experience."[69] So framed, Kripal thinks that "the erotic" is a term in

---

[65] Ibid., 34; Kakar, "Tantra and Tantric Healing," 155–179.
[66] Kripal, *Kali's Child*, 358, n. 71.   [67] Ibid., 24.   [68] Ibid., 23.   [69] Ibid., 23.

which "the horizons of religious experience and psychoanalysis can meet in the act of interpretation."[70] In the specific case of Ramakrishna and his tantric sensibility, this can be done only if one modifies the Freudian view of the "body," which is to say, of the instincts. While Kripal does not mention Rolland, it is pertinent to again recall he had suggested that psychoanalysts look closer at the reality of Hindu views on human physiology as implied in the notions of kundalini and the chakra system. From the tantric perspective, sexuality and aggression are understood as important energies, but, because they are framed as belonging to the lower chakras (specifically the first three chakras), their ultimate importance is relativized with respect to the higher, transmuted spiritual energies found in the higher chakras. As one proceeds upward through various meditational practices, sexual and aggressive drives are literally "alchemically transformed" into a refined spiritual energy. The tantric "body" is one that "goes beyond" the Freudian body in its postulation of an innate energy that is at once biological, psychological, and religious. Those psycho-physiological structures known as chakras and the mystical understanding they bequeath become the markers of development and "ascent." The outcome of this dialogical give-and-take, then, is that Freudian libido-based notions of development and sublimation are turned on their head, being relativized with respect to a tantric physiology and its aim of "realization." As has been said, from the standpoint of the successful tantric, "Freud only got to the third Chakra."[71]

If this is the case, and one wishes to dialogically conjoin psychoanalysis and tantric views on the ascent of Eros, one must utilize transformational theory. Kripal obliges by drawing on Lacan's commentary on Bernini's statue, "The Ecstasy of Saint Teresa," in answering the question: "And what is her *jouissance*, her *coming* from?":

Lacan was clear enough about his own answer to where Teresa was "coming from." He rejected the notion that the mystical can be reduced to sexuality and instead speculated that such ecstatic experiences of a *"jouissance* which goes beyond" issue forth from our own ontological ground.... Ramakrishna in *samadhi*, not unlike Bernini's "Teresa in Ecstasy," is obviously "coming." But "what is his *jouissance*, his *coming* from?"... I have respected the religious world of Tantra and have chosen to interpret Ramakrishna's mystico-erotic experiences within that universe. I would argue, then, that the saint's experiences were "coming from" the ontological ground of his Tantric world.... I would insist,

[70] Ibid.   [71] Ibid., 43.

moreover, that such a realization be understood on its own terms, as a genuine religious experience.[72]

While legitimating Ramakrishna's vision as touching noumenal ground, Kripal also goes on to argue for the benefit of an *inclusive* psychoanalytic approach. Drawing on Paul Ricoeur, he posits in the ascent of Ramakrishna's Eros both a progressive (cultural-mystical) and regressive (psychoanalytic) meaning. Adding the anthropologist Gananath Obeyesekere's cultural take on Ricoeur's dialectic between Freudian *arche* and religious *telos*, Kripal paves the way for the application of a reflexive, inclusive approach:

But sometimes, in exceptional cases, we find genuine two-way "symbols" that function *both* as symptoms, hearkening back to the original crisis, *and* as numinous symbols, pointing to a resolution of the crisis, greater meaning, and what Obeyesekere calls a "radical transformation of one's being." Obeyesekere identifies Ramakrishna as one of those "exceptional cases" in which the symptom became a symbol and turned a crisis into an experience of the sacred: "Ramakrishna's Hinduism permits the progressive development of the personal symbol.... To Ramakrishna his own mother is mother Kali who is *the* Mother and the guiding principle of cosmic creativity. Through Kali, Ramakrishna has achieved trance and knowledge of a radically different order from the others, and he can progress to the heart of a specifically Hindu reality that is essentially salvific.'... Here, then, is where I would locate the meaning of Ramakrishna's *eros* – both in his obvious infatuation with his boy disciples, an infatuation somehow connected with the archaic "regressive" motivations of his own personal history... *and* in a "progressive," essentially mystical, order of rapture and vision ... what was once a crisis became the secret, not only of his mystical and charismatic success, but of his very divinity. Kali's iconographic form was the primary symbolic focus of this transformation, of this dialectical movement back and forth between the regressive and the progressive.[73]

Importantly, while Kripal spies elements of an unresolved homoeroticism in Ramakrishna's *arche*, he is willing to concede to Kakar that, as a result of the religious transformation achieved through religious practices, such energies could well have culminated in the establishment of a divine androgyny.[74]

Finally, with respect to this and other cases, adaptive/transformational analyses cannot wholly dispense with classic-reductive models when properly qualified and judiciously applied. For example, we saw at the

---

[72] Ibid., 326. [73] Ibid., 323–324.
[74] While not apparent in his written corpus, Kripal has orally affirmed this (personal communication).

end of Chapter 6 how the Buddhist psychoanalysts Jack Engler and Jeff Rubin warned that even supposed Buddhist "masters" evince pathology. Conventional and contemplative lines of development do not necessarily proceed in a linear fashion but should be understood as interactive. In other words, contemplative achievements do not necessarily leave behind developmental determinants. Such cautionary tales are portable. The guru scandals involving sexual perversions, power, and the expression of archaic forms of grandiosity are evidence in this regard, as are theological formulations and mystical movements tied to racism, misogyny, and nationalism (e.g., what we earlier referred to as "Zen nationalism"). In such cases, then, classic-reductive studies can be likened to sentries standing guard at the top steps of the basement, ready to be employed when the occasion demands.[75]

---

[75] Rubin offers a good example of the interactive (and not linear) view of development and what we call an inclusive psychoanalytic theory in his case history analysis of Louis Nordstrom, who suffered from debilitating developmental trauma yet was also heralded as a Zen master. See C. Brown, "Enlightenment Therapy," New York Times, April 26, 2009, www.nytimes.com/2009/04/26/magazine/26zen-t.html.

Conclusion

Psychoanalytic Spirituality

During the course of this volume we have become familiar with three basic psychoanalytic approaches (i.e., classic-reductive, adaptive, transformational) as they emerged from Freud and developed through history, as well as the multiple enterprises (psychology *of*, psycho-spirituality, the *dialogical* projects) animating the psychology *and* religion movement. Through various cautionary tales, siphoned through the latter projects and advances in psychoanalytic theory, we arrived at the need for a *reflexive, dialogical, inclusive* psychoanalytic theory of religion, as well as portable lessons that can further its application. At the very least, we now see that a simple "cookie-cutter" approach to religious phenomena that emphasizes *only* the Oedipal in a classic-reductive sense is altogether too narrow. While the latter has its value when judiciously applied, the contemporary state of both psychoanalysis and the academic study of religion is far more sophisticated than that of Freud's era. The psychoanalytic theory of religion must follow suit and implement proper revisions lest it be marginalized as a tool for the investigation of religious phenomena.

To supplement the above we will, in this concluding chapter, shift our gaze to acknowledge another facet of the engagement between psychoanalysis and religion, namely, its cultural consequences. In so doing, we return full circle to the poem that started this work, W. H. Auden's "In Memory of Sigmund Freud," in which he framed Freud's impact on contemporary culture with the following words: "to us he is no more a person / now but a whole climate of opinion / under whom we conduct our different lives." What Auden meant was that our era, our cultural soup, is undeniably "therapeutic." A reigning impact of that culture on our view of religion is best summed up by Paul Ricoeur's "hermeneutics of suspicion" – one that consists in the *deconstruction* of any and all religious expressions as but projections of unconscious contents. Yet this is only half the story. The net effect of the narrative offered in this volume suggests that psychoanalytic modes of thought and clinical spaces have contributed to an alteration of how we think of religion in a *constructive* sense. In furthering this line of thought, we will highlight two ways in which this is the case: (1) by creating a "therapeutic" cultural super-ego to offset the "unpsychological" proceedings of the religious cultural super-ego and (2) by enabling the pursuit of an unchurched, inner-worldly spirituality. Certainly, the notion of "psychoanalytic spirituality," the title of this conclusion, would be anathema to Freud. However, it would not be received as such by Kohut and his valorization of Dag Hammarskjöld's "unchurched" form of rational mysticism. In an indirect, unintended sense, and certainly against the wishes of its founder, psychoanalysis has helped gin up a post-institutional, psychoanalytically informed spirituality. To show how this is the case involves once again tinkering with the definitional problem of religion, this time as framed by the "other" social sciences.[1]

THE EMERGENCE OF THE THERAPEUTIC CULTURAL SUPER-EGO

Sociological and anthropological perspectives on psychoanalysis, religion, and culture help us answer a few key questions: How did the morphing to a therapeutic culture happen? What were its mechanisms, and what cultural strands contributed to its ascendancy? How does it mark a difference with the religious cultures of the past? What is meant by a term such as "psychoanalytic spirituality"?

Auden's poem reflects a shift in the cultural super-ego. Recall that Freud, especially in *Future of an Illusion* and *Civilization and Its Discontents*, was adamantly opposed to what he called the "unpsychological" proceedings of the cultural (religious) super-ego, endeavoring to replace it with his secular cure of souls. While cautioning against any tendency to see him

---

[1] See William B. Parsons, "Psychoanalytic Spirituality," in *Spirituality and Religion: Psychoanalytic Perspectives. The Annual of Psychoanalysis*, ed. J. Weiner and J. Anderson (Catskill, NY: Mental Health Resources, 2007), 83–96. To be sure, any attempt at cultural analysis such as the one we are undertaking must do away with the concept of cause in favor of a Weberian elective affinity, the latter being further complicated not only because of the degree of difficulty involved in isolating and naming such multiple, diverse cultural strands but also because of the degree of impossibility involved in how they morph through their interaction. What is offered here, then, is but a small contribution to untangling that knot.

as a prophet, also recall how in *Civilization and Its Discontents* he noted that "the super-ego of an epoch of civilization ... is based on the impression left behind by the personalities of great leaders – men of overwhelming force of mind."[2] It is here that the "other" social sciences fill Freud's methodological gap. Indeed, there are a few seminal studies that, in attempting to account for the shift to a therapeutic culture, have provided a psycho-social infrastructure to Auden's more poetic observation. Prominent among them is Philip Rieff's now classic work *The Triumph of the Therapeutic.*[3] In articulating a theory of how cultural change occurs, Rieff's thesis was informed by the eminent sociological theorist Max Weber. In his *The Protestant Ethic and the Spirit of Capitalism*, Weber sought to show how charismatic figures and their original ideas (in this case those of Protestant reformers like John Calvin and Martin Luther), mediated through institutional structures and their accoutrements (like the Church, priests, and pastoral handbooks), could end up affecting what Weber called "whole groups of peoples." In the case of the early Protestants, Weber noted the significance of one particular "idea," the doctrine of predestination, defined simply as the directive of a wholly transcendent and unreachable God, who, in his majesty, had appointed some people to heaven, others to hell. As Weber frames it, in that era the average Protestant churchgoer was anxious in the extreme about salvation and sought pastoral advice as to how to ascertain the certainty of being predestined for heaven. Pastors and their handbooks counseled hard work along with an ascetic attitude toward what was inevitably the accumulation of money and worldly matters. The aim was not riches but to gain assurance of salvation, and the everyday Protestant literally created the certitude of salvation through hard work "in the world" (i.e., "inner-worldly"). To describe how this behavioral shift affected society, Weber used a conceptual term, the fabled "ideal type," which, in the case of the early Protestants, he dubbed the "inner-worldly ascetic." Weber argued that a new form of capitalism (for it had existed before) based on continual growth and the reinvestment of profit was not a normal phenomenon but a steroidal form created by salvation anxiety (hence the "spirit" of capitalism). Through time, the valorization of the Protestant "work ethic" has become part of our cultural super-ego.

This is where Rieff picks up the thread of Weber's argument. He sees Freud and his fellow psychologists as the new "idea" men and the

---

[2] Freud, *Civilization and Its Discontents*, S.E. 21: 141.
[3] Philip Rieff, *The Triumph of the Therapeutic* (New York: Harper, 1966).

psychological clinic as the new institutional mechanism for disseminating theories about the nature of the person, our predicament in life, and what to do about it. Indeed, as suggested above, Freud himself adopts a strategy close to this Weberian line of thought (even if not methodologically articulated as such). For Rieff, the consequences were quite extraordinary and involved a shift from what he called "positive communities "to "negative communities." Up until the twentieth century, diverse human civilizations had been "positive communities," their defining characteristic being the elaboration of a cultural symbolic in which the controls and restraints on instinctual behavior outweighed permissions for their release, hence valorizing community over individual self-interest. In such communities there exists a "language of faith," which can take many forms but is always deemed authoritative. This is the famed Freudian cultural super-ego, which is idealized and internalized, serving to keep the "lower" socially disruptive instinctual forces (sex and aggression) in check through repression and guilt. Represented institutionally by the church, positive communities reintegrate those suffering from anomie and neuroses through what Rieff calls "commitment therapies." The latter are those therapies that, as Freud saw, are typical of all forms of religious healing, enabling the afflicted to encounter their unconscious in a symbolic and therefore "experience-distant" manner. Religious narratives, mediated through rituals and the commanding, idealized figure of a religious functionary (e.g., priests), serve to edify and release aggressive and sexual tensions while facilitating the reinternalization of the cultural super-ego. All commitment therapies, then, are suggestive-supportive in nature, being in the service of the reigning sociopolitical and cultural symbolic.

Negative communities, on the other hand, are historically new and traceable to the effects of the originative psychologists, of which Rieff thinks Freud is the most important. Negative communities champion not so much "suggestive-supportive" but "analytic" and "uncovering" forms of therapy. The aim is to engage the unconscious directly ("Where Id was, there Ego shall be"), thus widening the ego and a sense of one's unique individuality. An "analytic attitude" of observation, detachment, and tolerance of psychical discontents replaces the "language of faith" and the command to repress. The result is the likelihood of becoming disillusioned (or "deconverted") from the reigning cultural symbolic, the collapse of the authority of the religious cultural super-ego, and the replacement of the church as a monitoring institution with the more reflective, therapeutically inclined institution of the clinic and its valorization of the uniqueness of the individual.

The Clinic and Social Spaces

Rieff's distinction between the social spaces of the church and clinic, their relation to the cultural super-ego, and their respective contributions to cultural change can be further nuanced. Our use of the term "social space" here is modeled after the classic example of a house: we perform different tasks in kitchens, bedrooms, living rooms, and bathrooms, and one does not usually do in the kitchen what one does in the bathroom. Following the example of the anthropologist Mary Douglas, social spaces provide the context for definitions: one's dirty boots are not prohibited in the hall foyer but are so on the kitchen table. Similarly, churched and clinical social spaces are ruled, socializing the participants into at times incommensurate ways of thinking about self, world, and Other. For example, in a fundamentalist religious social space where scripture, understood as eternal, unchangeable, and revealed, is summoned for memorization, there is little, if any, room for critical thought and deidealization. On the contrary, what is valorized is the internalization of an ethos and truth that cannot, under any circumstances, be deidealized (where deidealization is understood as the psychoanalytic infrastructure of belief: belief necessitates idealization). To act or even to think otherwise is, in fact, to risk communal ostracization, excommunication, or even to incur violence.

In contrast, psychological social spaces are often critical of the cultural super-ego and, as a result, are potentially transgressive and revolutionary. Here the work of another anthropologist, Victor Turner, pays dividends in rethinking the nature of "what happens" in the clinical encounter. One can think of the doors that demarcate the psychoanalytic ritualized social space as symbolic of the repression barrier and hence of the cultural super-ego, which by definition is composed of what the sociologist Emile Durkheim would call categorization schemes and "collective representations" (i.e., what society has collectively framed as being of value, such as ideologies). The actual therapeutic space, on the other hand, is what Turner calls "liminal" (social spaces bereft of any social structure or the socialization process, the psychoanalytic correlate being the inner space of the unconscious).[4] What is valorized and authorized in clinical spaces, then, is the de-repression and full expression of potentially socially transgressive desires, thoughts, and actions. In essence, one outcome of the social space of the clinic is liberative in nature, designed to change the content of the reigning cultural super-ego.

---

[4] V. Turner, *The Ritual Process* (Ithaca, NY: Cornell University Press, 1969).

It is this "resocialization" into a new, authorized mode of introspection that has potentially revolutionary consequences. For example, the cultural legitimacy of the clinic has promoted a greater tolerance for sexual fantasies as well as sexual aims aside from those of heterosexual monogamy (which Freud critiqued as one facet of the religious cultural super-ego that fermented *Unbehagen*, or uneasiness). Again, even if Freud himself was (as we have seen) "unreflexive" about cultural constructions of gender, one can, in separating Freud's creation of a socially legitimated clinical space from his male-centered and unreflexive metapsychology, view the "liminality" of the clinic as a progressive social space in which women (starting with Freud's daughter Anna) have historically been afforded an opportunity to explore their inner space, theorize about it, and, as a result, help change not only psychoanalytic theory but also patriarchal social structures. That this is so is evinced by what some call the feminist revolution in psychoanalytic theory (i.e., the ascendancy of object-relations theory). From this perspective, the cultural trend toward gender equality, the legitimation of alternative sexual orientations, and awareness of the unconscious origins of racial prejudice owe something to the liminal space of the clinic. And, as we have seen throughout this study, authorizing new modes of thinking about self, other, and culture has led, with respect to religion, to the fabled Ricoeurian "hermeneutics of suspicion" where religion is understood as not from the hand of the divine but as disguised projections of unconscious desire. Once de-repressed and worked through in the clinical social space, a new, more critical relation of the self to religion and the cultural super-ego (and hence "religion") can take place. It is in this sense that psychoanalytic therapy can be framed as a form of "secular ritual" that resocializes one and authorizes potentially transgressive social action.

The above can be framed as constituting a *constructive* contribution to religion and culture. Many social scientists have observed that, historically speaking, religion has maintained a functional value: it provides ideologies, values, and orientations that answer questions concerning gender identity, sexual orientation, the nature of the universe, social relations, group solidarity, and the meaning of life. If all of the latter have been the province of religion, and psychoanalytic thought and practice have authorized transgressive forms of the same, then what we have is nothing less than an alteration of the content and functional import of Durkheim's collective representations, now psychoanalytically understood as providing the content of the cultural super-ego. The ritualistic expressions of the clinically based individuating imagination, entangled with social spaces like the university, the hospital, visual media (movies, television), and social media, have functioned to offer an outlet for every unconscious wish and identity need. New models for and forms of thinking about key concepts like self, gender, race, and sexuality have been authorized over and against those found in religious narratives. In other words, psychoanalysis has served not only to deconstruct but also to replace standard religious framings and done so by offering a much wider set of models to accord with the diversity of individual proclivities. We are far beyond Freud, for the clinical space "entangled" with others has influenced Weber's "whole groups of peoples." As Auden put it, Freud (and we can add his heirs) is no longer just a person now, but a "whole climate" that has altered our culture toward the therapeutic.

PSYCHOANALYSIS AND INNER-WORLDLY MYSTICISM

There is another way in which psychoanalysis can be framed as offering a constructive response, namely, by contributing to the valorization and cultivation of what Weber called "inner-worldly mysticism."

To see this clearly, we turn to a different series of Rieff's reflections on the change from a religious to a therapeutic culture. He thinks that the inner world of the average Protestant was much more anxious and guilt-ridden than their fellow Catholics. This is so, for the latter's religious world was more magical and enchanted, being populated by a host of saintly intermediaries to God. The power of such intermediaries alongside the church, confessional (an early form of therapy), and a more developed monastic system gave the believer a psychological release from guilt and anxiety and a greater assurance of salvation. In contrast, the more "disenchanted" Protestant, who lacked such institutionally available releases, was, relatively speaking, more anxious, guilty, and neurotic, and so particularly ripe for being attracted to psychoanalytic therapy. The success and widespread appeal of psychoanalysis in the postwar Protestant United States was in part due to the ability of Freud's psychology, whose theory and practice focused on the super-ego, guilt, and anxiety, to address the historically conflicted psychological world of the inner-worldly ascetic. Culturally speaking, then, Rieff's conclusion is not a surprise: classic Freudian psychoanalysis fits hand-in-glove with Protestant inner-worldly asceticism.[5]

---

[5] P. Rieff, *The Feeling Intellect* (Chicago: University of Chicago Press, 1990). To be sure, other religious denominations and traditions, as well as their scholarly representatives (e.g., Hans Kung, Mircea Eliade, Martin Buber, D. T. Suzuki), took to dialogue with psychoanalysis during the postwar period. At the same time, it is still the case that the most

What Rieff did not speak to, but which we intimated to be the case in previous chapters by way of using a sociology of knowledge approach, is how the development of new cultural soils has occasioned advances in psychoanalytic theory: ego psychology and object-relations theory. Indeed, the gradual formulation of reflective, dialogical, inclusive psychoanalytic studies can be said to correlate with the emergence of such multiple cultural soils. Concentrating on just one such cultural development, we can add to that list by being more specific with the emergence and acceptance of transformational theory (an indispensable contributor to psychoanalytic spirituality). The ideal type that is best correlated with the emergence of the latter is not the inner-worldly ascetic but what Weber called the inner-worldly mystic. Elaborated further by Roland Robertson, the inner-worldly mystic is described as a modern form of adaptation to a culture characterized by the rise of individualism, a pluralistic religious surround, and access to multiple types of introspective techniques. Robertson traces the fermentation of this cultural soil to those of the baby-boomer generation (some of whom are now practicing analysts) in the essentially "liminal" decade of the 1960s. Viewed in the context of the capitalistic ethos, inner-worldly mysticism expresses the need to work "in the world" while striving for wholeness and the actualization of the "self." Therapy, yoga, meditation, dietary and exercise programs, and the individualistic, eclectic "supermarket" approach to religion are part and parcel of inner-worldly mysticism.[6] Empirical studies tend to back this up, as they estimate that between 20 and 30 percent of the current population have chosen to express their religious sentiments in this unchurched, spiritual manner (e.g., being "spiritual but not religious").[7]

---

creative, popular, and powerful form of the dialogue between depth-psychology and religion during the mid-twentieth century was that between psychoanalysis and Protestant theology, the predominant issues being the nature of sin, determinism, freedom, guilt, and the "heteronomous" God (see Jonte-Pace and Parsons, eds., *Religion and Psychology*). Indeed, a survey of the faculty and courses in the "psychology of religion" at major universities and seminaries (e.g., Yale, Harvard, Chicago, Union) during this era reveals an overwhelming focus on a Protestant response to psychoanalysis. Given that, demographically speaking, the United States was also overwhelmingly Protestant during that era, it should come as no surprise that Rieff's focus, writing mainly in the 1960s, would reflect such a cultural soil. That said, it is also the case, as we have suggested, that multiple other cultural soils affected the shape of psychoanalysis and its related projects.

[6] R. Robertson. *Meaning and Change* (New York: New York University Press, 1978).
[7] See William B. Parsons, ed., *Being Spiritual but Not Religious: Past, Present, Future(s)* (New York: Routledge, 2018).

It appears that psychoanalytic therapy has been incorporated into this inner-worldly regimen. As previously noted, contemporary psychoanalytic literature has catalogued how spirituality has crept into multiple aspects of the practice of analysts and of the therapeutic expectations of analysands. To cite but a few examples, the British psychoanalyst Nina Coltart, referring to matters of technique, speaks of "bare attention," a Buddhist meditative term, and how the practice of it has helped her to empathize with her analysands. For Coltart, "bare attention" is commensurate with Bion's concept of "O." Coltart speaks of the two coalescing in a state that she sees as being "unthought-out, involving a quality of intuitive apperception of another person's evolving truth."[8] The training analyst Michael Eigen, particularly influenced by Jewish mysticism and Zen, refers to psychoanalytic therapy as "a psychospiritual journey," further arguing that meditative practices and psychoanalysis are not separate but part of an allied process of growth.[9] The training analyst Paul Cooper thinks that spiritual practices have influenced multiple dimensions of psychoanalytic therapy (e.g., theory, technique, training, and supervision) and draws attention to the important empirical fact that many of his analysands understand psychoanalytic therapy as part of their spiritual growth. There is, thinks Cooper, an undeniable cultural drift in this direction.[10] These observations indicate that psychoanalytic therapy is engaging a new social base and that the latter is at least in part responsible for not only implementing developments in theory but also legitimating the spiritual concerns of both analysts and analysands. In sum, psychoanalysis has shifted from accommodating the psychology of the inner-worldly ascetic to being driven by the needs of the inner-worldly mystic, hence contributing to the establishment of a psychoanalytic spirituality.

Ideally, the continued development of psychoanalytic spirituality will proceed by creating dialogical bridges between clinicians, culture theorists, philosophers, comparativists, theologians, and religious adepts. The progression of the work will be powered by those analysts and analysands who are engaged not only in psychoanalytic therapy but also in the various physical and mental practices offered in spiritual communities east and west. Their insistence on change and expansion will come from hard-won experience and insight. This social base is likely here to stay, and will influence psychoanalysis for years to come.

---

[8] See Molino, ed., *The Couch and the Tree*, 77.   [9] Ibid., 225.   [10] Ibid.

Bibliography

Abel, E. "Race, Class, and Psychoanalysis? Opening Questions." In *Conflicts in Feminism*, ed. Marianne Hirsch and E. F. Keller. New York: Routledge, 1990: 184–204.
Akhtar, S. ed. *The Crescent and the Couch*. New York: Jason Aronson, 2008.
Aktar, S., and P. Tummala-Narra. "Psychoanalysis in India." In *Freud along the Ganges*, ed. S. Aktar. New Delhi: Stanza, 2008: 3–28.
Albright, W. F. *From the Stone Age to Christianity*. Baltimore: Johns Hopkins University Press, 1946.
Anzieu, D. *Freud's Self-Analysis*. London: Hogarth Press and the Institute of Psychoanalysis, 1986.
Aronson, H. *Buddhist Practice on Western Ground*. Boston: Shambala, 2004.
Assmann, J. *Moses the Egyptian*. Cambridge, MA: Harvard University Press, 1998.
Augustine, St. *The Confessions of St. Augustine*, trans. Rex Warner. New York: Mentor, 1963.
Bakan, D. "Augustine's *Confessions*: The Unentailed Self." In D. Capps and J. Dittes, eds., *The Hunger of the Heart*, 109–116.
Beers, W. "The Confessions of St. Augustine: Narcissistic Elements." *American Imago* 45 (1988): 107–125.
Beit-Hallahmi, B. "Psychology of Religion 1880–1930: The Rise and Fall of a Psychological Movement." *Journal of the History of Behavioral Sciences* 10 (1974): 84–90.
Benslama, F. *Psychoanalysis and the Challenge of Islam*. Minneapolis: University of Minnesota Press, 2009.
Berger, P. *The Sacred Canopy*. New York: Anchor Books, 1990 [1967].
Bernstein, R. *Freud and the Legacy of Moses*. Cambridge: Cambridge University Press, 1998.
Bettelheim, B. *Freud and Man's Soul*. New York: Vintage, 1983.
Bibring, E. "The Development and Problems of the Theory of the Instincts." *The International Journal of Psychoanalysis* 22 (1941): 102–131.
Bingaman, K. *Freud and Faith*. Albany: State University of New York Press, 2003.

Blackstone, J. *The Empathic Ground*. Albany: State University of New York Press, 2007.

Borch-Jacobsen, M. *Making Minds and Madness: From Hysteria to Depression*. Cambridge: Cambridge University Press, 2009.

Bose, G. "The Psychological Outlook of Hindu Philosophy." *Indian Journal of Psychology* 5 (1930): 119–146.

Brickman, C. *Aboriginal Populations in the Mind*. New York: Columbia University Press, 2003.

Brown, C. "Enlightenment Therapy." *New York Times*, April 26, 2009. www.nytimes.com/2009/04/26/magazine/26zen.

Brown, P. *Augustine of Hippo*. Berkeley: University of California Press, 1969.

Browning, D. *Religious Thought and the Modern Psychologies*. Philadelphia: Fortress Press, 1987.

Capps, D. "Augustine as Narcissist: Of Grandiosity and Shame." In D. Capps and J. Dittes, eds., *The Hunger of the Heart*, 169–185.

Capps, D., and J. Dittes, eds. *The Hunger of the Heart: Reflections on the Confessions of Augustine*. Monograph Series 8. West Lafayette, IN: Society for the Scientific Study of Religion, 1990.

Certeau, M. de "Mysticism." *Diacritics* 22 (1992): 11–25.

Chodorow, N. *The Reproduction of Mothering*. Berkeley: University of California Press, 1978.

Cooper, P. "The Disavowal of the Spirit: Integration and Wholeness in Buddhism and Psychoanalysis." In *The Couch and the Tree*, ed. A. Molino. New York: North Point Press, 1998: 231–246.

Zen Insight, Psychoanalytic Action. New York: Routledge, 2019.

Cooper-White, P. *Shared Wisdom*. New York: Augsburg, 2004

Courcelle, P. *Recherches sur les "Confessions" de S. Augustin*. Paris: Boccard, 1968.

Crews, F. *Freud: The Making of an Illusion*. New York: Metropolitan Books, 2017.

Cross, A. *When Heaven and Earth Collide: Racism, Southern Evangelicals, and the Better Way of Jesus*. Montgomery, AL: New South Books, 2014.

Daly, M. *The Church and the Second Sex*. Boston: Beacon Press, 1986 [1968].

Deikman, A. "Deautomatization and the Mystic Experience." In *Understanding Mysticism*, ed. R. Woods. Garden City, NY: Image Books: 240–260.

Dittes, J. "Continuities between the Life and Thought of Augustine." In D. Capps and J. Dittes, eds., *The Hunger of the Heart*, 117–133.

Dixon, S. *Augustine: The Scattered and Gathered Self*. St. Louis, MO: Chalice Press, 1999.

Douglas, M. "The Effects of Modernization on Religious Change." In *Religion and America: Spiritual Life in a Secular Age*, ed. M. Douglas and S. Tipton. Boston: Beacon Press, 1982.

Drescher, E. *Choosing Our Religion: The Spiritual Lives of America's Nones*. New York: Oxford University Press, 2016.

Durkheim, E. *The Elementary Forms of Religious Life*. New York: Free Press, 1995 [1912].

El Shakry, O. *The Arabic Freud*. Princeton, NJ: Princeton University Press, 2017.

Ellenberger, E. *The Discovery of the Unconscious*. New York: Basic Books, 1970.

Engler, J. "Therapeutic Aims in Psychotherapy and Buddhism." In *Transformations in Consciousness*, ed. K. Wilber, J. Engler, and D. Brown. Boston: Shambala, 1986: 17–52.
Epstein, M. *Thoughts without a Thinker*. New York: Basic Books, 1995.
Erikson, E. *Identity and the Life Cycle*. New York: W. W. Norton, 1994 [1959].
— *Young Man Luther*. New York: W. W. Norton, 1958.
Evans, R. B., and W. A. Koelch. "Psychoanalysis arrives in America: The 1909 Psychology Conference at Clark University." *American Psychologist* 40, no. 8 (1985): 942–948.
Fanon, F. *Black Skin, White Masks*. New York: Grove Press, 2008 [1952].
Forman, R. C., ed. *The Problem of Pure Consciousness*. New York: Oxford University Press, 1990.
Fowler, J. *Stages of Faith*. New York: Harper, 1995 [1979].
Fredriksen, P. "Augustine and His Analysts: The Possibility of a Psychohistory." *Soundings* 61 (1978): 206–227.
Freud, A. *The Ego and the Mechanisms of Defence*. New York: Routledge, 1992 [1936].
Freud, S. "A Letter from Freud." *The American Journal of Psychiatry* 107 (1951): 786–787.
— *The Origins of Psychoanalysis: Letters to Wilhelm Fliess*, ed. M. Bonaparte. New York: Basic Books, 1954.
— *The Standard Edition of the Complete Psychological Works of Sigmund Freud* [S.E.], vols. 1–24, trans. and ed. J. Strachey. London: Hogarth Press.
— (1893). *Studies on Hysteria*. S.E. 2: 1–335.
— (1900). *The Interpretation of Dreams*. S.E. 4–5.
— (1901) *On Dreams*. S.E. 5: 629–722.
— (1901) *The Psychopathology of Everyday Life*. S.E. 6: 1–291.
— (1905) *Three Essays on Sexuality*. S.E. 7: 125–245.
— (1905) "On Psychotherapy." S.E. 7: 257–270.
— (1907) "Obsessive Acts and Religious Practices." S.E. 9: 115–128.
— (1909) "Analysis of a Phobia in a Five-Year-Old Boy." S.E. vol. 10: 3–152.
— (1910). *Five Lectures on Psychoanalysis*. S.E. 11: 3–56.
— (1913) *Totem and Taboo*. S.E. 13: 1–162.
— (1914) "The Moses of Michelangelo." S.E. 13: 210–236.
— (1915) "Thoughts for the Times on War and Death." S.E. 14: 273–300.
— (1916) *Introductory Lectures on Psychoanalysis*. S.E. 16: 243–483.
— (1918) "From the History of an Infantile Neurosis." S.E. 17: 3–122.
— (1921) *Group Psychology and the Analysis of the Ego*. S.E. 18: 67–143.
— (1923) "A Seventeenth-Century Demonological Neurosis." S.E. 19: 69–108.
— (1923) *The Ego and the Id*. S.E. 19: 3–59.
— (1927) *The Future of an Illusion*. S.E. 21: 1–56.
— (1928) *A Religious Experience*. S.E. 21: 167–172.
— (1930) *Civilization and Its Discontents*. S.E. 21: 57–146.
— (1933) *New Introductory Lectures on Psychoanalysis*. S.E. 22: 3–184.
— (1933) "Femininity." S.E. 22: 112–135.
— (1933) "Dreams and Occultism." S.E: 22: 31–56.
— (1933) "The Dissection of the Psychical Personality." S.E. 22: 57–80.

(1933) "The Question of a *Weltanschuung*." S.E. 22: 158–184.
(1936) "A Disturbance of Memory on the Acropolis." S.E. 22: 239–248.
(1939) *Moses and Monotheism* S.E. 23: 3–137.
Freud, S., and Oskar Pfister. *Psychoanalysis and Faith: The Letters of Sigmund Freud and Oskar Pfister*, ed. H. Meng and E. L. Freud. New York: Basic Books, 1963.
Fuller, Robert C. *Stairways to Heaven*. Boulder, CO: Westview Press, 2000.
Garb, J. *Shamanic Trance in Modern Kabbalah*. Chicago: University of Chicago Press, 2011.
Gay, P. *Freud: A Life for Our Time*. New York: W. W. Norton, 1988.
A Godless Jew. New Haven, CT: Yale University Press, 1987.
Geertz, C. *The Interpretation of Cultures*. New York: Basic Books, 1973.
Gilman, S. *Freud, Race, and Gender*. Princeton, NJ: Princeton University Press, 1993.
Gombrich, R. "Review of *The Oceanic Feeling*, by Jeffrey Masson." *Journal of the Royal Asiatic Society* 1 (1983): 75–78.
Greenberg, J., and S. Mitchell. *Object Relations in Psychoanalytic Theory*. Cambridge, MA: Harvard University Press, 1983.
Grinstein, A. *Sigmund Freud's Dreams*. New York: International Universities Press, 1980.
Grünbaum, A. *The Foundations of Psychoanalysis*. Berkeley: University of California Press, 1984.
Halbfass, W. "Review of *The Oceanic Feeling*, by Jeffrey Masson." *Journal of Asian Studies* 41 (1982): 387–388.
Hamman, J. "The Reproduction of the Hypermasculine Male: Select Subaltern Views." *Pastoral Psychology* 66 (2017): 799–818.
Harding, C., et al., eds. *Religion and Psychotherapy in Modern Japan*. New York: Routledge, 2015.
Hartmann, H. *Ego Psychology and the Problem of Adaptation*. New York: International Universities Press, 1958.
Hewitt, M. *Freud on Religion*. Durham, UK: Acumen, 2014.
Hiltebeitel, A. *Freud's India: Sigmund Freud and India's First Psychoanalyst Girindrasekhar Bose*. New York: Oxford University Press, 2018.
Homans, P. "The Psychology and Religion Movement." In *The Encyclopedia of Religion*, ed. Mircea Eliade. New York: Macmillan, 1987: 22: 64–77.
The Ability to Mourn. Chicago: University of Chicago Press, 1989.
Jung in Context. Chicago: University of Chicago Press, 1989.
Theology after Freud. New York: Bobbs-Merrill, 1970.
Hughes, H. S. *The Sea Change: The Migration of Social Thought, 1930–1965*. New York: Harper and Row, 1975.
Jacoby, M. *Individuation and Narcissism*. New York: Routledge, 1990.
James, W. *The Varieties of Religious Experience*. New York: Modern Library, 1929.
Jones, E. *The Life and Work of Sigmund Freud*, 3 vols. New York: Basic Books, 1953–1957.
Jones, J. *Blood That Cries out from the Earth*. New York: Oxford University Press, 2008.
Contemporary Psychoanalysis and Religion: Transference and Transcendence. New Haven, CT: Yale University Press, 1993 [1991].
Religion and Psychology in Transition: Psychoanalysis, Feminism, and Theology. New Haven, CT: Yale University Press, 1996.

Jonte-Pace, D. "Analysts, Critics, and Inclusivists: Feminist Voices in the Psychology of Religion." In Jonte-Pace and Parsons, eds., *Religion and Psychology: Mapping the Terrain*, 129–148.
"Augustine on the Couch: Psychohistorical (Mis)readings of the Confessions." *Religion* 23 (1993): 71–83.
"Psychoanalysis, Colonialism, and Modernity: Reflections on Brickman's *Aboriginal Populations in the Mind*." *Religious Studies Review* 32, no. 1 (2006): 1–4.
Speaking the Unspeakable. Berkeley: University of California Press, 2001.
Jonte-Pace, D., and W. B. Parsons, eds. *Religion and Psychology: Mapping the Terrain*. New York: Routledge, 2001.
Jung, C. *Psychology and Religion*. New Haven, CT: Yale University Press, 1977 [1938].
Kakar, S. "The Guru as Healer." In S. Kakar, *The Analyst and the Mystic*. Chicago: University of Chicago Press, 1991: 35–54.
The Inner World. New York: Oxford University Press, 1979.
"Reflections on Psychoanalysis, Indian Culture, and Mysticism." *Journal of Indian Philosophy* 20 (1982): 289–297.
Shamans, Mystics, and Doctors. New York: Alfred A. Knopf, 1982.
Katz, S., ed. *Mysticism and Philosophical Analysis*. New York: Oxford University Press, 1980.
Khanna, R. *Dark Continents: Psychoanalysis and Colonialism*. Durham, NC: Duke University Press, 2003.
Kirkpatrick, L. "An Attachment-Theory Approach to the Psychology of Religion." *The International Journal for the Psychology of Religion* 2, no. 1 (1992): 3–28.
Klein, D. B. *Jewish Origins of the Psychoanalytic Movement*. Chicago: University of Chicago Press, 1981.
Kohut, H. "Forms and Transformations of Narcissism." In *The Search for the Self*, 2 vols., ed. P. Ornstein. New York: International Universities Press, 1978: 427–460.
"On Leadership." In *Self Psychology and the Humanities*, ed. C. Strozier. New York: W. W. Norton, 1985: 51–72.
Kohut, H., and E. Wolf. "The Disorders of the Self and their Treatment: An Outline." *International Journal of Psychoanalysis* 59 (1978): 413–425.
Kripal, J. *Esalen: America and the Religion of No Religion*. Chicago: University of Chicago Press, 2011.
Kali's Child: The Mystical and the Erotic in the Life and Teachings of Ramakrishna. Chicago: University of Chicago Press, 1995.
Kris, E. *Psychoanalytic Explorations in Art*. New York: International Universities Press, 1952.
Kristeva, J. *In the Beginning Was Love: Psychoanalysis and Faith*, trans. A. Goldhammer. New York: Columbia University Press, 1989.
Küng, H. *Freud and the Problem of God*. New Haven, CT: Yale University Press, 1990.
Lacan, J. "God and the Jouissance of Women." In *Feminine Sexuality: Jacques Lacan and the École Freudian*, ed. J. Mitchell and J. Rose. New York: W. W. Norton, 1982: 137–149.

Laderman, G. *Sacred Matters*. New York: New Press, 2010.
Lasch, C. *The Culture of Narcissism*. New York: W. W. Norton, 1979.
Lorand, J. *The Fetish Revisited: Marx, Freud, and the Gods Black People Make*. Durham, NC: Duke University Press, 2018.
Malinowski, B. *Sex and Repression in Savage Society*. London: Forgotten Books, 2012 [1927].
Masson, J., and C. Hanly. "A Critical Examination of the New Narcissism." *International Journal of Psychoanalysis* 57 (1976): 49–66.
Masson, J., and T. C. Masson, "The Study of Mysticism: A Criticism of W. T. Stace." *Journal of Indian Philosophy* 4 (1976): 109–125.
Masson, J. M. *The Assault on Truth: Freud's Suppression of the Seduction Theory*, 3rd ed. New York: HarperCollins, 1992 [1984].
"Indian Psychotherapy?" *Journal of Indian Philosophy* 7 (1979): 327–332.
The Oceanic Feeling. Dordrecht: D. Riedel, 1980.
"The Psychology of the Ascetic." *Journal of Asian Studies* 35 (1976): 611–625.
McCutcheon, T. *Studying Religion*. New York: Routledge, 2018.
McGinn, B. *The Foundations of Mysticism*. New York: Crossroad, 1991.
McGrath, W. *Freud's Discovery of Psychoanalysis: The Politics of Hysteria*. Ithaca, NY: Cornell University Press, 1986.
"Freud as Hannibal: The Politics of the Brother Band." *Central European History* 7 (1974): 31–57.
McGuire, W. ed. *The Freud–Jung Letters*. Princeton, NJ: Princeton University Press, 1974.
McMahon, R. *Augustine's Prayerful Ascent: An Essay on the Literary Form of the Confessions*. Athens: University of Georgia Press, 1990.
Meissner, W. W. *Freud and Psychoanalysis*. Notre Dame: University of Notre Dame Press, 2000.
Psychoanalysis and Religious Experience. New Haven, CT: Yale University Press, 1984.
Mitchell, J. *Psychoanalysis and Feminism*, 2nd ed. New York: Basic Books, 2000 [1974].
Miller, C., and N. Carlin. "Joel Osteen as Cultural Self-Object: Meeting the Needs of the Group Self and Its Individual Members in and from the Largest Church in America." *Pastoral Psychology* 59 (2010): 27–51.
Miller, J. "Interpretations of Freud's Jewishness 1924–1974." *Journal of the History of Behavioral Sciences* 17 (1981): 357–374.
Molino, A., ed. *The Couch and the Tree*. New York: North Point, 1998.
Obeyesekere, G. *The Work of Culture*. Chicago: University of Chicago Press, 1990.
Ornston, D., ed. *Translating Freud*. New Haven, CT: Yale University Press, 1992.
Osborne, A. *Ramana Maharshi and the Path of Self-Knowledge*. New York: Samuel Weiser, 1973.
Parsons, A. "Is the Oedipus Complex Universal?" In *Man and His Culture: Psychoanalytic Anthropology after Totem and Taboo*, ed. W. Muensterberger. New York: Taplinger, 1970: 331–384.
Parsons, T. *Social Structure and Personality*. New York: Simon and Schuster, 2007 [1964].
Parsons, W. B., ed. *Being Spiritual but Not Religious: Past, Present, Future(s)*. New York: Routledge, 2018.

The Enigma of the Oceanic Feeling. New York: Oxford University Press, 1999.
Freud and Augustine in Dialogue. Charlottesville: University of Virginia Press, 2013
"Freud's Encounter with Hinduism." In *Vishnu on Freud's Desk*, ed. T. G. Vaidyanathan and J. Kripal. Delhi: Oxford University Press, 1999: 41–80.
"Mysticism: An Overview." In *Oxford Research Encyclopedia of Religion*, ed. J. Barton, 2019. https://oxfordre.com/religion/view/10.1093/acrefore/9780199340378.001.0001/acrefore-9780199340378-e-55.
"Psychoanalysis Meets Buddhism." In *Changing the Scientific Study of Religion: Beyond Freud?*, ed. J. Belzen. New York: Springer, 2009: 179–210.
"Psychoanalytic Spirituality." In *Spirituality and Religion: Psychoanalytic Perspectives*, ed. J. Weiner and J. Anderson. Catskill, NY: Mental Health Resources: 83–96.
"Psychology of Religion." In *The Encyclopedia of Religion*, 2nd ed., ed. L. Jones. New York: Macmillan, 2005: 7473–7481.
"The Psychology of Religion: An Overview." In *Social Religion*, ed. W. B. Parsons. New York: Macmillan, 2016: 3–22.
ed. *Teaching Mysticism.* New York: Oxford University Press, 2011.
"Themes and Debates in the Psychology-Comparativist Dialogue." In Jonte-Pace and Parsons, eds., *Religion and Psychology: Mapping the Terrain*, 229–253.
Paul, R. *Moses and Civilization.* New Haven, CT: Yale University Press, 1996.
Pfister, O. "The Illusion of the Future: A Friendly Disagreement with Prof. Sigmund Freud." *International Journal of Psychoanalysis* 74 (1993): 557–579.
Pinn, A. *Terror and Triumph.* Minneapolis, MN: Fortress Press, 2003.
Rainey, R. *Freud as Student of Religion.* Atlanta, GA: Scholar's Press, 1975.
Rappaport, D. *The Structure of Psychoanalytic Theory.* New York: International Universities Press, 1960.
Rice, E. *Freud and Moses: The Long Journey Home.* Albany: State University of New York Press, 1990.
Ricoeur, P. *Freud and Philosophy.* New Haven, CT: Yale University Press, 1970.
Rieff, P. *The Feeling Intellect.* Chicago: University of Chicago Press, 1990.
Freud: The Mind of the Moralist. Chicago: University of Chicago Press, 1959.
"The Meaning of History and Religion in Freud's Thought." In *Psychoanalysis and History*, ed. B. Mazlish. Englewood Cliffs, NJ: Prentice Hall, 1963: 3–41.
The Triumph of the Therapeutic. New York: Harper, 1966.
Rizzuto, A. M. *The Birth of the Living God.* Chicago: University of Chicago Press, 1979.
Robertson. R. *Meaning and Change.* New York: New York University Press, 1978.
Rolland, R. *The Life of Ramakrishna.* Calcutta: Advaita Ashrama, 1965.
Rubin, J. *Psychotherapy and Buddhism.* New York: Plenum Press, 1996.
Said, E. *Freud and the Non-European.* New York: Verso, 2003.
Samuels, A. *Jung and the Post-Jungians.* New York: Routledge, 1986.
Schorske, C. *Fin-de-Siècle Vienna.* New York: Vintage, 1981.
Sil, N. *Ramakrishna Paramahamsa: A Psychological Profile.* Leiden: Brill, 1991.
Simon, E. "Sigmund Freud the Jew." *Leo Baeck Institute Yearbook* 2 (1957): 302–305.
Sinha, T. C. "Development of Psycho-analysis in India." *International Journal of Psychoanalysis* 47 (1966): 427–439.
Smith, J. Z. *Imagining Religion.* Chicago: University of Chicago Press, 1988.
"Religion, Religions, Religious." In *Critical Terms for Religious Studies*, ed. M. Taylor. Chicago: University of Chicago Press, 1998: 269–284.

Smith, W. C. *The Meaning and End of Religion*. Minneapolis, MN: Fortress Press, 1991 [1962].

Spero, M. H. "Self-Effacement and Self-Inscription: Reconsidering Freud's Anonymous Moses of Michelangelo." *Psychoanalysis and Contemporary Thought* 24 (2002): 359–462.

Sulloway F. *Freud, Biologist of the Mind: Beyond the Psychoanalytic Legend*. Cambridge, MA: Harvard University Press, 1992 [1979].

Tauber, A. I. *Freud, the Reluctant Philosopher*. Princeton, NJ: Princeton University Press, 2010.

Teresa, St. *The Interior Castle*, trans. K. Kavanaugh and O. Rodriguez. New York: Paulist Press, 1979.

TeSelle, E. "Augustine as Client and as Theorist." In Capps and Dittes, eds., *The Hunger of the Heart*, 185–216.

Tillich, P. *The Courage to Be*. New Haven, CT: Yale University Press, 1952.

The Dynamics of Faith. New York: Harper, 2009 [1956].

The Meaning of Health. Berkeley: North Atlantic Press, 1984 [1961].

Turner, V. *The Ritual Process*. Ithaca, NY: Cornel University Press, 1969.

Vaidyanathan, T. G., and J. Kripal, eds. *Vishnu on Freud's Desk*. New Delhi: Oxford University Press, 1999.

Van Herik, J. *Freud on Femininity and Faith*. Berkeley: University of California Press, 1982.

Victoria, B. D. *Zen at War*. Lanham, MD: Rowman & Littlefield, 2006.

Zen War Stories. New York: Routledge, 2003.

Wacker, G. *America's Pastor: Billy Graham and the Shaping of a Nation*. Cambridge, MA: Harvard University Press, 2014.

Wallace, E. *Freud and Anthropology*. New York: International Universities Press, 1983.

Wallwork, E. *Psychoanalysis and Ethics*. New Haven, CT: Yale University Press, 1991.

Webb, R., and M. Sells. "Lacan and Bion: Psychoanalysis and the Mystical Language of Unsaying." *Theory and Psychology* 5 (1995): 195–215.

Weinstein F., and G. Platt. *Psychoanalytic Sociology*. Baltimore: Johns Hopkins University Press, 1973.

Welbon, G. *The Western Interpreters of the Buddhist Nirvana*. Chicago: University of Chicago Press, 1968.

Whitebook, J. *Freud: An Intellectual Biography*. Cambridge: Cambridge University Press, 2017.

Whitmont, Edward C. *The Symbolic Quest*. Princeton, NJ: Princeton University Press, 1991 [1969].

Winnicott, D. W. *Playing and Reality*. New York: Penguin, 1971.

Wulff, D. M. *Psychology of Religion: Classic and Contemporary*, 2nd ed. New York: John Wiley and Sons, 1997.

Wulff, D. M. "Psychology of Religion: An Overview." In Jonte-Pace and Parsons, eds., *Religion and Psychology: Mapping the Terrain*, 15–29.

Yearly, Y. "Freud as Critic and Creator of Cosmogonies and Their Ethics." In *Cosmogony and Ethical Order*, ed. R. Lovin and F. Reynolds. Chicago: University of Chicago Press, 1985: 381–413.

Yerushalmi, Y. *Freud's Moses: Judaism Terminable and Interminable*. New Haven, CT: Yale University Press, 1991.

Zock, H. *A Psychology of Ultimate Concern*. Amsterdam: Rodopi, 1990.

Index

abandoned object-cathexis, 189
Above the Battle (Rolland), 133–134
Acropolis, 162–163
adaptive approach, 24–25, 99–101, 196–197, 221, 250
adolescence, 34, 45, 190–192, 229–233
adulthood, 190–191, 218, 233–241
Advaita Vedanta, 171–173
African American religion, 119–120
ahimsa, 193
Akhenaten, 88–89
Allport, Gordon, 14–15
ambiguity, 68–69
Amenhotep IV, 82–83
Amitabha, 174–176
anal stage, 9, 137–138
anatta (no-self), 163–165
Andreas-Salomé, Lou, 138–139
animism, 66–67, 129–130
  narcissism and, 68–69
  psychological logic behind, 67
  worldview of, 67–68
"Anna O," 7
anthropology, 45–47
  "evolutionary" anthropological theorists, 55
  psychoanalytic, 54–55, 72–73
  socio-evolutionism, 75–76
  theological, 125–126
  Totem and Taboo and, 70–71
anti-Semitism, 36–37, 39
  academic atmosphere of, 49–50
  Catholic, 41

Christianity and, 40–41, 104–105
complicity in, 39–40
cultural, 37–38
fascism and, 133–134
increase in, 85
antisocial tendencies, 110–112, 114
apophatic theology, 234–235
applied psychoanalysis, 24, 29–30, 143, 149–150, 188, 249–250
archaic heritage, 71–72
arche, 254–255
archetypes, 13, 53–54, 167–168
assimilation, 32, 36–37, 41–42
Assmann, Jan, 89–90
atheism, 29–30, 45
Atkinson, J. J., 57
Aton (sun god), 82–83
Atonism, 88–89
attachment theory, 130–131
Auden, W. H., 1, 256–258
Augustine (saint), 221, 223–226
  adolescence of, 229–233
  adulthood of, 233–241
  Confessions, 222–224, 227–228, 230, 236, 240–241
  conflicted sexuality of, 227
  developmental infrastructure of, 225–226
  education of, 227–228
  God-representation and, 222–223
  materiality and, 228–229
  mother of, 224, 238–239

273

Augustine (saint) (cont.)
  mysticism and, 235–236
  religious nature of, 228
automatization, 212–213

Bakan, David, 225–226
Barca, Hamilcar, 40–41
basement theology, 165, 225, 229
beatific vision, 236
Beauvoir, Simone de, 77–78
to become (*werden*), 48–49
behaviorism, 14
Beit-Hallahmi, Benjamin, 14
Bengali Vaishnavism, 167–168
Berger, Peter, 109–110, 126–127
Berkeley-Hill, Owen, 76–77
Bettelheim, Bruno, 47–48
Bhagavad Gita, 158–161, 173–174, 242–243
bhavas, 250–251
biblical figures, 34
Bion, Wilfred, 210–211, 264
Blackstone, Judith, 240
Bleuler, Paul Eugen, 5
B'nai B'rith, 42–44, 49–50
Boas, Franz, 70–71
Boniface (saint), 94
Book of Hosea, 85–86
Bose, Girindrasekhar, 3–5, 20, 42–43, 73, 168–174, 177, 210
Bowlby, John, 130
brainwashing, 77
Breasted, J. H., 81–82
Breuer, Josef, 7, 35–36
Brown, Peter, 231
Browning, Don, 148–149
Brücke, Ernst, 29, 36
Bucke, Richard Maurice, 3–5
Buddhism, 151–152, 164–166, 184–185.
  See also relevant terminology"common-man's," 168–169
  Mahayana values, 174–176
  practices of, 181–182
  psychology-comparativist dialogue and, 240
  psychology-theology dialogue and, 185–186
  Pure Land, 174–178
  Zen, 211

Campbell, Joseph, 14–15
Capps, Donald, 240–241

Carlin, Nathan, 203
castration, 9, 177
  anxiety, 17–19, 62
  guilt and, 103–104
  phylogenetically buried memory of, 84
  psychological reality of, 9–10
categorical imperative, 58–59
catharsis, 7
Catholicism, 34–35, 41, 65–66, 142–143, 262–263
celibacy, 244
Certeau, Michel de, 166–167
chakras, lower, 252–253
Charcot, Jean Martin, 3–5, 7, 35–36
chariot metaphor, 216–217
children, 56–57, 97, 102–103
Christian Socialist Party, 36–37
Christianity, 31–32, 39–40, 64, 81, 121–122, 151–152, 225, 230, 234, 236–237
  anti-Semitism and, 40–41, 104–105
  conversion, 223–224
  Feuerbach on, 45–46
  reconversion to, 101–105
  totemism and, 60–64
Church Fathers, 165–166
Cicero, 231–232
civil religion, 118
civilization, 36, 55, 64–65, 75–76, 97–98, 139, 144
  advancement of, 116
  characterizations of, 106
  continued survival of, 59–60
  course of, 105–106
  danger to, 114
  development of, 140
  growing uneasiness of humans in, 95
  kept whole, 94, 112
  material and mental assets of, 106–108
  origin myth of, 137
  relations between people mediated by, 145–146
  secularization and, 137
  unity and, 137–138
  vehicles of, 114–115
Civilization and Its Discontents (Freud), 36–37, 64–65, 130, 147–148, 153–154
  critiques of, 148–150
  cultural super-ego and, 257–258
  Eastern religions and, 152–153
  first chapter of, 158–159

Future of an Illusion and, 95
  general frame of, 137–139
  narrative at beginning of, 133–134
  preliminary title of, 133
  programs for life and, 164
Clark University, 3–5, 70–71, 135–136
classic-reductive approach, 24–25, 221, 227–229, 250
classic-reductive model, 96–99, 223–226
classic-reductive studies, 223–224, 246–249
clinical space, 144–145, 259–260
Coe, George, 3–5
collective guilt, 64
collective mind, 54, 61–63, 91–92
collective representations, 259–261
collective unconscious, 5–13, 53–54
colonialism, 196–197, 248–250
Coltart, Nina, 264
commitment therapies, 258–259
common unhappiness, 146, 148
"common-man's" religion, 117–120, 134–135, 157–158, 168–169, 176–177
communion, 64, 205–206
comparative study of religions, 55, 88–89
The Concept of Repression (Bose), 171
Confessions (St. Augustine), 222–224, 227–228, 230, 236, 240–241
conflict model, 10–11
consciousness, 5–13, 65–67
constructivism, 168, 239–240
contextualism, 168
conversion, case of, 101–105
Cooper, Paul, 183, 264
Copernicus, 65–66, 98
coping theory, 15
correlational scale, 14–15
creationism, 98
credo quia absurdum, 157
critical theorists, 78–79
cross-cultural applied psychoanalysis, 249–250
cultural interests, 35–36
cultural relativism, 249–250
cultural super-ego, 106–107, 110–112, 144–145, 257–258, 260
  content of, 139–140, 259–261
  deconstruction of, 147–148
  reinternalization of, 258–259
  religious, 145, 165, 193–194, 259
  therapeutic, 147–148, 257–259
cultural works, 29–30
culture, evolution of, 64–66, 68–69

da Vinci, Leonardo, 100–101
Daly, Claude Dagmar, 76–77
Darwin, Charles, 29, 57, 65–66, 144–145
deautomatization, 212–213, 239–240
deconstruction, 256–257
defense mechanisms, 72–73
deidealization, 231–233, 260
Deikman, Arthur, 212–213, 239–240
déjà vu, 163–164
Delacroix, Henri, 3–5
delusion, 204–205
depersonalization, 163–164
depth psychology, 5, 240–241
derealization, 162–163
desire
  of id, 64–65, 84, 139
  somatically based, 8–9
  unconscious, 10–11, 252
developmental considerations, 34–35
developmental determinism, 119–120
developmental directionality, 60–61
developmental infrastructure, 39, 46–47, 51–52, 165, 201–202, 225–226, 239–240
developmental line of sexual instinct, 9
developmental milestones, 199–200
developmental second chance, 202–203
dialogical approach, 221
dialogical critiques, 179–187
dialogical projects, 20–21, 24–26, 125–126, 145, 196, 256
dialogue, 249–255
dim nostalgias, 194–195
Dionysius, 210–211
disillusionment, 65–66, 112–113
"A Disturbance of Memory on the Acropolis" (Freud), 162–163
"The Diver" (Schiller), 159
Divine, 221–222
divine androgyny, 251–252, 254–255
divine retribution, 94
Dorje, Lama Namgyal, 178–179
Douglas, Mary, 260
dream associations, 30
dreams, 38–41, 68
dreamwork, 38, 68
drives (*triebe*), 58–59
dualism, 231

Durkheim, Émile, 54–55, 118, 127, 259–261

early childhood, 190–191
Eastern religions, 152–153, 162–165, 179, 183, 186–187
ego, 10–11, 122–123
  autonomous, 182–183
  development of, 190–191
  executive, 14–15
  id and, 211–212
  individuation of, 218
  as mechanism, 189
  regression in service of, 194–195
The Ego and the Id (Freud), 216–217
ego psychology, 14–15, 189, 249–250
  emergence of, 189–190
  hypnosis and, 212–213
  key formulations of, 190–197
  postwar capitalistic culture and, 197–198
Egyptian culture, 34
Eigen, Michael, 264
Electra complex, 9–10
empathy, 116, 214–215, 251–252
Empedocles, 30, 45–46, 108–109, 137–138, 148–149
emptiness, 122–123
Engler, Jack, 185–186, 240, 254–255
enlightenment, 95
The Enneads (Plotinus), 217, 234–235
entheogens, 6–7
envy, 57
epigenesis, 191–192
epistemology, 95–99, 169–170, 204–205
Epstein, Mark, 184–185, 240
Erikson, Erik, 14–15, 45, 92–93, 100, 148, 171, 232–233, 239–240
  ego psychology and, 189, 249–250
  epigenesis and, 191–192
  life-cycle theory and, 190–191
  moratoriums and, 194, 231–232
  nostalgia and, 209–210
  Silesius and, 234–235
  Young Man Luther, 195–196
Eros, 137–139, 142–143, 242, 244
  ascent of, 216–218
  Ramakrishna and, 246–248
Esalen Institute, 179–180
The Essence of Christianity (Feuerbach), 45–46
ethical capacities, 190–191

ethical maturity, 84
ethics, 58–59
ethnopsychologies, 21
Europe, 3–5
evil, 231, 236
evolutionary drift of history, 65–66
evolutionary schema, 66–67
Exodus, 81–82
experience-distant, 2, 104
experience-near, 2
experimental psychology, 54
external reality, 67–68, 145–146, 204–205, 216

faith, language of, 258–259
fascism, 80–81, 133–134, 184
father-religion, 64
Faust (Goethe), 47–48
Faustus, 232–233
female development, 77–78
female divinities, 191–192
female sexuality, 10
feminism, 128–130
Ferrer, Jorge, 15
Feuerbach, Ludwig, 45–47, 68, 121–122
Fingarette, Hebert, 182–183
fixation, 75–76
Flournoy, Theodore, 3–5
flow states, 186–187
folklore, 13
fornication, 227
Francis (saint), 146–147
Frankl, Victor, 14–15
fraternal solidarity, 35
Fredriksen, Paula, 227
free association, 7–8, 155
freedom, 34
Freiberg, Moravia, 32
Freud, Sigmund. *See also specific topics*
  external critiques of, 23
  humanistic, 31
  internal critiques of, 23
  nephew John, 35
Fromm, Erich, 181–182
Future of an Illusion (Freud), 22–23, 36, 45–46, 49, 51, 59–60, 64–65, 116, 137–138
  agenda of, 133
  argument of, 95–96
  St. Boniface and, 94
  Civilization and Its Discontents and, 95

critiques of, 99–116
cultural super-ego and, 257–258
Kosawa on, 176
on material and mental assets of civilization, 106–108
Pfister and, 121–122
prophetic call to arms in, 105–106
reflexivity and, 128–130
A Religious Experience and, 101–102
religious intent and, 216
Rolland and, 133–134, 158–159
sociological responses to, 126–128
on super-ego, 110

Galileo, 65–66, 98
Gandhi, Mahatma, 152, 179–180, 193–194, 196
Geertz, Clifford, 119–120
gender, 62–63, 77–78, 108–109
cultural constructions of, 261
essentialism, 129–130
identifications, 145, 221–222, 251
in *Totem and Taboo*, 75–76
German Anthropological Society, 54–55
German nationalist students, 36–37
Girgensohn, Karl, 3–5
God, 63–64, 90–91, 101–102, 131–132, 262–263. *See also* Yahweh
classic-reductive studies and, 223–224
cultural containers of, 99–100
Father-, 83–84, 117–118
above God, 125–126
heteronomous, 228, 262–263
object-, 228–229
Silesius and, 234–235
unsophisticated understanding of, 223
God-representation, 205–209, 221–223, 229, 231–232, 238
Goethe, Johann, 45–48, 108–109
Goethe Prize, 30, 159
Goetz, Bruno, 160
Golden Calf, 44–45
Gombrich, Richard, 248–249
Gospel of St. John, 121–122
Grabbe, Christian, 155
grace, 102–103
Great Depression, 14
group identification, 108
Group Psychology and the Analysis of the Ego (Freud), 216

group therapy, 194
guilt, 58–79, 107–110, 122–123, 140–141, 233, 262–263
castration and, 103–104
heightening of, 112, 140
oedipal victory and, 163
gurus, 201–203

Haeckel, Ernst, 63, 71–72
Haizmann, Christoph, 99–100, 195–196
Halbfass, Wilhelm, 248–249
Hall, G. Stanley, 3–5
Hammarskjöld, Dag, 92–93, 218–220, 256–257
Hammerschlag, Samuel, 33–34
Hannibal (Grabbe), 155
Hannibal fantasy, 31–32, 34–35, 39–41
happiness, 144, 146–147
Hartmann, Heinz, 212–213
heavenly powers, 148–149
heliocentrism, 65–66, 98
hermeneutical method, 124–125
hermeneutics of suspicion, 148–149, 256–257, 261
heterosexual monogamy, 144–145, 261
Hewitt, Marsha, 130–131
Hillman, James, 14–15
Hiltebeitel, A., 171–173
Hinduism, 146–147, 151–152, 163–166
"common-man's," 168–169
Rolland on, 171–173
historical development, 53, 60–64
historical traumas, 61–62
Hocking, W. E., 3–5
Holy Trinity, 154–155
Homans, Peter, 125–126
homo religiosus, 193–194
homosexuality, 101
Horney, Karen, 180–181
human aggression, 59–60
human development, 55
human personality, 48–49, 106, 120–121
humanism, 47–48, 95
humanistic Freud, 31
humanistic psychoanalysis, 47–48
humanistic psychology, 14–15, 19
humanitarianism, 133–134
hypnosis, 212–213
hysteria, 7, 35–36

id, 10–11, 75, 122–123
    desire of, 64–65, 84, 139
    dynamic upsurge of, 189–190
    ego and, 211–212
idealization, 111–112, 225–226, 232–233, 260
idealized objects, 189
Ikhnaton, 82–83
illusion, 97, 204–205
Imago (journal), 52–53, 80–81
immanence, 125–126
immediate gratification, 84
immediate luminousness, 6
inclusive formula, 188–189
inclusive psychoanalytic approach, 221, 254
inclusivity, 23–26, 145
Indian Psychoanalytic Society, 171
individual psychology, 73–74
individualism, 126–127, 263
individuation, 13, 218
ineffability, 135–136, 234–235
instinct theory, 30, 168–171
instinctual gratification, 85
instinctual renunciation, 41–42
institutional religion, 157–158
internalization, 111–112
The Interpretation of Dreams (Freud), 35–36
intrapsychic conflict, 11–12
intuition, 169–170
intuitive psychologists, 216
inwardness, 116
Islam, 81, 87–88, 165–166
Italy, 39

James, William, 3–7, 12–13, 119, 154–155
    mysticism and, 135–136, 166–167
    paranormal and, 213–214
Janet, Pierre, 3–5
jealousy, 57
Jesus, 64, 123–124
Jewish cultural self-objects, 45
Jewish orthodoxy, 32
Jewish Press Centre, 32–33
jiriki, 174–176
jivatman, 171–173
John of the Cross (saint), 210–211
Jones, Ernst, 1–2, 57, 71–72
Jones, James, 125–126
Jonte-Pace, Diane, 78–79
jouissance, 217–218, 253–254

Judaism, 31–34, 41, 43–44, 49–50, 151–152
    continuance of, 89–90
    Freud drawn to, 92–93
    identity and, 92–94
    Jewish orthodoxy, 32
    monotheism and, 81
    Moses and, 82–85
    Moses, murdered by Jews, 85–86
    pre-history of, 81–82
Judeo-Christian tradition, 144–145, 201–202
Jung, Carl, 3–5, 12–13, 35, 53–54, 119, 166–167
    abdicated role as heir of psychoanalytic movement, 44
    Durkheim and, 127
    as heir to psychoanalytic throne, 42–43
    influence of, 14–15
    Oedipus complex and, 71–72
    paranormal and, 213–214
    Self archetype and, 167–168
    Totem and Taboo and, 90–91

Kakar, Sudhir, 92–93, 178–179, 196–197, 202–203, 214–215, 240, 249–252
Kali, 242, 244–245, 247–248
Kalika Purana (Hindu scriptural text), 17–19
Kant, Immanuel, 45–46, 58–59, 143, 169–170, 210–211
Kennedy, John F., 106–107
Kierkegaard, Soren, 196
Kirkpatrick, Lee, 130–131
Kohut, Heinz, 90–93, 148, 199–201, 218–220, 249–250, 256–257
Kondo, Akihisa, 180–181
Kosawa, Heisaku, 3–5, 20, 42–43, 73, 168–169, 174–178
Kripal, Jeffrey, 247–248, 252–255
Kris, Ernst, 14–15, 194–195
Krishna, 242
Krishnaprem, Yogi Sri, 167–168
Külpe, Oswald, 3–5
Kulturarbeit, 47–48
kundalini, 170–171

Lacan, Jacques, 217–218, 250, 252
Lakewood megachurch, 203
Lamarck, Jean-Baptiste, 61–62, 71–72, 75–76

latent dream wishes, 38
Leopoldstädter Gymnasium, 33–34
Leseverein der deutschen Studenten, 35–37
Leuba, James, 3–5
Levi, 81–82
libido, 9–10, 34–35, 190–191, 196
life-cycle theory, 190–193, 196–197
liminality, 5–7, 261, 263
limitlessness, 136, 155–156
lives-cycles theory, 240
Logos (Reason), 36
logotherapy, 14–15
Lueger, Karl, 36–37, 39, 42, 141–142

magical practices, 67. *See also* superstition
Maharshi, Sri Ramana, 154–155, 218
Mahayana values, 174–176
Malinowski, Bronislaw, 73–74
Manicheanism, 229–234, 236
manifest dreams, 38
manifest motives, 96
Maréchal, Joseph, 3–5
Marx, Karl, 106
Maslow, Abraham, 14–15, 19, 167–168
masochism, 112
mass psychology, 60
Masson, Jeffrey, 246–248, 252
master–disciple relationships, 184
materiality, 228–229
matriarchal religion, 60
Maupin, Ed, 182–183
maya (illusion), 163–165
meaninglessness, 122–123, 197–198
medical materialism, 36
meditational practices, 180
megachurches, 201–203
Meissner, W. W., 88–89
metaphysics, 46–47, 51–52
metapsychology, 29, 51–52, 249–250, 261
Meyer, Eduard, 81–82, 86
Meyers–Briggs Type Indicator, 14–15
Meynert, Theodor, 36
Michelangelo, 44–45
Miller, Christine, 203
mindfulness, 181
mirroring, 91–92
misogyny, 69–70
Mitra, S. C., 171
moksha, 178–179, 208–209, 214–215

monotheism, 60, 71–72, 94
declining, 64–65
developments in, 86–88
Judaism and, 81
male-gendered, 62–63
origins of, 80–81
psychological determinants of, 89
return of phylogenetic repressed and, 87–88
Totem and Taboo and, 83
moral education, 143
moral helpfulness, 6
moral hypocrisy, 46–47
morality, 34, 55–64, 193–194
moratoriums, 45, 194, 229–232
Morel, Ferdinand, 3–5
Mosaic prophetic self-consciousness, 49–50
Moses, 44–45, 81–86, 88–89
"The Moses of Michelangelo" (Freud), 43–44
Moses and Monotheism (Freud), 43–44, 52, 64–65
argument of, 81
critiques of, 88–94
organizational strategy of, 80–81
Totem and Taboo and, 81
mother goddesses, 62–63
Mother Mary, 191–192
Mount Sinai, 83–84
Multatuli, 98–99
must, shall be (*soll*), 48–49
Myers, Frederic, 3–5, 212–214
mystical epistemology, 169–170
mystical experiences, 5–7, 155, 157–162, 165–166, 236–237
mystical phenomena, 154–155
mystical practices, 157–162, 211–212
mystical psychoanalysis, 218–220
mysticism, 135–136
St. Augustine and, 235–236
Christian, 217–218
definitional problem of, 165–168
everywhere, 168
inner-worldly, 262–264
process dimension of, 220
psychoanalytic understanding of, 136–137, 152–153
rational, 256–257
Rolland and, 166–167, 218
rubric of, 153

narcissism, 15, 67–68, 92, 142–143, 184–185
  animism and, 68–69
  cosmic, 218–220
  developmental line of, 89, 189, 199–200
  early formation, 177
  labile, 18–19, 98
  masculine, 40–41
  overcoming, 181–182
  primary, 136, 155–156, 199–200
  species, 65–66
Naropa University, 179–180
Nazis, 14, 32
negative communities, 258–259
Neumann, Erich, 14–15
neuroses, 46–47, 62–63, 147–148
neurotic misery, 146, 148
neurotic symptoms, 10–11
neurotics, 67, 110–112
New Introductory Lectures on Psychoanalysis (Freud), 47
New Testament, 234
Nietzsche, Friedrich, 30, 45–46
nirvana principle, 164
noesis, 135–136, 169–170
nomos (ordered and meaningful worldview), 109–110
noninstitutional cultural expressions, 127
non-psychoanalytic psychologies, 14–15
North America, 3–5
no-self (anatta), 163–165
nostalgia, 209–210
Nothnagel, Hermann, 36
noumenon (thing-in-itself), 210–211, 254
nuclear family, 203

Obeyesekere, Gananath, 254
object-God, 228–229
object-love, 9
object-relational theorists, 236–237
object-relations, 15, 90–92, 184–185, 197–198, 232–233
  attachment theory, 130–131
  sexual, 60–61
object-relations theory, 249–250
obsessional neurosis, 11–12
oceanic feeling, 133–137, 152–153, 155–156, 158–159, 218–220
  crucial aspects of, 156–157
  interpretation of, 153–154, 157
  nature of, 166–167

  of omnipotence, 199–200
  residues of, 182–183
oedipal competition, 230
oedipal conflict, 223
oedipal dynamic, 104
oedipal period, 15
oedipal reductionism, 25–26
oedipal triangle, 52, 73
oedipal victory, 163
Oedipus complex, 9, 21, 103–104
  conflicted attitudes found in, 56–57
  discovering, 34–35
  dissolving, 122
  Jung and, 71–72
  primacy of, 53–54
  sexual object-relations and, 60–61
  unconscious ambivalence and, 58–59
  universality of, 23–24, 77–78
"On Dreams" (Freud), 68
"On Psychotherapy" (Freud), 100–101
ontogenetic dimension, 62
ontos, 18–19
oral stage, 9
ordered and meaningful worldview (*nomos*), 109–110
orginological effects of religion, 6
oriental renaissance, 152
orientalism, 79, 196–197, 248–250
origin myth, 58–59, 137
original sin, 58–79, 227
Osteen, Joel, 203
Ostia vision, 236–239
Otto, Rudolph, 119
Outler, A. C., 240–241

paranormal, 213–214
parental units, 139–140
parents, 32, 200–201
Parsons, Ann, 73–74
Parsons, Talcott, 75
particularity, 42
passivity, 135–136
pastoral psychology, 20, 122–123, 126, 191–192
patriarchy, 62–63, 71–72, 83
Paul (saint), 87–88, 141–142
Paul, Robert, 89–90
peak experiences, 167–168
penis envy, 9–10
perennialism, 153, 168
personality types, 14–15

personhood, 122
pessimism, 138–139
Pfister, Oskar, 20, 31–32, 42–43, 49, 100–101, 116, 173–174, 228
   definitional strategy of religion, 122
   Future of an Illusion and, 121–122
   pastoral psychology and, 126, 191–192
   psychology-theology dialogue and, 124–125, 241
   structural elements laid down by, 122–123
Phaedrus (Plato), 216–217
phallic phase, 9–10
phallic stage, 9
phenomenological-existential psychologies, 14–15
philosophical reasonableness, 6
phylogenesis, 63, 71–72
phylogenetic dimension, 62
phylogenetic hypothesis, 91–92
phylogenetic repressed, return of the, 81, 85–88
phylogenetic unconscious, 62–63, 71–73
Pinn, Anthony, 119–120
Plato, 45–46, 108–109, 216–217, 247–248, 252
pleasure principle, 8–9, 139, 145–146, 207–208
Plotinus, 217, 234–235
politics, 35–37, 40–42, 46–47
positive communities, 258–259
postwar capitalistic culture, 197–198
practical theology, 20
pragmatic effects of religion, 6
Pratt, James Bisset, 3–5
praxis, 47, 78–79
prayer, 205–206, 223–224
pre religion, 53
prejudice, 36–37
pre-oedipal developmental stage, 130–131, 136, 155–156, 190–191
prestige of consciousness, 65–66
primal crime, 60–64
primal deed, 137
primal father, 57–79
"primal fantasies," 62
primitive religion, 52–53
primitivity, 75–76
privatization, 126–127
programs for life, 164
projection, 10–11, 131–132

The Protestant Ethic and the Spirit of Capitalism (Weber), 257–258
Protestantism, 121–122, 142–143, 174–176, 262–263
   theology, 122, 262–263
   work ethic and, 257–258
psychic phenomena, 214–215
psychoanalysis
   applied, 24, 29–30, 143, 149–150, 188, 249–250
   creation of, 36
   cross-cultural applied, 249–250
   humanistic, 47–48
   mystical, 218–220
   redemptive mission of, 41–45
psychoanalytic anthropology, 54–55, 72–73
psychoanalytic clinical sessions, 1
psychoanalytic cultural universe, 1–2
psychoanalytic epistemology, 204–205
psychoanalytic hermeneutical applications, 215
psychoanalytic investigation, 30, 55
psychoanalytic methodology, 20, 78–79
psychoanalytic motto, 47–50, 116, 181–182
psychoanalytic practice, 2
psychoanalytic programs for life, 145–147
Psychoanalytic Quarterly (journal), 76–77
psychoanalytic sequence of groups, 86–87
psychoanalytic sociology, 72–73
psychoanalytic spirituality, 264
psychoanalytic theories of religion, 2, 22–23
psychoanalytic theory, 61–62, 71–72, 76–77, 145, 149–150, 194–195, 222, 256
   developments in, 72–73
   evolving nature of, 242
   falsification of, 220
   feminist revolution in, 261
   psychology-comparativist dialogue relativizing, 185–186
   revisions in, 74–75
psychoanalytic therapy, 105–106, 146, 183, 264
psychoanalytic thought, 2
psychoanalytic universalism, 248
psychoanalytic universals, 178–179
psychoanalytic view of time and history, 60–61
psychological analysis, 134–135
psychological development, 77–78

"The Psychological Outlook of Hindu Philosophy" (Bose), 173–174
"Psychological Problems in Anthropology" (Boas), 70–71
psychological processes, 5–7
psychological universalism, 249–250
psychological wisdom, 193–194
psychology and religion movement, 2–5, 14–16, 19, 23
  enterprises animating, 256
  first period of, 119
  oriental renaissance and, 152
  third period of, 88–89
  World War II and, 188
  Wundt and, 54
psychology as religion, 16, 19
psychology of religion, 16–17, 19–21, 54, 256, 262–263
psychology of unconscious, 51–52
psychology-comparativist dialogue, 16, 20, 24, 152–153, 174
  Buddhism and, 240
  relativizing psychoanalytic theory, 185–186
  Rolland and, 167, 211–212
  sophistication of, 179–180
psychology-theology dialogue, 16, 24, 103, 116–117, 122–125, 132, 185–186, 222–223, 241
The Psychopathology of Everyday Life (Freud), 51
psycho-sexual developmental scheme, 56–74
psychosocial moratoriums, 194
psycho-spirituality, 16, 19, 256
psychotherapy, 100–101
puberty, 9
Puranas, 242–243
Pure Land Buddhism, 174–178

Quest Scale, 15
"The Question of a Weltanschauung?" (Freud), 68–69

race, 75–76, 128–130
racism, 69–70, 119–120
radical empiricism, 6–7
Ramakrishna, 152–153, 163–164, 170–171, 176–177, 221, 242–245, 252, 254
  arche of, 254–255
  Eros and, 246–248

Kakar on, 249–252
Kali and, 244–245
Masson on, 246–247
secret talk and, 243
tantric mystical physiology and, 244
Rangtong meditational insight, 240
Real Self, 180–181
reality principle, 10–11, 145–146, 207–208
Reason (*Logos*), 36
recapitulation theory, 63
reductionism, 19, 79
reflectivity, 249–252
reflexive approach, 221
reflexive critiques, 176–179
reflexivity, 23–26, 72–76, 145, 148, 180
  adaptive view of religion and, 196–197
  Future of an Illusion and, 128–130
  lack of, 116–117, 179
  transformational perspectives on, 252–255
regression, 75–76, 136, 158–159, 194–195, 211–212
religion. *See also specific religions*
  decline of, 112–114, 126–127
  definitional debate over, 117–120, 134–135, 176
  matriarchal, 60
  origins of, 55–64, 69–70
  pragmatic effects of, 6
  primitive, 52–53
  traditional, 65–66
  Western, 55
religious behavior, 14–15
religious commands, 58–59
religious doctrines, 139–143
A Religious Experience (Freud), 101–102
religious forms of therapy, 104–105
religious ideation, 131–132
religious institutions, 194
religious intent, 216–218
religious mendacity, 69–70
religious narratives, 131–132, 206–207
religious phenomena, 205–206
religious practices, 205–206, 211–215
religious prescriptions for happiness, 144
religious programs for life, 145–147
religious therapies, 218–220
Religious Viewpoints Scale, 15
religious worldviews, 66–69
religiously driven repressive educational norms, 115–116

reminiscences, 60–61
renunciation, 47–48, 116
repression, 7–8, 10–11, 114–115
resocialization, 261
"return of the repressed," 60–62, 101
Ricoeur, Paul, 1–2, 20, 88, 124–125, 254, 256–257, 261
Rieff, Philip, 257–259, 262–263
right-brain artistic activities, 186–187
rituals, 52, 110–112
Rizzuto, Ana-Maria, 205–208, 231–232, 236–237
Robertson, Roland, 263
Rolland, Romain, 20, 42–43, 133–137, 152–154, 168–171, 211
 "A Disturbance of Memory on the Acropolis" and, 162–163
 ethno-psychological critique of, 176–177
 Future of an Illusion and, 133–134, 158–159
 on Hinduism, 171–173
 Kripal and, 252–253
 limited nature of Freud's correspondence with, 156–157
 mysticism and, 166–167, 218
 psychology-comparativist dialogue and, 167, 211–212
 as silent interlocutor, 137
Rome neurosis, 31–32, 34–35, 39, 41
Rorschach tests, 184
Rose, Jacqueline, 42
Rubin, Jeff, 186–187, 254–255

sahaja samadhi, 154–155
Salpêtrière, 7, 35–36
San Francisco Zen Center, 179–180
satyagraha, 193
Schiller, Friedrich, 30, 108–109, 159–160
Schopenhauer, Arthur, 30, 45–46
Schreber, Daniel, 246–247
Schwab, Raymond, 152
Scopes monkey trial, 98
The Second Sex (Beauvoir), 77–78
secularization, 53, 94, 112–114, 126–128, 137
seduction theory, 63, 71–72
self-analysis, 30
Self archetype, 167–168
self-consciousness, 49–50
self-critique, 231

self-esteem, 85, 199–201
self-knowledge, 116
self-objects, 43–45, 202–203, 233
 of power, 200–201
Self psychology, 199–201
self-reflective awareness, 2
Sellin, Ernst, 85–86
sexual development, 60–61, 72–73, 115–116
sexual drives, 108
sexual fantasies, 261
sexual identity, 108–109
sexual instinct, 9
Shakespeare, William, 30, 45–46, 108–109
Shakti, 245
Shentong meditational insight, 240
Sil, Narasingha, 246–248
Silesius, Angelus, 209–211, 234–235, 239–240
Sinha, Tarun, 171
Smith, Robertson, 57
social dislocation, 36, 59–60
social institutions, 35–36
social justice, 34
social obligations, 21–22
social sciences, 54–55
social space, 116, 259–260
socialization, 13
societal set of laws and morals, 53
socio-evolutionism, 93–94
sociohistorical arguments, 95–96, 105–106, 114
sociopolitical authoritarianism, 41
soll (must, shall be), 48–49
somatically based desire, 8–9
son-religion, 64
Spiderman (fictional character), 107–108, 200
spiritual marriage, 154–155
stages, 125–126
Stanley, Henry Morton, 77–78
Starbuck, E. D., 3–5
Sterba, Richard, 174
structural model of mind, 8–9, 72–73
structure building, 47–48
subconscious, 5–13
subjectivity, 186–187
subject–object split, 181–182
sublimation, 9–11, 41–42, 47–48, 113–114, 116, 250–251
suffering, 145–146

suggestion, 77
suggestive-supportive therapy, 100–101
sun god Aton, 82–83
super-ego, 10–11, 58–59, 62, 69–70, 75, 122–123. *See also* cultural super-ego
  determinants of, 143
  Future of an Illusion on, 110
  individual, 110
  religious, 140
  rituals and, 110–112
  unconscious and, 225
supernatural reality, 51–52
superstition, 11–12, 67, 87
Suzuki, D. T., 180–182

The Symposium (Plato), 216–217, 244
taboos, 58–59, 137
Tantra, 242–243, 251–252
tantric mystical physiology, 244
tariki, 174–176
"Der Taucher" (Schiller), 159–162
telepathy, 213–215
Teresa of Avila (saint), 154–155, 217–218
Tertullian, 157
Thanatos, 137–139, 142–143, 164
theodicy, 102–103
theological anthropology, 125–126
theological neo-orthodoxy, 14
theology, 120–126, 203
  apophatic, 234–235
  Protestant, 122, 262–263
therapeutic atmosphere, 2
therapeutic era, 1
therapeutic intervention, 101
therapeutic violence, 176–177
thing-in-itself (noumenon), 210–211, 254
thou shalts, 18–19
thought-transference, 214–215
Tillich, Paul, 20, 119–120, 122–123, 125–126, 210, 228, 241
torokashi, 177–178
totem meals, 57
Totem and Taboo (Freud), 52, 57, 59–64, 81, 112
  anthropology and, 70–71
  critiques of, 69–79
  cultural super-ego and, 110–112
  evolutionary schema and, 66–67
  Jung and, 90–91
  Kosawa on, 176
  Moses and Monotheism and, 81

  on patriarchy and monotheism, 83
  preface of, 58–59
  race and gender in, 75–76
  on return of phylogenetic repressed, 87–88
  socio-evolutionism and, 93–94
  super-ego and, 58–59
  thesis advocated in, 89–90
totemism, 53, 55–56, 58–79, 118, 129
  Christianity and, 60–64
  creation of, 87–88
  primal deed and, 137
  social scientific theorizing on, 57
traditional religion, 65–66
trance states, 212
transcendence, 125–126
transference, 7–8, 90–91, 125–126, 182–183
transformational approach, 24–25, 218–221
transformational reflections, 213–214
transiency, 135–136, 157
transitional objects, 204–205
transitional phenomena, 204
transpersonal psychology, 15, 19
tribalism, 36–37, 39, 46–47, 69–70, 142–143
triebe (drives), 58–59
Trieste, 162–163
The Triumph of the Therapeutic (Rieff), 257–258
Trungpa, Chogyam, 179–180
Turner, Victor, 260
Tylor, Edward Burnett, 54–55

unbehagen, 133, 139–145, 156–157, 162–165
unconscious, 5–15, 53–54, 98
  ambivalence, 58–59
  desires, 10–11, 252
  fantasies, 1
  latent dream wishes in, 38
  monitoring and containing, 104–105
  personal, 84
  phylogenetic, 62–63, 71–73
  primordial depths of, 214–215
  psychological conflict, 7
  psychology of, 51–52
  reformulating, 209–211
  super-ego and, 225
  transformational dimension to, 211–212

unity, 135–138
universal obsessional neurosis, 110–112
University of Bordeaux, 54–55
University of Vienna, 35–38, 42, 45, 49–50
Upanishads, 171–174, 208–209, 242–243
Urbarmachung, 47–48

Varieties of Religious Experience (James), 119, 135–136, 154–155
Vishnu, 171, 242
Vivekananda, 152–153, 163–164, 242

Wallwork, E., 148–149
Weber, Max, 257–259, 262
Weismann, August, 71–72
Weltanschauung, 66–69
werden (to become), 48–49
Western religion, 55
wholeheartedness, 180–181
Wilber, Ken, 15
Wilhelm, Friedrich, 42–43
Winckelmann, Johann Joachim, 39–40
Winnicott, D. W., 132, 204–205, 221–222, 249–250
World War I, 44, 133–134
World War II, 188
World's Parliament of Religions, 151–152
Wundt, Wilhelm, 3–5, 54

Yahweh, 86
Yearly, Lee, 148–149
Yerushalmi, Yosef, 89–90
yoga, 146–147, 169–170
young adulthood, 190–191
Young Man Luther (Erikson), 195–196

Zen Buddhism, 182–183, 211
Zen Buddhism and Psychoanalysis (Fromm), 181–182
Zen nationalism, 184
Zuider Zee, 47–48

CPSIA information can be obtained
at www.ICGtesting.com
Printed in the USA
LVHW080920030821
694401LV00004B/310